P9-CJD-278

A DOCUMENTARY HISTORY OF AMERICAN LIFE

General Editor: **David Donald,** *The Johns Hopkins University*

1. *Settlements to Society: 1584–1763*
   JACK P. GREENE, *University of Michigan*

2. *Colonies to Nation: 1763–1789*
   JACK P. GREENE, *University of Michigan*

3. *The Great Republic: 1789–1845*
   WILSON SMITH, *University of California, Davis*

4. *Democracy on Trial: 1845–1877*
   ROBERT W. JOHANNSEN, *University of Illinois*

5. *Shaping the Industrial Republic: 1877–1898*
   ROBERT A. LIVELY, *Princeton University*

6. *Progressivism and Postwar Disillusionment: 1898–1928*
   DAVID A. SHANNON, *University of Maryland*

7. *Depression, Recovery, and War: 1929–1945*
   ALFRED B. ROLLINS, JR., *Harpur College, State University of New York*

8. *Anxiety and Affluence: 1945–1965*
   ERNEST R. MAY, *Harvard University*

1945–1965

Edited by **ERNEST R. MAY**

Harvard University

Volume 8

A Documentary History of American Life

General Editor: **David Donald**

The Johns Hopkins University

McGRAW-HILL BOOK COMPANY

New York St. Louis San Francisco

Toronto London Sydney

Selection 12 is from *Decision in Germany* by Lucius D. Clay. Copyright 1950 by Lucius D. Clay. Reprinted by permission of Doubleday & Company, Inc.

Selection 18 is from *Memoirs* by Harry S. Truman. *Life* Magazine © 1956 Time, Inc. All Rights Reserved.

Selection 20 is from *Bill Mauldin in Korea* by Bill Mauldin. Copyright by William Mauldin.

Selection 22 is reprinted from *Foreign Affairs,* July, 1947. Copyright by the Council on Foreign Relations, Inc., New York.

"Fire!" (Selection 37) is from *The Herblock Book* (Beacon Press, 1952).

"We Now Have New and Important Evidence" (Selection 37) is from *The Herblock Book* (Beacon Press, 1952).

Selection 42 is reprinted with permission of The Macmillan Company from *The Other America* by Michael Harrington. Copyright © Michael Harrington 1962.

Selection 43 is from *The Organization Man* by William H. Whyte, Jr. Copyright © 1956 by William H. Whyte, Jr. Reprinted by permission of Simon and Schuster, Inc., and distributed in the British Commonwealth by Jonathan Cape Limited.

Selection 43 is from *On the Road* by Jack Kerouac. Copyright © 1955, 1957 by Jack Kerouac. Reprinted by permission of The Viking Press, Inc.

Selection 44 is from *Stride toward Freedom: The Montgomery Story* by Martin Luther King, Jr. Copyright © by Martin Luther King, Jr. Used by permission of Harper & Row, Publishers, Incorporated.

ANXIETY AND AFFLUENCE: 1945–1965

Library of Congress Catalog Card Number 66-14810

1234567890 HD 7321069876

FOREWORD

The history of the United States is more a matter of record than is that of any other major world power that has ever existed. The beginnings of our nation are not shrouded in myth or in medieval obscurity, for they can be traced in the precise and explicit directives which the English sovereigns gave their subjects who went to explore or inhabit the New World. At the other end of the time scale, the government of the United States has swiftly moved to declassify and to help publish even the "top secret" papers of World War II and after. For every intervening period the documentary record is voluminous and comprehensive.

A Documentary History of American Life presents an extensive, representative sampling of that vast record. It differs in a number of important ways from the several collections of documents already available to teachers and students. In the first place, it provides the most extensive coverage yet attempted for the entire history of America, from the first expedition of Walter Raleigh through the "Great Society" message to Congress by President Lyndon B. Johnson. The eight volumes of this series, containing approximately 2 million words, afford for the first time a canvas of sufficient size on which to present the panorama of the American past in its full complexity and detail. Moreover, the scope of the series allows the publication of all the significant portions of each document, not merely of selected snippets. Of course, not even a work of this size can include every document relating to American history, but for most students there is abundance here, and each teacher can choose those writings which best fit the needs of his particular courses.

A second major feature of the series is its variety. The seven editors, who have worked closely together during the preparation of these books, agree in rejecting the old notion that a document is necessarily a law, a treaty, or a Supreme Court decision. All these, to be sure, are here present, but so are diary accounts, contemporary letters, essays, poems, and cartoons. All the volumes include documents to illustrate our social, economic, and intellectual, as well as our political and diplomatic, history.

The series is further distinguished by its pedagogical usefulness. Teachers themselves, the seven editors are alert to the problems of college teaching in an age when classes are large and much of the actual instruction must be done by beginning instructors often only a few steps ahead of their pupils. Not just documents are needed, but documents whose relevance is explained and whose implications are explored. For each document, or group of documents, in this series, therefore, there is a full editorial introduction and a brief bibliographical note.

As a result, *A Documentary History of American Life* offers a rich fare to both beginning and advanced students who seek to know our country's history. The editors present these volumes in the profound conviction that only if our citizens understand the past can they intelligently face the future.

The Johns Hopkins University *David Donald*

PREFACE

This volume treats aspects of our own age. That age began just at the end of World War II, with the flash of atomic explosions over Hiroshima and Nagasaki. Except on desolate proving grounds, such explosions have not been seen since. But our age has been influenced, more than anything else, by the knowledge that they may occur and that, if they do, all or most of mankind may die.

Since the documents in this volume illustrate our age, many show, in one way or another, the fear of nuclear catastrophe that broods with all of us. In some documents, the fear is on the surface. The American government proposes a Baruch Plan or signs a limited test-ban treaty. Beatniks pursue pleasure aimlessly, asking why they should take thought for a tomorrow that may not be.

In other documents, fear is there but is not stated. It is the force that puts restraint and caution into words of presidents and secretaries of state speaking of Greece, Berlin, China, Korea, the Middle East, and Cuba.

In still other documents, the fear is present but darkly masked. This is the case in the documents that illustrate the almost incredible Red Scare of the late 1940s and early 1950s.

But anxiety is not the only characteristic of our age. In Jean-Paul Sartre's *No Exit,* three disagreeable characters find that they are in hell and are condemned to live with one another for eternity. In the last line of the play, one of them says, "Well, let's get on with it." Americans, though living in the nuclear age, have gotten on with quite a number of things.

Since World War II, Americans have come to grips with several long-standing political problems. Consensus has developed on issues that, in earlier decades, were divisive. Emerging from the racking Depression preceding World War II, Americans have also built an economy that, in spite of all we know about it, retains some of the qualities of a miracle. Their nation is the first in all of history in which a majority of the people have been well-off. Having built this economy, Americans have begun to take thought about learning and art and beauty and other things that may make a rich society a great society. Perhaps most impressive of all, Americans have, under the unnerving shadows of the bomb and the cold war, succeeded in preserving most and expanding some of the liberties that were ideals of earlier, simpler, and less crisis-ridden ages.

The documents in this volume illustrate not only the anxieties of our age but also some of its accomplishments.

Ernest R. May

PART FOUR Catastrophe in Asia

PART FIVE Conflict in Korea

PART SIX Policies for the Long Pull

PART SEVEN Traces of a Mild Thaw

PART EIGHT The Great Red Scare

PART NINE Restless Opulence

PRELUDE

The Dawn of the Atomic Age

SELECTION 1

United States Strategic Bombing Survey, "The Effects of the Atomic Bomb at Hiroshima and Nagasaki"

On May 7, 1945, General Dwight D. Eisenhower cabled Washington: "The mission of this Allied Force was fulfilled at 0241, local time." That morning at Reims representatives of the German high command had signed articles of complete and unconditional surrender. In Europe, World War II was over.

In the Far East the United States and its Allies still had a ferocious war on their hands. In 1944 they had at last broken the outer ring of Japanese defenses, moved back into Burma and the Philippines, begun to retake territory in China, and captured islands in the Marshall chain. Early in 1945 a dogged, bloody campaign resulted in the conquest of Iwo Jima, an island 750 miles from Japan proper. An even bloodier campaign continuing through the spring yielded control of Okinawa, a larger island only 325 miles from Japan. With the war in Europe over, the next step in the Far East seemed a massive effort to conquer Japan itself.

In the meantime, American, British, and Canadian scientists perfected a stupendous new weapon—the atomic bomb.

The President of the United States faced the question of whether or how to use the atomic bomb to hasten victory. Franklin D. Roosevelt had died in April, 1945. Harry S. Truman was now in his place. The burden of decision lay on him. Advised that the alternative to using the bomb was an invasion of Japan that might cost a million American lives, Truman ordered that atomic bombs be dropped on the Japanese cities of Hiroshima and Nagasaki.

The President's momentous decision has been analyzed in, among other works, Elting E. Morison, Turmoil and Tradition: A Life of Henry L. Stimson (1960), *a biography of the Secretary of War; Louis Morton, "The Decision to Use the Atomic Bomb,"* Foreign Affairs *(January, 1957), pages 334–353, which is based on extensive use of classified military and naval documents; and Herbert Feis,* Japan Subdued *(1961), which draws on classified State Department material. The indispensable account of the actual making of the atomic bomb is Richard G. Hewlett and Oscar E. Anderson, Jr.,* The New World, 1939–1946 *(1962), which is the first volume of the official history of the United States Atomic Energy Commission. By far the best account of Japanese reactions is Robert J. C. Butow,* Japan's Decision to Surrender *(1954).*

Hiroshima and Nagasaki were the only places where atomic weapons were actually used in combat. Much of the thought of the post-World War II era, both governmental and nongovernmental, was to be influenced by memory of what happened to those two cities.

Descriptions are numerous. Among the best are John Hersey, Hiroshima *(1947), Robert Jungk,* Brighter than a Thousand Suns *(1958), and Fletcher Knebel and Charles W. Bailey, II,* No High Ground *(1960). None has been more influential than the official description prepared by the Strategic Bombing*

Survey, a joint Army-Navy organization created in 1944 to study the military, economic, and political effects of strategic bombing in all theaters of World War II. The following excerpts are from the special report of the United States Strategic Bombing Survey, The Effects of the Atomic Bomb at Hiroshima and Nagasaki *(Government Printing Office, 1946), pages 3–23.*

A. THE ATTACKS AND DAMAGE

The Attacks

A single atomic bomb, the first weapon of its type ever used against a target, exploded over the city of Hiroshima at 0815 on the morning of 6 August 1945. Most of the industrial workers had already reported to work, but many workers were enroute and nearly all the school children and some industrial employees were at work in the open on the program of building removal to provide firebreaks and disperse valuables to the country. The attack came 45 minutes after the "all clear" had been sounded from a previous alert. Because of the lack of warning and the populace's indifference to small groups of planes, the explosion came as an almost complete surprise, and the people had not taken shelter. Many were caught in the open, and most of the rest in flimsily constructed homes or commercial establishments.

The bomb exploded slightly northwest of the center of the city. Because of this accuracy and the flat terrain and circular shape of the city, Hiroshima was uniformly and extensively devastated. Practically the entire densely or moderately built-up portion of the city was leveled by blast and swept by fire. A "fire-storm," a phenomenon which has occurred infrequently in other conflagrations, developed in Hiroshima: fires springing up almost simultaneously over the wide flat area around the center of the city drew in air from all directions. The inrush of air easily overcame the natural ground wind, which had a velocity of only about 5 miles per hour. The "fire-wind" attained a maximum velocity of 30 to 40 miles per hour 2 to 3 hours after the explosion. The "fire-wind" and the symmetry of the built-up center of the city gave a roughly circular shape to the 4.4 square miles which were almost completely burned out.

The surprise, the collapse of many buildings, and the conflagration contributed to an unprecedented casualty rate. Seventy to eighty thousand people were killed, or missing and presumed dead, and an equal number were injured. The magnitude of casualties is set in relief by a comparison with the Tokyo fire raid of 9–10 March 1945, in which, though nearly 16 square miles were destroyed, the number killed was no larger, and fewer people were injured.

At Nagasaki, 3 days later, the city was scarcely more prepared, though vague references to the Hiroshima disaster had appeared in the newspaper of 8 August. From the Nagasaki Prefectural Report on the bombing something of the shock of the explosion can be inferred:

> The day was clear with not very much wind—an ordinary midsummer's day. The strain of continuous air attack on the city's population and the severity of the summer had vitiated enthusiastic air raid precautions. Previously, a general alert had been sounded at 0748, with a raid alert at 0750; this was canceled at 0830, and the alertness of the people was dissipated by a great feeling of relief.

The city remained on the warning alert, but when two B–29's were again sighted coming in the raid signal was not given immediately; the bomb was dropped at 1102 and the raid signal was given a few minutes later, at 1109. Thus only about 400 people were in the city's tunnel shelters, which were adequate for about 30 per cent of the population.

> When the atomic bomb exploded, an intense flash was observed first, as though a large amount of magnesium had been ignited, and the scene grew hazy with white smoke. At the same time at the center of the explosion, and a short while later in other areas, a tremendous roaring sound was heard and a crushing blast wave and intense heat were felt. The people of Nagasaki, even those who lived on the outer edge of the blast, all felt as though they had sustained a direct hit, and the whole city suffered damage such as would have resulted from direct hits everywhere by ordinary bombs.
>
> The zero area, where the damage was most severe, was almost completely wiped out and for a short while after the explosion no reports came out of that area. People who were in comparatively damaged areas reported their condition under the impression that they had received a direct hit. If such a great amount of damage could be wreaked by a near miss, then the power of the atomic bomb is unbelievably great.

In Nagasaki, no fire storm arose, and the uneven terrain of the city confined the maximum intensity of damage to the valley over which the bomb exploded. The area of nearly complete devastation was thus much smaller; only about 1.8 square miles. Casualties were lower also; between 35,000 and 40,000 were killed, and about the same number injured. People in the tunnel shelters escaped injury, unless exposed in the entrance shaft. . . .

The Nagasaki Prefectural Report describes vividly the impress of the bomb on the city and its inhabitants:

> Within a radius of 1 kilometer from ground zero, men and animals died almost instantaneously from the tremendous blast pressure and heat; houses and other structures were smashed, crushed and scattered; and fires broke out. The strong complex steel members of the structures of the Mitsubishi Steel Works were bent and twisted like jelly and the roofs of the reinforced

concrete National Schools were crumpled and collapsed, indicating a force beyond imagination. Trees of all sizes lost their branches or were uprooted or broken off at the trunk. . . .

B. GENERAL EFFECTS

1. Casualties

The most striking result of the atomic bombs was the great number of casualties. The exact number of dead and injured will never be known because of the confusion after the explosions. Persons unaccounted for might have been burned beyond recognition in the falling buildings, disposed of in one of the mass cremations of the first week of recovery, or driven out of the city to die or recover without any record remaining. No sure count of even the preraid populations existed. Because of the decline in activity in the two port cities, the constant threat of incendiary raids, and the formal evacuation programs of the Government, an unknown number of the inhabitants had either drifted away from the cities or been removed according to plan. In this uncertain situation, estimates of casualties have generally ranged between 100,000 and 180,000 for Hiroshima, and between 50,000 and 100,000 for Nagasaki. The Survey believes the dead at Hiroshima to have been between 70,000 and 80,000, with an equal number injured; at Nagasaki over 35,000 dead and somewhat more than that injured seems the most plausible estimate.

Most of the immediate casualties did not differ from those caused by incendiary or high-explosive raids. The outstanding difference was the presence of radiation effects, which became unmistakable about a week after the bombing. At the time of impact, however, the causes of death and injury were flash burns, secondary effects of blast and falling debris, and burns from blazing buildings. No records are available that give the relative importance of the various types of injury, especially for those who died immediately after the explosion. Indeed, many of these people undoubtedly died several times over, theoretically, since each was subjected to several injuries, any one of which would have been fatal. The Hiroshima prefectural health department placed the proportion of deaths from burns (flash or flame) at 60 percent, from falling debris at 30 percent, and from other injuries at 10 percent; it is generally agreed that burns caused at least 50 percent of the initial casualties. Of those who died later, an increasing proportion succumbed to radiation effects.

The seriousness of these radiation effects may be measured by the fact that 95 percent of the traced survivors of the immediate explosion who were within 3,000 feet suffered from radiation disease. Colonel Stafford Warren, in his testimony before the Senate Committee on Atomic Energy, estimated that radiation was responsible for 7 to 8 percent of the total deaths in the two cities. Most medical investigators who spent some time in the areas feel that this estimate is far too low; it is generally felt that no less than 15 to 20 percent of the deaths were from radiation. In addition, there were an equal number who were casualties but survived, as well as uncounted thousands who probably were affected by the gamma rays but not enough to produce definite illness.

A plausible estimate of the importance of the various causes of death would range as follows:

Flash burns, 20 to 30 percent.
Other injuries, 50 to 60 percent.
Radiation sickness, 15 to 20 percent.

If we examine the nature of the casualties under each group of causes we find familiar and unfamiliar effects.

Flash Burns. The flash of the explosion, which was extremely brief, emitted radiant heat travelling at the speed of light. Flash burns thus followed the explosion instantaneously. The fact that relatively few victims suffered burns of the eyeballs should not be interpreted as an indication that the radiant heat followed the flash, or that time was required to build up to maximum heat intensity. The explanation is simply that the structure of the eye is more resistant to heat than is average human skin, and near ground zero the recessed position of the eyeball offered protection from the overhead explosion. Peak temperatures lasted only momentarily.

Survivors in the two cities stated that people who were in the open directly under the explosion of the bomb were so severely burned that the skin was charred dark brown or black and that they died within a few minutes or hours.

Among the survivors, the burned areas of the skin showed evidence of burns almost immediately after the explosion. At first there was marked redness, and other evidence of thermal burns appeared within the next few minutes or hours, depending on the degree of the burn. Uninfected burns healed promptly without any unusual clinical features, according to the Japanese physicians who attended the cases. American medical observers noted only a tendency to formation of excess scar tissue, which could be satisfactorily explained as the result of malnutrition and the large degree of secondary infection that complicated healing of the burns. There were also a few instances of burns healing with contractures and limitation of the mobility of certain joints, such as the elbows or knees. In many instances, these primary burns of minor nature were completely healed before patients developed evidence of radiation effects.

Because of the brief duration of the flash wave and the shielding effects of almost any objects—leaves and clothing as well as buildings—there were many interesting cases of protection. The radiant heat came in a direct line like light, so that the area burned corresponded to this directed exposure. Persons whose sides were toward the explosion often showed definite burns of both sides of the back while the hollow of the back escaped. People in buildings or houses were apparently burned only if directly exposed through the windows. The most striking instance was that of a man writing before a window. His hands were seriously burned but his exposed face and neck suffered only slight burns due to the angle of entry of the radiant heat through the window.

Flash burns were largely confined to exposed areas of the body, but on occasion would occur through varying thicknesses of clothing. Generally speaking, the thicker the clothing the more likely it was to give complete protection against flash burns. One woman was burned over the shoulder except for a T-shaped area about one-fourth inch in breadth; the T-shaped area corresponded to an increased thickness of the clothing from the seam of the garment. Other people were burned through a single thickness of kimono but were unscathed or only slightly affected underneath the lapel. In other instances, skin was burned beneath tightly fitting clothing but was unburned beneath loosely fitting portions. Finally, white or light colors reflected heat and afforded some protection; people wearing black or dark-colored clothing were more likely to be burned.

Other Injuries. Because of the combination of factors at the area near the center of the explosion, the casualty effects of blast are hard to single out. If it is remembered that even directly under the explosion, people were several hundred feet away from the air-burst, it will be easier to understand why true blast effects were relatively rare. Only toward the periphery of the affected zone was the blast effect lateral and likely to throw people violently against buildings, and at the periphery the intensity of the blast had fallen off sharply. Comparatively few instances were reported of arms or legs being torn from the body by flying debris. Another indication of the rarity of over-pressure is the scarcity of ruptured eardrums. Among 106 victims examined by the Japanese in Hiroshima on 11 and 12 August, only three showed ruptured eardrums; a study done in October at the Omura hospital near Nagasaki revealed that only two of 92 cases had ruptured eardrums. Only at Nagasaki were there reports of over-pressure in the shock wave. Some of the dead were said by survivors to have had their abdomens ruptured and intestines protruding; others were reported to have protruding eyes and tongues, and to have looked as if they had drowned. Thorough check by Allied investigators discredited these stories as evidence of direct blast effects; the normal effects of blast are internal hemorrhage and crushing. These external signs point to injuries from debris rather than blast.

Injuries produced by falling and flying debris were much more numerous, and naturally increased in number and seriousness nearer the center of the affected area. The collapse of the buildings was sudden, so that thousands of people were pinned beneath the debris. Many were able to extricate themselves or received aid in escaping, but large numbers succumbed either to their injuries or to fire before they could be extricated. The flimsiness of Japanese residental construction should not be allowed to obscure the dangers of collapse; though the walls and partitions were light, the houses had heavy roof timbers and heavy roof tiles. Flying glass from panels also caused a large number of casualties, even up to 15,000 feet from ground zero.

The number of burns from secondary fires was slight among survivors, but it was probable that a large number of the deaths in both cities came from the burning of people caught in buildings. Eyewitness accounts agree that many fatalities occurred in this way, either immediately or as a result of the lack of care for those who did extricate themselves with serious burns. There are no references, however, to people in the streets succumbing either to heat or to carbon monoxide as they did in Tokyo or in Hamburg, Germany. A few burns resulted from clothing set afire by the flash wave, but in most cases people were able to beat out such fires without serious injury to the skin.

Radiation Disease. The radiation effects upon survivors resulted from the gamma rays liberated by the fission process rather than from induced radio-activity or the lingering radio-activity of deposits of primary fission products. Both at Nagasaki and at Hiroshima, pockets of radio-activity have been detected where fission products were directly deposited, but the degree of activity in these areas was insufficient to produce casualties. Similarly, induced radio-activity from the interaction of neutrons with matter caused no authenticated fatalities. But the effects of gamma rays—here used in a general sense to include all penetrating high-frequency radiations and neutrons that caused injury—are well established, even though the Allies had no observers in the affected areas for several weeks after the explosions.

Our understanding of radiation casualties is not complete. In part the deficiency is in our basic knowledge of how radiation affects animal tissue. In the words of Dr. Robert Stone of the Manhattan Project, "The fundamental mechanism of the action of radiation on living tissues has not been understood. All methods of treatment have therefore been symptomatic rather than specific. For this reason, studies into the fundamental nature of the action of radiation have been carried on to some extent, the limitation being that it was unlikely that significant results could be obtained during the period of war."

According to the Japanese, those individuals very near the center of the explosion but not affected by flash burns or secondary injuries became ill within 2 or 3 days. Bloody diarrhea followed, and the victims expired, some within 2 to 3 days after the onset and the majority within a week. Autopsies showed remarkable changes in the blood picture—almost complete absence of white blood cells, and deterioration of bone marrow. Mucous membranes of the throat, lungs, stomach, and the intestines showed acute inflammation.

The majority of the radiation cases, who were at greater distances, did not show severe symptoms until 1 to 4 weeks after the explosion, though many felt weak and listless on the following day. After a day or two of mild nausea and vomiting, the appetite improved and the person felt quite well until symptoms reappeared at a later date. In the opinion of some Japanese physicians, those who rested or subjected themselves to less physical exertion showed a longer delay before the onset of subsequent symptoms. The first signs of recurrence were loss of appetite, lassitude, and general discomfort. Inflammation of the gums, mouth, and pharynx appeared next. Within 12 to 48 hours, fever became evident. In many instances it reached only 100° Fahrenheit and remained for only a few days. In other cases, the temperature went as high as 104° or 106° Fahrenheit. The degree of fever apparently had a direct relation to the degree of exposure to radiation. Once developed, the fever was usually well sustained, and in those cases terminating fatally it continued high until the end. If the fever subsided, the patient usually showed a rapid disappearance of other symptoms and soon regained his feeling of good health. The other symptoms commonly seen were shortage of white corpuscles, loss of hair, inflammation and gangrene of the gums, inflammation of the mouth and pharynx, ulceration of the lower gastro-intestinal tract, small livid spots (petechiae) resulting from escape of blood into the tissues of the skin or mucous membrane, and larger hemorrhages of gums, nose and skin.

Loss of hair usually began about 2 weeks after the bomb explosion, though in a few instances it is reported to have begun as early as 4 to 5 days afterward. The areas were involved in the following order of frequency with variations depending on the degree of exposure: scalp, armpits, beard, pubic region, and eyebrows. Complete baldness was rare. Microscopic study of the body areas involved has shown atrophy of the hair follicles. In those patients who survived after 2 months, however, the hair has commenced to regrow. An interesting but unconfirmed report has it that loss of the hair was less marked in persons with grey hair than in those with dark hair.

A decrease in the number of white blood corpuscles in the circulating blood appears to have been a constant accompaniment of radiation disease, even existing in some milder cases without other radiation effects. The degree of leukopenia was probably the most accurate index of the amount of radiation a person received. The normal white blood count averages 5,000 to 7,000: leukopenia is indicated by a count of 4,000 or less. The white blood count in the more severe cases ranged from 1,500 to 0, with almost entire disappearance of the bone marrow. The moderately severe cases showed evidence of degeneration of bone marrow and total white blood counts of 1,500 to 3,000. The milder cases showed white blood counts of 3,000 to 4,000 with more minor degeneration changes in the bone marrow. The changes in the system for forming red blood corpuscles developed later, but were equally severe.

Radiation clearly affected reproduction, though the extent has not been determined. Sterility has been a common finding throughout Japan, especially under the conditions of the last 2 years, but there are signs of an increase in the Hiroshima and Nagasaki areas to be attributed to the radiation. Sperm counts done in Hiroshima under American supervision revealed low sperm counts or complete aspermia for as long as 3 months afterward in males who were within 5,000 feet of the center of the explosion. Cases dying of radiation disease showed clear effects on spermatogenesis. Study of sections of ovaries from autopsied radiation victims has not yet been completed. The effects of the bomb on pregnant women are marked, however. Of women in various stages of pregnancy who were within 3,000 feet of ground zero, all known cases have had miscarriages. Even up to 6,500 feet they have had miscarriages or premature infants who died shortly after birth. In the group between 6,500 and 10,000 feet, about one-third have given birth to apparently normal children. Two months after the explosion, the city's total incidence of miscarriages, abortions, and premature births was 27 percent as compared with a normal rate of 6 percent. Since other factors than radiation contributed to this increased rate, a period of years will be required to learn the ultimate effects of mass radiation upon reproduction.

Treatment of victims by the Japanese was limited by the lack of medical supplies and facilities. Their therapy consisted of small amounts of vitamins, liver extract, and an occasional blood transfusion. Allied doctors used penicillin and plasma with beneficial effects. Liver extract seemed to benefit the few patients on whom it was used: It was given in small frequent doses when available. A large percentage of the cases died of secondary disease, such as septic bronchopneumonia or tuberculosis, as a result of lowered resistance. Deaths from radiation began about a week after exposure and reached a peak in 3 to 4 weeks. They had practically ceased to occur after 7 to 8 weeks.

Unfortunately, no exact definition of the killing power of radiation can yet be given, nor a satisfactory account of the sort and thickness of concrete or earth that will shield people. From the definitive report of the Joint Commission will come more nearly accurate statements on these matters. In the meanwhile the awesome lethal effects of the atomic bomb and the insidious additional peril of the gamma rays speak for themselves.

There is reason to believe that if the effects of blast and fire had been entirely absent from the bombing, the number of deaths among people within a radius of one-half mile from ground zero would have been almost as great as the actual figures and the deaths among those within 1 mile would have been only slightly less. The principal difference would have been in the time of the deaths. Instead of being killed outright as were most of these victims, they would have survived for a few days or even 3 or 4 weeks, only to die eventually of radiation disease. . . .

2. Morale[1]

As might be expected, the primary reaction to the bomb was fear—uncontrolled terror, strengthened by the sheer horror of the destruction and suffering witnessed and experienced by the survivors. Between one-half and two-thirds of those interviewed in the Hiroshima and Nagasaki areas confessed having such reactions, not just for the moment but for some time. As two survivors put it:

> Whenever a plane was seen after that, people would rush into their shelters: They went in and out so much that they did not have time to eat. They were so nervous they could not work.
>
> After the atomic bomb fell, I just couldn't stay home. I would cook, but while cooking I would always be watching out and worrying whether an atomic bomb would fall near me.

[1] An U. S. S. B. S. Morale division team interviewed a scientifically selected sample of almost 250 persons: 128 from Hiroshima and Nagasaki cities, and 120 from the immediately surrounding areas. The same standard questions were put to these people and similar groups in representative Japanese cities.

The behavior of the living immediately after the bombings, as described earlier, clearly shows the state of shock that hindered rescue efforts. A Nagasaki survivor illustrates succinctly the mood of survivors:

> All I saw was a flash and I felt my body get warm and then I saw everything flying around. My grandmother was hit on the head by a flying piece of roof and she was bleeding * * * I became hysterical seeing my grandmother bleeding and we just ran around without knowing what to do.
>
> I was working at the office. I was talking to a friend at the window. I saw the whole city in a red flame, then I ducked. The pieces of the glass hit my back and face. My dress was torn off by the glass. Then I got up and ran to the mountain where the good shelter was.

The two typical impulses were those: Aimless, even hysterical activity or flight from the city to shelter and food. . . .

There is no doubt that the bomb was the most important influence among the people of these areas in making them think that defeat was inevitable. . . .

Typical comments of survivors were:

> If the enemy has this type of bomb, everyone is going to die, and we wish the war would hurry and finish.
>
> I did not expect that it was that powerful. I thought we have no defense against such a bomb.
>
> One of my children was killed by it, and I didn't care what happened after that.

Other reactions were found. In view of their experiences, it is not remarkable that some of the survivors (nearly one-fifth) hated the Americans for using the bomb or expressed their anger in such terms as "cruel," "inhuman," and "barbarous."

> * * * they really despise the Americans for it, the people all say that if there are such things as ghosts, why don't they haunt the Americans?
>
> When I saw the injured and killed, I felt bitter against the enemy.
>
> After the atomic bomb exploded, I felt that now I must go to work in a munitions plant * * * My sons told me that they wouldn't forget the atomic bomb even when they grow up.

The reaction of hate and anger is not surprising, and it is likely that in fact it was a more extensive sentiment than the figures indicate, since unquestionably many respondents, out of fear or politeness, did not reveal their sentiments with complete candor. Despite this factor, the frequency of hostile sentiments seems low. Two percent of the respondents even volunteered the observation that they did not blame the United States for using the bomb. There is evidence that some hostility was turned against their own Government, either before or after the surrender, although only a few said they wondered why their nation could not have made the bomb. In many instances the reaction was simply one of resignation. A common comment was, "Since it was war, it was just shikata-ga-nai (Too bad)."

Admiration for the bomb was more frequently expressed than anger.

Over one-fourth of the people in the target cities and surrounding area said they were impressed by its power and by the scientific skill which underlay its discovery and production.

Of greater significance are the reactions of the Japanese people as a whole. The two raids were all-Japan events and were intended so: The Allied Powers were trying to break the fighting spirit of the Japanese people and their leaders, not just of the residents of Hiroshima and Nagasaki. Virtually all the Japanese people had a chance to react to the bomb though the news had not reached to full spread at the time of the surrender. By the time the interviewing was done, only about 2 percent of the population in rural areas and 1 percent in the cities had not heard of the bomb.

The reactions found in the bombed cities appeared in the country as a whole—fear and terror, anger and hatred against the users, admiration for the scientific achievement—though in each case with less intensity. The effect of the bomb on attitudes toward the war in Japan as a whole was, however, much less marked than in the target cities. While 40 percent of the latter respondents reported defeatist feelings induced by the bomb, 28 percent of those in the islands as a whole attributed such reactions to the news of the bomb. . . .

3. The Japanese Decision to Surrender

The further question of the effects of the bombs on the morale of the Japanese leaders and their decision to abandon the war is tied up with other factors. The atomic bomb had more effect on the thinking of Government leaders than on the morale of the rank and file of civilians outside of the target areas. It cannot be said, however, that the atomic bomb convinced the leaders who effected the peace of the necessity of surrender. The decision to seek ways and means to terminate the war, influenced in part by knowledge of the low state of popular morale, had been taken in May 1945 by the Supreme War Guidance Council.

As early as the spring of 1944, a group of former prime ministers and others close to the Emperor had been making efforts toward bringing the war to an end. This group, including such men as Admiral Okada, Admiral Yonai, Prince Konoye, and Marquis Kido, had been influential in effecting Tojo's resignation and in making Admiral Suzuki Prime Minister after Koiso's fall. Even in the Suzuki cabinet, however, agreement was far from unanimous. The Navy Minister, Admiral Yonai, was sympathetic, but the War Minister, General Anami, usually represented the fight-to-the-end policy of the Army. In the Supreme War Guidance Council, a sort of inner cabinet, his adherence to that line was further assured by the participation of the Army and Navy chiefs of staff, so that on the peace issue this organization was evenly divided, with these three opposing the Prime Minister, Foreign Minister, and Navy Minister. At any time military (especially Army) dissatisfaction with the Cabinet might have eventuated at least in its fall and possibly in the "liquidation" of the antiwar members.

Thus the problem facing the peace leaders in the Government was to bring about a surrender despite the hesitation of the War Minister and the opposition of the Army and Navy chiefs of staff. This had to be done, moreover, without precipitating counter measures by the Army which would eliminate the entire peace group. This was done ultimately by bringing the Emperor actively into the decision to accept the Potsdam terms. So long as the Emperor openly supported such a policy and could be presented to the country as doing so, the military, which had fostered and lived on the idea of complete obedience to the Emperor, could not effectively rebel.

A preliminary step in this direction had been taken at the Imperial Conference on 26 June. At this meeting, the Emperor, taking an active part despite his custom to the contrary, stated that he desired the development of a plan to end the war as well as one to defend the home islands. This was followed by a renewal of earlier efforts to get the Soviet Union to intercede with the United States, which were effectively answered by the Potsdam Declaration on 26 July and the Russian declaration of war on 9 August.

The atomic bombings considerably speeded up these political maneuverings within the government. This in itself was partly a morale effect, since there is ample evidence that members of the Cabinet were worried by the prospect of further atomic bombings, especially on the remains of Tokyo. The bombs did not convince the military that defense of the home islands was impossible, if their behavior in Government councils is adequate testimony. It did permit the Government to say, however, that no army without the weapon could possibly resist an enemy who had it, thus saving "face" for the Army leaders and not reflecting on the competence of Japanese industrialists or the valor of the Japanese soldier. In the Supreme War Guidance Council voting remained divided, with the war minister and the two chiefs of staff unwilling to accept unconditional surrender. There seems little doubt, however, that the bombing of Hiroshima and Nagasaki weakened their inclination to oppose the peace group.

The peace effort culminated in an Imperial conference held on the night of 9 August and continued into the early hours of 10 August, for which the stage was set by the atomic bomb and the Russian war declaration. At this meeting the Emperor, again breaking his customary silence, stated specifically that he wanted acceptance of the Potsdam terms.

A quip was current in high Government circles at this time that the atomic bomb was the real Kamikaze, since it saved Japan from further useless slaughter and destruction. It is apparent that in the atomic bomb the Japanese found the opportunity which they had been seeking, to break the existing deadlock within the Government over acceptance of the Potsdam terms.

PART ONE

A Different Kind of Normalcy

SELECTION 

The Taft-Hartley Act

With the surrender of Japan, on August 14, 1945, World War II came to an end.

Many expected the aftermath of this war to be like the aftermath of World War I. Then, the American people had fled to the "normalcy" represented by Warren Harding and Calvin Coolidge. They turned abruptly away from the progressive reform movement symbolized by Theodore Roosevelt's "Square Deal" and Woodrow Wilson's "New Freedom." At least, so it seemed. The general expectation was that the people would now turn away, equally abruptly, from the progressive reform movement symbolized by Franklin Roosevelt's "New Deal."

The congressional elections of 1946 bore out this expectation. Eleven Democratic Senators and fifty-four Democratic Representatives lost their seats. For the first time since 1931, the Republicans had majorities in both houses.

By itself, Republican control of Congress was not return to normalcy. That had to wait until 1948 when, almost everyone assumed, a Republican President would replace Harry S. Truman. In the meantime, the champions of normalcy had to content themselves with minor steps such as forcing pell-mell demobilization of the armed forces, ending wartime price controls, cutting income taxes, and reducing agricultural price supports.

The one large step open to the Republicans in Congress was to rewrite the labor legislation of the New Deal Era. The National Labor Relations Act of 1935, better known as the Wagner Act, had enabled labor unions to gain power equal to, perhaps even greater than, that of all but the largest business corporations. Many Republicans felt that the Wagner Act had been wrong in principle. They were strengthened in this conviction by the fact that labor unions actively and enthusiastically supported their Democratic opponents. With Representative Fred Hartley, Jr., of New Jersey in the foreground, Republicans in the House drew up a bill that would have voided the Wagner Act and deprived unions of the rights to insist on collective bargaining, negotiate for a closed shop, resist the formation of company unions, or call on the Federal government to aid in curbing unfair practices by employers. The Hartley bill would have returned labor unions to the legal status they occupied in the 1920s.

The Republican leader in the Senate, Robert A. Taft of Ohio, was a more judicious man than Representative Hartley. Although personally an archconservative, Taft doubted both the wisdom and the practicality of trying to do as Hartley and his colleagues wished. Rewriting Hartley's bill, Taft strove to make it one that would primarily remove inequities most keenly protested by employers. The Wagner Act itemized unfair labor practices forbidden to employers. Taft concentrated on drawing up a list of unfair labor practices to be forbidden to unions.

The resultant Taft-Hartley Act, passed into law in spite of President Truman's veto, aroused fierce controversy. Terming it a "slave labor act," union leaders objected in particular to two sections of Title I, Section 8, which itemized the practices to be forbidden unions, and Section 14(b), which allowed states to pass right-to-work laws prohibiting closed-shop agreements. Union leaders also objected strongly to Title II, which authorized the President, in certain circumstances, to order strikers back to work. What union leaders feared was that Republican appointees on the National Labor Relations Board would hamstring collective bargaining, that states by the score would forbid the closed shop, and that unsympathetic Presidents would act as strikebreakers. As it turned out, these fears were only partly justified. Although leaders of organized labor continued to denounce the Taft-Hartley Act, they found in time that they could live with most of its provisions.

Taft's role in drafting the Taft-Hartley Act is sketched in William S. White, The Taft Story *(1954). H. A. Millis and E. C. Brown,* From the Wagner Act to Taft-Hartley *(1950), and C. O. Gregory,* Labor and the Law *(1949), describe the legal and political background. The following document consists of excerpts from the Taft-Hartley Act, taken from* United States Statutes at Large, *volume 61, pages 136–160.*

TITLE I—AMENDMENT OF NATIONAL LABOR RELATIONS ACT

Sec. 101. The National Labor Relations Act, [i.e., the Wagner Act (*ed.*)] is hereby amended to read as follows: . . .

"Rights of Employees

"*Sec. 7.* Employees shall have the right to self-organization, to form, join, or assist labor organizations, to bargain collectively through representatives of their own choosing, and to engage in other concerted activities for the purpose of collective bargaining or other mutual aid or protection, and shall also have the right to refrain from any or all of such activities except to the extent that such right may be affected by an agreement requiring membership in a labor organization as a condition of employment as authorized in section 8 (a) (3).

"Unfair Labor Practices

"*Sec. 8.* (a) It shall be an unfair labor practice for an employer—

"(1) to interfere with, restrain, or coerce employees in the exercise of the rights guaranteed in section 7;

"(2) to dominate or interfere with the formation or administration of any labor organization or contribute financial or other support to it. . . . ;

"(3) by discrimination in regard to hire or tenure of employment or any term or condition of employment to encourage or discourage membership in any labor organization: *Provided,* That nothing in this Act, or in any other statute of the United States, shall preclude an employer from making an agreement with a labor organization (not established, maintained, or assisted by any action defined in section 8 (a) of this Act as an unfair labor practice) to require as a condition of employment membership therein on or after the thirtieth day following the beginning of such employment or the effective date of such agreement, whichever is the later, (i) if such labor organization is the representative of the employees as provided in section 9 (a), in the appropriate collective-bargaining unit covered by such agreement when made; and (ii) if, following the most recent election held as provided in section 9 (e) the Board shall have certified that at least a majority of the employees eligible to vote in such election have voted to authorize such labor organization to make such an agreement: *Provided further,* That no employer shall justify any discrimination against an employee for nonmembership in a labor organization (A) if he has reasonable grounds for believing that such membership was not available to the employee on the same terms and conditions generally applicable to other members, or (B) if he has reasonable grounds for believing that membership was denied or terminated for reasons other than the failure of the employee to tender the periodic dues and the initiation fees uniformly required as a condition of acquiring or retaining membership;

"(4) to discharge or otherwise discriminate against an employee because he has filed charges or given testimony under this Act;

"(5) to refuse to bargain collectively with the representatives of his employees, subject to the provisions of section 9 (a).

"(b) It shall be an unfair labor practice for a labor organization or its agents—

"(1) to restrain or coerce (A) employees in the exercise of the rights guaranteed in section 7: *Provided,* That this paragraph shall not impair the right of a labor organization to prescribe its own rules with respect to the acquisition or retention of membership therein; or (B) an employer in the selection of his representatives for the purposes of collective bargaining or the adjustment of grievances;

"(2) to cause or attempt to cause an employer to discriminate against an employee in violation of subsection (a) (3) or to discriminate against an employee with respect to whom membership in such organization has been denied or terminated on some ground other that his failure to tender the periodic dues and the initiation fees uniformly required as a condition of acquiring or retaining membership;

"(3) to refuse to bargain collectively with an employer, provided it is the representative of his employees subject to the provisions of section 9 (a);

"(4) to engage in, or to induce or encourage the employees of any employer to engage in, a strike or a concerted refusal in the course of their employment to use, manufacture, process, transport, or otherwise handle or work on any goods, articles, materials, or commodities or to perform any services, where an object thereof is: (A) forcing or requiring any employer or self-employed person to join any labor or employer organization or any employer or other person to cease using, selling, handling, transporting, or otherwise dealing in the products of any other producer, processor, or manufacturer, or to cease doing business with any other person; (B) forcing or requiring any other employer to recognize or bargain with a labor organization as the representative of his employees unless such labor organization has been certified as the representative of such employees under the provisions of section 9; (C) forcing or requiring any employer to recognize or bargain with a particular labor organization as the representative of his employees if another labor organization has been certified as the representative of such employees under the provisions of section 9; (D) forcing or requiring any employer to assign particular work to employees in a particular labor organization or in a particular trade, craft, or class rather than to employees in another labor organization or in another trade, craft, or class, unless such employer is failing to conform to an order or certification of the Board determining the bargaining representative for employees performing such work: *Provided,* That nothing contained in this subsection (b) shall be construed to make unlawful a refusal by any person to enter upon the premises of any employer (other than his own employer), if the employees of such employer are engaged in a strike ratified or approved by a representative of such employees whom such employer is required to recognize under this Act;

"(5) to require of employees covered by an agreement authorized under subsection (a) (3) the payment, as a condition precedent to becoming a member of such organization, of a fee in an amount which the Board finds excessive or discriminatory under all the circumstances . . . ; and

"(6) to cause or attempt to cause an employer to pay or deliver or agree to pay or deliver any money or other thing of value, in the nature of an exaction, for services which are not performed or not to be performed.

"(c) The expressing of any views, argument, or opinion, or the dissemination thereof, whether in written, printed, graphic, or visual form, shall not constitute or be evidence of an unfair labor practice under any of the provisions of this Act, if such expression contains no threat of reprisal or force or promise of benefit.

"(d) For the purposes of this section, to bargain collectively is the performance of the mutual obligation of the employer and the representative of the employees to meet at reasonable times and confer in good faith with respect to wages, hours, and other terms and conditions of employment, or the negotiation of an agreement, or any question arising thereunder, and the execution of a written contract incorporating any agreement reached if requested by either party, but such obligation does not compel either party to agree to a proposal or require the making of a concession: *Provided,* That where there is in effect a collective-bargaining contract covering employees in an industry affecting commerce, the duty to bargain collectively shall also mean that no party to such contract shall terminate or modify such contract, unless the party desiring such termination or modification—

"(1) serves a written notice upon the other party to the contract of the proposed termination or modification sixty days prior to the expiration date thereof, or in the event such contract contains no expiration date, sixty days prior to the time it is proposed to make such termination or modification;

"(2) offers to meet and confer with the other party for the purpose of negotiating a new contract or a contract containing the proposed modifications;

"(3) notifies the Federal Mediation and Conciliation Service within thirty days after such notice of the existence of a dispute, and simultaneously therewith notifies any State or Territorial agency established to mediate and conciliate disputes within the State or Territory where the dispute occurred, provided no agreement has been reached by that time; and

"(4) continues in full force and effect, without resorting to strike or lock-out, all the terms and conditions of the existing contract for a period of sixty days after such notice is given or until the expiration date of such contract, whichever occurs later:

The duties imposed upon employers, employees, and labor organizations by paragraphs (2), (3), and (4) shall become inapplicable upon an intervening certification of the Board, under which the labor organization or individual, which is a party to the contract, has been superseded as or ceased to be the representative of the employees subject to the provisions of section 9 (a), and the duties so imposed shall not be construed as requiring either party to discuss or agree to any modification of the terms and conditions contained in a contract for a fixed period, if such modification is to become effective before such terms and conditions can be reopened under the provisions of the contract. Any employee who engages in a strike within the sixty-day period specified in this subsection shall lose his status as an employee of the employer engaged in the particular labor dispute, for the purposes of sections 8, 9, and 10 of this Act, as amended, but such loss of status for such employee shall terminate if and when he is reemployed by such employer.

"Representatives and Elections

"Sec. 9. (a) Representatives designated or selected for the purposes of collective bargaining by the majority of the employees in a unit appropriate for such purposes, shall be the exclusive representatives of all the employees in such unit for the purposes of collective bargaining in respect to rates of pay, wages, hours of employment, or other conditions of employment. . . .

"(b) The Board shall decide in each case whether, in order to assure to employees the fullest freedom in exercising the rights guaranteed by this Act, the unit appropriate for the purposes of collective bargaining shall be the employer unit, craft unit, plant unit, or subdivision thereof. . . .

"(c) (1) Whenever a petition shall have been filed, in accordance with such regulations as may be prescribed by the Board—

"(A) by an employee or group of employees or any individual or labor organization acting in their behalf alleging that a substantial number of employees (i) wish to be represented for collective bargaining and that their employer declines to recognize their representative as the representative defined in section 9 (a), or (ii) assert that the individual or labor organization, which has been certified or is being currently recognized by their employer as the bargaining representative, is no longer a representative as defined in section 9 (a); or

"(B) by an employer, alleging that one or more individuals or labor organizations have presented to him a claim to be recognized as the representative defined in section 9 (a);

the Board shall investigate such petition and if it has reasonable cause to believe that a question of representation affecting commerce exists shall provide for an appropriate hearing upon due notice. Such hearing may be conducted by an officer or employee of the regional office, who shall not make any recommendations with respect thereto. If the Board finds upon the record of such hearing that such a question of representation exists, it shall direct an election by secret ballot and shall certify the results thereof. . . .

"(3) No election shall be directed in any bargaining unit or any subdivision within which, in the preceding twelve-month period, a valid election shall have been held. Employees on strike who are not entitled to reinstatement shall not be eligible to vote. In any election where none of the choices on the ballot receives a majority, a run-off shall be conducted, the ballot providing for a selection between the two choices receiving the largest and second largest number of valid votes cast in the election. . . .

"(e) (1) Upon the filing with the Board by a labor organization, which is the representative of employees as provided in section 9 (a), of a petition alleging that 30 per centum or more of the employees within a unit claimed to be appropriate for such purposes desire to authorize such labor organization to make an agreement with the employer of such employees requiring membership in such labor organization as a condition of employment in such unit, upon an appropriate showing thereof the Board shall, if no question of representation exists, take a secret ballot of such employees, and shall certify the results thereof to such labor organization and to the employer. . . .

"(h) No investigation shall be made by the Board of any question affecting commerce concerning the representation of employees, raised by a labor organization under subsection (c) of this section, no petition under section 9 (e) (1) shall be entertained, and no complaint shall be issued pursuant to a charge made by a labor organization . . . , unless there is on file with the Board an affidavit executed contemporaneously or within the preceding twelve-month period by each officer of such labor organization and the officers of any national or international labor organization of which it is an affiliate or constituent unit that he is not a member of the Communist Party or affiliated with such party, and that he does not believe in, and is not a member of or supports any organization that believes in or teaches, the overthrow of the United States Government by force or by any illegal or unconstitutional methods. . . .

"Limitations

"*Sec. 13.* Nothing in this Act, except as specifically provided for herein, shall be construed so as either to interfere with or impede or diminish in any way the right to strike, or to affect the limitations or qualifications on that right.

"*Sec. 14.* (a) Nothing herein shall prohibit any individual employed as a supervisor from becoming or remaining a member of a labor organization, but no employer subject to this Act shall be compelled to deem individuals defined herein as supervisors as employees for the purpose of any law, either national or local, relating to collective bargaining.

"(b) Nothing in this Act shall be construed as authorizing the execution or application of agreements requiring membership in a labor organization as a condition of employment in any State or Territory in which such execution or application is prohibited by State or Territorial law. . . .

TITLE II—CONCILIATION OF LABOR DISPUTES IN INDUSTRIES AFFECTING COMMERCE; NATIONAL EMERGENCIES

Sec. 202. (a) There is hereby created an independent agency to be known as the Federal Mediation and Conciliation Service (herein referred to as the "Service". . . .

Sec. 203. (a) It shall be the duty of the Service, in order to prevent or minimize interruptions of the free flow of commerce growing out of labor disputes, to assist parties to labor disputes in industries affecting commerce to settle such disputes through conciliation and mediation.

(b) The Service may proffer its services in any labor dispute in any industry affecting commerce, either upon its own motion or upon the request of one or more of the parties to the dispute, whenever in its judgment such dispute threatens to cause a substantial interruption of commerce. The Director and the Service are directed to avoid attempting to mediate disputes which would have only a minor effect on interstate commerce if State or other conciliation services are available to the parties. Whenever the Service does proffer its services in any dispute, it shall be the duty of the Service promptly to put itself in communication with the parties and to use its best efforts, by mediation and conciliation, to bring them to agreement.

(c) If the Director is not able to bring the parties to agreement by conciliation within a reasonable time, he shall seek to induce the parties voluntarily to seek other means of settling the dispute without resort to strike, lock-out, or other coercion, including submission to the employees in the bargaining unit of the employer's last offer of settlement for approval or rejection in a secret ballot. The failure or refusal of either party to agree to any procedure suggested by the Director shall not be deemed a violation of any duty or obligation imposed by this Act.

(d) Final adjustment by a method agreed upon by the parties is hereby declared to be the desirable method for settlement of grievance disputes arising over the application or interpretation of an existing collective-bargaining agreement. The Service is directed to make its conciliation and mediation services available in the settlement of such grievance disputes only as a last resort and in exceptional cases.

Sec. 204. (a) In order to prevent or minimize interruptions of the free flow of commerce growing out of labor disputes, employers and employees and their representatives, in any industry affecting commerce, shall—

(1) exert every reasonable effort to make and maintain agreements concerning rates of pay, hours, and working conditions, including provision for adequate notice of any proposed change in the terms of such agreements;

(2) whenever a dispute arises over the terms or application of a collective-bargaining agreement and a conference is requested by a party or prospective party thereto, arrange promptly for such a conference to be held and endeavor in such conference to settle such dispute expeditiously; and

(3) in case such dispute is not settled by conference, participate fully and promptly in such meetings as may be undertaken by the Service under this Act for the purpose of aiding in a settlement of the dispute. . . .

National Emergencies

Sec. 206. Whenever in the opinion of the President of the United States, a threatened or actual strike or lock-out affecting an entire industry or a substantial part thereof engaged in trade, commerce, transportation, transmission, or communication among the several States or with foreign nations, or engaged in the production of goods for commerce, will, if permitted to occur or to continue, imperil the national health or safety, he may appoint a board of inquiry to inquire into the issues involved in the dispute and to make a written report to him within such time as he shall prescribe. Such report shall include a statement of the facts with respect to the dispute, including each party's statement of its position but shall not contain any recommendations. The President shall file a copy of such report with the Service and shall make its contents available to the public. . . .

Sec. 208. (a) Upon receiving a report from a board of inquiry the President may direct the Attorney General to petition any district court of the United States having jurisdiction of the parties to enjoin such strike or lock-out or the continuing thereof, and if the court finds that such threatened or actual strike or lock-out—

(i) affects an entire industry or a substantial part thereof engaged in trade, commerce, transportation, transmission, or communication among the several States or with foreign nations, or engaged in the production of goods for commerce; and

(ii) if permitted to occur or to continue, will imperil the national health or safety, it shall have jurisdiction to enjoin any such strike or lock-out, or the continuing thereof, and to make such other orders as may be appropriate. . . .

Sec. 209. (a) Whenever a district court has issued an order under section 208 enjoining acts or practices which imperil or threaten to imperil the national health or safety, it shall be the duty of the parties to the labor dispute giving rise to such order to make every effort to adjust and settle their differences, with the assistance of the Service created by this Act. Neither party shall be under any duty to accept, in whole or in part, any proposal of settlement made by the Service.

(b) Upon the issuance of such order, the President shall reconvene the board of inquiry which has previously reported with respect to the dispute. At the end of a sixty-day period (unless the dispute has been settled by that time), the board of inquiry shall report to the President the current position of the parties and the efforts which have been made for settlement, and shall include a statement by each party of its position and a statement of the employer's last offer of settlement. The President shall make such report available to the public. The National Labor Relations Board, within the succeeding fifteen days, shall take a secret ballot of the employees of each employer involved in the dispute on the question of whether they wish to accept the final offer of settlement made by their employer as stated by him and shall certify the results thereof to the Attorney General within five days thereafter.

Sec. 210. Upon the certification of the results of such ballot or upon a settlement being reached, whichever happens sooner, the Attorney General shall move the court to discharge the injunction, which motion shall then be granted and the injunction discharged. When such motion is granted, the President shall submit to the Congress a full and comprehensive report of the proceedings, including the findings of the board of inquiry and the ballot taken by the National Labor Relations Board, together with such recommendations as he may see fit to make for consideration and appropriate action. . . .

TITLE III

Suits by and against Labor Organizations

Sec. 301. (a) Suits for violation of contracts between an employer and a labor organization representing employees in an industry affecting commerce as defined in this Act, or between any such labor organizations, may be brought in any district court of the United States having jurisdiction of the parties, without respect to the amount in controversy or without regard to the citizenship of the parties.

(b) Any labor organization which represents employees in an industry affecting commerce as defined in this Act and any employer whose activities affect commerce as defined in this Act shall be bound by the acts of its agents. Any such labor organization may sue or be sued as an entity and in behalf of the employees whom it represents in the courts of the United States. Any money judgment against a labor organization in a district court of the United States shall be enforceable only against the organization as an entity and against its assets, and shall not be enforceable against any individual member or his assets. . . .

Boycotts and Other Unlawful Combinations

Sec. 303. (a) It shall be unlawful, for the purposes of this section only, in an industry or activity affecting commerce, for any labor organization to engage in, or to induce or encourage the employees of any employer to engage in, a strike or a concerted refusal in the course of their employment to use, manufacture, process, transport, or otherwise handle or work on any goods, articles, materials, or commodities or to perform any services, where an object thereof is—

(1) forcing or requiring any employer or self-employed person to join any labor or employer organization or any employer or other person to cease using, selling, handling, transporting, or otherwise dealing in the products of any other producer, processor, or manufacturer, or to cease doing business with any other person;

(2) forcing or requiring any other employer to recognize or bargain with a labor organization as the representative of his employees unless such labor organization has been certified as the representative of such employees under the provisions of section 9 of the National Labor Relations Act;

(3) forcing or requiring any employer to recognize or bargain with a particular labor organization as the representative of his employees if another labor organization has been certified as the representative of such employees under the provisions of section 9 of the National Labor Relations Act;

(4) forcing or requiring any employer to assign particular work to employees in a particular labor organization or in a particular trade, craft, or class rather than to employees in another labor organization or in another trade, craft, or class unless such employer is failing to conform to an order or certification of the National Labor Relations Board determining the bargaining representative for employees performing such work. Nothing contained in this subsection shall be construed to make unlawful a refusal by any person to enter upon the premises of any employer (other than his own employer), if the employees of such employer are engaged in a strike ratified or approved by a representative of such employees whom such employer is required to recognize under the National Labor Relations Act.

(b) Whoever shall be injured in his business or property by reason or any violation of subsection (a) may sue therefore in any district court of the United States subject to the limitations and provisions of section 301 hereof without respect to the amount in controversy, or in any other court having jurisdiction of the parties, and shall recover the damages by him sustained and the cost of the suit.

Restriction on Political Contributions

Sec. 304. Section 313 of the Federal Corrupt Practices Act, 1925 (U. S. C., 1940 edition, title 2, sec. 251; Supp. V, title 50, App., sec. 1509), as amended, is amended to read as follows:

"*Sec. 313.* It is unlawful for any national bank, or any corporation organized by authority of any law of Congress, to make a contribution or expenditure in connection with any election to any political office, or in connection with any primary election or political convention or caucus held to select candidates for any political office, or for any corporation whatever, or any labor organization to make a contribution or expenditure in connection with any election at which Presidential and Vice Presidential electors or a Senator or Representative in, or a Delegate or Resident Commissioner to Congress are to be voted for, or in connection with any primary election or political convention or caucus held to select candidates for any of the foregoing offices, or for any candidate, political committee, or other person to accept or receive any contribution prohibited by this section. Every corporation or labor organization which makes any contribution or expenditure in violation of this section shall be fined not more than $5,000; and every officer or director of any corporation, or officer of any labor organization, who consents to any contribution or expenditure by the corporation or labor organization, as the case may be, in violation of this section shall be fined not more than $1,000 or imprisoned for not more than one year, or both. For the purposes of this section 'labor organization' means any organization of any kind, or any agency or employee representation committee or plan, in which employees participate and which exists for the purpose, in whole or in part, of dealing with employers concerning grievances, labor disputes, wages, rates of pay, hours of employment, or conditions of work."

Strikes by Government Employees

Sec. 305. It shall be unlawful for any individual employed by the United States or any agency thereof including wholly owned Government corporations to participate in any strike. Any individual employed by the United States or by any such agency who strikes shall be discharged immediately from his employment, and shall forfeit his civil service status, if any, and shall not be eligible for reemployment for three years by the United States or any such agency. . . .

SELECTION 3

The Fair Deal: Harry S. Truman, State of the Union Address, 1949

In 1948, to their dismay, the Republicans failed to capture the Presidency. Although nearly all the polls showed their candidate, Thomas E. Dewey, a sure winner, Truman won by more than two million votes. In addition, the Democratic party regained control of both houses of Congress. The people seemed to have decisively rejected a return to normalcy.

Now President in his own right, Truman put forward a legislative program. Much of it was identical with Roosevelt's New Deal. Truman's adoption of the label "Fair Deal" seemed more than anything else an effort to coin a slogan of his own. A studious reader of Truman's public papers may, however, discern a slight difference between the New Deal and the Fair Deal. Whereas Roosevelt had spoken simply of the government's duty to aid the poor, Truman spoke of a special duty to aid those to whom society had denied equal opportunities for education and advancement—particularly ethnic and racial minorities.

Truman's hopes and disappointments are fully expressed in his own Memoirs (two volumes, 1955). His record in office is chronicled in W. F. Zornow, America at Mid-century: The Truman Administration; the Eisenhower Administration *(1959), and analyzed in Louis W. Koenig,* The Truman Administration *(1956). The following document is Truman's first State of the Union message after his 1948 victory. The basic statement of his program, it is taken from* Vital Speeches, *volume 15 (Jan. 15, 1949), pages 194–197.*

Mr. President, Mr. Speaker, Members of the Congress: I am happy to report to this Eighty-first Congress that the state of the union is good. Our nation is better able than ever before to meet the needs of the American people, and to give them their fair chance in the pursuit of happiness. This great Republic is foremost among the nations of the world in the search for peace.

During the last sixteen years the American people have been creating a society which offers new opportunities for every man to enjoy his share of the good things of life.

In this society we are conservative about the values and principles which we cherish; but we are forward-looking in protecting those values and principles and in extending their benefits. We have rejected the discredited theory that the fortunes of the nation should be in the hands of a privileged few. We have abandoned the "trickle-down" concept of national prosperity.

Instead, we believe that our economic system should rest on a democratic foundation and that wealth should be created for the benefit of all.

The recent election shows that the people of the United States are in favor of this kind of society and want to go on improving it.

The American people have decided that poverty is just as wasteful and just as unnecessary as preventable disease. We have pledged our common resources to help one another in the hazards and struggles of individual life. We believe that no unfair prejudice or artificial distinction should bar any citizen of the United States of America from an education, or from good health, or from a job that he is capable of performing.

The attainment of this kind of society demands the best efforts of every citizen in every walk of life, and it imposes increasing responsibilities on the Government.

The Government must work with industry, labor and the farmers in keeping our economy running at full speed. The Government must see that every American has a chance to obtain his fair share of our increasing abundance. These responsibilities go hand in hand.

We cannot maintain prosperity unless we have a fair distribution of opportunity and a widespread consumption of the products of our factories and farms.

Our Government has undertaken to meet these responsibilities.

We have made tremendous public investments in highways, hydroelectric power projects, soil conservation and reclamation. We have established a system of social security. We have enacted laws protecting the rights and the welfare of our working people and the income of our farmers.

These Federal policies have paid for themselves many times over. They have strengthened the material foundations of our democratic ideals. Without them our present prosperity would be impossible.

Reinforced by these policies, our private enterprise system has reached new heights of production. Since the boom year of 1929, while our population has increased by only 20 per cent, our agricultural production has increased by 45 per cent, and our industrial production has increased by 75 per cent. We are turning out far more goods and more wealth per worker than we have ever done before.

This progress has confounded the gloomy prophets—at home and abroad—who predicted the downfall of American capitalism. The people of the United States, going their own way, confident in their own powers, have achieved the greatest prosperity the world has ever seen.

But, great as our progress has been, we still have a long way to go.

As we look around the country many of our shortcomings stand out in bold relief.

We are suffering from excessively high prices.

Our production is still not large enough to satisfy our demands.

Our minimum wages are far too low.

Small business is losing ground to growing monopoly.

Our farmers still face an uncertain future. And too many of them lack the benefits of our modern civilization.

Some of our natural resources are still being wasted.

We are acutely short of electric power, although the means for developing such power are abundant.

Five million families are still living in slums and firetraps. Three million families share their homes with others.

Our health is far behind the progress of medical science. Proper medical care is so expensive that it is out of reach of the great majority of our citizens.

Our schools, in many localities, are utterly inadequate.

Our democratic ideals are often thwarted by prejudice and intolerance.

Each of these shortcomings is also an opportunity—an opportunity for the Congress and the President to work for the good of the people.

Our first great opportunity is to protect our economy against the evils of "boom and bust."

This objective cannot be attained by Government alone. Indeed, the greater part of the task must be performed by individual efforts under our system of free enterprise. We can keep our present prosperity, and increase it, only if free enterprise and free Government work together to that end.

We cannot afford to float ceaselessly on a post-war boom until it collapses. It is not enough merely to prepare to weather a recession if it comes. Instead, government and business must work together constantly to achieve more and more jobs and more and more production—which mean more and more prosperity for all the people.

The business cycle is man-made; and men of good-will, working together, can smooth it out.

So far as business is concerned, it should plan for steady, vigorous expansion—seeking always to increase its output, lower its prices, and avoid the vices of monopoly and restrictions. So long as business does this, it will be contributing to continued prosperity and it will have the help and encouragement of the Government. . . .

One of the most important factors in maintaining prosperity is the Government's fiscal policy. At this time it is essential not only that the Federal budget be balanced but also that there be a substantial surplus to reduce inflationary pressures and to permit a sizeable reduction in the national debt, which now stands as $252 billion.

I recommend, therefore, that the Congress enact new tax legislation to bring in an additional $4 billion of Government revenue. This should come principally from additional corporate taxes. A portion should come from revised estate and gift taxes. Consideration should be given to raising personal income tax rates in the middle and upper brackets.

If we want to keep our economy running to high gear we must be sure that every group has the incentive to make its full contribution to the national welfare. At present the working men and women of the nation are unfairly discriminated against by a statute that abridges their rights, curtails their constructive efforts and hampers our system of free collective bargaining. That statute is the Labor-Management Relations Act of 1947, sometimes called the Taft-Hartley Act.

That act should be repealed.

The Wagner Act should be reenacted. . . .

The health of our economy and its maintenance at high levels further require that the minimum wage fixed by law should be raised to at least 75 cents an hour.

If our free enterprise economy is to be strong and healthy we must reinvigorate the forces of competition. We must assure small business the freedom and opportunity to grow and prosper. To this purpose, we should strengthen our anti-trust laws by closing those loopholes that permit monopolistic mergers and consolidations.

Our national farm program should be improved—not only in the interest of the farmers but for the lasting prosperity of the whole nation. Our goals should be abundant farm production and parity income for agriculture. Standards of living on the farm should be just as good as anywhere else.

Farm price supports are an essential part of our program to achieve these ends. Price supports should be used to prevent farm price declines which are out of line with general price levels, to facilitate adjustments in production to consumer demands, and to promote good land use. Our price support legislation must be adapted to these objectives. The authority of the Commodity Credit Corporation to provide adequate storage space for crops should be restored.

Our program for farm prosperity should also seek to expand the domestic market for agricultural products, particularly among low income groups, and to increase and stabilize foreign markets.

We should give special attention to extending modern conveniences and services to our farms. Rural electrification should be pushed forward. And in considering legislation relating to housing, education, health and social security, special attention should be given to rural problems.

Our growing population and the expansion of our economy depends upon the wise management of our land, water, forest and mineral wealth. In our present dynamic economy the task of conservation is not to lock up our resources, but to develop and improve them. Failure, today, to make the investments which are necessary to support our progress in the future would be false economy.

We must push forward the development of our rivers for power, irrigation, navigation and flood control. We should apply the lessons of our Tennessee Valley experience to our other great river basins.

I again recommend action be taken by the Congress to approve the St. Lawrence Seaway and Power Project. This is about the fifth time I've recommended it.

We must adopt a program for the planned use of the petroleum reserves under the sea, which are—and must remain—vested in the Federal Government. We must extend our programs of soil conservation. We must place our forests on a sustained yield basis and encourage the development of new sources of vital minerals.

In all this we must make sure that the benefits of these public undertakings are directly available to the people. Public power should be carried to consuming areas by public transmission lines where necessary to provide electricity at the lowest possible rates. Irrigation waters should serve family farms and not land speculators.

The Government has still other opportunities—to help raise the standard of living of our citizens. These opportunities lie in the fields of social security, health, education, housing and civil rights.

The present coverage of the social security laws is altogether inadequate, and benefit payments are too low. One-third of our workers are not covered. Those who receive old age and survivors insurance benefits receive an average payment of only $25 a month. Many others who cannot work because they are physically disabled are left to the mercy of charity.

We should expand our social security program, both as to the size of the benefits and extent of coverage, against the economic hazards due to unemployment, old age, sickness, and disability.

We must spare no effort to raise the general level of health in this country. In a nation as rich as ours it is a shocking fact that tens of millions lack adequate medical care. We are short of doctors, hospitals and nurses. We must remedy these shortages. Moreover, we need—and we must have without further delay—a system of pre-paid medical insurance which will enable every American to afford good medical care.

It is equally shocking that millions of our children are not receiving a good education. Millions of them are in overcrowded, obsolete buildings. We are short of teachers, because teachers' salaries are too low to attract new teachers, or to hold the ones we have. All these school problems will become much more acute as a result of the tremendous increase in the enrollment in our elementary schools in the next few years.

I cannot repeat too strongly my desire for prompt Federal financial aid to the states to help them operate and maintain their school systems.

The Governmental agency which now administers the programs of health, education and social security should be given full departmental status.

The housing shortage continues to be acute. As an immediate step, the Congress should enact the provisions of low-rent public housing, slum clearance, farm housing and housing research which I have repeatedly recommended. The number of low-rent public housing units provided for in the legislation should be increased to 1,000,000 units in the next seven years. Even this number of units will not begin to meet our need for new housing.

Most of the houses we need will have to be built by private enterprise, without public subsidy. By producing too few rental units and too large a proportion of high-priced houses, the building industry is rapidly pricing itself out of the market. Building costs must be lowered.

The Government is now engaged in a campaign to induce all segments of the building industry to concentrate on the production of lower priced housing. Additional legislation to encourage such housing will be submitted.

The authority which I have requested to allocate materials in short supply and to impose price ceilings on such materials, could be used, if found necessary, to channel more materials into homes large enough for family life at prices which wage earners can afford.

The driving force behind our progress is our faith in our democratic institutions. That faith is embodied in the promise of equal rights and equal opportunities which the founders of our republic proclaimed to their countrymen and to the whole world.

The fulfillment of this promise is among the highest purposes of Government.

We stand at the opening of an era which can mean either great achievement or terrible catastrophe for ourselves and for all mankind.

The strength of our nation must continue to be used in the interest of all our people rather than a privileged few. It must continue to be used unselfishly in the struggle for world peace and the betterment of mankind the world over.

This is the task before us.

It is not an easy one. It has many complications, and there will be strong opposition from selfish interests.

I hope for cooperation from farmers, from labor, and from business. Every segment of our population and every individual have a right to expect from our Government a fair deal. . . .

Eisenhower on Modern Republicanism

Few of Truman's hopes were realized. Although the Democratic party maintained majorities in Congress, many of the Democrats, especially from the South, were conservatives. Blocs of Republicans and conservative Democrats dominated both houses, with the result that little of the Fair Deal was enacted into law.

Between 1948 and 1952, conditions in the country changed markedly. As documents in later chapters illustrate, the nation became engaged in a cold war with the Soviet Union; it found itself involved in a real war in Korea; and, at home, in spite of unparalleled prosperity, people succumbed to exaggerated fears of a domestic Communist menace. As of 1952, feeling was widespread that the successive Democratic administrations had made serious mistakes in foreign affairs, mishandled the Korean conflict, and underestimated the Communist threat at home. In addition, instances of corruption had come to light, some of them involving associates of the President. All signs indicated that voters would this time respond favorably to the Republican cry that it was "time for a change."

Many Republicans wanted as their presidential candidate the man who symbolized conservative opposition to the New Deal and Fair Deal—Robert A. Taft. Others, especially in Eastern cities, were opposed to Taft, largely because he seemed an unregenerate isolationist. Banding together, these Eastern Republicans championed the nomination of Dwight D. Eisenhower, a war hero with no political past but with a known attachment to internationalism. The battle for the nomination was fierce. The first ballot at the Republican convention was close. In the end, Eisenhower emerged as victor.

This time, Republican prophecies of victory were accurate. Eisenhower was elected President by a huge popular margin. At the same time, Republicans captured slim majorities in both houses of Congress. At last, it seemed, normalcy was at hand.

In practice, however, Eisenhower proved less conservative than his party. While he cut back Federal spending, he made few moves to end the welfare programs of the New Deal and Fair Deal. As time passed, he became convinced that a few further programs were in order.

After the death of Senator Taft in 1954, Eisenhower found himself more and more at odds with the Republican leadership in Congress. Even before he became a candidate for reelection in 1956, he spoke to intimates about the possibility of calling for formation of a new party, combining middle-of-the-road Republicans and Democrats and leaving out the reactionary wing of the GOP. He did not act on this thought. He ran again as a regular Republican candidate and won by an even larger margin than in 1952.

Surprisingly, Eisenhower's 1956 victory was not accompanied by Republican victories in congressional races. The House and Senate, which the Democrats had captured in 1954, remained under Democratic control. From that time on, Eisenhower in practice worked more with middle-of-the-road Democrats than with congressmen of his own party. Together, he and Lyndon B. Johnson of Texas, the Democratic leader in the Senate, engineered the passage of laws making modest beginnings toward Federal aid to education and greater protection for the voting rights of racial minorities.

Eisenhower labeled his position "Modern Republicanism." In a press conference in November, 1956, he outlined the meaning of this phrase. In a speech to Republican party workers in June, 1957, he elaborated on it. Both documents are reproduced below. In them, one can see how the idea of return to normalcy, after the model of the 1920s, had disappeared. The new conservatism, as voiced by Eisenhower, was committed to perpetuation of most of the changes wrought by the reformers of the 1930s and 1940s. The fullest account of Eisenhower's administration is his own The White House Years *(two volumes, 1963, 1965). Sherman Adams,* Firsthand Report *(1961) is by the White House chief of staff; E. J. Hughes,* Ordeal of Power *(1963) is a perceptive analysis by a onetime speech writer for the President. The two documents below are from* Public Papers of the Presidents: Dwight D. Eisenhower, 1956 *(1957), pages 1102–1103 and* ibid., 1957 *(1958), pages 448–458.*

PRESS CONFERENCE REMARKS, NOVEMBER 14, 1956

Q. Raymond P. Brandt, St. Louis Post-Dispatch: Mr. President, on Tuesday night you spoke of Modern Republicanism. What are your plans for greater effort to bring about cooperation with a certain group of your party in Congress to assert your leadership for Modern Republicanism?

The President: I would say this: in these 4 years ahead of us I intend to work for such a concept industriously and incessantly. I think that there is before the American people now, including even these people that you rather allowed to stay anonymous—[*laughter*]—that must convince even them that some change in the understanding that the public has of the Republican Party is necessary.

Now, I think I can tell you in a few sentences what I think about Modern Republicanism.

It is a type of political philosophy that recognizes clearly the responsibility of the Federal Government to take the lead in making certain that the productivity of our great economic machine is distributed so that no one will suffer disaster, privation, through no fault of his own. Now, this covers the wide field of education and health, and so on.

We believe likewise in the free enterprise system. We believe that it is free enterprise that has brought these blessings to America.

Therefore, we are going to try our best to preserve that free enterprise, and put all of these problems in the hands of localities and the private enterprise of States wherever we can. It happens that the great difference, as I see it, between myself and people of a philosophy that believes in centralized government, is that I believe to have this free enterprise healthy, you must have, first, integrity in your fiscal operations of the Government; second, you must preserve a sound dollar or all of our plans for social security and pensions for the aged fall by the wayside, they are no good; and thirdly, in this dispersion of power.

Now, that, at home, as I see it, represents Modern Republicanism.

ADDRESS TO REPUBLICAN PARTY WORKERS, JUNE 7, 1957

. . . Representative government can succeed only where there are healthy, responsible political parties. These parties must have at the center and core of their being the same dedication to the service of our nation as inspires the men of our armed services.

This sense of patriotism is felt by both of America's great parties—in this matter let no one anywhere in the world think Americans are divided.

But one thing more is necessary: A political party must stand for something—policies that it believes will advance the best interests of the entire nation. It must stand for principles and programs that the sovereign voters of the country can clearly see, identify and judge.

So what do we as Republicans stand for?

Why have we joined together in a national organization? And why do hundreds and thousands of Republicans work side by side—often without recognition or distinction or reward—in tasks assigned by this organization to which we all belong?

We do this because we have been drawn together by a set of common beliefs and principles respecting government and its relationship to other governments, to our own economy and to each individual citizen.

These beliefs are plainly stated in our Declarations of Faith and our Declarations of Determination which are the Republican National Platform of 1956. As we read and re-read that platform—a practice which I commend to all of you—it becomes very clear that the modern Republican Party stands one hundred percent for the basic principles of Republicanism that have been its guide since the days of its founding.

Some of the features of those beliefs:

We believe in integrity in government—not government by crony.

We believe that whatever can be done by private effort should be done by private effort rather than by the government—and not the other way round.

We believe that, if a job must be done by government, it should whenever possible be done by State and local government rather than by the Federal government—and not the other way round. We oppose unnecessary centralization of power.

We believe in a sound dollar—not a rubber dollar.

And therefore, we believe that a government should operate on a balanced budget and not go into debt except in emergencies—we reject deficit spending as a fiscal policy for America.

We believe that we should work to reduce taxes—not raise them; as we also seek to reduce our huge national debt.

And as we think, ladies and gentlemen, over the record of the past four years, let us not forget that the greatest tax cut in history was granted by the Republicans in power in Congress and the Administration. And we have paid something on our national debt.

We believe in vigorous and impartial enforcement of the laws.

We believe that private business is a healthy force which is the foundation of our prosperity, and should be respected and encouraged—not bullied and abused. And the fact that the four-year period since the reintroduction of this attitude into government has also been the period of the greatest sustained growth in jobs, production and incomes of all modern peace times is not, may I say, a mere congenial coincidence.

We believe that government can and should discharge its constitutional duty to promote the general well-being of its citizens—and can do so without excessive centralization.

We believe that to preserve our own freedom we must concern ourselves with the security of other free nations constantly exposed to the threat of domination by international communism. Nothing today can present more danger to us than a retreat to the folly of isolationism.

We believe in the pre-eminence of the individual citizen and his rights—with the government his servant, not his master or his keeper.

It is principles like these, then, that not only draw us together, but also set us apart from the easy-spending, paternalistic, business-baiting inflationists who were so influential for years before 1953.

But, while our principles have remained unchanged for a hundred years, the problems to which these principles must be applied have changed radically and rapidly.

Fortunately, one of the most all-pervading principles of our Party—and one most important to us today—is the willingness to adapt our basic convictions imaginatively to current problems.

We recall those ringing words spoken by Lincoln at a time of great tension and change. He said, "The dogmas of the quiet past, are inadequate to the stormy present. The occasion is piled high with difficulty, and we must rise with the occasion. As our case is new, so we must think anew, and act anew."

My friends, it comes down to this simple statement: It is the problems that change; the principles do not.

Let us look at several examples in government.

Agriculture. Because of the unique exposure of the farmer to economic forces over which he has no control, and the dependency of the nation upon our agricultural economy, the Federal government must concern itself in practical ways to assist in assuring a sound farm economy and income. That's the principle.

Now, one application of this principle a hundred years ago: A Federal Homestead Act, passed under Lincoln, providing free quarter sections of land to settlers. That's what they did a hundred years ago.

The application today: a new set of Federal actions, such as sensible price supports, the Soil Bank, stepped-up Federal research, and development of markets.

It is the problem that has changed; the principle has not.

Education. The principle: Education is vital to free government and it is a local matter; the Federal government should do only what has to be done toward provision of adequate education that State and local governments cannot do, things which will never allow the Federal government to become a controlling factor.

One application a hundred years ago: the Land Grant Act sponsored by Congressman Justin Smith Morrill, one of the organizers of the Republican Party from Vermont. That Federal Act made possible the growth of higher education in many places where it otherwise could not have begun or would have had great difficulty in starting.

The application today: emergency Federal help to assist the States to knock out a schoolroom deficit resulting from the national—not local—disasters of depression and war.

It is the problem that has changed; not the principle. . . .

We must not forget that to be truly conservative today is to be alert to the dangers of loose spending and of tampering with our nation's fiscal integrity. It involves, also, providing those things which would keep this country healthy, strong, growing and secure. . . .

We believe that our principles and our program truly reflect the aspirations of the overwhelming majority of Americans. There are those who rationalize a narrower point of view by saying they would rather be right than win. If such were the issue, all of us would agree. But this is not the issue. The Republican Party can and will be both right and win. It will do so because its central core of conviction is what America believes and wants today.

If we unite behind these principles and programs that the American people have so emphatically endorsed—my friends, we just can't lose!

The key to victory is unity.

As for myself, I welcome every person who believes in the principles our Platform expresses.

The great main stream of our cause is broad enough to include the oldest and finest of our conservative traditions, along with the most up to date application of those traditions to the age of automation and the atom.

Certainly none of us would want to be guilty of the supreme suicidal folly of forfeiting victory for vital principles, in order to indulge too long our differences as to the tactics to use.

Consider the alternative!

Suppose we go down to defeat? Suppose we go down to defeat because of these tactical differences, in support, we think, of the same principles? Will the Administration that follows be more to the liking of any Republican? I think we know the answer to that one.

Who wants to go back on the New-Deal Fair-Deal toboggan of loose spending, centralization, punishment of business and fiscal irresponsibility?

Of this there is no danger, if we close ranks now!

Lincoln said, in one of his most powerful statements, "We succeed only by concert. It is not," he said, " 'can any of us imagine better?' but," the question is, " 'can we all do better?' "

Certainly, each of us thinks he can "imagine better" than the Platform on which the Party has agreed. But this is not the question. The time is here for doing.

My fellow Republicans: I believe in the Republican Party, with all my heart. I believe in its capacity, in positions of political leadership, to serve our country today more effectively than can any other. I accepted nomination for this office, and again re-nomination, because I believed this, and because I believed in Republican principles of good government. I still believe those things. Every act of this Administration, of all my principal associates and myself stands witness to this fact.

Above all, I sincerely believe, as I said at last summer's convention, that the Republican Party can, should and must be the Party of the Future. It can and should be an instrument through which the American people, by the grace of God, carry our country forward to new heights of well-being, justice, harmony and peace.

Thanks very much, my friends.

Goodbye.

The New Frontier: John F. Kennedy, State of the Union Address, 1961

In 1960 the Republican candidate for the Presidency was Richard M. Nixon. For eight years Eisenhower's Vice President, Nixon stood forth as a champion of Modern Republicanism. The Democratic candidate was Senator John F. Kennedy of Massachusetts. A middle-of-the-roader who had generally followed Lyndon Johnson's lead in the Senate, Kennedy had few issues to raise against his opponent. Kennedy could simply call for larger-scale programs more vigorously administered. The chief point of public discussion during the campaign was the fact that Kennedy was a Roman Catholic, the first of his faith to seek the Presidency since Al Smith in 1928.

In the upshot, Kennedy won. His margin was a scant 120,000 votes.

Despite the absence of issues in the campaign and the closeness of the final vote, Kennedy's victory had great significance. It symbolized the end of the Anglo-Saxon Protestant's assured dominance in American politics. Perhaps more important, it symbolized a transfer of power from the old to the young. At forty-three, Kennedy was the youngest man ever to be elected President. Although Nixon, too, was in his mid-forties, his links were with the old guard of his party. Kennedy, with great physical vitality, a crisp intelligence, a pragmatic mind, cultivated tastes, and deep reserves of self-confidence, represented a wholly new generation, with a new style in leadership. Kennedy's style and personality were to have great impact not only on his contemporaries but on all the youth of his day.

J. M. Burns, John F. Kennedy *(1960) is a preelection biography; T. H. White,* The Making of the President, 1960 *(1961) is a superb account of the election campaign; Theodore Sorenson,* Kennedy *(1965) is an analytical account by Kennedy's closest aide; A. M. Schlesinger, Jr.,* A Thousand Days *(1965) is a powerful narrative by a historian who was also close to Kennedy and served on his White House staff.*

Such changes as were wrought by Kennedy's election were changes in style more than changes in program. The document that follows is Kennedy's first State of the Union message. It sets forth his program, the slogan for which was the "New Frontier." Though considerably bolder than Modern Republicanism, this program contained relatively little that had not been in the programs of Roosevelt, Truman, and Eisenhower.

The text is taken from The Public Papers of the Presidents: John F. Kennedy, 1961 *(1962), pages 19–28.*

. . . It is a pleasure to return from whence I came. You are my oldest friends in Washington, and this House is my oldest home. It was here, more than fourteen years ago, that I first took the oath of Federal office. It was here, for fourteen years, that I gained both knowledge and inspiration from members of both parties in both Houses, from your wise and generous leaders, and from the pronouncements which I can vividly recall, sitting where you now sit, including the programs of two great Presidents, the undimmed eloquence of Churchill, the soaring idealism of Nehru, the steadfast words of General de Gaulle. To speak from this same historic rostrum is a sobering experience. To be back among so many friends is a happy one.

I am confident that that friendship will continue. Our Constitution wisely assigns both joint and separate roles to each branch of the government; and a President and a Congress who hold each other in mutual respect will neither permit nor attempt any trespass. For my part, I shall withhold from neither the Congress nor the people any fact or report, past, present or future, which is necessary for an informed judgment of our conduct and hazards. I shall neither shift the burden of executive decisions to the Congress, nor avoid responsibility for the outcome of those decisions.

I speak today in an hour of national peril and national opportunity. Before my term has ended, we shall have to test anew whether a nation organized and governed such as ours can endure. The outcome is by no means certain. The answers are by no means clear. All of us together—this Administration, this Congress, this nation—must forge those answers.

But today, were I to offer, after little more than a week in office, detailed legislation to remedy every national ill, the Congress would rightly wonder whether the desire for speed had replaced the duty of responsibility.

My remarks, therefore, will be limited. But they will also be candid. To state the facts frankly is not to despair the future nor indict the past. The prudent heir takes careful inventory of his legacies, and gives a faithful accounting to those whom he owes an obligation of trust. And, while the occasion does not call for another recital of our blessings and assets, we do have no greater asset than the willingness of a free and determined people, through its elected officials, to face all problems frankly and meet all dangers free from panic or fear.

The present state of our economy is disturbing. We take office in the wake of seven months of recession, three and one-half years of slack, seven years of diminished economic growth, and nine years of falling farm income.

Business bankruptcies have reached their highest level since the Great Depression. Since 1951 farm income has been squeezed down by 25 per cent. Save for a brief period in 1958, insured unemployment is at the highest peak in our history. Of some five and one-half million Americans who are without jobs, more than one million have been searching for work for more than four months. And during each month some 150,000 workers are exhausting their already meager jobless benefit rights.

Nearly one-eighth of those who are without jobs live almost without hope in nearly one hundred depressed and troubled areas. The rest include new school graduates unable to use their talents, farmers forced to give up their part-time jobs which helped balance their family budgets, skilled and unskilled workers laid off in such important industries as metals, machinery, automobiles and apparel.

Our recovery from the 1958 recession, moreover, was anemic and incomplete. Our Gross National Product never regained its full potential. Unemployment never returned to normal levels. Maximum use of our national industrial capacity was never restored.

In short, the American economy is in trouble. The most resourceful industrialized country on earth ranks among the last in the rate of economic growth. Since last spring our economic growth rate has actually receded. Business investment is in a decline. Profits have fallen below predicted levels. Construction is off. A million unsold automobiles are in inventory. Fewer people are working, and the average work week has shrunk well below forty hours. Yet prices have continued to rise, so that now too many Americans have *less* to spend for items that cost *more* to buy.

Economic prophecy is at best an uncertain art, as demonstrated by the prediction one year ago from this same podium that 1960 would be, and I quote, "the most prosperous year in our history." Nevertheless, forecasts of continued slack and only slightly reduced unemployment through 1961 and 1962 have been made with alarming unanimity, and this Administration does not intend to stand helplessly by.

We cannot afford to waste idle hours and empty plants while awaiting the end of the recession. We must show the world what a free economy can do, to reduce unemployment, to put unused capacity to work, to spur new productivity, and to foster higher economic growth within a range of sound fiscal policies and relative price stability.

I will propose to the Congress within the next fourteen days measures to improve unemployment compensation through temporary increases in duration on a self-supporting basis; to provide more food for the families of the unemployed, and to aid their needy children; to redevelop our areas of chronic labor surplus; to expand the services of the U.S. Employment Offices; to stimulate housing and construction; to secure more purchasing power for our lowest-paid workers by raising and expanding the minimum wage; to offer tax incentives for sound plant investment; to increase the development of natural resources; to encourage price stability; and to take other steps aimed at insuring a prompt recovery and paving the way for increased long-range growth. This is not a partisan program concentrating on our weaknesses; it is, I hope, a national program to realize our national strength. . . .

The current Federal budget for fiscal 1961 is almost certain to show a net deficit. The budget already submitted for fiscal 1962 will remain in balance only if the Congress enacts all the revenue measures requested, and only if an earlier and sharper upturn in the economy than my economic advisers now think likely produces the tax revenues estimated. Nevertheless, a new Administration must of necessity build on the spending and revenue estimates already submitted. Within that framework, barring the development of urgent national defense needs or a worsening of the economy, it is my current intention to advocate a program of expenditures which, including revenues from a stimulation of the economy, will not of and by themselves unbalance the earlier budget.

However, we will do what must be done. For our national household is cluttered with unfinished and neglected tasks. Our cities are being engulfed in squalor. Twelve long years after Congress declared our goal to be "a decent home and a suitable environment for every American family," we still have 25 million Americans living in substandard homes. A new housing program under a new Housing and Urban Affairs Department will be needed this year.

Our classrooms contain two million more children than they can properly have room for, taught by ninety thousand teachers not properly qualified to teach. One-third of our most promising high school graduates are financially unable to continue the development of their talents. The war babies of the 1940's, who overcrowded our schools in the 1950's, are now descending in 1960 upon our colleges—with two college students for every one, ten years from now—and our colleges are ill prepared. We lack the scientists, the engineers and the teachers our world obligations require. We have neglected oceanography, saline water conversion and the basic research that lies at the root of all progress. Federal grants for both higher and public school education can no longer be delayed.

Medical research has achieved new wonders, but these wonders are too often beyond the reach of too many people, owing to a lack of income (particularly among the aged), a lack of hospital beds, a lack of nursing homes and a lack of doctors and dentists. Measures to provide health care for the aged under Social Security, and to increase the supply of both facilities and personnel, must be undertaken this year.

Our supply of clean water is dwindling. Organized and juvenile crimes cost the taxpayers millions of dollars each year, making it essential that we have improved enforcement and new legislative safeguards. The denial of constitutional rights to some of our fellow Americans on account of race, at the ballot box and elsewhere, disturbs the national conscience, and subjects us to the charge of world opinion that our democracy is not equal to the high promise of our heritage. Morality in private business has not been sufficiently spurred by morality in public business. A host of problems and projects in all fifty states, though not possible to include in this message, deserves, and will receive, the attention of both the Congress and the Executive Branch. . . . In the words of a great President, whose birthday we honor today, closing his final State of the Union Message sixteen years ago, "We pray that we may be worthy of the unlimited opportunities that God has given us."

Toward a New Congress: "Baker v. Carr"

In November, 1963, Kennedy was assassinated by a madman. As of that date, little of the New Frontier had been translated into law. Like Roosevelt, Truman, and even Eisenhower, Kennedy had been frustrated by opposition from the congressional coalition of conservative Republicans and Southern Democrats.

Soon, however, the logjam began to break. Congress passed a major civil rights act. (See Part Nine below.) After stepping up aid to higher education, it finally enacted legislation for improving elementary and secondary schools. Congress also agreed to federally financed medical care for the aged.

One reason for the passage of this legislation was careful planning by Kennedy before his death. Another was that his Vice President and successor was Lyndon B. Johnson, one of the most skilled legislative managers in the history of Congress. But still another was that the Congress itself was undergoing change; and a major reason for that was a decree by the Supreme Court signifying that Congress would have to become more representative of America's changed population.

The America of the 1960s was nearly 80 per cent urban. The composition of few state legislatures reflected that fact. Rural areas were heavily overrepresented, and urban areas underrepresented. State legislatures so composed then decided the composition and boundaries of congressional districts. The result naturally was that rural areas received preference. It was not uncommon for an urban congressional district to contain half a million voters while a rural district contained fewer than 100,000. The rural population was overrepresented in Congress as well as in state legislatures. And, by and large, the rural minority cared less than the urban majority about civil rights, schools, medical care for the aged, and other elements in the New Deal, the Fair Deal, Modern Republicanism, and the New Frontier.

Ruling, in 1961, in the case of Baker et al. v. Carr et al., *the Supreme Court held that the overrepresentation of rural areas in state legislatures was contrary to the Constitution. The suit had been brought by a group of Tennessee voters. The basis of the suit was the fact that the Tennessee legislature had not been reapportioned since 1901. Changes over the years had made some legislative districts much more populous than others, yet these districts still had but one representative in Nashville.*

Baker and the other Tennessee voters claimed that the result was to deny them the equal protection of the laws guaranteed by the Fourteenth Amendment. They had asked a Federal district court to order Joe C. Carr, the secretary of state of Tennessee, and other Tennessee officials, to reapportion the state legislature. The district court had dismissed their suit. One stated reason was that the case was "political" and hence outside the jurisdiction of the Federal judiciary. A second stated reason was that the ground of complaint was insufficient.

The Supreme Court reversed the decision of the district court. Eight justices, one abstaining, ruled that the issue was one on which the Federal courts had jurisdiction. They also ruled that the plaintiffs had ample ground for filing suit. The most lucid analysis of the issues and the Court's decision is R. G. McCloskey, "The Supreme Court, 1961 Term, Foreword: The Reapportionment Case," Harvard Law Review *(November, 1962), pages 54–74.*

Although the immediate effect of the decision was simply that the case be heard again in the lower court, the long-term effect was to command the states to reapportion their legislatures so that districts would be more nearly equal in population. Acting in accordance with this decision, courts thereafter ordered state after state to effect such reforms.

The document that follows is excerpted from the opinion of the Court as delivered by Mr. Justice Brennan. It is taken from United States Supreme Court Reports, *Volume 369 (1961–1962), pages 186–237.*

This civil action was brought under 42 U. S. C. §§ 1983 and 1988 to redress the alleged deprivation of federal constitutional rights. The complaint, alleging that by means of a 1901 statute of Tennessee apportioning the members of the General Assembly among the State's 95 counties, "these plaintiffs and others similarly situated, are denied the equal protection of the laws accorded them by the Fourteenth Amendment to the Constitution of the United States by virtue of the debasement of their votes," was dismissed by a three-judge court convened under 28 U. S. C. § 2281 in the Middle District of Tennessee. The court held that it lacked jurisdiction of the subject matter and also that no claim was stated upon which relief could be granted. . . . We hold that the dismissal was error, and remand the cause to the District Court for trial and further proceedings consistent with this opinion.

The General Assembly of Tennessee consists of the Senate with 33 members and the House of Representatives with 99 members. The Tennessee Constitution provides in Art. II as follows:

> Sec. 3. Legislative authority—Term of office.—The Legislative authority of this State shall be vested in a General Assembly, which shall consist of a Senate and House of Representatives, both dependent on the people; who shall hold their offices for two years from the day of the general election.
>
> Sec. 4. Census.—An enumeration of the qualified voters, and an apportionment of the Representatives in the General Assembly, shall be made in the year one thousand eight hundred and seventy-one, and within every subsequent term of ten years.
>
> Sec. 5. Apportionment of representatives.—The number of Representatives shall, at the several periods of making the enumeration, be apportioned among the several counties or districts, according to the number of qualified voters in each; and shall not exceed seventy-five, until the population of the State shall be one million and a half, and shall never exceed ninety-nine; Provided, that any county having two-thirds of the ratio shall be entitled to one member.
>
> Sec. 6. Apportionment of senators.—The number of Senators shall, at the several periods of making the enumeration, be apportioned among the several counties or districts according to the number of qualified electors in each, and shall not exceed one-third the number of representatives. In apportioning the Senators among the different counties, the fraction that may be lost by any county or counties, in the apportionment of members to the House of Representatives, shall be made up to such county or counties in the Senate, as near as may be practicable. When a district is composed of two or more counties, they shall be adjoining; and no county shall be divided in forming a district.

Thus, Tennessee's standard for allocating legislative representation among her counties is the total number of qualified voters resident in the respective counties, subject only to minor qualifications. Decennial reapportionment in compliance with the constitutional scheme was effected by the General Assembly each decade from 1871 to 1901. The 1871 apportionment was preceded by an 1870 statute requiring an enumeration. The 1881 apportionment involved three statutes, the first authorizing an enumeration, the second enlarging the Senate from 25 to 33 members and the House from 75 to 99 members, and the third apportioning the membership of both Houses. In 1891 there were both an enumeration and an apportionment. In 1901 the General Assembly abandoned separate enumeration in favor of reliance upon the Federal Census and passed the Apportionment Act here in controversy. In the more than 60 years since that action, all proposals in both Houses of the General Assembly for reapportionment have failed to pass.

Between 1901 and 1961, Tennessee has experienced substantial growth and redistribution of her population. In 1901 the population was 2,020,616, of whom 487,380 were eligible to vote. The 1960 Federal Census reports the State's population at 3,567,089, of whom 2,092,891 are eligible to vote. The relative standings of the counties in terms of qualified voters have changed significantly. It is primarily the continued application of the 1901 Apportionment Act to this shifted and enlarged voting population which gives rise to the present controversy.

Indeed, the complaint alleges that the 1901 statute, even as of the time of its passage, "made no apportionment of Representatives and Senators in accordance with the constitutional formula . . . , but instead arbitrarily and capriciously apportioned representatives in the Senate and House without reference . . . to any logical or reasonable formula whatever." It is further alleged that "because of the population changes since 1900, and the failure of the Legislature to reapportion itself since 1901," the 1901 statute became "unconstitutional and obsolete." Appellants also argue that, because of the composition of the legislature effected by the 1901 Apportionment Act, redress in the form of a state constitutional amendment to change the entire mechanism for reapportioning, or any other change short of that, is difficult or impossible. The complaint concludes that "these plaintiffs and others similarly situated, are denied the equal protection of the laws accorded them by the Fourteenth Amendment to the Constitution of the United States by virtue of the debasement of their votes." They seek a declaration that the 1901 statute is unconstitutional and an injunction restraining the appellees from acting to conduct any further elections under it. They also pray that unless and until the General Assembly enacts a valid reapportionment, the District Court should either decree a reapportionment by mathematical application of the Tennessee constitutional formulae to the most recent Federal Census figures, or direct the appellees to conduct legislative elections, primary and general, at large. They also pray for such other and further relief as may be appropriate.

I. THE DISTRICT COURT'S OPINION AND ORDER OF DISMISSAL

Because we deal with this case on appeal from an order of dismissal granted on appellees' motions, precise identification of the issues presently confronting us demands clear exposition of the grounds upon which the District Court rested in dismissing the case. The dismissal order recited that the court sustained the appellees' grounds "(1) that the Court lacks jurisdiction of the subject matter, and (2) that the complaint fails to state a claim upon which relief can be granted. . . . "

In the setting of a case such as this, the recited grounds embrace two possible reasons for dismissal:

First: That the facts and injury alleged, the legal bases invoked as creating the rights and duties relied upon, and the relief sought, fail to come within that language of Article III of the Constitution and of the jurisdictional statutes which define those matters concerning which United States District Courts are empowered to act;

Second: That, although the matter is cognizable and facts are alleged which establish infringement of appellants' rights as a result of state legislative action departing from a federal constitutional standard, the court will not proceed because the matter is considered unsuited to judicial inquiry or adjustment.

We treat the first ground of dismissal as "lack of jurisdiction of the subject matter." The second we consider to result in a failure to state a justiciable cause of action.

The District Court's dismissal order . . . reveals that the court rested its dismissal upon lack of subject-matter jurisdiction and lack of a justiciable cause of action without attempting to distinguish between these grounds. After noting that the plaintiffs challenged the existing legislative apportionment in Tennessee under the Due Process and Equal Protection Clauses, and summarizing the supporting allegations and the relief requested, the court stated[1]

> The action is presently before the Court upon the defendants' motion to dismiss predicated upon three grounds: first, that the Court lacks jurisdiction of the subject matter; second, that the complaints fail to state a claim upon which relief can be granted; and third, that indispensable party defendants are not before the Court.

The court proceeded to explain its action as turning on the case's presenting a "question of the distribution of political strength for legislative purposes." For,[2]

> From a review of [numerous Supreme Court] . . . decisions there can be no doubt that the federal rule, as enunciated and applied by the Supreme Court, is that the federal courts, whether from a lack of jurisdiction or from the inappropriateness of the subject matter for judicial consideration, will not intervene in cases of this type to compel legislative reapportionment.

The court went on to express doubts as to the feasibility of the various possible remedies sought by the plaintiffs. 179 F. Supp., at 827–828. Then it made clear that its dismissal reflected a view not of doubt that violation of constitutional rights was alleged, but of a court's impotence to correct that violation:[3]

> With the plaintiffs' argument that the legislature of Tennessee is guilty of a clear violation of the state constitution and of the rights of the plaintiffs the Court entirely agrees. It also agrees that the evil is a serious one which should be corrected without further delay. But even so the remedy in this situation clearly does not lie with the courts. It has long been recognized and

[1] 179 F. Supp., at 826.
[2] 179 F. Supp., at 826.
[3] 179 F. Supp., at 828.

is accepted doctrine that there are indeed some rights guaranteed by the Constitution for the violation of which the courts cannot give redress.

In light of the District Court's treatment of the case, we hold today only (a) that the court possessed jurisdiction of the subject matter; (b) that a justiciable cause of action is stated upon which appellants would be entitled to appropriate relief; and (c) because appellees raise the issue before this Court, that the appellants have standing to challenge the Tennessee apportionment statutes. Beyond noting that we have no cause at this stage to doubt the District Court will be able to fashion relief if violations of constitutional rights are found, it is improper now to consider what remedy would be most appropriate if appellants prevail at the trial.

II. JURISDICTION OF THE SUBJECT MATTER

The District Court was uncertain whether our cases withholding federal judicial relief rested upon a lack of federal jurisdiction or upon the inappropriateness of the subject matter for judicial consideration—what we have designated "nonjusticiability." The distinction between the two grounds is significant. It the instance of nonjusticiability, consideration of the cause is not wholly and immediately foreclosed; rather, the Court's inquiry necessarily proceeds to the point of deciding whether the duty asserted can be judicially identified and its breach judicially determined, and whether protection for the right asserted can be judicially molded. In the instance of lack of jurisdiction the cause either does not "arise under" the Federal Constitution, laws or treaties (or fall within one of the other enumerated categories of Art. III, § 2), or is not a "case or controversy" within the meaning of that section; or the cause is not one described by any jurisdictional statute. Our conclusion . . . that this cause presents no nonjusticiable "political question" settles the only possible doubt that it is a case or controversy. Under the present heading of "Jurisdiction of the Subject Matter" we hold only that the matter set forth in the complaint does arise under the Constitution. . . .

Article III, § 2, of the Federal Constitution provides that "The judicial Power shall extend to all Cases, in Law and Equity, arising under this Constitution, the Laws of the United States, and Treaties made, or which shall be made, under their Authority. . . ." It is clear that the cause of action is one which "arises under" the Federal Constitution. The complaint alleges that the 1901 statute effects an apportionment that deprives the appellants of the equal protection of the laws in violation of the Fourteenth Amendment. Dismissal of the complaint upon the ground of lack of jurisdiction of the subject matter would, therefore, be justified only if that claim were "so attenuated and unsubstantial as to be absolutely devoid of merit," *Newburyport Water Co.* v. *Newburyport,* 193 U. S. 561, 579, or "frivolous," *Bell* v. *Hood,* 327 U. S. 678, 683. . . . Since the District Court obviously and correctly did not deem the asserted federal constitutional claim unsubstantial and frivolous, it should not have dismissed the complaint for want of jurisdiction of the subject matter. . . .

Since the complaint plainly sets forth a case arising under the Constitution, the subject matter is within the federal judicial power defined in Art. III, § 2, and so within the power of Congress to assign to the jurisdiction of the District Courts. Congress has exercised that power in 28 U. S. C. § 1343 (3):

> The district courts shall have original jurisdiction of any civil action authorized by law to be commenced by any person . . . [t]o redress the deprivation, under color of any State law, statute, ordinance, regulation, custom or usage, of any right, privilege or immunity secured by the Constitution of the United States. . . .

. . . We hold that the District Court has jurisdiction of the subject matter of the federal constitutional claim asserted in the complaint.

III. STANDING

A federal court cannot "pronounce any statute, either of a State or of the United States, void, because irreconcilable with the Constitution, except as it is called upon to adjudge the legal rights of litigants in actual controversies." *Liverpool Steamship Co.* v. *Commissioners of Emigration,* 113 U. S. 33, 39. Have the appellants alleged such a personal stake in the outcome of the controversy as to assure that concrete adverseness which sharpens the presentation of issues upon which the court so largely depends for illumination of difficult constitutional questions? This is the gist of the question of standing. It is, of course, a question of federal law.

The complaint was filed by residents of Davidson, Hamilton, Knox, Montgomery, and Shelby Counties. Each is a person allegedly qualified to vote for members of the General Assembly representing his county. These appellants sued "on their own behalf and on behalf of all qualified voters of their respective counties, and further, on behalf of all voters of the State of Tennessee who are similarly situated. . . ." The appellees are the Tennessee Secretary of State, Attorney General, Coordinator of Elections, and members of the State Board of Elections; the members of the State Board are sued in their own right and also as representatives of the County Election Commissioners whom they appoint.

We hold that the appellants do have standing to maintain this suit. . . .

These appellants seek relief in order to protect or vindicate an interest of their own, and of those similarly situated. Their constitutional claim is, in substance, that the 1901 statute constitutes arbitrary and capricious state action, offensive to the Fourteenth Amendment in its irrational disregard of the standard of apportionment prescribed by the State's Constitution or of any standard, effecting a gross disproportion of representation to voting population. The injury which appellants assert is that this classification disfavors the voters in the counties in which they reside, placing them in a position of constitutionally unjustifiable inequality *vis-à-vis* voters in irrationally favored counties. A citizen's right to a vote free of arbitrary impairment by state action has been judicially recognized as a right secured by the Constitution, when such impairment resulted from dilution by a false tally, cf. *United States* v. *Classic,* 313 U. S. 299; or by a refusal to count votes from arbitrarily selected precincts, cf. *United States* v. *Mosley,* 238 U. S. 383, or by a stuffing of the ballot box, cf. *Ex parte Siebold,* 100 U. S. 371; *United States* v. *Saylor,* 322 U. S. 385.

It would not be necessary to decide whether appellants' allegations of impairment of their votes by the 1901 apportionment will, ultimately, entitle them to any relief, in order to hold that they have standing to seek it. If such impairment does produce a legally cognizable injury, they are among those who have sustained it. . . .

IV. JUSTICIABILITY

In holding that the subject matter of this suit was not justiciable, the District Court relied on *Colegrove* v. *Green* . . . [328 U. S. 549, *(ed.)*] and subsequent *per curiam* cases. The court stated: "From a review of these decisions there can be no doubt that the federal rule . . . is that the federal courts . . . will not intervene in cases of this type to compel legislative reapportionment." 179 F. Supp., at 826. We understand the District Court to have read the cited cases as compelling the conclusion that since the appellants sought to have a legislative apportionment held unconstitutional, their suit presented a "political question" and was therefore nonjusticiable. We hold that this challenge to an apportionment presents no nonjusticiable "political question." The cited cases do not hold the contrary.

Of course the mere fact that the suit seeks protection of a political right does not mean it presents a political question. . . . Rather, it is argued that apportionment cases, whatever the actual wording of the complaint, can involve no federal constitutional right except one resting on the guaranty of a republican form of government, and that complaints based on that clause have been held to present political questions which are nonjusticiable.

We hold that the claim pleaded here neither rests upon nor implicates the Guaranty Clause and that its justiciability is therefore not foreclosed by our decisions of cases involving that clause. The District Court misinterpreted *Colegrove* v. *Green* and other decisions of this Court on which it relied. Appellants' claim that they are being denied equal protection is justiciable. . . .

It is apparent that several formulations which vary slightly according to the settings in which the questions arise may describe a political question, although each has one or more elements which identify it as essentially a function of the separation of powers. Prominent on the surface of any case held to involve a political question is found a textually demonstrable constitutional commitment of the issue to a coordinate political department; or a lack of judicially discoverable and manageable standards for resolving it; or the impossibility of deciding without an initial policy determination of a kind clearly for nonjudicial discretion; or the impossibility of a court's undertaking independent resolution without expressing lack of the respect due coordinate branches of government; or an unusual need for unquestioning adherence to a political decision already made; or the potentiality of embarrassment from multifarious pronouncements by various departments on one question.

Unless one of these formulations is inextricable from the case at bar, there should be no dismissal for nonjusticiability on the ground of a political question's presence. The doctrine of which we treat is one of "political questions," not one of "political cases." The courts cannot reject as "no law suit" a bona fide controversy as to whether some action denominated "political" exceeds constitutional authority. . . .

But it is argued that this case shares the characteristics of . . . cases concerning the Constitution's guaranty, in Art. IV, § 4, of a republican form of government. . . .

The Court has . . . refused to resort to the Guaranty Clause—which alone had been invoked for the purpose—as the source of a constitutional standard for invalidating state action. . . .

We come, finally, to the ultimate inquiry whether our precedents as to what constitutes a nonjusticiable "political question" bring the case before us under the umbrella of that doctrine. A natural beginning is to note whether any of the common characteristics which we have been able to identify and label descriptively are present. We find none: The question here is the consistency of state action with the Federal Constitution. We have no question decided, or to be decided, by a political branch of government coequal with this Court. Nor do we risk embarrassment of our government abroad, or grave disturbance at home if we take issue with Tennessee as to the constitutionality of her action here challenged. Nor need the appellants, in order to succeed in this action, ask the Court to enter upon policy determinations for which judicially manageable standards are lacking. Judicial standards under the Equal Protection Clause are well developed and familiar, and it has been open to courts since the enactment of the Fourteenth Amendment to determine, if on the particular facts they must, that a discrimination reflects *no* policy, but simply arbitrary and capricious action.

This case does, in one sense, involve the allocation of political power within a State, and the appellants might conceivably have added a claim under the Guaranty Clause. Of course, as we have seen, any reliance on that clause would be futile. But because any reliance on the Guaranty Clause could not have succeeded it does not follow that appellants may not be heard on the equal protection claim which in fact they tender. True, it must be clear that the Fourteenth Amendment claim is not so enmeshed with those political question elements which render Guaranty Clause claims nonjusticiable as actually to present a political question itself. But we have found that not to be the case here. . . .

We conclude then the nonjusticiability of claims resting on the Guaranty Clause which arises from their embodiment of questions that were thought "political," can have no bearing upon the justiciability of the equal protection claim presented in this case. Finally, we emphasize that it is the involvement in Guaranty Clause claims of the elements thought to define "political questions," and no other feature, which could render them nonjusticiable. Specifically, we have said that such claims are not held non-justiciable because they touch matters of state governmental organization. . . .

Article I, §§ 2, 4, and 5, and Amendment XIV, § 2, relate only to congressional elections and obviously do not govern apportionment of state legislatures. However, our decisions in favor of justiciability even in light of those provisions plainly afford no support for the District Court's conclusion that the subject matter of this controversy presents a political question. . . .

We conclude that the complaint's allegations of a denial of equal protection present a justiciable constitutional cause of action upon which appellants are entitled to a trial and a decision. The right asserted is within the reach of judicial protection under the Fourteenth Amendment.

The judgment of the District Court is reversed and the cause is remanded for further proceedings consistent with this opinion.

PART TWO

The Onset of a Cold War

SELECTION 

"The Iron Curtain": Winston S. Churchill, Address at Fulton, Missouri, March 12, 1946

Dominating American life for a decade after World War II was the tense relationship with the Soviet Union, popularly termed the cold war. Even before Germany's surrender in 1945, the American-Soviet relationship had become strained. The Soviet government installed Communist regimes in Poland and elsewhere in Eastern Europe in spite of American protests based on the Yalta agreements and other wartime accords.

President Truman sent a special envoy to Moscow to seek understanding with the Soviet Premier, Josef Stalin. He himself talked with Stalin at Potsdam in July, 1945. Diplomatic notes passed back and forth. Endless meetings were held of a Council of Foreign Ministers, on which sat the United States Secretary of State and the foreign ministers of Britain, France, and the U.S.S.R. All to no avail.

As time passed, the Soviets became more truculent rather than more conciliatory. Communist regimes in Eastern Europe entrenched themselves. Soviet-backed Communists waged war in Greece, seeking to conquer that country. The Soviet government pressed Turkey to cede certain districts on the Turkish-Soviet frontier. Despite a wartime promise of speedy withdrawal, Soviet troops remained in occupation of northern Iran. At the meetings of foreign ministers, the Soviet representative demanded portions of former Italian colonies in North Africa. Gradually, American officials and the American public began to believe that the Soviet Union was bent on building a Communist empire and that it would halt its expansion only when forced to do so.

With this conviction, the American government took steps to block further Soviet expansion. From then on, relations between the two powers bordered on a state of war.

Hugh Seton-Watson, Neither War nor Peace *(1960) describes the context of the Soviet-American split. Kenneth Ingram,* History of the Cold War *(1955) is a brief, balanced chronicle; D. F. Fleming,* The Cold War and Its Origins *(Two volumes, 1960) is a longer chronicle, presenting the Soviet side in a favorable and the American side in an unfavorable light; John Lukacs,* A History of the Cold War *(1961) is an attempt to analyze the underlying sources of conflict; and J. W. Spanier,* American Foreign Policy since World War II *(1960) is an attempt to appraise America's decisions and performance.*

At an early date, a tocsin, calling Americans to resist Soviet imperialism, was sounded by an Englishman. Britain's wartime leader, Winston Churchill, voted out of office in 1945, visited the United States in 1946. At Westminster College in Fulton, Missouri, he received an honorary degree. With President Truman sitting on the platform behind him, Churchill warned in ringing tones that the Soviet Union had enclosed Eastern Europe behind an "iron curtain." A portion of his speech follows. It is taken from Vital Speeches, *volume 12 (Mar. 15, 1946), pages 331–332.*

. . . A shadow has fallen upon the scenes so lately lighted by the Allied victory. Nobody knows what Soviet Russia and its Communist international organization intends to do in the immediate future, or what are the limits, if any, to their expansive and proselytizing tendencies. I have a strong admiration and regard for the valiant Russian people and for my war-time comrade, Marshal Stalin. There is sympathy and good will in Britain—and I doubt not here also—toward the peoples of all the Russias and a resolve to persevere through many differences and rebuffs in establishing lasting friendships. We understand the Russians need to be secure on her western frontiers from all renewal of German aggression. We welcome her to her rightful place among the leading nations of the world. Above all we welcome constant, frequent and growing contacts between the Russian people and our own people on both sides of the Atlantic. It is my duty, however, to place before you certain facts about the present position in Europe—I am sure I do not wish to, but it is my duty, I feel, to present them to you.

From Stettin in the Baltic to Triest in the Adriatic, an iron curtain has descended across the Continent. Behind that line lie all the capitals of the ancient states of central and eastern Europe. Warsaw, Berlin, Prague, Vienna, Budapest, Belgrade, Bucharest and Sofia, all these famous cities and the populations around them lie in the Soviet sphere and all are subject in one form or another, not only to Soviet influence but to a very high and increasing measure of control from Moscow. Athens alone, with its immortal glories, is free to decide its future at an election under British, American and French observation. The Russian-dominated Polish government has been encouraged to make enormous and wrongful inroads upon Germany, and mass expulsions of millions of Germans on a scale grievous and undreamed of are now taking place. The Communist parties, which were very small in all these eastern states of Europe, have been raised to pre-eminence and power far beyond their numbers and are seeking everywhere to obtain totalitarian control. Police governments are prevailing in nearly every case, and so far, except in Czechoslovakia, there is no true democracy. Turkey and Persia are both profoundly alarmed and disturbed at the claims which are made upon them and at the pressure being exerted by the Moscow government. An attempt is being made by the Russians in Berlin to build up a quasi-Communist party in their zone of occupied Germany by showing special favors to groups of Left-Wing German leaders. At the end of the fighting last June, the American and British armies withdrew westward, in accordance with an earlier agreement, to a depth at some points 150 miles on a front of nearly 400 miles to allow the Russians to occupy this vast expanse of territory which the western democracies had conquered. If now the Soviet government tries, by separate action, to build up a pro-Communist Germany in their areas this will cause new serious difficulties in the British and American zones, and will give the defeated Germans the power of putting themselves up to auction between the Soviets and western democracies. Whatever conclusions may be drawn from these facts—and facts they are—this is certainly not the liberated Europe we fought to build up. Nor is it one which contains the essentials of permanent peace.

The safety of the world, ladies and gentlemen, requires a new unity in Europe from which no nation should be permanently outcast.

It is impossible not to comprehend—twice we have seen them drawn by irresistible forces in time to secure the victory but only after frightful slaughter and devastation have occurred. Twice the United States has had to send millions of its young men to fight a war, but now war can find any nation between dusk and dawn. Surely we should work within the structure of the United Nations and in accordance with our charter. That is an open course of policy.

In front of the iron curtain which lies across Europe are other causes for anxiety. In Italy the Communist party is seriously hampered by having to support the Communist trained Marshal Tito's claims to former Italian territory at the head of the Adriatic. Nevertheless the future of Italy hangs in the balance. Again one cannot imagine a regenerated Europe without a strong France. All my public life I have worked for a strong France and I never lost faith in her destiny, even in the darkest hours. I will not lose faith now. However, in a great number of countries, far from the Russian frontiers and throughout the world, Communist fifth columns are established and work in complete unity and absolute obedience to the directions they receive from the Communist center. Except in the British Commonwealth and in this United States, where Communism is in its infancy, the Communist parties or fifth columns constitute a growing challenge and peril to Christian civilization. These are somber facts for any one to have to recite on the morrow of a victory gained by so much splendid comradeship in arms and in the cause of freedom and democracy, and we should be most unwise not to face them squarely while time remains.

The outlook is also anxious in the Far East and especially in Manchuria. The agreement which was made at Yalta, to which I was a party, was extremely favorable to Soviet Russia, but it was made at a time when no one could say that the German war might not extend all through the summer and autumn of 1945 and when the Japanese war was expected to last for a further eighteen months from the end of the German war. In this country you are all so well informed about the Far East, and such devoted friends of China, that I do not need to expatiate on the situation there.

I have felt bound to portray the shadow which, alike in the West and in the East, falls upon the world. I was a minister at the time of the Versailles treaty and a close friend of Mr. Lloyd George. I did not myself agree with many things that were done, but I have a very vague impression in my mind of that situation, and I find it painful to contrast it with that which prevails now. In those days there were high hopes and unbounded confidence that the wars were over, and that the League of

Nations would become all-powerful. I do not see or feel the same confidence or even the same hopes in the haggard world at this time.

On the other hand I repulse the idea that a new war is inevitable; still more that it is imminent. It is because I am so sure that our fortunes are in our own hands and that we hold the power to save the future, that I feel the duty to speak out now that I have an occasion to do so. I do not believe that Soviet Russia desires war. What they desire is the fruits of war and the indefinite expansion of their power and doctrines. But what we have to consider here today while time remains, is the permanent prevention of war and the establishment of conditions of freedom and democracy as rapidly as possible in all countries. Our difficulties and dangers will not be removed by closing our eyes to them. They will not be removed by mere waiting to see what happens; nor will they be relieved by a policy of appeasement. What is needed is a settlement and the longer this is delayed the more difficult it will be and the greater our dangers will become. From what I have seen of our Russian friends and allies during the war, I am convinced that there is nothing they admire so much as strength, and there is nothing for which they have less respect than for military weakness. For that reason the old doctrine of a balance of power is unsound. We cannot afford, if we can help it, to work on narrow margins, offering temptations to a trial of strength. If the western democracies stand together in strict adherence to the principles of the United Nations Charter, their influence for furthering these principles will be immense and no one is likely to molest them. If, however, they become divided or falter in their duty, and if these all-important years are allowed to slip away, then indeed catastrophe may overwhelm us all.

Last time I saw it all coming, and cried aloud to my fellow countrymen and to the world, but no one paid any attention. Up till the year 1933 or even 1935, Germany might have been saved from the awful fate which has overtaken her and we might all have been spared the miseries Hitler let loose upon mankind. There never was a war in all history easier to prevent by timely action than the one which has just desolated such great areas of the globe. It could have been prevented without the firing of a single shot, and Germany might be powerful, prosperous and honored today, but no one would listen and one by one we were all sucked into the awful whirlpool. We surely must not let that happen again. This can only be achieved by reaching now, in 1946, a good understanding on all points with Russia under the general authority of the United Nations Organization and by the maintenance of that good understanding through many peaceful years, by the world instrument, supported by the whole strength of the English-speaking world and all its connections.

Let no man underrate the abiding power of the British Empire and Commonwealth. Because you see the forty-six millions in our island harassed about their food supply, of which they grew only one half, even in war time, or because we have difficulty in restarting our industries and export trade after six years of passionate war effort, do not suppose that we shall not come through these dark years of privation as we have come through the glorious years of agony, or that half a century from now you will not see seventy or eighty millions of Britons spread about the world and united in defense of our traditions, our way of life and of the world causes we and you espouse. If the population of the English-speaking commonwealth be added to that of the United States, with all that such co-operation implies in the air, on the sea and in science and industry, there will be no quivering, precarious balance of power to offer its temptation to ambition or adventure. On the contrary, there will be an overwhelming assurance of security. If we adhere faithfully to the charter of the United Nations and walk forward in sedate and sober strength, seeking no one's land or treasure, or seeking to lay no arbitrary control on the thoughts of men, if all British moral and material forces and convictions are joined with your own in fraternal association, the highroads of the future will be clear, not only for us but for all, not only for our time but for a century to come.

A Voice of Protest: Henry A. Wallace, Address at Madison Square Garden, September 12, 1946

Churchill's "iron curtain" speech put into words feelings that had been growing on many Americans. But not on all. To a number, the Soviet seizure of control in Eastern Europe was a source of irritation but not alarm. Their feeling was that the United States should seek understandings with the Soviet Union, avoiding at almost any cost the development of antagonism.

The leading spokesman for this point of view was Henry A. Wallace. A former Vice President, Wallace was Secretary of Commerce in Truman's Cabinet. The document that follows is part of a speech that Wallace delivered in Madison Square Garden on September 12, 1946. Although Wallace claimed in the speech that President Truman had approved its text, Truman subsequently denied having done so. Truman rebuked Wallace, and Wallace resigned from the Cabinet, thereafter to become a more and more passionate advocate of a point of view that had fewer and fewer adherents. In 1948, Wallace was to run as a third-party candidate for the Presidency and to poll a pathetically small number of votes. In 1946, however, he appeared to be representative of a significant current in American thought.

An extract from Wallace's Madison Square Garden speech follows. It is taken from Vital Speeches, *volume 12 (Oct. 1, 1946), pages 738–741.*

. . . Tonight I want to talk about peace—and how to get peace. Never have the common people of all lands so longed for peace. Yet, never in a time of comparative peace have they feared war so much.

Up till now peace has been negative and unexciting. War has been positive and exciting. Far too often, hatred and fear, intolerance and deceit have had the upper hand over love and confidence, trust and joy. Far too often, the law of nations has been the law of the jungle; and the constructive spiritual forces of the Lord have bowed to the destructive forces of Satan.

During the past year or so, the significance of peace has been increased immeasurably by the atom bomb, guided missiles and airplanes which soon will travel as fast as sound. Make no mistake about it—another war would hurt the United States many times as much as the last war. We cannot rest in the assurance that we invented the atom bomb—and therefore that this agent of destruction will work best for us. He who trusts in the atom bomb will sooner or later perish by the atom bomb—or something worse.

I say this as one who steadfastly backed preparedness throughout the Thirties. We have no use for namby-pamby pacifism. But we must realize that modern inventions have now made peace the most exciting thing in the world—and we should be willing to pay a just price for peace. If modern war can cost us $400 billion, we should be willing and happy to pay much more for peace. But certainly, the cost of peace is to be measured not in dollars but in the hearts and minds of men.

The price of peace—for us and for every nation in the world—is the price of giving up prejudice, hatred, fear, and ignorance. . . .

The Republican party is the party of economic nationalism and political isolation—and as such is as anachronistic as the dodo and as certain to disappear. The danger is that before it disappears it may enjoy a brief period of power during which it can do irreparable damage to the United States and the cause of world peace.

Governor Dewey has expressed himself as favoring an alliance of mutual defense with Great Britain as the key to our foreign policy.* This may sound attractive because we both speak the same language and many of our customs and traditions have the same historical background. Moreover, to the military men, the British Isles are our advanced air base against Europe.

Certainly we like the British people as individuals. But to make Britain the key to our foreign policy would be, in my opinion, the height of folly. We must not let the reactionary leadership of the Republican party force us into that position. We must not let British balance-of-power manipulations determine whether and when the United States gets into war.

Make no mistake about it—the British imperialistic policy in the Near East alone, combined with Russian retaliation, would lead the United

*[The reference is to Governor Thomas E. Dewey of New York, who had been the Republican nominee for the Presidency in 1944 and was to be again in 1948 (*ed.*)]

States straight to war unless we have a clearly-defined and realistic policy of our own.

Neither of these two great powers wants war now, but the danger is that whatever their intentions may be, their current policies may eventually lead to war. To prevent war and insure our survival in a stable world, it is essential that we look abroad through our own American eyes and not through the eyes of either the British Foreign Office or a pro-British or anti-Russian press.

In this connection, I want one thing clearly understood. I am neither anti-British nor pro-British—neither anti-Russian nor pro-Russian. And just two days ago, when President Truman read these words, he said that they represented the policy of his administration.

I plead for an America vigorously dedicated to peace—just as I plead for opportunities for the next generation throughout the world to enjoy the abundance which now, more than ever before, is the birthright of man.

To achieve lasting peace, we must study in detail just how the Russian character was formed—by invasions of Tartars, Mongols, Germans, Poles, Swedes, and French; by the czarist rule based on ignorance, fear and force; by the intervention of the British, French and Americans in Russian affairs from 1919 to 1921; by the geography of the huge Russian land mass situated strategically between Europe and Asia; and by the vitality derived from the rich Russian soil and the strenuous Russian climate. Add to all this the tremendous emotional power which Marxism and Leninism gives to the Russian leaders—and then we can realize that we are reckoning with a force which cannot be handled successfully by a "Get tough with Russia" policy. "Getting tough" never brought anything real and lasting—whether for schoolyard bullies or businessmen or world powers. The tougher we get, the tougher the Russians will get.

Throughout the world there are numerous reactionary elements which had hoped for Axis victory—and now profess great friendship for the United States. Yet, these enemies of yesterday and false friends of today continually try to provoke war between the United States and Russia. They have no real love of the United States. They only long for the day when the United States and Russia will destroy each other.

We must not let our Russian policy be guided or influenced by those inside or outside the United States who want war with Russia. This does not mean appeasement.

We most earnestly want peace with Russia—but we want to be met half way. We want cooperation. And I believe that we can get cooperation once Russia understands that our primary objective is neither saving the British Empire nor purchasing oil in the Near East with the lives of American soldiers. We cannot allow national oil rivalries to force us into war. All of the nations producing oil, whether inside or outside of their own boundaries, must fulfill the provisions of the United Nations Charter and encourage the development of world petroleum reserves so as to make the maximum amount of oil available to all nations of the world on an equitable peaceful basis—and not on the basis of fighting the next war.

For her part, Russia can retain our respect by cooperating with the United Nations in a spirit of openminded and flexible give-and-take.

The real peace treaty we now need is between the United States and Russia. On our part, we should recognize that we have no more business in the *political* affairs of Eastern Europe than Russia has in the *political* affairs of Latin America, Western Europe and the United States. We may not like what Russia does in Eastern Europe. Her type of land reform, industrial expropriation, and suppression of basic liberties offends the great majority of the people of the United States. But whether we like it or not the Russians will try to socialize their sphere of influence just as we try to democratize our sphere of influence. This applies also to Germany and Japan. We are striving to democratize Japan and our area of control in Germany, while Russia strives to socialize eastern Germany.

As for Germany, we all must recognize that an equitable settlement, based on a unified German nation, is absolutely essential to any lasting European settlement. This means that Russia must be assured that never again can German industry be converted into military might to be used against her—and Britain, Western Europe and the United States must be certain that Russia's Germany policy will not become a tool of Russian design against Western Europe.

The Russians have no more business in stirring up native communists to political activity in Western Europe, Latin America and the United States than we have in interfering in the politics of Eastern Europe and Russia. We know what Russia is up to in Eastern Europe, for example, and Russia knows what we are up to. We cannot permit the door to be closed against our trade in Eastern Europe any more than we can in China. But at the same time we have to recognize that the Balkans are closer to Russia than to us—and that Russia cannot permit either England or the United States to dominate the politics of that area.

China is a special case and although she holds the longest frontier in the world with Russia, the interests of world peace demand that China remain free from any sphere of influence, either politically or economically. We insist that the door to trade and economic development opportunities be left wide open in China as in all the world. However, the open door to trade and opportunities for economic development in China are meaningless unless there is a unified and peaceful China—built on the cooperation of the various groups in that country and based on a hands-off policy of the outside powers.

We are still arming to the hilt. Our excessive expenses for military purposes are the chief cause for our unbalanced budget. If taxes are to be lightened we must have the basis of a real peace with Russia—a peace that cannot be broken by extremist propagandists. We do not want our course determined for us by master minds operating out of London, Moscow or Nanking.

Russian ideas of social-economic justice are going to govern nearly a third of the world. Our ideas of free enterprise democracy will govern much of the rest. The two ideas will endeavor to prove which can deliver the most satisfaction to the common man in their respective areas of political dominance. But by mutual agreement, this competition should be put on a friendly basis and the Russians should stop conniving against us in certain areas of the world just as we should stop scheming against them in other parts of the world. Let the results of the two systems speak for themselves.

Meanwhile, the Russians should stop teaching that their form of communism must, by force if necessary, ultimately triumph over democratic capitalism—while we should close our ears to those among us who would have us believe that Russian communism and our free enterprise system cannot live, one with another, in a profitable and productive peace.

Under friendly peaceful competition the Russian world and the American world will gradually become more alike. The Russians will be forced to grant more and more of the personal freedoms; and we shall become more and more absorbed with the problems of social-economic justice.

Russia must be convinced that we are not planning for war against her and we must be certain that Russia is not carrying on territorial expansion or world domination through native communists faithfully following every twist and turn in the Moscow party line. But in this competition, we must insist on an open door for trade throughout the world. There will always be an ideological conflict—but that is no reason why diplomats cannot work out a basis for both systems to live safely in the world side by side.

Once the fears of Russia and the United States Senate have been allayed by practical regional political reservations, I am sure that concern over the veto power would be greatly diminished. Then the United Nations would have a really great power in those areas which are truly international and not regional. In the world-wide, as distinguished from the regional field, the armed might of the United Nations should be so great as to make opposition useless. Only the United Nations should have atomic bombs and its military establishment should give special emphasis to air power. It should have control of the strategically located air bases with which the United States and Britain have encircled the world. And not only should individual nations be prohibited from manufacturing atomic bombs, guided missiles and military aircraft for bombing purposes, but no nation should be allowed to spend on its military establishment more than perhaps 15 per cent of its budget.

Practically and immediately, we must recognize that we are not yet ready for World Federation. Realistically, the most we can hope for now is a safe reduction in military expense and a long period of peace based on mutual trust between the Big Three.

During this period, every effort should be made to develop as rapidly as possible a body of international law based on moral principles and not on the Machiavellian principles of deceit, force and distrust—which, if continued, will lead the modern world to rapid disintegration.

In brief, as I see it today, the World Order is bankrupt—and the United States, Russia and England are the receivers. These are the hard facts of power politics on which we have to build a functioning, powerful United Nations and a body of international law. And as we build, we must develop fully the doctrine of the rights of small peoples as contained in the United Nations Charter. This law should ideally apply as much to Indonesians and Greeks as to Bulgarians and Poles—but practically, the application may be delayed until both British and Russians discover the futility of their methods.

In the full development of the rights of small nations, the British and Russians can learn a lesson from the Good Neighbor policy of Franklin Roosevelt. For under Roosevelt, we in the Western Hemisphere built a workable system of regional internationalism that fully protected the sovereign rights of every nation—a system of multilateral action that immeasurably strengthened the whole of world order.

In the United States an informed public opinion will be all-powerful. Our people are peace-minded. But they often express themselves too late—for events today move much faster than public opinion. The people here, as everywhere in the world, must be convinced that another war is not inevitable. And through mass meetings such as this, and through persistent pamphleteering, the people can be organized for peace—even though a large segment of our press is propagandizing our people for war in the hope of scaring Russia. And we who look on this war-with-Russia talk as criminal foolishness must carry our message direct to the people—even though we may be called communists because we dare to speak out.

I believe that peace—the kind of peace I have outlined tonight—is the basic issue, both in the Congressional campaign this fall and right on through the Presidential election in 1948. How we meet this issue will determine whether we live not in "one world" or "two worlds"—but whether we live at all.

SELECTION 

The Baruch Plan: Bernard M. Baruch, Address to the United Nations Atomic Energy Commission, June 14, 1946

In 1946, neither the government nor the public was ready to accept the idea that understanding with the Soviet Union was out of the question. Without necessarily sharing all of Henry Wallace's views, many people still felt that all could be made right if Americans could somehow convince the Russians that they meant no ill.

During 1946, the American government matured a plan for international control of nuclear weapons. Prepared by a committee headed by Dean G. Acheson and David E. Lilienthal, this plan was presented to the United Nations Atomic Energy Commission by Bernard M. Baruch. It became known as the Baruch Plan. The purposes behind it, as Baruch's presentation address made plain, were two. One was to move toward an international arrangement designed to ensure that these terrifying weapons would never be used in future warfare. The second was to offer the Russians tangible evidence that the United States did not intend to use its temporary nuclear monopoly to impose its will upon them.

To the astonishment of both American officials and the American public, the Soviet Union rejected the Baruch Plan. It put forward alternative proposals that did not involve international control, and stood firmly by these alternative proposals. The reason—or at least one reason—came to light in 1949, when it was disclosed that the U.S.S.R. was engaged in an all-out program to develop atomic weapons of its own. At the time, the Soviet position seemed to most Americans incomprehensible. Russia's spurning of what most Americans viewed as a well-intentioned and generous proposal persuaded many that Soviet intentions were mischievous and hostile. Afterward, many more were willing to believe that the Soviets were capable of understanding no language except that of force.

Firsthand material on the development of the Baruch Plan appears in B. M. Baruch, The Public Years *(1960) and* The Journals of David E. Lilienthal *(two volumes, 1964). The document that follows is Baruch's address presenting the American plan to the UN Atomic Energy Commission. It is taken from the* State Department Bulletin, *volume 14 (June 23, 1964), pages 1059–1062.*

. . . The United States proposes the creation of an International Atomic Development Authority, to which should be entrusted all phases of the development and use of atomic energy, starting with the raw material and including—

1. Managerial control or ownership of all atomic-energy activities potentially dangerous to world security.
2. Power to control, inspect, and license all other atomic activities.
3. The duty of fostering the beneficial uses of atomic energy.
4. Research and development responsibilities of an affirmative character intended to put the Authority in the forefront of atomic knowledge and thus to enable it to comprehend, and therefor to detect, misuse of atomic energy. To be effective, the Authority must itself be the world's leader in the field of atomic knowledge and development and thus supplement its legal authority with the great power inherent in possession of leadership in knowledge.

I offer this as a basis for beginning our discussion.

But I think the peoples we serve would not believe—and without faith nothing counts—that a treaty, merely outlawing possession or use of the atomic bomb, constitutes effective fulfilment of the instructions to this Commission. Previous failures have been recorded in trying the method of simple renunciation, unsupported by effective guaranties of security and armament limitation. No one would have faith in that approach alone.

Now, if ever, is the time to act for the common good. Public opinion supports a world movement toward security. If I read the signs aright, the peoples want a program not composed merely of pious thoughts but of enforceable sanctions—an international law with teeth in it.

We of this nation, desirous of helping to bring peace to the world and realizing the heavy obligations upon us arising from our possession of the means of producing the bomb and from the fact that it is part of our armament, are prepared to make our full contribution toward effective control of atomic energy.

When an adequate system for control of atomic energy, including the renunciation of the bomb as a weapon, has been agreed upon and put into effective operation and condign punishments set up for violations of the rules of control which are to be stigmatized as international crimes, we propose that—

1. Manufacture of atomic bombs shall stop;
2. Existing bombs shall be disposed of pursuant to the terms of the treaty; and
3. The Authority shall be in possession of full information as to the know-how for the production of atomic energy.

Let me repeat, so as to avoid misunderstanding: My country is ready to make its full contribution toward the end we seek, subject of course to our constitutional processes and to an adequate system of control becoming fully effective, as we finally work it out.

Now as to violations: In the agreement, penalties of as serious a nature as the nations may wish and as immediate and certain in their execution as possible should be fixed for—

1. Illegal possession or use of an atomic bomb;
2. Illegal possession, or separation, of atomic material suitable for use in an atomic bomb;
3. Seizure of any plant or other property belonging to or licensed by the Authority;
4. Wilful interference with the activities of the Authority;
5. Creation or operation of dangerous projects in a manner contrary to, or in the absence of, a license granted by the international control body.

It would be a deception, to which I am unwilling to lend myself, were I not to say to you and to our peoples that the matter of punishment lies at the very heart of our present security system. It might as well be admitted, here and now, that the subject goes straight to the veto power contained in the Charter of the United Nations so far as it relates to the field of atomic energy. The Charter permits penalization only by concurrence of each of the five great powers—the Union of Soviet Socialist Republics, the United Kingdom, China, France, and the United States.

I want to make very plain that I am concerned here with the veto power only as it affects this particular problem. There must be no veto to protect those who violate their solemn agreements not to develop or use atomic energy for destructive purposes.

The bomb does not wait upon debate. To delay may be to die. The time between violation and preventive action or punishment would be all too short for extended discussion as to the course to be followed.

As matters now stand several years may be necessary for another country to produce a bomb, *de novo*. However, once the basic information is generally known, and the Authority has established producing plants for peaceful purposes in the several countries, an illegal seizure of such a plant might permit a malevolent nation to produce a bomb in 12 months, and if preceded by secret preparation and necessary facilities perhaps even in a much shorter time. The time required—the advance warning given of the possible use of a bomb—can only be generally estimated but obviously will depend upon many factors, including the success with which the Authority has been able to introduce elements of safety in the design of its plants and the degree to which illegal and secret preparation for the military use of atomic energy will have been eliminated. Presumably no nation would think of starting a war with only one bomb.

This shows how imperative speed is in detecting and penalizing violations.

The process of prevention and penalization—a problem of profound statecraft—is, as I read it, implicit in the Moscow statement, signed by the Union of Soviet Socialist Republics, the United States, and the United Kingdom a few months ago.

But before a country is ready to relinquish any winning weapons it must have more than words to reassure it. It must have a guarantee of safety, not only against the offenders in the atomic area but against the illegal users of other weapons—bacteriological, biological, gas—perhaps—why not?—against war itself.

In the elimination of war lies our solution, for only then will nations cease to compete with one another in the production and use of dread "secret" weapons which are evaluated solely by their capacity to kill. This devilish program takes us back not merely to the Dark Ages but from cosmos to chaos. If we succeed in finding a suitable way to control atomic weapons, it is reasonable to hope that we may also preclude the use of other weapons adaptable to mass destruction. When a man learns to say "A" he can, if he chooses, learn the rest of the alphabet too.

Let this be anchored in our minds:

Peace is never long preserved by weight of metal or by an armament race. Peace can be made tranquil and secure only by understanding and agreement fortified by sanctions. We must embrace international cooperation or international disintegration.

Science has taught us how to put the atom to work. But to make it work for good instead of for evil lies in the domain dealing with the principles of human duty. We are now facing a problem more of ethics than of physics.

The solution will require apparent sacrifice in pride and in position, but better pain as the price of peace than death as the price of war.

I now submit the following measures as representing the fundamental features of a plan which would give effect to certain of the conclusions which I have epitomized.

1. General. The Authority should set up a thorough plan for control of the field of atomic energy, through various forms of ownership, dominion, licenses, operation, inspection, research, and management by competent personnel. After this is provided for, there should be as little interference as may be with the economic plans and the present private, corporate, and state relationships in the several countries involved.

2. Raw Materials. The Authority should have as one of its earliest purposes to obtain and maintain complete and accurate information on world supplies of uranium and thorium and to bring them under its dominion. The precise pattern of control for various types of deposits of such materials will have to depend upon the geological, mining, refining, and economic facts involved in different situations.

The Authority should conduct continuous surveys so that it will have the most complete knowledge of the world geology of uranium and thorium. Only after all current information on world sources of uranium and thorium is known to us all can equitable plans be made for their production, refining, and distribution.

3. Primary Production Plants. The Authority should exercise complete managerial control of the production of fissionable materials. This means that it should control and operate all plants producing fissionable materials in dangerous quantities and must own and control the product of these plants.

4. Atomic Explosives. The Authority should be given sole and exclusive right to conduct research in the field of atomic explosives. Research activities in the field of atomic explosives are essential in order that the Authority may keep in the forefront of knowledge in the field of atomic energy and fulfil the objective of preventing illicit manufacture of bombs. Only by maintaining its position as the best-informed agency will the Authority be able to determine the line between intrinsically dangerous and non-dangerous activities.

5. Strategic Distribution of Activities and Materials. The activities entrusted exclusively to the Authority because they are intrinsically dangerous to security should be distributed throughout the world. Similarly, stockpiles of raw materials and fissionable materials should not be centralized.

6. Non-dangerous Activities. A function of the Authority should be promotion of the peacetime benefits of atomic energy.

Atomic research (except in explosives), the use of research reactors, the production of radioactive tracers by means of non-dangerous reactors, the use of such tracers, and to some extent the production of power should be open to nations and their citizens under reasonable licensing arrangements from the Authority. Denatured materials, whose use we know also requires suitable safeguards, should be furnished for such purposes by the Authority under lease or other arrangement. Denaturing seems to have been overestimated by the public as a safety measure.

7. Definition of Dangerous and Non-dangerous Activities. Although a reasonable dividing line can be drawn between dangerous and non-dangerous activities, it is not hard and fast. Provision should, therefore, be made to assure constant reexamination of the questions and to permit revision of the dividing line as changing conditions and new discoveries may require.

8. Operations of Dangerous Activities. Any plant dealing with uranium or thorium after it once reaches the potential of dangerous use must be not only subject to the most rigorous and competent inspection by the Authority, but its actual operation shall be under the management, supervision, and control of the Authority.

9. Inspection. By assigning intrinsically dangerous activities exclusively to the Authority, the difficulties of inspection are reduced. If the Authority is the only agency which may lawfully conduct dangerous activities, then visible operation by others than the Authority will constitute an unambiguous danger signal. Inspection will also occur in connection with the licensing functions of the Authority.

10. Freedom of Access. Adequate ingress and egress for all qualified representatives of the Authority must be assured. Many of the inspection activities of the Authority should grow out of, and be incidental to, its other functions. Important measures of inspection will be associated with the tight control of raw materials, for this is a keystone of the plan. The continuing activities of prospecting, survey, and research in relation to raw materials will be designed not only to serve the affirmative development functions of the Authority but also to assure that no surreptitious operations are conducted in the raw-materials field by nations or their citizens.

11. Personnel. The personnel of the Authority should be recruited on a basis of proven competence but also so far as possible on an international basis.

12. Progress by Stages. A primary step in the creation of the system of control is the setting forth, in comprehensive terms, of the functions, responsibilities, powers, and limitations of the Authority. Once a charter for the Authority has been adopted, the Authority and the system of control for which it will be responsible will require time to become fully organized and effective. The plan of control will, therefore, have to come into effect in successive stages. These should be specifically fixed in the charter or means should be otherwise set forth in the charter for transitions from one stage to another, as contemplated in the resolution of the United Nations Assembly which created this Commission.

13. Disclosures. In the deliberations of the United Nations Commission on Atomic Energy, the United States is prepared to make available the information essential to a reasonable understanding of the proposals which it advocates. Further disclosures must be dependent, in the interests of all, upon the effective ratification of the treaty. When the Authority is actually created, the United States will join the other nations in making available the further information essential to that organization for the performance of its functions. As the successive stages of international control are reached, the United States will be prepared to yield, to the extent required by each stage, national control of activities in this field to the Authority.

14. International Control. There will be questions about the extent of control to be allowed to national bodies, when the Authority is established. Purely national authorities for control and development of atomic energy should to the extent necessary for the effective operation of the Authority be subordinate to it. This is neither an endorsement nor a disapproval of the creation of national authorities. The Commission should evolve a clear demarcation of the scope of duties and responsibilities of such national authorities.

And now I end. I have submitted an outline for present discussion. . . .

All of us are consecrated to making an end of gloom and hopelessness. It will not be an easy job. The way is long and thorny, but supremely worth traveling. All of us want to stand erect, with our faces to the sun, instead of being forced to burrow into the earth, like rats.

The pattern of salvation must be worked out by all for all. . . .

The Truman Doctrine: Harry S. Truman, Special Message to Congress, March 12, 1947

After World War II, the British government aided the Greek and Turkish governments in their resistance to Communist pressure. Early in 1947, Britain notified Washington that it could not afford to continue this aid. The exactions of six years of war, capped by a bruising winter in 1946, had so strained England that she was near the bottom of her resources. The United States would either have to take over the support of Greece and Turkey or look on while these nations were drawn into the Soviet orbit.

Truman's decision was to act. On March 12, 1947, he went before Congress to propose that the United States extend aid to Greece and Turkey. In effect, he also proposed that the United States formally abandon its historic policy of avoiding entanglement in European politics. Approved overwhelmingly by Congress, this "Truman Doctrine" marked the first step toward active American resistance to Communist expansion. The document that follows is the text of Truman's message. It is taken from Eighty-first Congress, first session, Senate Document Number 123, Senate Foreign Relations Committee, A Decade of American Foreign Policy, 1941–1949, *pages 1253–1257.*

Mr. President, Mr. Speaker, Members of the Congress of the United States:

The gravity of the situation which confronts the world today necessitates my appearance before a joint session of the Congress.

The foreign policy and the national security of this country are involved.

One aspect of the present situation, which I wish to present to you at this time for your consideration and decision, concerns Greece and Turkey.

The United States has received from the Greek Government an urgent appeal for financial and economic assistance. Preliminary reports from the American Economic Mission now in Greece and reports from the American Ambassador in Greece corroborate the statement of the Greek Government that assistance is imperative if Greece is to survive as a free nation.

I do not believe that the American people and the Congress wish to turn a deaf ear to the appeal of the Greek Government.

Greece is not a rich country. Lack of sufficient natural resources has always forced the Greek people to work hard to make both ends meet. Since 1940 this industrious and peace-loving country has suffered invasion, four years of cruel enemy occupation, and bitter internal strife.

When forces of liberation entered Greece they found that the retreating Germans had destroyed virtually all the railways, roads, port facilities, communications, and merchant marine. More than a thousand villages had been burned. Eighty-five percent of the children were tubercular. Livestock, poultry, and draft animals had almost disappeared. Inflation had wiped out practically all savings.

As a result of these tragic conditions, a militant minority, exploiting human want and misery, was able to create political chaos which, until now, has made economic recovery impossible.

Greece is today without funds to finance the importation of those goods which are essential to bare subsistence. Under these circumstances the people of Greece cannot make progress in solving their problems of reconstruction. Greece is in desperate need of financial and economic assistance to enable it to resume purchases of food, clothing, fuel, and seeds. These are indispensable for the subsistence of its people and are obtainable only from abroad. Greece must have help to import the goods necessary to restore internal order and security so essential for economic and political recovery.

The Greek Government has also asked for the assistance of experienced American administrators, economists, and technicians to insure that the financial and other aid given to Greece shall be used effectively in creating a stable and self-sustaining economy and in improving its public administration.

The very existence of the Greek state is today threatened by the terrorist activities of several thousand armed men, led by Communists, who defy the Government's authority at a number of points, particularly along the northern boundaries. A commission appointed by the United Nations Security Council is at present investigating disturbed conditions in northern Greece and alleged border violations along the frontier between Greece on the one hand and Albania, Bulgaria, and Yugoslavia on the other.

Meanwhile, the Greek Government is unable to cope with the situation. The Greek Army is small and poorly equipped. It needs supplies and equipment if it is to restore authority to the Government throughout Greek territory.

Greece must have assistance if it is to become a self-supporting and self-respecting democracy.

The United States must supply that assistance. We have already extended to Greece certain types of relief and economic aid, but these are inadequate.

There is no other country to which democratic Greece can turn.

No other nation is willing and able to provide the necessary support for a democratic Greek Government.

The British Government, which has been helping Greece, can give no further financial or economic aid after March 31. Great Britain finds itself under the necessity of reducing or liquidating its commitments in several parts of the world, including Greece.

We have considered how the United Nations might assist in this crisis. But the situation is an urgent one requiring immediate action, and the United Nations and its related organizations are not in a position to extend help of the kind that is required.

It is important to note that the Greek Government has asked for our aid in utilizing effectively the financial and other assistance we may give to Greece, and in improving its public administration. It is of the utmost importance that we supervise the use of any funds made available to Greece, in such a manner that each dollar spent will count toward making Greece self-supporting, and will help to build an economy in which a healthy democracy can flourish.

No government is perfect. One of the chief virtues of a democracy, however, is that its defects are always visible and under democratic processes can be pointed out and corrected. The Government of Greece is not perfect. Nevertheless it represents 85 percent of the members of the Greek Parliament who were chosen in an election last year. Foreign observers, including 692 Americans, considered this election to be a fair expression of the views of the Greek people.

The Greek Government has been operating in an atmosphere of chaos and extremism. It has made mistakes. The extension of aid by this country does not mean that the United States condones everything that the Greek Government has done or will do. We have condemned in the past, and we condemn now, extremist measures of the right or the left. We have in the past advised tolerance, and we advise tolerance now.

Greece's neighbor, Turkey, also deserves our attention.

The future of Turkey as an independent and economically sound state is clearly no less important to the freedom-loving peoples of the world than the future of Greece. The circumstances in which Turkey finds itself today are considerably different from those of Greece. Turkey has been spared the disasters that have beset Greece. And during the war the United States and Great Britain furnished Turkey with material aid.

Nevertheless, Turkey now needs our support.

Since the war Turkey has sought additional financial assistance from Great Britain and the United States for the purpose of effecting that modernization necessary for the maintenance of its national integrity.

That integrity is essential to the preservation of order in the Middle East.

The British Government has informed us that, owing to its own difficulties, it can no longer extend financial or economic aid to Turkey.

As in the case of Greece, if Turkey is to have the assistance it needs, the United States must supply it. We are the only country able to provide that help.

I am fully aware of the broad implications involved if the United States extends assistance to Greece and Turkey, and I shall discuss these implications with you at this time.

One of the primary objectives of the foreign policy of the United States is the creation of conditions in which we and other nations will be able to work out a way of life free from coercion. This was a fundamental issue in the war with Germany and Japan. Our victory was won over countries which sought to impose their will, and their way of life, upon other nations.

To insure the peaceful development of nations, free from coercion, the United States has taken a leading part in establishing the United Nations. The United Nations is designed to make possible lasting freedom and independence for all its members. We shall not realize our objectives, however, unless we are willing to help free peoples to maintain their free institutions and their national integrity against aggressive movements that seek to impose upon them totalitarian regimes. This is no more than a frank recognition that totalitarian regimes imposed upon free peoples, by direct or indirect aggression, undermine the foundations of international peace and hence the security of the United States.

The peoples of a number of countries of the world have recently had totalitarian regimes forced upon them against their will. The Government of the United States has made frequent protests against coercion and intimidation, in violation of the Yalta agreement, in Poland, Rumania, and Bulgaria. I must also state that in a number of other countries there have been similar developments.

At the present moment in world history nearly every nation must choose between alternative ways of life. The choice is too often not a free one.

One way of life is based upon the will of the majority, and is distinguished by free institutions, representative government, free elections, guaranties, of individual liberty, freedom of speech and religion, and freedom from political oppression.

The second way of life is based upon the will of a minority forcibly imposed upon the majority. It relies upon terror and oppression, a controlled press and radio, fixed elections, and the suppression of personal freedoms.

I believe that it must be the policy of the United States to support free peoples who are resisting attempted subjugation by armed minorities or by outside pressures.

I believe that we must assist free peoples to work out their own destinies in their own way.

I believe that our help should be primarily through economic and financial aid which is essential to economic stability and orderly political processes.

The world is not static, and the *status quo* is not sacred. But we cannot allow changes in the *status quo* in violation of the Charter of the United Nations by such methods as coercion, or by such subterfuges as political infiltration. In helping free and independent nations to maintain their freedom, the United States will be giving effect to the principles of the Charter of the United Nations.

It is necessary only to glance at a map to realize that the survival and integrity of the Greek nation are of grave importance in a much wider situation. If Greece should fall under the control of an armed minority, the effect upon its neighbor, Turkey, would be immediate and serious. Confusion and disorder might well spread throughout the entire Middle East.

Moreover, the disappearance of Greece as an independent state would have a profound effect upon those countries in Europe whose peoples are struggling against great difficulties to maintain their freedoms and their independence while they repair the damages of war.

It would be an unspeakable tragedy if these countries, which have struggled so long against overwhelming odds, should lose that victory for which they sacrificed so much. Collapse of free institutions and loss of independence would be disastrous not only for them but for the world. Discouragement and possibly failure would quickly be the lot of neighboring peoples striving to maintain their freedom and independence.

Should we fail to aid Greece and Turkey in this fateful hour, the effect will be far-reaching to the West as well as to the East.

We must take immediate and resolute action.

I therefore ask the Congress to provide authority for assistance to Greece and Turkey in the amount of $400,000,000 for the period ending June 30, 1948. In requesting these funds, I have taken into consideration the maximum amount of relief assistance which would be furnished to Greece out of the $350,000,000 which I recently requested that the Congress authorize for the prevention of starvation and suffering in countries devastated by the war.

In addition to funds, I ask the Congress to authorize the detail of American civilian and military personnel to Greece and Turkey, at the request of those countries, to assist in the tasks of reconstruction, and for the purpose of supervising the use of such financial and material assistance as may be furnished. I recommend that authority also be provided for the instruction and training of selected Greek and Turkish personnel.

Finally, I ask that the Congress provide authority which will permit the speediest and most effective use, in terms of needed commodities, supplies, and equipment, of such funds as may be authorized.

If further funds, or further authority, should be needed for purposes indicated in this message, I shall not hesitate to bring the situation before the Congress. On this subject the Executive and Legislative branches of the Government must work together.

This is a serious course upon which we embark.

I would not recommend it except that the alternative is much more serious.

The United States contributed $341,000,000,000 toward winning World War II. This is an investment in world freedom and world peace.

The assistance that I am recommending for Greece and Turkey amounts to little more than one-tenth of one percent of this investment. It is only common sense that we should safeguard this investment and make sure that it was not in vain.

The seeds of totalitarian regimes are nurtured by misery and want. They spread and grow in the evil soil of poverty and strife. They reach their full growth when the hope of a people for a better life has died.

We must keep that hope alive.

The free peoples of the world look to us for support in maintaining their freedoms.

If we falter in our leadership, we may endanger the peace of the world—and we shall surely endanger the welfare of our own Nation.

Great responsibilities have been placed upon us by the swift movement of events.

I am confident that the Congress will face these responsibilities squarely.

SELECTION 11

The Marshall Plan: George C. Marshall, Address at Harvard University, June 5, 1947

In 1947, Greece and Turkey were not the only zones of peril. All Western Europe had been impoverished by the war. In every country, Communists were active, working openly or secretly to promote discontent and political instability.

Looking at the European scene, American officials felt that the entire Continent was in danger of falling to the Communists. This could be prevented, they concluded, only if the United States mounted a massive attack on the economic conditions that bred discontent and instability. Such an attack, they also concluded, would require 10 to 20 billion dollars of direct American economic aid. J. M. Jones, The Fifteen Weeks *(1955) is a firsthand account of activity within the American government during this period of scrutiny.*

Discussions with European statesmen and particularly with England's Foreign Secretary, Ernest Bevin, developed a course of action that seemed likely to succeed. In spite of the staggering estimate of probable costs, President Truman decided to go ahead. His Secretary of State by this time was George C. Marshall, the wartime Chief of Staff of the Army. In June, 1947, Secretary Marshall was to receive an honorary degree at Harvard University, and it was decided that Marshall should use this occasion to announce the decision.

In his address, Marshall invited European governments to get together, frame plans for the economic rebuilding of the Continent, and then put specific requests for funds before the United States government. Significantly, he invited the Soviet Union and its East European satellites to join in the planning. Even now, the American government was not willing to take the position that co-operation with the Communist nations was impossible. In any case, the assumption in Washington was that economic recovery would forestall the spread of communism even if nations already Communist participated in the recovery.

The document below is the text of Marshall's address at Harvard—the basic statement of what was to become known as the "Marshall Plan." It is taken from the State Department Bulletin, *volume 17 (June 15, 1947), pages 1159–1160.*

I need not tell you gentlemen that the world situation is very serious. That must be apparent to all intelligent people. I think one difficulty is that the problem is one of such enormous complexity that the very mass of facts presented to the public by press and radio make it exceedingly difficult for the man in the street to reach a clear appraisement of the situation. Furthermore, the people of this country are distant from the troubled areas of the earth and it is hard for them to comprehend the plight and consequent reactions of the long-suffering peoples, and the effect of those reactions on their governments in connection with our efforts to promote peace in the world.

In considering the requirements for the rehabilitation of Europe, the physical loss of life, the visible destruction of cities, factories, mines, and railroads was correctly estimated, but it has become obvious during recent months that this visible destruction was probably less serious than the dislocation of the entire fabric of European economy. For the past 10 years conditions have been highly abnormal. The feverish preparation for war and the more feverish maintenance of the war effort engulfed all aspects of national economies. Machinery has fallen into disrepair or is entirely obsolete. Under the arbitrary and destructive Nazi rule, virtually every possible enterprise was geared into the German war machine. Long-standing commercial ties, private institutions, banks, insurance companies, and shipping companies disappeared, through loss of capital, absorption through nationalization, or by simple destruction. In many countries, confidence in the local currency has been severely shaken. The breakdown of the business structure of Europe during the war was complete. Recovery has been seriously retarded by the fact that two years after the close of hostilities a peace settlement with Germany and Austria has not been agreed upon. But even given a more prompt solution of these difficult problems, the rehabilitation of the economic structure of Europe quite evidently will require a much longer time and greater effort than had been foreseen.

There is a phase of this matter which is both interesting and serious. The farmer has always produced the foodstuffs to exchange with the city dweller for the other necessities of life. This division of labor is the basis of modern civilization. At the present time it is threatened with breakdown. The town and city industries are not producing adequate goods to exchange with the food-producing farmer. Raw materials and fuel are in short supply. Machinery is lacking or worn out. The farmer or the peasant cannot find the goods for sale which he desires to purchase. So the sale of his farm produce for money which he cannot use seems to him an unprofitable transaction. He, therefore, has withdrawn many fields from crop cultivation and is using them for grazing. He feeds more grain to stock and finds for himself and his family an ample supply of food, however short he may be on clothing and the other ordinary gadgets of civilization. Meanwhile people in the cities are short of food and fuel. So the governments are forced to use their foreign money and credits to procure these necessities abroad. This process exhausts funds which are urgently needed for reconstruction. Thus a very serious situation is rapidly developing which bodes no good for the world. The modern system of the division of labor upon which the exchange of products is based is in danger of breaking down.

The truth of the matter is that Europe's requirements for the next three or four years of foreign food and other essential products—principally from America—are so much greater than her present ability to pay that she must have substantial additional help or face economic, social, and political deterioration of a very grave character.

The remedy lies in breaking the vicious circle and restoring the confidence of the European people in the economic future of their own countries and of Europe as a whole. The manufacturer and the farmer throughout wide areas must be able and willing to exchange their products for currencies the continuing value of which is not open to question.

Aside from the demoralizing effect on the world at large and the possibilities of disturbances arising as a result of the desperation of the people concerned, the consequences to the economy of the United States should be apparent to all. It is logical that the United States should do whatever it is able to do to assist in the return of normal economic health in the world, without which there can be no political stability and no assured peace. Our policy is directed not against any country or doctrine but against hunger, poverty, desperation, and chaos. Its purpose should be the revival of a working economy in the world so as to permit the emergence of political and social conditions in which free institutions can exist. Such assistance, I am convinced, must not be on a piecemeal basis as various crises develop. Any assistance that this Government may render in the future should provide a cure rather than a mere palliative. Any government that is willing to assist in the task of recovery will find full cooperation, I am sure, on the part of the United States Government. Any government which maneuvers to block the recovery of other countries cannot expect help from us. Furthermore, governments, political parties, or groups which seek to perpetuate human misery in order to profit therefrom politically or otherwise will encounter the opposition of the United States.

It is already evident that, before the United States Government can proceed much further in its efforts to alleviate the situation and help start the European world on its way to recovery, there must be some agreement among the countries of Europe as to the requirements of the situation and the part those countries themselves will take in order to give proper effect to whatever action might be undertaken by this Government. It would be neither fitting nor efficacious for this Government to undertake to draw up unilaterally a program designed to place Europe on its feet economically. This is the business of the Europeans. The initiative, I think, must come from Europe. The role of this country should consist of friendly aid in the drafting of a European program and of later support of such a program so far as it may be practical for us to do so. The program should be a joint one, agreed to by a number, if not all, European nations.

An essential part of any successful action on the part of the United States is an understanding on the part of the people of America of the character of the problem and the remedies to be applied. Political passion and prejudice should have no part. With foresight, and a willingness on the part of our people to face up to the vast responsibility which history has clearly placed upon our country, the difficulties I have outlined can and will be overcome.

PART THREE

Between Peace and War

SELECTION 12

The Berlin Blockade: From Lucius D. Clay, "Decision in Germany"

With each month, the antagonism between the United States and the Soviet Union sharpened. In 1948, Soviet-backed Communists seized power in Czechoslovakia. In Italy, the first postwar election became a fierce contest between American-supported Christian Democrats and Soviet-supported Communists, with the Christian Democrats winning a narrow victory. In Yugoslavia, the government of Marshal Josip Broz Tito, while remaining Communist, broke with the Soviet Union, and the United States almost immediately gave Tito support.

Germany then became the storm center. There, the United States, Britain, France, and the U.S.S.R. were supposed to exercise joint control. In fact, combined action had proved almost impossible, and western Germany, controlled by the three Western powers, had grown more and more distinct from the eastern zone controlled by the Soviets.

After the Marshall Plan went into effect, the Western powers concerted policies so that their zones in Germany could participate in Europe's effort to achieve economic recovery. This was done in spite of loud and determined protest from Moscow.

Several steps were taken by the Western powers. One was currency reform for the west German occupation zones. The American, British, and French zones established a single currency convertible to other European currencies. Western Germany thus became able to trade with Western Europe. A second step was to ease the postvictory restraints on German industrial development, allowing the reopening and rebuilding of manufacturing plants in the Rhine and Ruhr basins.

Soviet officials and the Communist press charged the Western powers with aggressive motives. The Soviet Union retaliated against currency reform measures in the Western zones of Germany by closing the border of the Soviet occupation zone. The city of Berlin, deep within the Soviet zone, was nominally under four-power control. Actually, like Germany itself, it was divided into a Western sector and a Soviet sector. The effect of the closing of the border was to cut off communication between the Western powers and their sector of Berlin. The Soviet action was therefore spoken of as "the Berlin blockade."

After debating various alternatives, the American government decided on a massive effort to supply Berlin by air. The Soviets, though halting rail and road traffic, did not interfere with the movement of aircraft. The airlift to Berlin proved successful. The Western sector of Berlin was rescued. In 1949, the Soviet Union lifted the blockade. In the meantime, however, the United States and the Soviet Union had seemed to teeter on the edge of war.

Most of the available evidence on the prolonged crisis is in firsthand accounts such as President Truman's Memoirs *(two volumes, 1955). The only scholarly study, W. P. Davidson,* The Berlin Blockade *(1958), concentrates on reactions of the Berlin populace. The description below is taken from the memoirs of the general who was in command of American occupation forces in Germany. It is from Lucius D. Clay,* Decision in Germany *(Doubleday, 1950), pages 358–362, 374, 368, 381–382, 390–391.*

. . . on . . . March 31, 1948, the Soviet Military Administration issued an order which prevented the movement of military passenger trains across the border en route to Berlin unless baggage and passengers were checked by their personnel. This was a direct violation of our right to be in Berlin and of the oral agreement with Marshal Zhukov in which it had been specified that our personnel would be subject to neither customs nor border controls. If these controls were accepted American personnel would be subject to seizure by Soviet police, and rough handling of our people might result.

The following day, in implementation of this order, Soviet representatives decreed that no freight could leave Berlin by rail unless permission had been granted by the Russian Kommandatura. This put the Soviet authorities in Berlin in full control of its trade. We could not accept this principle. As a result our incoming traffic was limited to civil and military freight, while trains returning from Berlin were empty.

The Soviet deputy military governor, General Dratvin, wrote to my deputy, General Hays, to announce the details of their search procedure. I reported this letter and my proposed reply at once in a teleconference with the Department of the Army. I suggested that we accept a compromise measure under which the train commanders would furnish certified passenger lists and documentation to Soviet inspectors. I added:

> We cannot permit our military trains to be entered [for such purposes] by representatives of other powers, and to do so would be inconsistent with the free and unrestricted right of access in Berlin which was the condition precedent to our evacuation of Saxony and Thuringia.

This reply was approved and dispatched to General Dratvin. It was rejected by Soviet representatives.

I also reported my intent to send a test train with a few armed guards on board across the border to see if the Russians would actually stop it by force or by sidetracking. The train progressed some distance into the Soviet Zone but was finally shunted off the main line by electrical switching to a siding, where it remained for a few days until it withdrew rather ignominiously. It was clear the Russians meant business.

During this teleconference I thought I detected some apprehension on the part of Secretary Royall and his advisers that a firm stand on our part might develop incidents involving force which would lead to war. Therefore I expressed my opinion that weakness on our part would cost important prestige and that if war were desired by the Soviet Government it would not be averted by weakness. I added:

> I do not believe this means war. . . . Please understand we are not carrying a chip on our shoulder and will shoot only for self-protection. I do not believe we will have to do so.

Because of the six hours' difference in time between Berlin and Washington these telecons usually took place in the late evening, as four o'clock in the afternoon in Washington was ten o'clock at night in Berlin. To go to this telecon I had excused myself from dinner in my home with my French and British colleagues. We had been discussing our course of action, and I rushed home to continue this discussion. General Bradley* had ended the telecon with:

> Thanks muchly. This has been an arduous day and we appreciate your co-operation.

I could admit that it had been already, though the discussion with my colleagues lasted for several additional hours. We agreed not to accept the Soviet restrictions and to maintain a common front.

On April 2 the Department of the Army again requested a teleconference in which it stated that pressures were rising at home for the withdrawal of our families and that many responsible persons believed it unthinkable that they should stay in Berlin. I reported that we could support the Americans in Berlin indefinitely with a very small airlift and that we should not evacuate our dependents. Just prior to a meeting with my staff a few days before, I had been told that a number of applications had been received from our officers and officials in Berlin requesting permission for their families to be returned to the United States. I took the opportunity afforded by the staff meeting to state that it was unbecoming to an American to show any signs of nervousness. If there were those who felt uneasy I would be glad to arrange for their return home and a request to this effect would not discredit the applicant. On the other hand, I wanted no one with me in Berlin who had sent his family home, and therefore a request to go home would apply to all members of the family. While I had expected some increase in applications, the result of my statement was the opposite and almost all of the applications previously received were withdrawn. Therefore I felt that I could say accurately in my reply to the Department of the Army:

> Evacuation in face of the Italian elections and European situation is to me almost unthinkable. Our women and children can take it, and they ap-

*[General of the Army Omar N. Bradley, then Chief of Staff of the United States Army (*ed.*).]

preciate import. There are few here who have any thought of leaving unless required to do so.

The next move of the Soviet representatives to extend the blockade was to stop outgoing passenger trains, including the international train, the Nord Express. This led to another teleconference with the Department of the Army on April 10 in which Royall stated that while there was no change in the Department's position that we should remain in Berlin, the question was under constant discussion in Washington and he wanted to have my views once more. In my reply I stated that we should not leave Berlin unless driven out by force. I thought that the extension of the blockade to cut food off from the German population in Berlin might succeed in forcing us out but I doubted if the Russians would be so foolish as to make a move which would alienate the German population completely. I continued:

> We have lost Czechoslovakia. Norway is threatened. We retreat from Berlin. When Berlin falls, western Germany will be next. If we mean . . . to hold Europe against Communism, we must not budge. We can take humiliation and pressure short of war in Berlin without losing face. If we withdraw, our position in Europe is threatened. If America does not understand this now, does not know that the issue is cast, then it never will and communism will run rampant. I believe the future of democracy requires us to stay. . . . This is not heroic pose because there will be nothing heroic in having to take humiliation without retaliation.

So we remained in Berlin. Many British and French dependents were evacuated to their zones. While we had planned a substantial transfer in view of increased work in Frankfurt resulting from bi-zonal fusion, we slowed it down to avoid misunderstanding. In point of fact the international excitement which had resulted from the imposition of the blockade against Allied personnel and supplies did not last long. Our remaining in Berlin, dependent on air supply and cut off from the rest of the world by land and water, was soon taken for granted. The small airlift we started to meet our needs did not have the dramatic appeal of the great airlift that later supplied all the civilian population of western Berlin.

In April the Russians expelled our Signal Corps teams, which were stationed in the Soviet Zone to maintain repeater stations through which communication lines passed from Berlin to our zone. They had been there since the 1945 agreement covering our entry into Berlin.

We were soon convinced that it was only a question of time until the blockade was extended against the German civilian population. In May the Soviet representatives established new and impossible documentation requirements for the movement of military and civilian freight into Berlin. In June our civil supply trains were held up on various pretexts, and occasionally cars were cut off from civilian freight and mail trains and disappeared. On June 10 Soviet representatives tried to remove switching locomotives and railroad cars from our sector of Berlin, and we had to stop them with armed guards. On June 18 they began to stop at the border a large percentage of the cars which carried freight for Berlin on the grounds of "bad order." Finally, on June 24, all rail traffic between the western zones and Berlin was stopped by the Soviet Military Administration. Technical difficulties were the alleged reason. These "technical difficulties" soon extended to canal and highway, and by August 4 the blockade by land and water was complete. . . .

The care with which the Russians avoided measures which would have been resisted with force had convinced me that the Soviet Government did not want war although it believed that the Western Allies would yield much of their position rather than risk war. On July 10, I reported this conviction to our government, suggesting that we advise the Soviet representatives in Germany that under our rights to be in Berlin we proposed on a specific date to move in an armed convoy which would be equipped with the engineering material to overcome the technical difficulties which the Soviet representatives appeared unable to solve. I made it clear that I understood fully the risk and its implications and that this was a decision which could be made only by government. No armed convoy could cross the border without the possibility of trouble. In my view the chances of such a convoy being met by force with subsequent developments of hostilities were small. I was confident that it would get through to Berlin and that the highway blockade would be ended. When our government turned down my suggestion, I understood its desire to avoid this risk of armed conflict until the issue had been placed before the United Nations. I shall always believe that the convoy would have reached Berlin.

On July 19, I repeated these views in a cable which, paraphrased in part, said:

> I feel that the world is now facing the most vital issue that has developed since Hitler placed his political aggression under way. In fact the Soviet government has a greater strength under its immediate control than Hitler had to carry out his purpose. Under the circumstances which exist today, only we can assert world leadership. Only we have the strength to halt this aggressive policy here and now. It may be too late the next time. I am sure that determined action will bring it to a halt now without war. It can be stopped only if we assume some risk. . . .

During this crisis Murphy and I were summoned to Washington to report to the National Security Council where, some months before, both Ambassador Smith and I had predicted trouble in Berlin. On July 20, I reported the existing situation in a meeting attended by President Truman, Secretaries Marshall, Forrestal, Royall, Symington, Sullivan, Under Secretary Lovett, and the Joint Chiefs of Staff. I asserted my confidence that, given the planes, we could remain in Berlin indefinitely without war and that our departure would be a serious if not disastrous blow to the maintenance of freedom in Europe. I asked for 160 C-54s, a plane which would carry ten tons of cargo as compared to the two and a half tons carried by the C-47. Symington and General Hoyt Vandenberg of the Air Forces said they could deliver these planes in a relatively short time. There was no dissent to my recommendations, which were approved by the National Security Council. When the Council adjourned, President Truman honored me by asking me to remain with him for further discussion, during which

I told him I was sure that the Berlin population would stand fast through the coming winter if it proved necessary. I left his office inspired by the understanding and confidence I received from him. . . .

Berlin under blockade was like a besieged city with only one supply line linking it to the Western world, the airlift bringing food, clothing, coal, raw materials, and medicines to the 2,500,000 men, women, and children in its western sectors. Operation Vittles, as the pilots designated the airlift, grew steadily from the few outmoded planes we had in Germany to the fleet of giant flying transports which on the record day delivered almost 13,000 tons to our three airports.

At the start our C-47s had flown the clock around; pilots, plane and ground crews worked far beyond normal hours to achieve a maximum effort. This effort showed the high number of landings which could be made, thus demonstrating that with larger planes we could sustain the Berlin population. It was a welcome sight to the pilots of the C-47s when the first C-54s began to arrive on June 30, 1948, from Alaska, Panama, and Hawaii. It was impressive to see these planes with their insignia indicating the parts of the world from which they had come to participate in the airlift.

In July when I visited Washington I had been promised more planes to give us a total of 160 C-54s, and as they came in squadron by squadron, our freight to Berlin increased consistently. We proved on Air Force Day our ability with planes on hand to bring in 6987.7 tons, and the replacement of C-47s still in operation would have given us the 8000 tons which was essential to a sustaining economy in Berlin. We believed that in good weather we had to be able to carry twice the minimum quota of 4000 tons, although this provided a substantial safety factor.

By December our daily average exceeded 4500 tons. In January and February it had climbed to 5500 tons. We were over the minimum quota of 4000 tons a day by a substantial margin. This minimum provided no fuel for either domestic heating or industrial production. It did supply coal to maintain the available electric generating facilities in the western sectors. . . .

On May 4 it was announced that the four occupying powers had agreed to lift the Berlin blockade, with trade conditions to be restored to the preblockade arrangements, on May 12, and that the foreign ministers would meet in Paris on May 23. I cabled to the Department of the Army immediately that we should continue the airlift until Berlin had adequate reserves of coal and food to carry it through another winter if the blockade should be resumed. This recommendation was approved and I announced it publicly in Germany on May 6.

At midnight on May 11–12 our trains and trucks crossed the borders en route to Berlin, without incident. Large numbers of correspondents from home and from other countries crossed the border in automobiles and as passengers in the first train. In Berlin it was a day of relaxation for the population with some evidence of a holiday spirit. However, the roar of the airlift still reminded them of their long siege. The blockade was lifted but the struggle for freedom was not yet over. The people had met a major test and were happy in the pride of accomplishment and determined to meet any further test in the same way. I did not meet the first incoming train, for though it represented a great victory, it was but one step forward in the fight for freedom. . . .

SELECTION 13

The Vandenberg Resolution: S.R. 239, June 11, 1948

With the passage of time, more and more Americans became convinced that the Soviet Union would heed no language except that of force. Many felt that the Russians might be deceived by the past record of the United States. Historically, the United States had not entangled itself in Europe, and, in both world wars, it had been slow to act. Many Americans feared that the Soviet government might move aggressively against Western Europe, calculating that the United States would not defend the Continent. Many also feared that Western Europeans might make the same mistake, assume that the United States would not defend them, and perhaps come to the conclusion that the safest course was to come to terms with Moscow.

During 1948, the American government encouraged European governments to form an alliance for mutual defense against possible Soviet aggression. Such an alliance was concluded at Brussels in March. In view of the weakness of postwar Europe, however, it seemed clear that this alliance alone might not be enough to deter the Soviets from attempting conquest of the Continent. It would be sure to be effective only if the United States became a party to it, thus announcing unequivocally that American power would be used to defend Western Europe from attack.

The idea of a military alliance with European nations was at variance with the tradition in American foreign policy of nonentanglement—a tradition first embodied in Washington's Farewell Address. Yet the idea won increasing support among leaders of both parties. Among them was Republican Senator Arthur Vandenberg of Michigan. Earlier one of the foremost isolationists, Vandenberg had changed his position, become a champion of a bipartisan foreign policy, and engineered Republican support for the establishment of the United Nations, the Baruch Plan, aid to Greece and Turkey, and the Marshall Plan. To test the sentiment of Congress on a possible military alliance with the nations of Western Europe, Vandenberg introduced a resolution stating that the United States would be prepared to join in regional defense arrangements affecting its own security. This resolution passed on June 11, 1948, 64 to 4.

Some background on the resolution is provided in A. H. Vandenberg, Jr.

(ed.), The Private Papers of Senator Vandenberg *(1952) and in H. B. Westerfield,* Foreign Policy and Party Politics: Pearl Harbor to Korea *(1955). The text of the Vandenberg Resolution, which follows, is taken from Eighty-eighth Congress, second session,* Congressional Record, *pages 6053–6054.*

Whereas peace with justice and the defense of human rights and fundamental freedoms require international cooperation through more effective use of the United Nations: Therefore be it

Resolved, That the Senate reaffirm the policy of the United States to achieve international peace and security through the United Nations so that armed force shall not be used except in the common interest, and that the President be advised of the sense of the Senate that this Government, by constitutional process, should particularly pursue the following objectives within the United Nations Charter:

1. Voluntary agreement to remove the veto from all questions involving pacific settlements of international disputes and situations, and from the admission of new members.
2. Progressive development of regional and other collective arrangements for individual and collective self-defense in accordance with the purposes, principles, and provisions of the Charter.
3. Association of the United States, by constitutional process, with such regional and other collective arrangements as are based on continuous and effective self-help and mutual aid, and as affect its national security.
4. Contributing to the maintenance of peace by making clear its determination to exercise the right of individual or collective self-defense under article 51 should any armed attack occur affecting its national security.
5. Maximum efforts to obtain agreements to provide the United Nations with armed forces as provided by the Charter, and to obtain agreement among member nations upon universal regulation and reduction of armaments under adequate and dependable guaranty against violation.
6. If necessary, after adequate effort toward strengthening the United Nations, review of the Charter at an appropriate time by a General Conference called under article 109 or by the General Assembly.

SELECTION 14

The North Atlantic Treaty, April 4, 1949

With the Vandenberg Resolution as encouragement, the Truman administration negotiated a defensive alliance with eleven other nations: Britain, France, Italy, Portugal, Belgium, Luxembourg, the Netherlands, Denmark, Norway, Iceland,

and Canada. Signed on April 4, 1949, it was ratified by the United States Senate in July by a vote of 82 to 13.

Out of this North Atlantic Treaty grew a North Atlantic Treaty Organization, or NATO, with military, naval, and air units under unified command. Later Greece and West Germany signed the treaty and became members. Two analyses of NATO are B. T. Moore, NATO and the Future of Europe *(1958) and R. E. Osgood,* NATO: The Entangling Alliance *(1962).*

The text of the treaty is taken from Eighty-first Congress, first session, Senate Document Number 123, Senate Foreign Relations Committee, A Decade of American Foreign Policy, 1941–49, *pages 1328–30.*

The Parties to this Treaty reaffirm their faith in the purposes and principles of the Charter of the United Nations and their desire to live in peace with all peoples and all governments.

They are determined to safeguard the freedom, common heritage and civilization of their peoples, founded on the principles of democracy, individual liberty and the rule of law.

They seek to promote stability and well-being in the North Atlantic area.

They are resolved to unite their efforts for collective defense and for the preservation of peace and security.

They therefore agree to this North Atlantic Treaty:

Article 1

The Parties undertake, as set forth in the Charter of the United Nations, to settle any international disputes in which they may be involved by peaceful means in such a manner that international peace and security, and justice, are not endangered, and to refrain in their international relations from the threat or use of force in any manner inconsistent with the purposes of the United Nations.

Article 2

The Parties will contribute toward the further development of peaceful and friendly international relations by strengthening their free institutions, by bringing about a better understanding of the principles upon which these institutions are founded, and by promoting conditions of stability and well-being. They will seek to eliminate conflict in their international economic policies and will encourage economic collaboration between any or all of them.

Article 3

In order more effectively to achieve the objectives of this Treaty, the Parties, separately and jointly, by means of continuous and effective self-help and mutual aid, will maintain and develop their individual and collective capacity to resist armed attack.

Article 4

The Parties will consult together whenever, in the opinion of any of them, the territorial integrity, political independence or security of any of the Parties is threatened.

Article 5

The Parties agree that an armed attack against one or more of them in Europe or North America shall be considered an attack against them all; and consequently they agree that, if such an armed attack occurs, each of them, in exercise of the right of individual or collective self-defense recognized by Article 51 of the Charter of the United Nations, will assist the Party or Parties so attacked by taking forthwith, individually and in concert with the other Parties, such action as it deems necessary, including the use of armed force, to restore and maintain the security of the North Atlantic area.

Any such armed attack and all measures taken as a result thereof shall immediately be reported to the Security Council. Such measures shall be terminated when the Security Council has taken the measures necessary to restore and maintain international peace and security.

Article 6

For the purpose of Article 5 an armed attack on one or more of the Parties is deemed to include an armed attack on the territory of any of the Parties in Europe or North America, on the Algerian departments of France, on the occupation forces of any Party in Europe, on the islands under the jurisdiction of any Party in the North Atlantic area north of the Tropic of Cancer or on the vessels or aircraft in this area of any of the Parties.

Article 7

This Treaty does not affect, and shall not be interpreted as affecting, in any way the rights and obligations under the Charter of the Parties which are members of the United Nations, or the primary responsibility of the Security Council for the maintenance of international peace and security.

Article 8

Each Party declares that none of the international engagements now in force between it and any other of the Parties or any third state is in conflict with the provisions of this Treaty, and undertakes not to enter into any international engagement in conflict with this Treaty.

Article 9

The Parties hereby established a council, on which each of them shall be represented, to consider matters concerning the implementation of this Treaty. The council shall be so organized as to be able to meet promptly at any time. The council shall set up such subsidiary bodies as may be necessary; in particular it shall establish immediately a defense committee which shall recommend measures for the implementation of Articles 3 and 5.

Article 10

The Parties may, by unanimous agreement, invite any other European state in a position to further the principles of this Treaty and to contribute to the security of the North Atlantic area to accede to this Treaty. Any state so invited may become a party to the Treaty by depositing its instrument of accession with the Government of the United States of America. The Government of the United States of America will inform each of the Parties of the deposit of each such instrument of accession.

Article 11

This Treaty shall be ratified and its provisions carried out by the Parties in accordance with their respective constitutional processes. The instruments of ratification shall be deposited as soon as possible with the Government of the United States of America, which will notify all the other signatories of each deposit. The Treaty shall enter into force between the states which have ratified it as soon as the ratifications of the majority of the signatories, including the ratifications of Belgium, Canada, France, Luxembourg, the Netherlands, the United Kingdom and the United States, have been deposited and shall come into effect with respect to other states on the date of the deposit of their ratifications.

Article 12

After the Treaty has been in force for ten years, or at any time thereafter, the Parties shall, if any of them so requests, consult together for the purpose of reviewing the Treaty, having regard for the factors then affecting peace and security in the North Atlantic area, including the development of universal as well as regional arrangements under the Charter of the United Nations for the maintenance of international peace and security.

Article 13

After the Treaty has been in force for twenty years, any Party may cease to be a party one year after its notice of denunciation has been given to the Government of the United States of America, which will inform the Governments of the other Parties of the deposit of each notice of denunciation.

Article 14

This Treaty, of which the English and French texts are equally authentic, shall be deposited in the archives of the Government of the United States of America. Duly certified copies thereof will be transmitted by that Government to the Governments of the other signatories.

In witness whereof, the undersigned plenipotentiaries have signed this Treaty.

Done at Washington, the fourth day of April, 1949.

PART FOUR

Catastrophe in Asia

SELECTION 

The Quest for Peace in China: President Truman's Instructions to General Marshall, December 15, 1945

In 1949, the center of the cold war suddenly shifted to Asia. There, the United States suffered a shattering reverse. The whole of China, with vast resources and a population estimated at over 400 million fell to the control of a Chinese Communist party. At that time, the Chinese Communists seemed willing servants of the Soviet Union. The Communist takeover of China appeared a great coup for the Kremlin.

The background of the Communist conquest of China is fantastically complicated. The American role was a small one. In the immediate aftermath, however, American attention naturally focused on the question of whether or not the United States, by doing more or less than it had done, could have altered the course of Chinese history.

During World War II, the United States had extended some aid to the non-Communist government of China headed by Generalissimo Chiang Kai-shek. Intent on prosecuting the war against Japan, the American government had urged Chiang to fight the Japanese rather than the Communists who were his rivals for power. Since the Communists were also battling the Japanese, the American government urged that the two Chinese factions cooperate. The intricate tale of America's wartime aid and advice is told in Herbert Feis, The China Tangle *(1953) and in more detail in three volumes by Riley Sunderland and C. F. Romanus—*Stilwell's Mission to China *(1953);* Stilwell's Command Problems *(1956); and* Time Runs Out in CBI *(1959).*

At the Yalta Conference early in 1945, the United States came to an understanding with the Soviet Union about postwar China. The American government had for some time been pressing Russia to enter the war against Japan. At Yalta, Soviet Premier Stalin made a final commitment to do so. His conditions were that, after the war, the Soviet Union receive the Kuril Islands and the southern half of Sakhalin Island and, jointly with China, manage the principal railroads in Manchuria and control the port of Dairen. In return, Stalin promised not only to participate in the Far Eastern war but also to sign a treaty of amity and commerce with the government of Chiang Kai-shek. These negotiations are described in E. R. May, "The United States, the Soviet Union, and the Far Eastern War, 1941–1945," Pacific Historical Review *(May, 1955), pages 153–174; J. L. Snell,* The Meaning of Yalta *(1956); and Herbert Feis,* Churchill, Roosevelt, Stalin *(1957).*

At a later date, the Yalta arrangements were to be viewed by some Americans as a betrayal of Nationalist China and the seed from which later events in China sprang. At the time, the concessions to the Soviet Union seemed a small price for Soviet participation in the war against Japan. In addition, the Yalta agreements seemed to promise that the Chinese would be able to work out their own destiny without interference from their powerful Communist neighbor.

After Japan's sudden and unexpected surrender, the United States used its influence in China to promote reconciliation between the Nationalists and Communists. At the time, it did not seem impossible for non-Communists and

Communists to work together in a coalition government. Such a government was functioning in Czechoslovakia, and it seemed a success. Only in 1948 did the Czech Communists betray their coworkers and seize power. Until that occurred, Americans assumed that a government like that in Czechoslovakia could be established in China. If so, it would bring a halt to China's civil warfare and allow its government to cope with grave and pressing economic problems.

In a campaign to induce Chinese Nationalists and Communists to negotiate with one another, the American government used all the weapons at its disposal —advice, exhortation, promises of aid in return for compromises, threats to deny aid if compromises were not made. With nothing availing, President Truman decided in December, 1945, to send a special representative to China to promote such negotiations. He selected General George C. Marshall, who had distinguished himself during the war as chief of staff of the United States Army. The President's instructions to Marshall were contained in the letter that appears below. A capsule statement of American policy at this time, it is taken from the so-called State Department White Paper—United States Department of State, U.S. Relations with China *(Publication number 3573: Government Printing Office, 1949), pages 605–606.*

Washington, December 15, 1945

My dear General Marshall:

On the eve of your departure for China I want to repeat to you my appreciation of your willingness to undertake this difficult mission.

I have the utmost confidence in your ability to handle the task before you but, to guide you in so far as you may find it helpful, I will give you some of the thoughts, ideas, and objectives which Secretary Byrnes and I have in mind with regard to your mission. . . .

The fact that I have asked you to go to China is the clearest evidence of my very real concern with regard to the situation there. Secretary Byrnes and I are both anxious that the unification of China by peaceful, democratic methods be achieved as soon as possible. It is my desire that you, as my Special Representative, bring to bear in an appropriate and practicable manner the influence of the United States to this end.

Specifically, I desire that you endeavor to persuade the Chinese Government to call a national conference of representatives of the major political elements to bring about the unification of China and, concurrently, to effect a cessation of hostilities, particularly in north China.

It is my understanding that there is now in session in Chungking a Peoples' Consultative Council made up of representatives of the various political elements, including the Chinese Communists. The meeting of this Council should furnish you with a convenient opportunity for discussions with the various political leaders.

Upon the success of your efforts, as outlined above, will depend largely, of course, the success of our plans for evacuating Japanese troops from China, particularly north China, and for the subsequent withdrawal of our own armed forces from China. I am particularly desirous that both be accomplished as soon as possible.

In your conversations with Chiang Kai-shek and other Chinese leaders you are authorized to speak with the utmost frankness. Particularly, you may state, in connection with the Chinese desire for credits, technical assistance in the economic field, and military assistance (I have in mind the proposed U. S. military advisory group which I have approved in principle), that a China disunited and torn by civil strife could not be considered realistically as a proper place for American assistance along the lines enumerated.

I am anxious that you keep Secretary Byrnes and me currently informed of the progress of your negotiations and of obstacles you may encounter. You will have our full support and we shall endeavor at all times to be as helpful to you as possible.

Sincerely yours,

HARRY TRUMAN

SELECTION 

The Fall of China: Excerpts from The State Department White Paper, 1949

General Marshall's mission failed. Conditions in China went from bad to worse. In 1949, Generalissimo Chiang Kai-shek and his government fled to the island of Taiwan, or Formosa, off the Chinese coast. The Communists were masters of all China.

Attempting to answer anguished questions about why China had fallen and whether the United States could have prevented it, the State Department put together the fat volume of narrative and documents that was to become known as the "White Paper." The following document is the letter of transmittal by Secretary of State Dean G. Acheson which was, in effect, an introduction to and summary of the volume. It is taken from pages iii–xvii of the White Paper.

The President: In accordance with your wish, I have had compiled a record of our relations with China, special emphasis being placed on the last five years. This record is being published and will therefore be available to the Congress and to the people of the United States.

Although the compilation is voluminous, it necessarily covers a relatively small part of the relations between China and the United States. Since the beginning of World War II, these relations have involved many Government departments and agencies. The preparation of the full historical record of that period is by no means yet complete. Because of the great current interest in the problems confronting China, I have not delayed publication until the complete analysis could be made of the archives of the National Military Establishment, the Treasury Department, the Lend-Lease Administration, the White House files and many other official sources. However, I instructed those charged with the compilation of this document to present a record which would reveal the salient facts which determined our policy toward China during this period and which reflect the execution of that policy. This is a frank record of an extremely complicated and most unhappy period in the life of a great country to which the United States has long been attached by ties of closest friendship. No available item has been omitted because it contains statements critical of our policy or might be the basis of future criticism. The inherent strength of our system is the responsiveness of the Government to an informed and critical public opinion. It is precisely this informed and critical public opinion which totalitarian governments, whether Rightist or Communist, cannot endure and do not tolerate.

The interest of the people and the Government of the United States in China goes far back into our history. Despite the distance and broad differences in background which separate China and the United States, our friendship for that country has always been intensified by the religious, philanthropic and cultural ties which have united the two peoples, and has been attested by many acts of good will over a period of many years, including the use of the Boxer indemnity for the education of Chinese students, the abolition of extraterritoriality during the Second World War, and our extensive aid to China during and since the close of the war. The record shows that the United States has consistently maintained and still maintains those fundamental principles of our foreign policy toward China which include the doctrine of the Open Door, respect for the administrative and territorial integrity of China, and opposition to any foreign domination of China. It is deplorable that respect for the truth in the compilation of this record makes it necessary to publish an account of facts which reveal the distressing situation in that country. I have not felt, however, that publication could be withheld for that reason.

The record should be read in the light of conditions prevailing when the events occurred. It must not be forgotten, for example, that throughout World War II we were allied with Russia in the struggle to defeat Germany and Italy, and that a prime object of our policy was to bring Russia into the struggle against Japan in time to be of real value in the prosecution of the war. In this period, military considerations were understandably predominant over all others. Our most urgent purpose in the Far East was to defeat the common enemy and save the lives of our own men and those of our comrades-in-arms, the Chinese included. We should have failed in our manifest duty had we pursued any other course.

In the years since V-J Day, as in the years before Pearl Harbor, military considerations have been secondary to an earnest desire on our part to assist the Chinese people to achieve peace, prosperity and internal stability. The decisions and actions of our Government to promote these aims necessarily were taken on the basis of information available at the time. Throughout this tragic period, it has been fully realized that the material aid, the military and technical assistance, and the good will of the United States, however abundant, could not of themselves put China on her feet. In the last analysis, that can be done only by China herself.

Two factors have played a major role in shaping the destiny of modern China.

The population of China during the eighteenth and nineteenth centuries doubled, thereby creating an unbearable pressure upon the land. The first problem which every Chinese Government has had to face is that of feeding this population. So far none has succeeded. The Kuomintang attempted to solve it by putting many land-reform laws on the statute books. Some of these laws have failed, others have been ignored. In no small measure, the predicament in which the National Government finds itself today is due to its failure to provide China with enough to eat. A large part of the Chinese Communists' propaganda consists of promises that they will solve the land problem.

The second major factor which has shaped the pattern of contemporary China is the impact of the West and of Western ideas. For more than three thousand years the Chinese developed their own high culture and civilization, largely untouched by outside influences. Even when subjected to military conquest the Chinese always managed in the end to subdue and absorb the invader. It was natural therefore that they should come to look upon themselves as the center of the world and the highest expression of civilized mankind. Then in the middle of the nineteenth century the heretofore impervious wall of Chinese isolation was breached by the West. These outsiders brought with them aggressiveness, the unparalleled development of Western technology, and a high order of culture which had not accompanied previous foreign incursions into China. Partly because of these qualities and partly because of the decay of Manchu rule, the Westerners, instead of being absorbed by the Chinese, introduced new ideas which played an important part in stimulating ferment and unrest.

By the beginning of the twentieth century, the combined force of overpopulation and new ideas set in motion that chain of events which can be called the Chinese revolution. It is one of the most imposing revolutions in recorded history and its outcome and consequences are yet to be foreseen. Out of this revolutionary whirlpool emerged the Kuomintang, first under the leadership of Dr. Sun Yat-sen, and later Generalissimo Chiang Kai-shek, to assume the direction of the revolution. The leadership of the Kuomintang was not challenged until 1927 by the Chinese Communist party which had been organized in the early twenties under the ideological impetus of the Russian revolution. It should be remembered that Soviet doctrine and practice had a measurable effect upon the thinking and principles of Dr. Sun Yat-sen, particularly in terms of economics and party organization, and that the Kuomintang and the Chinese Communists cooperated until 1927 when the Third International demanded a predominant position in the Government and the army. It was this demand which precipitated the break between the two groups. To a large extent the history of the period between 1927 and 1937 can be written in terms of the struggle for power between the Kuomintang and the Chinese Communists, with the latter apparently fighting a losing battle. During this period the Kuomintang made considerable progress in its efforts to unify the country and to build up the nation's financial and economic strength. Somewhere during this decade, however, the Kuomintang began to lose the dynamism and revolutionary fervor which had created it, while in the Chinese Communists the fervor became fanaticism.

Perhaps largely because of the progress being made in China, the Japanese chose 1937 as the departure point for the conquest of China proper, and the goal of the Chinese people became the expulsion of a brutal and hated invader. Chinese resistance against Japan during the early years of the war compelled the unqualified admiration of freedom-loving peoples throughout the world. Until 1940 this resistance was largely without foreign support. The tragedy of these years of war was that physical and human devastation to a large extent destroyed the emerging middle class which historically has been the backbone and heart of liberalism and democracy.

In contrast also to the unity of the people of China in the war against Japan were the divided interests of the leaders of the Kuomintang and of the Chinese Communists. It became apparent in the early forties that the leaders of the Government, just as much as the Communist leaders, were still as preoccupied with the internal struggle for power as they were with waging war against Japan. Once the United States became a participant in the war, the Kuomintang was apparently convinced of the ultimate defeat of Japan and saw an opportunity to improve its position for a show-down struggle with the Communists. The Communists, for their part, seemed to see in the chaos of China an opportunity to obtain that which had been denied them before the Japanese war, namely, full power in China. This struggle for power in the latter years of the war contributed largely to the partial paralysis of China's ability to resist.

It was precisely here that two of the fundamental principles of United States policy in regard to China—noninterference in its internal affairs and support of its unity and territorial integrity—came into conflict and that one of them also conflicted with the basic interests of the Allies in the war against Japan. It seemed highly probable in 1943 and 1944 that, unless the Chinese could subordinate their internal interests to the larger interest of the unified war effort against Japan, Chinese resistance would become completely ineffective and the Japanese would be able to deprive the Allies of valuable bases, operating points and manpower in China at a time when the outcome of the war against Japan was still far from clear. In this situation and in the light of the paramount necessity of the most vigorous prosecution of the war, in which Chinese interests were equally at stake with our own, traditional concepts of policy had to be adapted to a new and unprecedented situation.

After Pearl Harbor we expanded the program of military and economic aid which we had inaugurated earlier in 1941 under the Lend-Lease Act.

That program . . . was far from reaching the volume which we would have wished because of the tremendous demands on the United States from all theaters of a world-wide war and because of the difficulties of access to a China all of whose ports were held by the enemy. Nevertheless it was substantial.

Representatives of our Government, military and civilian, who were sent to assist the Chinese in prosecuting the war soon discovered that, as indicated above, the long struggle had seriously weakened the Chinese Government not only militarily and economically, but also politically and in morale. The reports of United States military and diplomatic officers reveal a growing conviction through 1943 and 1944 that the Government and the Kuomintang had apparently lost the crusading spirit that won them the people's loyalty during the early years of the war. In the opinion of many observers they had sunk into corruption, into a scramble for place and power, and into reliance on the United States to win the war for them and to preserve their own domestic supremacy. The Government of China, of course, had always been a one-party rather than a democratic government in the Western sense. The stresses and strains of war were now rapidly weakening such liberal elements as it did possess and strengthening the grip of the reactionaries who were indistinguishable from the war lords of the past. The mass of the Chinese people were coming more and more to lose confidence in the Government.

It was evident to us that only a rejuvenated and progressive Chinese Government which could recapture the enthusiastic loyalty of the people could and would wage an effective war against Japan. American officials repeatedly brought their concern with this situation to the attention of the Generalissimo and he repeatedly assured them that it would be corrected. He made, however, little or no effective effort to correct it and tended to shut himself off from Chinese officials who gave unpalatable advice. In addition to a concern over the effect which this atrophy of the central Chinese administration must have upon the conduct of the war, some American observers, whose reports are also quoted in the attached record, were concerned over the effect which this deterioration of the Kuomintang must have on its eventual struggle, whether political or military, with the Chinese Communists. These observers were already fearful in 1943 and 1944 that the National Government might be so isolating itself from the people that in the postwar competition for power it would prove itself impotent to maintain its authority. Nevertheless, we continued for obvious reasons to direct all our aid to the National Government.

This was of course the period during which joint prosecution of the war against Nazi Germany had produced a degree of cooperation between the United States and Russia. President Roosevelt was determined to do what he could to bring about a continuance in the postwar period of the partnership forged in the fire of battle. The peoples of the world, sickened and weary with the excesses, the horrors, and the degradation of the war, shared this desire. It has remained for the postwar years to demonstrate that one of the major partners in this world alliance seemingly no longer pursues this aim, if indeed it ever did.

When Maj. Gen. Patrick J. Hurley was sent by President Roosevelt to

Chungking in 1944 he found what he considered to be a willingness on the part of the National Government and the Chinese Communists to lay aside their differences and cooperate in a common effort. Already they had been making sporadic attempts to achieve this result.

Previously and subsequently, General Hurley had been assured by Marshal Stalin that Russia had no intention of recognizing any government in China except the National Government with Chiang Kai-shek as its leader. It may be noted that during the late war years and for a time afterwards Marshal Stalin reiterated these views to American officials. He and Molotov expressed the view that China should look to the United States as the principal possible source of aid. The sentiments expressed by Marshal Stalin were in large part incorporated in the Sino-Soviet treaty of 1945.

From the wartime cooperation with the Soviet Union and from the costly campaigns against the Japanese came the Yalta Agreement. The American Government and people awaited with intense anxiety the assault on the main islands of Japan which it was feared would cost up to a million American casualties before Japan was conquered. The atomic bomb was not then a reality and it seemed impossible that the war in the Far East could be ended without this assault. It thus became a primary concern of the American Government to see to it that the Soviet Union enter the war against Japan at the earliest possible date in order that the Japanese Army in Manchuria might not be returned to the homeland at the critical moment. It was considered vital not only that the Soviet Union enter the war but that she do so before our invasion of Japan, which already had been set for the autumn of 1945.

At Yalta, Marshal Stalin not only agreed to attack Japan within two or three months after V–E Day but limited his "price" with reference to Manchuria substantially to the position which Russia had occupied there prior to 1904. We for our part, in order to obtain this commitment and thus to bring the war to a close with a consequent saving of American, Chinese and other Allied lives, were prepared to and did pay the requisite price. Two facts must not, however, be lost sight of in this connection. First, the Soviet Union when she finally did enter the war against Japan, could in any case have seized all the territories in question and considerably more regardless of what our attitude might have been. Second, the Soviets on their side in the Sino-Soviet Treaty arising from the Yalta Agreement, agreed to give the National Government of China moral and material support and moreover formalized their assurances of noninterference in China's internal affairs. Although the unexpectedly early collapse of Japanese resistance later made some of the provisions of the Yalta Agreement seem unnecessary, in the light of the predicted course of the war at that time they were considered to be not only justified but clearly advantageous. Although dictated by military necessity, the Agreement and the subsequent Sino-Soviet Treaty in fact imposed limitations on the action which Russia would, in any case, have been in a position to take.

For reasons of military security, and for those only, it was considered too dangerous for the United States to consult with the National Government regarding the Yalta Agreement or to communicate its terms at once to Chungking. We were then in the midst of the Pacific War. It was felt that there was grave risk that secret information transmitted to the Nationalist capital at this time would become available to the Japanese almost immediately. Under no circumstances, therefore, would we have been justified in incurring the security risks involved. It was not until June 15, 1945, that General Hurley was authorized to inform Chiang Kai-shek of the Agreement.

In conformity with the Russian agreement at Yalta to sign a treaty of friendship and alliance with Nationalist China, negotiations between the two nations began in Moscow in July 1945. During their course, the United States felt obliged to remind both parties that the purpose of the treaty was to implement the Yalta Agreement—no more, no less—and that some of the Soviet proposals exceeded its provisions. The treaty, which was signed on August 14, 1945, was greeted with general satisfaction both in Nationalist China and in the United States. It was considered that Russia had accepted definite limitations on its activities in China and was committed to withhold all aid from the Chinese Communists. On September 10, however, our embassy in Moscow cautioned against placing undue confidence in the Soviet observance of either the spirit or letter of the treaty. The subsequent conduct of the Soviet Government in Manchuria has amply justified this warning.

When peace came the United States was confronted with three possible alternatives in China: (1) it could have pulled out lock, stock and barrel; (2) it could have intervened militarily on a major scale to assist the Nationalists to destroy the Communists; (3) it could, while assisting the Nationalists to assert their authority over as much of China as possible, endeavor to avoid a civil war by working for a compromise between the two sides.

The first alternative would, and I believe American public opinion at the time so felt, have represented an abandonment of our international responsibilities and of our traditional policy of friendship for China before we had made a determined effort to be of assistance. The second alternative policy, while it may look attractive theoretically and in retrospect, was wholly impracticable. The Nationalists had been unable to destroy the Communists during the 10 years before the war. Now after the war the Nationalists were, as indicated above, weakened, demoralized, and unpopular. They had quickly dissipated their popular support and prestige in the areas liberated from the Japanese by the conduct of their civil and military officials. The Communists on the other hand were much stronger than they had ever been and were in control of most of North China. Because of the ineffectiveness of the Nationalist forces which was later to be tragically demonstrated, the Communists probably could have been dislodged only by American arms. It is obvious that the American people would not have sanctioned such a colossal commitment of our armies in 1945 or later. We therefore came to the third alternative policy whereunder we faced the facts of the situation and attempted to assist in working out a *modus vivendi* which would avert civil war but nevertheless preserve and even increase the influence of the National Government.

As the record shows, it was the Chinese National Government itself which, prior to General Hurley's mission, had taken steps to arrive at a working agreement with the Communists. As early as September 1943 in addressing the Koumintang Central Executive Committee, the Generalissimo said, "we should clearly recognize that the Communist problem is a purely political problem and should be solved by political means." He repeated this view on several occasions. Comprehensive negotiations between representatives of the Government and of the Communists, dealing with both military cooperation and civil administration, were opened in Sian in May 1944. These negotiations, in which Ambassador Hurley later assisted at the invitation of both parties between August 1944 and September 1945, continued intermittently during a year and a half without producing conclusive results and culminated in a comprehensive series of agreements on the basic points on October 11, 1945, after Ambassador Hurley's departure from China and before General Marshall's arrival. Meanwhile, however, clashes between the armed forces of the two groups were increasing and were jeopardizing the fulfillment of the agreements. The danger of widespread civil war, unless the negotiations could promptly be brought to a successful conclusion, was critical. It was under these circumstances that General Marshall left on his mission to China at the end of 1945.

. . . Our policy at that time was inspired by the two objectives of bringing peace to China under conditions which would permit stable government and progress along democratic lines, and of assisting the National Government to establish its authority over as wide areas of China as possible. As the event proved, the first objective was unrealizable because neither side desired it to succeed: The Communists because they refused to accept conditions which would weaken their freedom to proceed with what remained consistently their aim, the communization of all China: the Nationalists because they cherished the illusion, in spite of repeated advice to the contrary from our military representatives, that they could destroy the Communists by force of arms.

The second objective of assisting the National Government, however, we pursued vigorously from 1945 to 1949. The National Government was the recognized government of a friendly power. Our friendship, and our right under international law alike, called for aid to the Government instead of to the Communists who were seeking to subvert and overthrow it. The extent of our aid to Nationalist China is set forth in detail in chapters V, VI, VII and VIII of the record and need not be repeated here. The National Government had in 1945, and maintained until the early fall of 1948, a marked superiority in manpower and armament over their rivals. Indeed during that period, thanks very largely to our aid in transporting, arming and supplying their forces, they extended their control over a large part of North China and Manchuria. By the time General Marshall left China at the beginning of 1947, the Nationalists were apparently at the very peak of their military successes and territorial expansion. The following year and a half revealed, however, that their seeming strength was illusory and that their victories were built on sand.

The crisis had developed around Manchuria, traditional focus of Russian and Japanese imperialism. On numerous occasions, Marshal Stalin had stated categorically that he expected the National Government to take over the occupation of Manchuria. In the truce agreement of January 10, 1946, the Chinese Communists agreed to the movement of Government troops into Manchuria for the purpose of restoring Chinese sovereignty over this area. In conformity with this understanding the United States transported sizable government armies to the ports of entry into Manchuria. Earlier the Soviet Army had expressed a desire to evacuate Manchuria in December 1945, but had remained an additional two or three months at the request of the Chinese Government. When the Russian troops did begin their evacuation, the National Government found itself with extended lines of communications, limited rolling stock and insufficient forces to take over the areas being evacuated in time to prevent the entry of Chinese Communist forces, who were already in occupation of the countryside. As the Communists entered, they obtained the large stocks of matériel from the Japanese Kwantung Army which the Russians had conveniently "abandoned." To meet this situation the National Government embarked on a series of military campaigns which expanded the line of its holdings to the Sungari River. Toward the end of these campaigns it also commenced hostilities within North China and succeeded in constricting the areas held by the Communists.

In the spring of 1946 General Marshall attempted to restore peace. This effort lasted for months and during its course a seemingly endless series of proposals and counterproposals were made which had little effect upon the course of military activities and produced no political settlement. During these negotiations General Marshall displayed limitless patience and tact and a willingness to try and then try again in order to reach agreement. Increasingly he became convinced, however, that twenty years of intermittent civil war between the two factions, during which the leading figures had remained the same, had created such deep personal bitterness and such irreconcilable differences that no agreement was possible. The suspicions and the lack of confidence were beyond remedy. He became convinced that both parties were merely sparring for time, jockeying for military position and catering temporarily to what they believed to be American desires. General Marshall concluded that there was no hope of accomplishing the objectives of his mission.

Even though for all practical purposes General Marshall, by the fall of 1946, had withdrawn from his efforts to assist in a peaceful settlement of the civil war, he remained in China until January 1947. One of the critical points of dispute between the Government and the Communists had been the convocation of the National Assembly to write a new constitution for China and to bring an end to the period of political tutelage and of one-party government. The Communists had refused to participate in the National Assembly unless there were a prior military settlement. The Generalissimo was determined that the Assembly should be held and the program carried out. It was the hope of General Marshall during the late months of 1946 that his presence in China would encourage the liberal elements in non-Communist China to assert themselves more forcefully than they had in the past and to exercise a leavening influence upon the absolutist control wielded by the reactionaries and the militarists. General Marshall remained in China until the Assembly had completed its work. Even though the proposed new framework of government appeared satisfactory, the evidence suggested that there had been little shift in the balance of power.

In his farewell statement, General Marshall announced the termination of his efforts to assist the Chinese in restoring internal peace. He described the deep-seated mutual suspicion between the Kuomintang and the Chinese Communist Party as the greatest obstacle to a settlement. He made it clear that the salvation of China lay in the hands of the Chinese themselves and that, while the newly adopted constitution provided the framework for a democratic China, practical measures of implementation by both sides would be the decisive test. He appealed for the assumption of leadership by liberals in and out of the Government as the road to unity and peace. With these final words he returned to Washington to assume, in January 1947, his new post as Secretary of State.

As the signs of impending disaster multiplied, the President in July 1947, acting on the recommendation of the Secretary of State, instructed Lt. Gen. Albert C. Wedemeyer to survey the Chinese scene and make recommendations. In his report, submitted on September 19, 1947, the General recommended that the United States continue and expand its policy of giving aid to Nationalist China, subject to these stipulations:

1. That China inform the United Nations of her request for aid.
2. That China request the United Nations to bring about a truce in Manchuria and request that Manchuria be placed under a Five-Power guardianship or a trusteeship.
3. That China utilize her own resources, reform her finances, her Government and her armies, and accept American advisers in the military and economic fields.

General Wedemeyer's report, which fully recognized the danger of Communist domination of all China and was sympathetic to the problems of the National Government, nevertheless listed a large number of reforms which he considered essential if that Government were to rehabilitate itself.

It was decided that the publication at that time of a suggestion for the alienation of a part of China from the control of the National Government, and for placing that part under an international administration to include Soviet Russia, would not be helpful. . . .

The reasons for the failures of the Chinese National Government appear in some detail in the attached record. They do not stem from any inadequacy of American aid. Our military observers on the spot have reported that the Nationalist armies did not lose a single battle during the crucial year of 1948 through lack of arms or ammunition. The fact was that the decay which our observers had detected in Chungking early in the war had fatally sapped the powers of resistance of the Kuomintang. Its leaders had proved incapable of meeting the crisis confronting them, its troops had lost the will to fight, and its Government had lost popular support. The Communists, on the other hand, through a ruthless discipline and fanatical zeal, attempted to sell themselves as guardians and liberators of the people.

The Nationalist armies did not have to be defeated; they disintegrated. History has proved again and again that a regime without faith in itself and an army without morale cannot survive the test of battle.

The record obviously can not set forth in equal detail the inner history and development of the Chinese Communist Party during these years. The principal reason is that, while we had regular diplomatic relations with the National Government and had the benefit of voluminous reports from our representatives in their territories, our direct contact with the Communists was limited in the main to the mediation efforts of General Hurley and General Marshall.

Fully recognizing that the heads of the Chinese Communist Party were ideologically affiliated with Moscow, our Government nevertheless took the view, in the light of the existing balance of forces in China, that peace could be established only if certain conditions were met. The Kuomintang would have to set its own house in order and both sides would have to make concessions so that the Government of China might become, in fact as well as in name, the Government of all China and so that all parties might function within the constitutional system of the Government. Both internal peace and constitutional development required that the progress should be rapid from one party government with a large opposition party in armed rebellion, to the participation of all parties, including the moderate non-communist elements, in a truly national system of government.

None of these conditions has been realized. The distrust of the leaders of both the Nationalist and Communist Parties for each other proved too deep-seated to permit final agreement, notwithstanding temporary truces and apparently promising negotiations. The Nationalists, furthermore, embarked in 1946 on an over-ambitious military campaign in the face of warnings by General Marshall that it not only would fail but would plunge China into economic chaos and eventually destroy the National Government. General Marshall pointed out that though Nationalist armies could, for a period, capture Communist-held cities, they could not destroy the Communist armies. Thus every Nationalist advance would expose their communications to attack by Communist guerrillas and compel them to retreat or to surrender their armies together with the munitions which the United States has furnished them. No estimate of a military situation has ever been more completely confirmed by the resulting facts.

The historic policy of the United States of friendship and aid toward the people of China was, however, maintained in both peace and war. Since V–J Day, the United States Government has authorized aid to Nationalist China in the form of grants and credits totaling approximately 2 billion dollars, an amount equivalent in value to more than 50 percent of the monetary expenditures of the Chinese Government and of proportionately greater magnitude in relation to the budget of that Government than the United States has provided to any nation of Western Europe since the end of the war. In addition to these grants and credits, the United States Government has sold the Chinese Government large quantities of military and civilian war surplus property with a total procurement cost of over 1 billion dollars, for which the agreed realization to the United States was 232 million dollars. A large proportion of the military supplies furnished the Chinese armies by the United States since V–J Day has, however, fallen into the hands of the Chinese Communists through the military ineptitude of the Nationalist leaders, their defections and surrenders, and the absence among their forces of the will to fight.

It has been urged that relatively small amounts of additional aid—military and economic—to the National Government would have enabled it to destroy communism in China. The most trustworthy military, economic, and political information available to our Government does not bear out this view.

A realistic appraisal of conditions in China, past and present, leads to the conclusion that the only alternative open to the United States was full-scale intervention in behalf of a Government which had lost the confidence of its own troops and its own people. Such intervention would have required the expenditure of even greater sums than have been fruitlessly spent thus far, the command of Nationalist armies by American officers, and the probable participation of American armed forces—land, sea, and air—in the resulting war. Intervention of such a scope and magnitude would have been resented by the mass of the Chinese people, would have diametrically reversed our historic policy, and would have been condemned by the American people.

It must be admitted frankly that the American policy of assisting the Chinese people in resisting domination by any foreign power or powers is now confronted with the gravest difficulties. The heart of China is in Communist hands. The Communist leaders have foresworn their Chinese heritage and have publicly announced their subservience to a foreign power, Russia, which during the last 50 years, under czars and Communists alike, has been most assiduous in its efforts to extend its control in the Far East. In the recent past, attempts at foreign domination have appeared quite clearly to the Chinese people as external aggression and as such have been bitterly and in the long run successfully resisted. Our aid and encouragement have helped them to resist. In this case, however, the foreign domination has been masked behind the facade of a vast crusading movement which apparently has seemed to many Chinese to be wholly indigenous and national. Under these circumstances, our aid has been unavailing.

The unfortunate but inescapable fact is that the ominous result of the civil war in China was beyond the control of the government of the United States. Nothing that this country did or could have done within the reasonable limits of its capabilities could have changed that result; nothing that was left undone by this country has contributed to it. It was the product of internal Chinese forces, forces which this country tried to influence but could not. A decision was arrived at within China, if only a decision by default.

And now it is abundantly clear that we must face the situation as it exists in fact. We will not help the Chinese or ourselves by basing our policy on wishful thinking. We continue to believe that, however tragic may be the immediate future of China and however ruthlessly a major portion of this great people may be exploited by a party in the interest of a foreign imperialism, ultimately the profound civilization and the democratic individualism of China will reassert themselves and she will throw off the foreign yoke. I consider that we should encourage all developments in China which now and in the future work toward this end.

In the immediate future, however, the implementation of our historic policy of friendship for China must be profoundly affected by current developments. It will necessarily be influenced by the degree to which the Chinese people come to recognize that the Communist regime serves not their interests but those of Soviet Russia and the manner in which, having become aware of the facts, they react to this foreign domination. One point, however, is clear. Should the Communist regime lend itself to the aims of Soviet Russian imperialism and attempt to engage in aggression against China's neighbors, we and the other members of the United Nations would be confronted by a situation violative of the principles of the United Nations Charter and threatening international peace and security.

Meanwhile our policy will continue to be based upon our own respect for the Charter, our friendship for China, and our traditional support for the Open Door and for China's independence and administrative and territorial integrity.

Respectfully yours,

DEAN ACHESON

Afterthoughts: Declaration by Eight Republican Senators, 1951

For all the haste in which it was compiled, the White Paper was a remarkably fair and judicious piece of work. The latest and most careful scholarly study, Tang Tsou, America's Failure in China, 1941–50 *(1963), in spite of its title, confirms most of the White Paper's judgments.*

At the time, many Americans were not able to accept the sobering conclusions presented in the White Paper. Many continued to believe that the United States could have saved Nationalist China. The document below is an excerpt from a report issued in 1951 by eight Republican Senators: Styles Bridges (N.H.), Alexander Wiley (Wis.), H. Alexander Smith (N.J.), Bourke B. Hickenlooper (Iowa), William F. Knowland (Calif.), Henry P. Cain (Wash.), Owen Brewster (Maine), and Ralph E. Flanders (Vt.). A capsule presentation of the viewpoint of critics of American Chinese policy, it is taken from the Eighty-second Congress, first session. Hearings before the Committee on Foreign Relations and the Armed Services Committee, United States Senate, Military Situation in the Far East, *pages 3591–3596.*

1. Yalta Is a Great Tragedy of American Diplomacy

The turning point of American foreign policy in the Far East was the Yalta Agreement of February 1945. The Secretary of State has vigorously defended the agreements made at Yalta as being essential to achieve the participation of Russia in the war against Japan. According to witnesses who defended the Yalta Agreement, the Japanese forces were then capable of terrific resistance. It was claimed that it would cost a million American casualties to invade the Japanese Islands. It was stated by the Secretary of State that, at the time of Yalta, we did not know whether or not we had an atomic bomb and, therefore, Russian military participation was essential.

The evidence of Gen. Patrick J. Hurley, Ambassador to China at this time, however, contradicts this "explanation" of Yalta. In the opinion of General Hurley:

"The surrender of the principles and objectives by the State Department at Yalta created the confusion, the crisis which confronts our Nation today."

General MacArthur referred to Yalta as a great tragedy, stating that "one of the gravest mistakes that was ever made was to permit the Soviet to come down into China at Port Arthur, Dairen, and other places of that sort."

Under questioning, it was established that at the time of Yalta the Japanese Navy was at the bottom of the ocean and American airpower had destroyed the Japanese industrial potential. Furthermore, with the economy of Japan dependent on imports, there was absolutely no doubt, from a military point of view, that the Japanese home army would wither on the vine.

The testimony of Admiral Leahy in I Was There was to the effect that it was not the intention of President Roosevelt to invade the Japanese islands, but rather to bring to bear the might of American naval and air power. Admiral Leahy states that he believed that Russia should not be asked to participate in the Japanese War, but that the military desired Russian participation and the President accepted their view.

Testimony has been introduced into the record by Senator Bridges that there was prepared by 50 specialists in the Military Intelligence Division, G–2, the War Department, a study evaluating the desirability of Russian participation in the Japanese War and concluding that such participation should be prevented. (When asked to produce this paper, the Defense Department replied that it has not been able to find the document in question.)

The final and overwhelming evidence is that Secretary of War Stimson and Gen. Leslie R. Groves, head of the Manhattan Engineer District (wartime atom bomb agency) before Yalta, went to President Roosevelt and told him that the atom bomb was a certainty and would be ready for use by midsummer of 1945. (Further, a Colonel Consodine of the Manhattan Engineer District flew to the island of Malta where he met with Secretary of State Stettinius and briefed him immediately prior to Yalta on the certainty of the atom bomb.)

This myth, that the Russian participation in the Japanese War was a military necessity has been refuted adequately. History will record that at Yalta the United States repudiated some of its solemn obligations, yielded to Russian imperialism, and gave way to appeasement which will be regretted for decades and all for mythical reasons. The true reason for Yalta remains an inscrutable mystery. The result of Yalta remains a triumph for Communist diplomacy.

From John Hay to Cordell Hull, America maintained the "open door" in China. At Yalta America slammed the "open door."

2. The Victory Won by Our Armed Forces in the Pacific Has Been Squandered by Our Diplomats

In the year 1945 the United States was the dominant military power in the Far Pacific. With the assistance of our allies, excluding Russia, we had crushed the military might of the Japanese Empire. Our military position was unchallenged. Our diplomats were in a most excellent position for negotiation to maintain peace and stability in the area.

Our Chinese allies on the mainland in 1946 had begun to hammer at the Communist forces in the civil war within their land. They were making considerable headway late in 1946 in defeating this armed revolutionary movement.

However, our diplomats gave away our victory in secret agreements, so that in the year 1951, our foreign policy in the Far East stands revealed as a complete failure. China is in the hands of the Red; communism has swept through Asia; and we are involved in a war. Only Japan has been kept in the camp of the Western Powers, and the explanation for that may largely be found in the fact that our State Department exercised little authority in that area.

While Secretary Acheson's policies and those of his predecessors were largely instrumental in making 450 million of our former Chinese allies into enemies, General MacArthur's policies were largely instrumental in making 80 million former Japanese enemies into our friends.

It is doubtful if the annals of history reveal any similar instance wherein the fruits of victory, gained at such terrific cost in lives and treasure, have been so recklessly thrown away.

3. It Has Been Impossible to Determine Who Wrote the Instructions for General Marshall on His Mission to China

On November 27, 1945, the President accepted the resignation of Ambassador Patrick Hurley and announced the same day the appointment of General of the Army George C. Marshall to serve as his special representative in China. In the instructions issued to General Marshall, the President directed that he bring to bear the influence of the United States to the end that the "unification of China by peaceful, democratic methods" might be achieved and concurrently to endeavor to effect a termination of the civil war between the Nationalists and the Communists.

This, of course, had to do with the efforts to bring about a coalition government in which the Communists were to participate alongside of the bitterly anti-Communist Nationalist Government headed by Generalissimo Chiang Kai-shek. The Communists themselves have told all the world that their intention in participating in democratic processes of government is only to be considered as a stepping stone toward the ultimate creation of a Marxist Communist state.

Who wrote the instructions for the Marshall mission still remains a mystery despite repeated attempts on the part of members of this committee to ascertain this fact. Secretary Marshall stated that he did not write the instructions in the Presidential directive to him. The Secretary of State states that Secretary Marshall sat down and wrote his own instructions.

Senator Smith (Republican, New Jersey) referred to a communication from which a correspondent gave some personal views on the MacArthur situation. The final paragraph of the letter reads as follows:

"General Marshall was appointed and on December 11, 1945, sat down with Dean Acheson to write out the instructions President Truman was to give him."

Senator Smith continued to read this letter. It contained reference to a report General MacArthur made in 1945 in which he evaluated the armed forces in China.

Having listened to the reading of the letter, General Marshall stated:

"In the first place I have not a recollection of that report of General MacArthur's, but I have a very decided recollection of the reference in there that I sat down in the State Department and drew up this policy. *I did not.*"

Senator Smith had previously asked:

"Do you recall who had a hand in the preparation of the directives that sent you to China?"

To which Secretary Marshall replied:

"At that time, Senator, Mr. Byrnes was Secretary of State, and I presume he had a hand in it; Mr. Acheson was Under Secretary of State, and I presume he had a hand in it; John Carter Vincent was the head of the China group in the State Department, certainly he had a hand in it. I do not know what others did.

"On my part, General Hull, who is now on duty in the Army headquarters, and was the head of the Operations Division during the war for me, he represented my interest so far as I was concerned in that, together with a man from Time magazine forces, who had helped me briefly in the latter part of the war in the preparation of my final report, and who the directorship of Time loaned me to take to China with me because he had been there throughout a good period of the war."

When Secretary Acheson testified on this subject, he supplied the Senators with his version of the Marshall instructions, which is shown in the transcript as follows:

Secretary Acheson said:

"At the end of November 1945, Secretary Byrnes and General Marshall met. This was after General Marshall had been asked to go to China.

"Secretary Byrnes read him a memorandum suggesting the outline of instructions for him. General Marshall did not approve it.

"General Marshall said that he would wish to try his own hand, assisted by some of his associates, in drafting the instructions.

"This he did; and a draft was prepared by him, in conjunction with four generals who were working very closely with General Marshall. This was submitted to Secretary Byrnes.

"On the 8th of December Secretary Byrnes made his suggestions to General Marshall, that is, suggestions of changes or alterations or additions to the draft prepared by General Marshall.

"General Marshall's draft, with Secretary Byrnes' suggestions, was discussed at a meeting in Secretary Byrnes' office on Sunday morning, December 9, 1945, by Secretary Byrnes, General Marshall, Mr. John Carter Vincent, General Hull, and myself. I was then Under Secretary of State.

"Those of us went over the instructions. General Marshall approved the suggestion made by Secretary Byrnes and we then had a completely agreed draft."

The testimony from these two Cabinet officers is obviously contradictory. It is impossible to determine who actually wrote the instructions for General Marshall which contained the coalition policy which cost us our Chinese allies.

4. Some United States Officials Were So Opposed to Chiang Kai-shek That They Were Automatically on the Side of the "Red Regime"

Evidence has been presented to the committee that some of the American officials assigned to assist the Nationalist Government of the Republic of China were so much opposed to Chiang and his government so as to be automatically on the side of the Chinese Communists.

This committee did not attempt to explore fully the importance and widespread ramifications of this situation. However, the sworn testimony presented to this committee cannot be ignored. If the personal feelings of American diplomats operate to thwart the policy of their Government, there is a situation created which demands a complete and thorough inquiry.

It appears unlikely to us that the executive branch will undertake to expose this situation to the light of day. The situation strongly suggests that an appropriate committee of Congress endeavor to investigate this question and recommend remedial legislation.

5. It Has Not Been the Consistent Policy of the United States to Support the Republic of China

The Secretary of State testified it is the "firm and continuing" policy of the United States to support the Nationalist Government of the Republic of China. He stated this policy has been pursued by our Nation from the outbreak of World War II down to this very day.

The evidence before the committee indicates that this policy has been neither firm nor continuous. On the contrary, the policy has been obscured by constant conflict within the State Department, in the press, and in public debate. There has not been and even today there is no unanimity of opinion in the Government on the subject of aid to the Republic of China.

A policy of supporting the Republic of China should have been the firm and continuing policy of the United States. President Chiang Kai-shek was and is the outstanding anti-Communist leader in Asia. Our enemy in Asia and throughout the world has been identified as Russian communism.

The administration cannot straddle the fence on this issue. It claims to have followed a policy of supporting Chiang. The China white paper is a blunt denial of Secretary Acheson's statement. We have not been convinced that Chiang lost China for any other reason than that he did not receive sufficient support, both moral and material, from the United States.

The importance of moral support in any conflict in Asia was emphasized by General Wedemeyer. He testified that lack of moral support was the key to the downfall of the Government of the Republic of China.

Evidence of the continuing lack of moral support can be found in the quixotic attacks leveled by administration stalwarts, both in and out of Government, against President Chiang and all those who want to support him in his 25 years of struggle against communism and aggression.

The record is replete with the evidence of the lack of material support. Such military equipment as China Nationalists received in the critical days of the war against the Communist regime has been described as "moldy," broken, lacking parts, etc. One shipment of automatic weapons arrived without magazines, in such shape the guns were of no more value than broomsticks.

Official Government reports show that since VJ-day our former enemies, Japan, Germany, and Italy, have each received more United States aid and assistance than our wartime ally and historic friend, the Republic of China.

The contention that the administration consistently and firmly supported the Chinese Republic is simply not true.

Further evidence that the administration did not support the Government of the Republic of China is shown in the orientation fact sheet "Army Talk." This was an official War Department Publication used in World War II to indoctrinate our soldiers. The issue, dated April 7, 1945, was entitled "Our Ally China" and the role of the Communists was discussed.

Throughout the article "Communist" was in quotation marks and it was pointed out that when we speak of the Chinese "Communist," we should remember that many competent observers say that they stand for something very different from what we ordinarily intend when we use the word "Communist." In the first place, unlike Communists of the orthodox type, they believe in the rights of private property and private enterprise. Their chief interest at present is to improve the economic position of Chinese farmers, many of whom own but little land themselves but rent their land in part or in whole from wealthy landlords. In the second place, the Chinese "Communists" are not like those in America, merely a small minority. With the sole exception of Kuomintang itself, they are easily China's most important single political group. They exercise almost independent control over many parts of North China, where they have been responsible for much of the continuing guerrilla activity against the Japanese."

This astonishing orientation sheet continues to say:

"The situation is so complex and has such an involved history, that it is very difficult for any outsider to say definitely who is right and who is wrong. Probably some degree of right and wrong attaches 'to both sides.' The Communists say that they are trying to carry out certain economic and political reforms that the Kuomintang has up to now been unable or unwilling to make. Some American and other observers who have visited the 'Communists' agree that their program is a moderate one and that the things they have been doing in their areas are quite in accord with what we think of as liberal democracy."

Concluding the orientation is a brief discussion of Our Basic Concern which contains the statement that "the issue in China is not so much the tension that exists between the National Government and the Chinese "Communists" as it is between those elements within each camp who place their personal prestige, ideas, and ambitions ahead of winning the war."

American soldiers desiring to obtain more facts in regard to the problem of our Chinese ally were given a reference for further reading. That reference was The Making of Modern China by Owen Lattimore.

6. If the Republic of China Had Received Effective Military Aid from the United States They Might Have Defeated the Communists

Early in 1948 there were three high American officials in China, who felt the need for immediate action if China was to continue free of Communist domination. These officials, Ambassador Leighton Stuart, ECA Mission Chief Roger Lapham, and Vice Admiral Oscar Badger, journeyed to the north of China to see for themselves what could be done to stall the Communist advance and place the initiative in the hands of the Nationalist forces. They were impressed with the appearance, actions, and spirit of the armies of Gen. Fu Tsu Yi as well as the military stature of General Fu.

At the time of this visit General Fu told the United States officials "that he could do little more than to keep the Communists out of the area with his equipped armies and that he was constantly employing them on a defensive basis to meet Communist thrusts from various directions." However, the general went on to say "that if he could obtain equipment for the four additional trained armies he would then be able to set up an offensive to the northeast stabilizing the Chinhuangtao Hulutal corridor and for the eventual relief of Mukden."

He explained "that in relieving Mukden he could reopen a channel of supply for about 300,000 of the best troops in China (many of them American trained and equipped) which were cut off there and were very lacking in American munitions."

Immediately after this conference with Gen. Fu Tsu Yi a recommendation was sent to the JCS specifically listing the equipment required, and which was estimated at a total value of $16 million. It was approved in July 1948 but no specific action was taken to implement the decision.

In November 1948, Admiral Badger received word that a ship was about to enter Tiensin with about 10 percent of the recommended equipment on board. He said:

"Well, that's pretty bad. It's too bad that isn't the full business, but maybe it will still have a morale effect."

After the cargo was unloaded, Admiral Badger received a communication from General Fu reporting the deficiencies of the weapons. Of the total number, 480 of the machine guns lacked spare parts, tripod mounts, etc.; Thompson submachine guns had no magazines or clips, no loading machines for the loading of ammunition belts, only a thousand of the light machine guns with mounts and only a thousand clips for the 2,280 light machine guns. General Fu's commentary on this deplorable situation was according to Admiral Badger along the following lines:

"The above-mentioned weapons are not in good condition and, for the most part, cannot be used. I do not know how or why these weapons were forwarded in an incomplete state."

As a result of the arrival of this long anticipated shipment of arms in such an unusable condition, General Fu's plans for an offensive collapsed. The troops were completely demoralized and in Admiral Badger's judgment this action "was the straw that broke the camel's back."

The myth that the Republic of China fell because the Chinese troops refused to fight is again refuted by sworn testimony.

7. The Propaganda Campaign against the Republic of China Was Vicious

We have been greatly disturbed by the evidence which shows the terrific impact of the propaganda campaign against the Chinese Nationalist Government, originated by forces both within and without the United States. The constant attacks upon the leadership of Chiang Kai-shek and the repeated assaults upon the alleged corruption and graft of his associates softened the fiber of Nationalist resistance, especially since many of these attacks originated within a nation which claimed to be aiding and supporting the Republic of China.

It is clear that the defection of a friend is more destructive of morale than the victory of an enemy.

8. The Administration Believed That the Chinese Communists Would Work in Harmony with the Nationalists in a Coalition Government

The habit of administration witnesses to contradict themselves during the course of this investigation did little to allay misgivings as to the conduct of our foreign affairs. Nowhere were these misgivings more pronounced than in discussions of the China policy when the Secretary of State was asked:

"Was there ever any chance in your opinion of actually bringing the two Chinese groups to work together in harmony?"

He replied "Yes, sir." He then went on to say "it was the view of all our military people that it was possible and it was the only way to get real Chinese fighting against the Japanese." In direct contradiction to this statement is the statement of Lieutenant General Wedemeyer who certainly can qualify as a military expert in the Far East, that "I told him [General Marshall] very frankly that in my judgment he could not accomplish that mission. His mission was one that I thought was just like mixing oil and water."

Later on the Secretary was asked if it was not the "objective" of Communists in every government in which they had a part, to take over that government "Lock, stock, and barrel." The Secretary admitted that it was and that just such "captures" had occurred in Bulgaria, Rumania, Hungary, Czechoslovakia, and Poland.

Yet the administration persisted in pushing for a coalition policy for years after the Japanese had surrendered. The contention was made that the United States desired a "unified" China. The effort to achieve such unification was to insist upon an alliance of the Nationalists with the forces committed to their destruction, the Chinese Communists.

The admission that a policy could not be successful and, at the same time, adherence to that same policy, is a self-indictment.

9. The Administration Has Been Unduly Preoccupied with the Defense of America in Europe to the Neglect of the Defense of America in Asia

Since the days of Pearl Harbor, the American people have become used to the terms "global strategy," "global responsibilities," etc., and yet it is apparent to the signers of this report that the administration and the State Department have considered the globe to be much larger in its European aspects than in its Asiatic aspects.

While granting the importance of Europe and while recognizing the military and economic potential of that continent, we cannot help but feel there has been a myopia approaching blindness whenever we have dealt with matters of the Pacific.

There has never been the same amount of effort expended on behalf of Asiatic matters by the State Department as there has been toward those of Europe. It is unfortunate, but true, that the State Department has been affected by a group who have interpreted Asiatic problems to the advantage of Russia rather than that of the United States. . . .

PART FIVE

Conflict in Korea

SELECTION 

Outbreak of Violence: From Harry S. Truman, "Memoirs"

The Truman administration had acted to check, or contain, Communist expansion in Europe. After the Communist takeover in China, it faced the question of whether or not it should take similar action in Asia and, if so, how.

As of the beginning of 1950, it seemed likely that the Communist surge would continue across the Formosa Straits. The position of Chiang Kai-shek and his refugee government seemed shaky. It commanded no more popularity among the Chinese on Taiwan than among Chinese on the mainland, and the Taiwanese, a separate race, were as unenthusiastic about Chinese rule as they had been, during the fifty years before 1945, about Japanese rule. American officials calculated that Taiwan could be kept out of Communist hands only if the United States interposed military force to protect it. They also calculated that, given the precarious situation in Europe, this force simply was not available. Reluctantly, therefore, the Truman administration decided to write off Taiwan.

In Southeast Asia, the situation was unclear. Little of the evidence, however, was encouraging. The French in Indochina, the British in Malaya, and the Dutch in the Netherlands East Indies were battling guerrillas. Although the guerrillas' battle cries were nationalistic, many of their leaders were Communists. The long-range prospect, in the judgment of most American experts, was that the colonial powers would ultimately lose out. Unless more force was interposed, the Communist empire would very likely spread from the Gulf of Tonkin to the Java Sea. The United States did not at the time have forces to contribute. In any case, there was considerable question in American minds as to whether it would be right to support colonial powers seeking to preserve their *empires. Although the United States lent some aid to the French in Indochina, it was on a small scale.*

The general conclusion of the Truman administration was that the United States should draw a line in Asia, as it had in Europe, but that the line in Asia should run through deep water. Addressing the National Press Club in January, 1950, Secretary of State Acheson defined America's "defense perimeter" in the Far East. It ran, he said, "along the Aleutians to Japan . . . and from the Ryukyus to the Philippine Islands." Taiwan and all parts of the Asian mainland were excluded.

Another area not included in the defense perimeter was Korea. There, at the end of World War II, American forces had taken over the half of the peninsula south of 38°, while Soviet forces occupied the half north of that parallel. After long, futile negotiations, the two nations failed to agree on terms for ending their occupation and establishing a united, independent Korean nation. In the end, UN-supervised elections were held in South Korea. A Republic of Korea was established, with the veteran right-wing nationalist, Syngman Rhee, at the head of its government. In North Korea, the Soviets established a separate People's Republic of Korea, the leaders of which were all Communists. Afterward, both South Korea and North Korea had at least nominal independence.

Secretary Acheson did not include South Korea within the American defense perimeter. One reason probably was concern lest such inclusion encourage Rhee to think he would have American backing in a war to conquer North Korea. The small American advisory mission in Seoul, the Korean capital, had warned repeatedly that there was danger of Rhee's taking such action.

Acheson included in his Press Club speech, however, a broad statement concerning the possibility of a military attack on some Asian nation outside the defense perimeter. In such an event, he said, "the initial reliance must be on the people attacked to resist it and then upon the commitments of the entire civilized world under the Charter of the United Nations which so far has not proved a weak reed to lean on by any people who are determined to protect their independence against outside aggression."

On June 25, 1950, the United States was suddenly faced with a challenge to this second doctrine. The North Korean People's Republic launched an offensive against South Korea. The zone of combat lay outside the carefully defined defense perimeter. On the other hand, the attack by North Korea was clearly the kind of aggression that the United Nations Charter was supposed to prevent.

At the moment that the crisis broke, President Truman was visiting his home in Independence, Missouri. The following document is his own account of how the American government reacted. It is taken from Harry S. Truman, Memoirs *(two volumes, Doubleday, 1955), volume II, pages 332–339.*

It was a little after ten in the evening, and we were sitting in the library of our home on North Delaware Street when the telephone rang. It was the Secretary of State calling from his home in Maryland.

"Mr. President," said Dean Acheson, "I have very serious news. The North Koreans have invaded South Korea."

My first reaction was that I must get back to the capital, and I told Acheson so. He explained, however, that details were not yet available and that he thought I need not rush back until he called me again with further information. In the meantime, he suggested to me that we should ask the United Nations Security Council to hold a meeting at once and declare that an act of aggression had been committed against the Republic of Korea. I told him that I agreed and asked him to request immediately a special meeting of the Security Council, and he said he would call me to report again the following morning, or sooner if there was more information on the events in Korea.

Acheson's next call came through around eleven-thirty Sunday morning, just as we were getting ready to sit down to an early Sunday dinner. Acheson reported that the U. N. Security Council had been called into emergency session. Additional reports had been received from Korea, and there was no doubt that an all-out invasion was under way there. The Security Council, Acheson said, would probably call for a cease-fire, but in view of the complete disregard the North Koreans and their big allies had shown for the U.N. in the past, we had to expect that the U.N. order would be ignored. Some decision would have to be made at once as to the degree of aid or encouragement which our government was willing to extend to the Republic of Korea.

I asked Acheson to get together with the Service Secretaries and the Chiefs of Staff and start working on recommendations for me when I got back. Defense Secretary Louis Johnson and Chairman of the Chiefs of Staff General Omar Bradley were on their way back from an inspection tour of the Far East. I informed the Secretary of State that I was returning to Washington at once.

The crew of the presidential plane Independence did a wonderful job. They had the plane ready to fly in less than an hour from the time they were alerted, and my return trip got under way so fast that two of my aides were left behind. They could not be notified in time to reach the airport.

The plane left the Kansas City Municipal Airport at two o'clock, and it took just a little over three hours to make the trip to Washington. I had time to think aboard the plane. In my generation, this was not the first occasion when the strong had attacked the weak. I recalled some earlier instances: Manchuria, Ethiopia, Austria. I remembered how each time that the democracies failed to act it had encouraged the aggressors to keep going ahead. Communism was acting in Korea just as Hitler, Mussolini, and the Japanese had acted ten, fifteen, and twenty years earlier. I felt certain that if South Korea was allowed to fall Communist leaders would be emboldened to override nations closer to our own shores. If the Communists were permitted to force their way into the Republic of Korea without opposition from the free world, no small nation would have the courage to resist threats and aggression by stronger Communist neighbors. If this was allowed to go unchallenged it would mean a third world war, just as similar incidents had brought on the second world war. It was also clear to me that the foundations and the principles of the United Nations were at stake unless this unprovoked attack on Korea could be stopped.

I had the plane's radio operator send a message to Dean Acheson asking him and his immediate advisers and the top defense chiefs to come to Blair House for a dinner conference.*

When the Independence landed, Secretary of State Acheson was waiting for me at the airport, as was Secretary of Defense Johnson, who himself had arrived only a short while before. We hurried to Blair House, where we were joined by the other conferees. Present were the three service Secretaries, Secretary of the Army Frank Pace, Secretary of the Navy Francis Matthews, and Secretary of the Air Force Thomas Finletter. There

*[The White House was then undergoing repairs. Temporarily, the President and his family were living in the Blair House across the street from the White House, on Pennsylvania Avenue (*ed.*).]

were the Joint Chiefs of Staff, General of the Army Omar N. Bradley, the Army Chief General Collins, the Air Force Chief General Vandenberg, and Admiral Forrest Sherman, Chief of Naval Operations. Dean Acheson was accompanied by Under Secretary Webb, Deputy Under Secretary Dean Rusk and Assistant Under Secretary John Hickerson, and Ambassador-at-Large Philip Jessup.

It was late, and we went at once to the dining room for dinner. I asked that no discussion take place until dinner was served and over and the Blair House staff had withdrawn. I called on Dean Acheson first to give us a detailed picture of the situation. Acheson read us the first report that had been received by the State Department from our Ambassador in Seoul, Korea, at nine twenty-six the preceding evening:

> According Korean army reports which partly confirmed by KMAG field advisor reports North Korean forces invaded ROK territory at several points this morning. Action was initiated about 4 A.M. Ongjin blasted by North Korean artillery fire. About 6 A.M. North Korean infantry commenced crossing parallel in Ongjin area, Kaesong area, Chunchon area and amphibious landing was reportedly made south of Kangnung on east coast. Kaesong was reportedly captured at 9 A.M., with some 10 North Korean tanks participating in operation. North Korean forces, spearheaded by tanks, reportedly closing in on Chunchon. Details of fighting in Kangnung are unclear, although it seems North Korean forces have cut highway. Am conferring with KMAG advisors and Korean officials this morning re situation.
>
> It would appear from nature of attack and manner in which it was launched that it constitutes all out offensive against ROK.
>
> MUCCIO

There were additional messages from Ambassador Muccio, too, giving more details, but all confirmed that a full-fledged attack was under way, and the North Koreans had broadcast a proclamation that, in effect, was a declaration of war.

Earlier that Sunday evening, Acheson reported, the Security Council of the United Nations had, by a vote of 9 to 0, approved a resolution declaring that a breach of the peace had been committed by the North Korean action and ordering the North Koreans to cease their action and withdraw their forces.

I then called on Acheson to present the recommendations which the State and Defense Departments had prepared. He presented the following recommendations for immediate action:

> 1. That MacArthur† should evacuate the Americans from Korea—including the dependents of the Military Mission—and, in order to do so, should keep open the Kimpo and other airports, repelling all hostile attacks thereon. In doing this, his air forces should stay south of the 38th parallel.
>
> 2. That MacArthur should be instructed to get ammunition and supplies to the Korean army by airdrop and otherwise.
>
> 3. That the Seventh Fleet should be ordered into the Formosa Strait to

† [General of the Army Douglas MacArthur, Supreme Commander for the Allied Powers in Tokyo, in charge of occupation forces in Japan (*ed.*).]

prevent the conflict from spreading to that area. The Seventh Fleet should be ordered from Cavite north at once. We should make a statement that the fleet would repel any attack on Formosa and that no attacks should be made from Formosa on the mainland.

At this point I interrupted to say that the Seventh Fleet should be ordered north at once but that I wanted to withhold making any statement until the fleet was in position.

After this report I asked each person in turn to state his agreement or disagreement and any views he might have in addition. Two things stand out in this discussion. One was the complete, almost unspoken acceptance on the part of everyone that whatever had to be done to meet this aggression had to be done. There was no suggestion from anyone that either the United Nations or the United States could back away from it. This was the test of all the talk of the last five years of collective security. The other point which stands out in my mind from the discussion was the difference in view of what might be called for. Vandenberg and Sherman thought that air and naval aid might be enough. Collins said that if the Korean army was really broken, ground forces would be necessary. But no one could tell what the state of the Korean army really was on that Sunday night. Whatever the estimates of the military might be, everyone recognized the situation as serious in the extreme.

I then directed that orders be issued to put the three recommendations into immediate effect.

As we continued our discussion, I stated that I did not expect the North Koreans to pay any attention to the United Nations. This, I said, would mean that the United Nations would have to apply force if it wanted its order obeyed.

General Bradley said we would have to draw the line somewhere. Russia, he thought, was not yet ready for war, but in Korea they were obviously testing us, and the line ought to be drawn now.

I said that most emphatically I thought the line would have to be drawn.

General Collins reported that he had had a teletype conference with General MacArthur. The Far East commander, he told us, was ready to ship ammunition and supplies to Korea as soon as he received the green light.

I expressed the opinion that the Russians were trying to get Korea by default, gambling that we would be afraid of starting a third world war and would offer no resistance. I thought that we were still holding the stronger hand, although how much stronger, it was hard to tell.

I asked the three Chiefs of Staff, Collins, Vandenberg, and Sherman, what information they had on Russian forces in the Far East. Then I asked Admiral Sherman what the location of the Seventh Fleet was. The admiral said the fleet was nearing the Philippines, two days out of Japan, and when I asked how long it would take to bring these ships to the Formosa Strait, he replied that it would take one and a half to two days.

I asked General Collins how many divisions we had in Japan and how long it would take to move two or three of them to Korea. The general gave the information.

Next I asked the Secretary of the Air Force Finletter and General Vandenberg what the present disposition of the Air Force was and how long it would take to reinforce our air units in the Far East.

I instructed the service chiefs to prepare the necessary orders for the eventual use of American units if the United Nations should call for action against North Korea, and meanwhile General MacArthur was directed to send a survey party to Korea to find out what kind of aid would be most effective and how the military forces available to the Far East commander might be used. He was also to furnish such ammunition and equipment to the Republic of Korea as he could spare, and was authorized to use air and naval cover to assure the delivery of these supplies and to protect the American dependents being evacuated from Korea. The Seventh Fleet was placed under MacArthur's command and was to have its base at Sasebo, Japan.

As the meeting adjourned, Acheson showed me a message which had reached him from John Foster Dulles, who had just returned to Tokyo from Korea. For some time Dulles had been at work for the State Department on the preparation of the peace treaty with Japan, and he too seemed to have little doubt about the course of action we had to take.

"It is possible," his message read, "that South Koreans may themselves contain and repulse attack, and, if so, this is best way. If, however, it appears they cannot do so then we believe that US force should be used even though this risks Russian counter moves. To sit by while Korea is overrun by unprovoked armed attack would start disastrous chain of events leading most probably to world war. We suggest that Security Council might call for action on behalf of the organization under Article 106 by the five powers or such of them as are willing to respond."

By Monday the reports from Korea began to sound dark and discouraging, and among the messages that arrived was one from Syngman Rhee asking for help in the telegraphic style of the State Department messages:

"Beginning in early morning 25 June, North Korean Communist Army began armed aggression against South. Your Excellency and Congress of US already aware of fact that our people, anticipating incident such as today's, established strong national defense force in order to secure bulwark of democracy in the east and to render service to world peace. We again thank you for your indispensable aid in liberating us and in establishing our Republic. As we face this national crisis, putting up brave fight, we appeal for your increasing support and ask that you at the same time extend effective and timely aid in order to prevent this act of destruction of world peace."

The Korean Ambassador, who brought me President Rhee's appeal, was downhearted almost to the point of tears. I tried to encourage him by saying that the battle had been going on for only forty-eight hours and other men in other countries had defended their liberties to ultimate victory under much more discouraging circumstances. I told him to hold fast—that help was on the way.

But the Republic of Korea troops were no match for the tanks and heavy weapons of the North Koreans. Seoul, the capital of Syngman Rhee's government, seemed doomed; Communist tanks were reported in the outskirts of the city. Rhee moved his government to Taegu, about one hundred and fifty miles to the south.

Throughout Monday the situation in Korea deteriorated rapidly. I called another meeting at Blair House Monday night. The same persons who attended the first meeting were again present except Secretary of the Navy Matthews, while Assistant Secretary of State Matthews took Rusk's place. MacArthur's latest message was alarming:

> . . . [*sic*] Piecemeal entry into action vicinity Seoul by South Korean Third and Fifth Divisions has not succeeded in stopping the penetration recognized as the enemy main effort for the past 2 days with intent to seize the capital city of Seoul. Tanks entering suburbs of Seoul. Govt transferred to south and communication with part of KMAG opened at Taegu. Ambassador and Chief KMAG remaining in the city. FEC mil survey group en route to Korea has been recalled, under this rapidly deteriorating situation.
>
> South Korean units unable to resist determined Northern offensive. Contributory factor exclusive enemy possession of tanks and fighter planes. South Korean casualties as an index to fighting have not shown adequate resistance capabilities or the will to fight and our estimate is that a complete collapse is imminent.

There was now no doubt! The Republic of Korea needed help at once if it was not to be overrun. More seriously, a Communist success in Korea would put Red troops and planes within easy striking distance of Japan, and Okinawa and Formosa would be open to attack from two sides.

I told my advisers that what was developing in Korea seemed to me like a repetition on a larger scale of what had happened in Berlin. The Reds were probing for weaknesses in our armor; we had to meet their thrust without getting embroiled in a world-wide war.

I directed the Secretary of Defense to call General MacArthur on the scrambler phone and to tell him in person what my instructions were. He was to use air and naval forces to support the Republic of Korea with air and naval elements of his command, but only south of the 38th parallel. He was also instructed to dispatch the Seventh Fleet to the Formosa Strait. The purpose of this move was to prevent attacks by the Communists on Formosa as well as forays by Chiang Kai-shek against the mainland, this last to avoid reprisal actions by the Reds that might enlarge the area of conflict.

I also approved recommendations for the strengthening of our forces in the Philippines and for increased aid to the French in Indo-China. Meanwhile the Security Council of the United Nations met again and adopted on June 27 the resolution calling on all members of the U.N. to give assistance to South Korea.

That same morning, Tuesday, I asked a group of congressional leaders to meet with me so that I might inform them on the events and the decisions of the past few days. With me that morning, in addition to the "Big Four" (Barkley, McFarland, Rayburn, McCormack), were Senators Connally, Wiley, Alexander Smith, George, Tydings, Bridges, and Thomas of Utah, and Representatives Kee, Eaton, Vinson, and Short. Acheson, Johnson, Pace, Matthews, Finletter, and the Joint Chiefs of Staff were present, with some of their aides.

I asked the Secretary of State to summarize the situation. Then I pointed out that it was the United Nations which had acted in this case and had acted with great speed. I read a statement which had already been prepared for release to the press later that day, and I asked for the views of the congressional leaders.

Senator Wiley asked what forces General MacArthur had dispatched so far. Secretary Johnson assured him that MacArthur had sent his air and naval units as soon as he had received his instructions to do so.

Senator Tydings said that his Armed Services Committee had that morning acted to extend the draft act and to give the President power to call out the National Guard.

Senator Smith commented that in Korea we would act as members of the U.N. rather than as a single nation. I said this was correct but pointed out that, so far as our action concerned Formosa, we were acting on our own and not on behalf of the U.N.

John McCormack wanted to know from Admiral Sherman if the Navy would not have to be enlarged, and Secretary Johnson replied that the Joint Chiefs had already begun to study such expansion of the services as might be needed but that a balanced program would be maintained.

Congressman Kee, Senator Connally, and the Secretary of State made several suggestions regarding the wording of the U.N. resolution, and Dewey Short expressed the hope that other nations would join in supporting the U.N. in this cause.

The congressional leaders approved of my action. On that same day Thomas E. Dewey, Republican leader, pledged his full support.

This is the statement I gave out to the press at the conclusion of this meeting with the congressional leaders:

June 27, 1950

STATEMENT BY THE PRESIDENT

In Korea the Government forces, which were armed to prevent border raids and to preserve internal security, were attacked by invading forces from North Korea. The Security Council of the United Nations called upon the invading troops to cease hostilities and to withdraw to the 38th parallel. This they have not done, but on the contrary have pressed the attack. The Security Council called upon all members of the United Nations to render every assistance to the United Nations in the execution of this resolution. In these circumstances I have ordered United States air and sea forces to give the Korean Government troops cover and support.

The attack upon Korea makes it plain beyond all doubt that Communism has passed beyond the use of subversion to conquer independent nations and will now use armed invasion and war. It has defied the orders of the Security Council of the United Nations issued to preserve international peace and security. In these circumstances the occupation of Formosa by Communist forces would be a direct threat to the security of the Pacific area and to United States forces performing their lawful and necessary functions in that area.

Accordingly I have ordered the Seventh Fleet to prevent any attack upon Formosa. As a corollary of this action I am calling upon the Chinese Government on Formosa to cease all air and sea operations against the mainland. The Seventh Fleet will see that this is done. The determination of the future status of Formosa must await the restoration of security in the Pacific, a peace settlement with Japan, or consideration by the United Nations.

I have also directed that United States Forces in the Philippines be strengthened and that military assistance to the Philippine Government be accelerated.

I have similarly directed acceleration in the furnishing of military assistance to the forces of France and the Associated States in Indo-China and the dispatch of a military mission to provide close working relations with those forces.

I know that all members of the United Nations will consider carefully the consequences of this latest aggression in Korea in defiance of the Charter of the United Nations. A return to the rule of force in international affairs would have far-reaching effects. The United States will continue to uphold the rule of law.

I have instructed Ambassador Austin, as the representative of the United States to the Security Council, to report these steps to the Council.

Our allies and friends abroad were informed through our diplomatic representatives that it was our feeling that it was essential to the maintenance of peace that this armed aggression against a free nation be met firmly. We let it be known that we considered the Korean situation vital as a symbol of the strength and determination of the West. Firmness now would be the only way to deter new actions, in other portions of the world. Not only in Asia but in Europe, the Middle East, and elsewhere the confidence of peoples in countries adjacent to Soviet Union would be very adversely affected, in our judgment, if we failed to take action to protect a country established under our auspices and confirmed in its freedom by action of the United Nations. . . .

Uniting for Peace: Resolution by the United Nations General Assembly, November 17, 1950

The United Nations organization had been able to take action against the aggression in Korea because the Soviet chief delegate had been absent. On his return, the Soviet veto stood in the way of further action at the Security Council level. The United States turned therefore to the General Assembly, where the veto did not operate. On November 17, 1950, the General Assembly passed what is known as the "Uniting for Peace" resolution. By means of this resolution, the intervention in Korea preserved its character as intervention in support of the UN Charter, even though the Security Council was not united. The text of the resolution is taken from UN General Assembly, fifth session, Official Records: Supplement Number 20 *(A/1775), pages 13–14.*

T*he General Assembly,*

Recognizing the profound desire of all mankind to live in enduring peace and security, and in freedom from fear and want,

Confident that, if all governments faithfully reflect this desire and observe their obligations under the Charter, lasting peace and security can be established,

Condemning the intervention of a State in the internal affairs of another State for the purpose of changing its legally established government by the threat or use of force,

1. *Solemnly* reaffirms that, whatever the weapons used, any aggression, whether committed openly, or by fomenting civil strife in the interest of a foreign Power, or otherwise, is the gravest of all crimes against peace and security throughout the world;

2. *Determines* that for the realization of lasting peace and security it is indispensable:

(1) That prompt united action be taken to meet aggression wherever it arises;

(2) That every nation agree:

(*a*) To accept effective international control of atomic energy, under the United Nations, on the basis already approved by the General Assembly in order to make effective the prohibition of atomic weapons;

(*b*) To strive for the control and elimination, under the United Nations, of all other weapons of mass destruction;

(*c*) To regulate all armaments and armed forces under a United Nations system of control and inspection, with a view to their gradual reduction;

(*d*) To reduce to a minimum the diversion for armaments of its human and economic resources and to strive towards the development of such resources for the general welfare, with due regard to the needs of the under-developed areas of the world;

3. *Declares* that these goals can be attained if all the Members of the United Nations demonstrate by their deeds their will to achieve peace.

SELECTION 

A Peculiar Kind of War: From "Bill Mauldin in Korea"

North Koreans at first careered through South Korean territory. By August, the South Korean army and the American troops sent to their aid were penned within a small area around the port of Pusan.

Meanwhile, however, marines and army troops from the United States had sped to Japan. Naval vessels and aircraft gathered there. General Douglas MacArthur, commander both of United States forces in the Far East and United Nations forces in Korea, soon had a formidable force at his disposal.

A master of amphibious strategy, MacArthur devised a plan to stage a landing behind the North Korean front. On September 15, his forces plunged ashore at Inchon on the western coast of Korea, well to the north of the Pusan perimeter.

With their communication and supply lines threatened, the North Koreans hastily retreated toward their homeland. MacArthur's men fanned out, recapturing all of South Korea. Then MacArthur, authorized to capture and destroy North Korea's forces, turned his troops northward. American and Allied units marched across the 38th parallel. The North Koreans fled before their advance. The official account of this stage of the war is R. E. Appleton, South to the Maktong, North to the Yalu *(1961).*

By November, MacArthur's forces were approaching the Yalu River, the boundary between Korea and China. Through various channels, Chinese Communist authorities warned the United Nations command to stop short of their frontier. MacArthur and his superiors in Washington scoffed at these warnings. Meeting President Truman on Wake Island in October, MacArthur predicted confidently that the fighting would be over in a matter of weeks.

This was not the case. The North Koreans suddenly began to put up more resistance. Chinese soldiers were discovered in the North Korean ranks. Peking said these Chinese were "volunteers." Then advancing American columns began to meet Chinese divisions. The Chinese Communists were intervening in force. As MacArthur said later, the United Nations command was now involved in "a new war."

Spread out on both sides of the Korean peninsula and lacking adequate train transportation and communications, American and Allied units had no choice but to run. Many were trapped. The agonies American troops experienced in fleeing from the Communists are brilliantly portrayed in S. L. A. Marshall, The River and the Gauntlet *(1958). By April, the United Nations command was desperately trying to establish a defense line somewhere near the 38th parallel.*

The fighting in Korea was of a kind that few Americans had experienced. It was not all-out warfare such as that in World War I and World War II. It was a limited war. Although costing more lives than most of the wars in American history, it was referred to officially as a "police action." Many Americans, including many in the fighting forces, found this kind of war hard to comprehend.

For men in the field, the idea of limited war was all the stranger because the fighting that did take place was so earnest. Conditions in Korea were rather like those in Italy, where some of the worst fighting of World War II had taken place. The forests and rocky hills of Korea made hard ground for battle. The enemy was implacable. When the Chinese captured men, they either treated them brutally or subjected them to mental torture known as "brainwashing," attempting to convert them to communism as, ages back, the Holy Inquisition had converted men to Christianity.

And, perhaps worse than anything else, the bad weather almost never let up. In winter, the ice and snow produced epidemics of frostbite. In summer, the mud was ankle-deep. Nothing captures this aspect of the fighting in Korea better than does the drawing by Bill Mauldin reproduced below from Bill Mauldin in Korea *(W. W. Norton, 1952), page 62.*

I swear even the mud is dusty

SELECTION 21

Removal of a General

After the Chinese intervention in Korea, a breach developed between MacArthur and his superiors in Washington.

During World War II, there had been frequent differences of opinion between

MacArthur on the one hand and Roosevelt and the Joint Chiefs of Staff on the other. Commanding American forces in the Southwest Pacific, MacArthur had always wanted that theater to be the central theater of the war. Although MacArthur never received the resources he requested, he performed brilliantly, directing the campaigns that regained New Guinea and the Philippine Islands from the Japanese.

After World War II, MacArthur did not come home, even for a ceremonial visit. He remained in the Far East. Commanding occupation forces in Japan, he guided that nation's economic recovery and its changeover from an authoritarian to a democratic system. His accomplishments in peace were even more remarkable than his accomplishments in war.

But MacArthur, absent from his country for a decade, lost touch with what was going on at home. Perhaps to a degree he lost touch with reality. Independent, proud, and vain by nature, he had had in Japan, for five years, the experience of being more than an emperor—almost a god.

In Korea, MacArthur was angered by the Chinese intervention. He proposed to Washington that, in the new war that had developed, China be treated as the enemy. Specifically, he proposed that the Chinese coast be blockaded, that bombing missions be carried out against Chinese territory beyond the Yalu, and that Chiang Kai-shek be given logistical and tactical support in attempting to return to the mainland.

On all counts, Washington rejected MacArthur's advice. The Truman administration was fearful that the Chinese would retaliate by bombing Japan or that Russian "volunteers" would appear in Korea. Even more, the administration feared that the United States, if drawn into larger-scale warfare in the Far East, would lose the capacity to defend Europe. President Truman commanded that the war in Korea remain a limited war.

Convinced that he was right and Truman wrong, MacArthur decided to appeal to American public opinion. Having been not only the champion of an Asia-first strategy during World War II but also the Army chief of staff who had dispersed the "bonus army" during the Hoover administration, he had many admirers on the right wing of the Republican party. MacArthur let these admirers know of the differences between his views and those of the Democratic President.

In a letter to the annual convention of the Veterans of Foreign Wars in 1950, MacArthur hinted at his differences with Truman. In conversations with reporters visiting Tokyo, he became increasingly outspoken. Finally, on March 20, 1951, he sent a letter to Joseph W. Martin, Jr., the Republican leader in the House of Representatives, and allowed the letter to be published. It said, among other things, "We must win. There is no substitute for victory."

Truman viewed many of MacArthur's actions as calculated insubordination. Because of MacArthur's abilities and prestige, the President hesitated to act; however, after the letter to Representative Martin, he felt that he had no choice. Truman consulted with his chiefs of staff and other advisers. Meanwhile, MacArthur flouted a Presidential directive forbidding military commanders to speak publicly of terms for ending the Korean conflict by announcing that he was prepared to meet with the enemy commanders at any time to discuss truce terms. Whatever objections Truman's advisers might have raised disappeared.

There seemed to everyone around the White House but one course that the President could follow. On April 11, 1951, Truman issued a brusque order relieving MacArthur of all his commands.

Truman's relief of MacArthur stirred more excitement in the United States than had any event since the Japanese surrender of 1945. At once, congressional opponents of the Truman administration were in full voice, taking the general's side. So were many newspapers.

Congress invited MacArthur to come to Capitol Hill to state his views. The general accepted. On his way to Washington, he received ecstatic welcomes in several cities.

After addressing a joint session of Congress, MacArthur was asked to testify before the Senate Foreign Relations and Armed Services Committees. These two committees joined forces to obtain a complete airing of the issues between the general and the President. They invited the Secretaries of State and Defense, the chiefs of staff, and other officials to follow MacArthur to the stand.

The issues in this controversy were grave and important ones. In dispute between MacArthur and the Truman administration was the long-standing question of whether American interests were greater in Asia than in Europe. In dispute, too, was the question of whether or not the United States could or should endure a stalemate in a limited war in order to prevent a greater war from erupting. And hanging over both these questions was the still larger question, of whether, in deciding a military issue, a civilian President, right or wrong, should prevail over a professional military leader.

Because of the gravity and importance of the issues, the controversy has produced a considerable literature. Arthur M. Schlesinger, Jr., and Richard Rovere, The General and the President *(1951) is a sprightly narrative, very much on Truman's side. Trumbull Higgins,* Korea and the Fall of MacArthur *(1960) is partial to MacArthur, at least in the strategic debate. J. W. Spanier,* The Truman-MacArthur Controversy and the Korean War *(1959) and W. W. Hoare, "Harry S. Truman," in E. R. May (ed.),* The Ultimate Decision *(1960), are judicious analyses written long after the fact.*

The first document reproduced below is MacArthur's address to the joint session of Congress. It is taken from Eighty-second Congress, first session, Congressional Record, *pages 4123–4125. The second document consists of excerpts from the subsequent hearings, including testimony by MacArthur, Secretary of Defense George C. Marshall, and the Chairman of the Joint Chiefs of Staff, General Omar N. Bradley. It is taken from Eighty-second Congress, first session, Hearings before the Foreign Relations Committee and Armed Services Committee, United States Senate,* Military Situation in the Far East, *pages 29–31, 99–103, 322–325, 351–353, 729–734, 752–753, 877–879.*

GENERAL DOUGLAS MACARTHUR, ADDRESS TO CONGRESS, APRIL 17, 1951

Mr. President, Mr. Speaker, distinguished Members of the Congress, I stand on this rostrum with a sense of deep humility and great pride; humility in the wake of those great American architects of our history who have stood here before me; pride in the reflection that this forum of legislative debate represents human liberty in the purest form yet devised. [Applause.]

Here are centered the hopes, and aspirations, and faith of the entire human race.

I do not stand here as advocate for any partisan cause, for the issues are fundamental and reach quite beyond the realm of partisan consideration. They must be resolved on the highest plane of national interest if our course is to prove sound and our future protected. I trust, therefore, that you will do me the justice of receiving that which I have to say as solely expressing the considered viewpoint of a fellow American. I address you with neither rancor nor bitterness in the fading twilight of life with but one purpose in mind, to serve my country. [Applause.]

The issues are global and so interlocked that to consider the problems of one sector oblivious to those of another is but to court disaster for the whole.

While Asia is commonly referred to as the gateway to Europe, it is no less true that Europe is the gateway to Asia, and the broad influence of the one cannot fail to have its impact upon the other.

There are those who claim our strength is inadequate to protect on both fronts, that we cannot divide our effort. I can think of no greater expression of defeatism. [Applause.] If a potential enemy can divide his strength on two fronts, it is for us to counter his effort.

The Communist threat is a global one. Its successful advance in one sector threatens the destruction of every other sector. You cannot appease or otherwise surrender to communism in Asia without simultaneously undermining our efforts to halt its advance in Europe. [Applause.]

Beyond pointing out these general truisms, I shall confine my discussion to the general areas of Asia. Before one may objectively assess the situation now existing there, he must comprehend something of Asia's past and the revolutionary changes which have marked her course up to the present. Long exploited by the so-called colonial powers, with little opportunity to achieve any degree of social justice, individual dignity, or a higher standard of life such as guided our own noble administration to the Philippines, the peoples of Asia found their opportunity in the war just past to throw off the shackles of colonialism and now see the dawn of new opportunity and heretofore unfelt dignity and the self-respect of political freedom.

Mustering half of the earth's population and 60 percent of its natural resources these peoples are rapidly consolidating a new force, both moral and material, with which to raise the living standard and erect adaptations of the design of modern progress to their own distinct cultural environments. Whether one adheres to the concept of colonization or not, this is the direction of Asian progress and it may not be stopped. It is a corollary to the shift of the world economic frontiers, as the whole epi-center of world affairs rotates back toward the area whence it started. In this situation it becomes vital that our own country orient its policies in consonance with this basic evolutionary condition rather than pursue a course blind to the reality that the colonial era is now past and the Asian peoples covet the right to shape their own free destiny. What they seek now is friendly guidance, understanding, and support, not imperious direction [applause]; the dignity of equality, not the shame of subjugation. Their prewar standard of life, pitifully low, is infinitely lower now in the devastation left in war's wake. World ideologies play little part in Asian thinking and are little understood. What the peoples strive for is the opportunity for a little more food in their stomachs, a little better clothing on their backs, a little firmer roof over their heads, and the realization of a normal nationalist urge for political freedom. These political-social conditions have but an indirect bearing upon our own national security, but do form a backdrop to contemporary planning which must be thoughtfully considered if we are to avoid the pitfalls of unrealism.

Of more direct and immediate bearing upon our national security are the changes wrought in the strategic potential of the Pacific Ocean in the course of the past war. Prior thereto, the western strategic frontier of the United States lay on the littoral line of the Americas with an exposed island salient extending out through Hawaii, Midway, and Guam to the Philippines. That salient proved not an outpost of strength but an avenue of weakness along which the enemy could and did attack. The Pacific was a potential area of advance for any predatory force intent upon striking at the bordering land areas.

All this was changed by our Pacific victory. Our strategic frontier then shifted to embrace the entire Pacific Ocean which became a vast moat to protect us as long as we held it. Indeed, it acts as a protective shield for all of the Americas and all free lands of the Pacific Ocean area. We control it to the shores of Asia by a chain of islands extending in an arc from the Aleutians to the Marianas held by us and our free allies.

From this island chain we can dominate with sea and air power every Asiatic port from Vladivostok to Singapore and prevent any hostile movement into the Pacific. Any predatory attack from Asia must be an amphibious effort. No amphibious force can be successful without control of the sea lanes and the air over those lanes in its avenue of advance. With naval and air supremacy and modest ground elements to defend bases, any major attack from continental Asia toward us or our friends of the Pacific would be doomed to failure. Under such conditions the Pacific no longer represents menacing avenues of approach for a prospective invader—it assumes instead the friendly aspect of a peaceful lake. Our line of defense is a natural one and can be maintained with a minimum of military effort and expense. It envisions no attack against anyone nor does it provide the bastions essential for offensive operations, but properly maintained would be an invincible defense against aggression.

The holding of this littoral defense line in the western Pacific is entirely dependent upon holding all segments thereof, for any major breach of that line by an unfriendly power would render vulnerable to determined attack every other major segment. This is a military estimate as to which I have yet to find a military leader who will take exception. [Applause.]

For that reason I have strongly recommended in the past as a matter of military urgency that under no circumstances must Formosa fall under Communist control. [Applause.]

Such an eventuality would at once threaten the freedom of the Philippines and the loss of Japan, and might well force our western frontier back to the coasts of California, Oregon, and Washington.

To understand the changes which now appear upon the Chinese mainland, one must understand the changes in Chinese character and culture over the past 50 years. China up to 50 years ago was completely nonhomogeneous, being compartmented into groups divided against each other. The war-making tendency was almost nonexistent, as they still followed the tenets of the Confucian ideal of pacifist culture. At the turn of the century, under the regime of Chan So Lin, efforts toward greater homogeneity produced the start of a nationalist urge. This was further and more successfully developed under the leadership of Chiang Kai-shek, but has been brought to its greatest fruition under the present regime, to the point that it has now taken on the character of a united nationalism of increasingly dominant aggressive tendencies. Through these past 50 years, the Chinese people have thus become militarized in their concepts and in their ideals. They now constitute excellent soldiers with competent staffs and commanders. This has produced a new and dominant power in Asia which for its own purposes is allied with Soviet Russia, but which in its own concepts and methods has become aggressively imperialistic with a lust for expansion and increased power normal to this type of imperalism. There is little of the ideological concept either one way or another in the Chinese make-up. The standard of living is so low and the capital accumulation has been so thoroughly dissipated by war that the masses are desperate and avid to follow any leadership which seems to promise the alleviation of local stringencies. I have from the beginning believed that the Chinese Communists' support of the North Koreans was the dominant one. Their interests are at present parallel to those of the Soviet, but I believe that the aggressiveness recently displayed not only in Korea, but also in Indochina and Tibet and pointing potentially toward the south, reflects predominantly the same lust for the expansion of power which has animated every would-be conqueror since the beginning of time. [Applause.]

The Japanese people since the war have undergone the greatest reformation recorded in modern history. With a commendable will, eagerness to learn, and marked capacity to understand, they have, from the ashes left in war's wake, erected in Japan an edifice dedicated to the primacy of individual liberty and personal dignity, and in the ensuing process there has been created a truly representative government, committed to the advance of political morality, freedom of economic enterprise and social justice. [Applause.] Politically, economically, and socially Japan is now abreast of many free nations of the earth and will not again fail the universal trust. That it may be counted upon to wield a profoundly beneficial influence over the course of events in Asia is attested by the magnificent manner in which the Japanese people have met the recent challenge of war, unrest, and confusion surrounding them from the outside, and checked communism within their own frontiers without the slightest slackening in their forward progress. I sent all four of our occupation divisions to the Korean battle front without the slightest qualms as to the effect of the resulting power vacuum upon Japan. The results fully justified my faith. [Applause.] I know of no nation more serene, orderly, and industrious—nor in which higher hopes can be entertained for future constructive service in the advance of the human race. [Applause.]

Of our former wards, the Philippines, we can look forward in confidence that the existing unrest will be corrected and a strong and healthy nation will grow in the longer aftermath of war's terrible destructiveness. We must be patient and understanding and never fail them, as in our hour of need they did not fail us. [Applause.] A Christian nation, the Philippines stand as a mighty bulwark of Christianity in the Far East, and its capacity for high moral leadership in Asia is unlimited.

On Formosa, the Government of the Republic of China has had the opportunity to refute by action much of the malicious gossip which so undermined the strength of its leadership on the Chinese mainland. [Applause.]

The Formosan people are receiving a just and enlightened administration with majority representation on the organs of government; and politically, economically, and socially appear to be advancing along sound and constructive lines.

With this brief insight into the surrounding areas I now turn to the Korean conflict. While I was not consulted prior to the President's decision to intervene in the support of the Republic of Korea, that decision from a military standpoint proved a sound one. [Applause.] As I say, a brief and sound one as we hurled back the invaders and decimated his forces. Our victory was complete and our objectives within reach when Red China intervened with numerically superior ground forces. This created a new war and an entirely new situation, a situation not contemplated when our forces were committed against the North Korean invaders, a situation which called for new decisions in the diplomatic sphere to permit the realistic adjustment of military strategy. Such decisions have not been forthcoming. [Applause.]

While no man in his right mind would advocate sending our ground forces into continental China—and such was never given a thought—the new situation did urgently demand a drastic revision of strategic planning if our political aim was to defeat this new enemy as we had defeated the old. [Applause.]

Apart from the military need as I saw it to neutralize sanctuary, protection given to the enemy north of the Yalu, I felt that military necessity in the conduct of the war made necessary:

First, the intensification of our economic blockade against China.

Second, the imposition of a naval blockade against the China coast.

Third, removal of restrictions on air reconnaissance of China's coastal areas and of Manchuria. [Applause.]

Fourth, removal of restrictions on the forces of the Republic of China on Formosa with logistical support to contribute to their effective operation against the Chinese mainland. [Applause.]

For entertaining these views all professionally designed to support our forces committed to Korea and bring hostilities to an end with the least possible delay and at a saving of countless American and Allied lives, I have been severely criticized in lay circles, principally abroad, despite my understanding that from a military standpoint the above views have been fully shared in the past by practically every military leader concerned with the Korean campaign, including our own Joint Chiefs of Staff. [Applause, the Members rising.]

I called for reinforcements, but was informed that reinforcements were not available. I made clear that if not permitted to utilize the friendly Chinese force of some 600,000 men on Formosa; if not permitted to blockade the China coast to prevent the Chinese Reds from getting succor from without; and if there were to be no hope of major reinforcements, the position of the command from the military standpoint forbade victory. We could hold in Korea by constant maneuver and at an approximate area where our supply advantages were in balance with the supply line disadvantages of the enemy, but we could hope at best for only an indecisive campaign, with its terrible and constant attrition upon our forces if the enemy utilized his full military potential. I have constantly called for the new political decisions essential to a solution. Efforts have been made to distort my position. It has been said in effect that I was a warmonger. Nothing could be further from the truth. I know war as few other men now living know it, and nothing to me is more revolting. I have long advocated its complete abolition as its very destructiveness on both friend and foe has rendered it useless as a means of settling international disputes. Indeed, on the 2d of September 1945, just following the surrender of the Japanese Nation on the battleship *Missouri,* I formally cautioned as follows:

> Men since the beginning of time have sought peace. Various methods through the ages have been attempted to devise an international process to prevent or settle disputes between nations. From the very start, workable methods were found insofar as individual citizens were concerned, but the mechanics of an instrumentality of larger international scope have never been successful. Military alliances, balances of power, leagues of nations, all in turn failed, leaving the only path to be by way of the crucible of war. The utter destructiveness of war now blots out this alternative. We have had our last chance. If we will not devise some greater and more equitable system, Armageddon will be at our door. The problem basically is theological and involves a spiritual recrudescence and improvement of human character that will synchronize with our almost matchless advances in science, art, literature, and all material and cultural developments of the past 2,000 years. It must be of the spirit if we are to save the flesh. [Applause.]

But once war is forced upon us, there is no other alternative than to apply every available means to bring it to a swift end. War's very object is victory—not prolonged indecision. [Applause.] In war, indeed, there can be no substitute for victory. [Applause.]

There are some who for varying reasons would appease Red China. They are blind to history's clear lesson. For history teaches with unmistakable emphasis that appeasement but begets new and bloodier war. It points to no single instance where the end has justified that means—where appeasement has led to more than a sham peace. Like blackmail, it lays the basis for new and successively greater demands, until, as in blackmail, violence becomes the only other alternative. Why, my soldiers asked of me, surrender military advantages to an enemy in the field? I could not answer. [Applause.] Some may say to avoid spread of the conflict into an all-out war with China; others, to avoid Soviet intervention. Neither explanation seems valid. For China is already engaging with the maximum power it can commit and the Soviet will not necessarily mesh its actions with our moves. Like a cobra, any new enemy will more likely strike whenever it feels that the relativity in military or other potential is in its favor on a world-wide basis.

The tragedy of Korea is further heightened by the fact that as military action is confined to its territorial limits, it condemns that nation, which it is our purpose to save, to suffer the devastating impact of full naval and air bombardment, while the enemy's sanctuaries are fully protected from such attack and devastation. Of the nations of the world, Korea alone, up to now, is the sole one which has risked its all against communism. The magnificence of the courage and fortitude of the Korean people defies description. [Applause.] They have chosen to risk death rather than slavery. Their last words to me were "Don't scuttle the Pacific." [Applause.]

I have just left your fighting sons in Korea. They have met all tests there and I can report to you without reservation they are splendid in every way. [Applause.] It was my constant effort to preserve them and end this savage conflict honorably and with the least loss of time and a minimum sacrifice of life. Its growing bloodshed has caused me the deepest anguish and anxiety. Those gallant men will remain often in my thoughts and in my prayers always. [Applause.]

I am closing my 52 years of military service. [Applause.] When I joined the Army even before the turn of the century, it was the fulfillment of all my boyish hopes and dreams. The world has turned over many times since I took the oath on the plain at West Point, and the hopes and dreams have long since vanished. But I still remember the refrain of one of the most popular barrack ballads of that day which proclaimed most proudly that—

"Old soldiers never die; they just fade away." And like the old soldier of that ballad, I now close my military career and just fade away—an old soldier who tried to do his duty as God gave him the light to see that duty.

Good-by.

EXCERPTS FROM THE MACARTHUR HEARINGS

Testimony by General of the Army Douglas MacArthur

Senator Alexander Wiley [(R., Wis.)]: You have indicated in your public addresses that there has been a failure to take certain needed political decisions in the Korean matter. Can you tell us what you think those decisions might well have been?

General MacArthur: I can tell you what I would have done.

Senator Wiley: Yes.

General MacArthur: I would have served—as soon as it became apparent that Red China was throwing the full might of its military force against our troops in Korea, I would have served warning on her that if she did not within a reasonable time discuss a cease-fire order, that the entire force of the United Nations would be utilized to bring to an end the predatory attack of her forces on ours.

In other words, I would have supplied her with an ultimatum that she would either come and talk terms of a cease fire within a reasonable period of time or her actions in Korea would be regarded as a declaration of war against the nations engaged there and that those nations would take such steps as they felt necessary to bring the thing to a conclusion. That is what I would have done, and I would still do it, Senator. . . .

Senator Wiley: General, when you were recalled when the message came through, were there any reasons assigned to your recall?

General MacArthur: The only reasons were contained in the order that I received and the reason that was given was that it was felt that I could not give my complete support to the policies of the United States and of the United Nations.

That reason seems to be to me—there was no necessity to give any reason.

Senator Wiley: I understand.

General MacArthur: But it seems to me to be completely invalid. I have not carried out every directive that I have ever received, but what I was trying to do was to find out what the directives were to be for the future.

I was operating in what I call a vacuum. I could hardly have been said to be in opposition to policies which I was not aware of even. I don't know what the policy is now. You have various potentials:

First is that you can go on and complete this war in the normal way and bring about just and honorable peace at the soonest time possible with the least loss of life by utilizing all of your potential.

The second is that you bring this thing to an end in Korea by yielding to the enemy's terms and on his terms.

The third is that you go on indecisively, fighting, with no mission for the troops except to resist and fight in this accordion fashion—up and down—which means that your cumulative losses are going to be staggering. It isn't just dust that is settling in Korea, Senator; it is American blood.

Now, my whole effort has been since Red China came in there to get some definition, military definition, of what I should do. There has been no change from the directions that I had—to clear North Korea.

As far as the United Nations are concerned, as far as the Joint Chiefs of Staff are concerned, my directives have been changed and I have been informed that my main objective, which takes precedence over everything else, was the security of my forces and the protection of Japan. And I have been operating on that.

Now, that is not a mission. . . .

Senator [*Brien*] *McMahon* [(D., Conn.)]: General, there are some fundamental basic differences between the Government and yourself as to the wisdom of the best course to pursue in the east; that is true?

General MacArthur: Naturally.

Senator McMahon: Do you consider, General, that it comes within the province of a theater commander to register publicly with persons in political life, or out of it for that matter, his differences of opinion while he is still in active charge of the theater?

General MacArthur: I believe the theater commander has the responsibility of registering his views as he might see fit, if they are honest views and not in contradiction to any implementing directives that he may have received.

I do not believe the implications of your question, that any segment of American society shall be so gagged that the truth and the full truth shall not be brought out.

I believe it is in the interest, the public interest, that diverse opinions on any controversial issue shall be fully aired.

I understand completely that the totalitarian and the Soviet method is entirely in contradiction to that, that they do muzzle certain segments of society. I do not believe that is the American way.

And if your question is intended to mean that I would be subservient to and not register within the proper processes my opinions, I would refute it at once.

Otherwise you do not get what is the foundation of the very liberty that we breathe, that the people are entitled to have the facts, that the judgment of the Government itself is subject to their opinion and to their control; and in order to exercise that, they are entitled to the truth, the whole truth, and nothing but the truth, Senator.

Senator McMahon: Now, let's assume, General, that one of your subordinate generals in the theater of your command had felt as you feel. He, too, is a military man and he, too, is subordinate to his higher command.

Do I take it that you would defend the right of a brigadier general on your staff to give his opinions as to the policy that was proceeding or that was being proceeded with by the Government of the United States?

General MacArthur: I wouldn't have a brigadier general or anyone else on my staff that didn't freely and frankly give me his opinions in contradiction to my own. The very value of a subordinate is the freedom with which he expresses his initiative.

I have frequently had officers under my command, not only in my staff, but in my command, that disagreed with me completely and I listened to them and on occasions they have convinced me that I was wrong and they were right. That, I believe, is fundamental.

Senator McMahon: Now, General, we are not talking about the same thing, I don't think. I fully agree with you that it would be a poor commander, a poor executive of any kind, who insisted on having "yes men" around him and wouldn't listen to what they had to say.

However, General, that isn't quite what I am talking about. I assume that you had the right and exercised it at any and all times to bring any views that you might have to the attention of your superior officers.

Do you wish the question read?

General MacArthur: I didn't get your——

Senator McMahon: Read the question, Mr. Reporter.

(The pending question was read by the reporter.)

General MacArthur: Naturally.

Senator McMahon: And you were never restricted in any way in bringing those recommendations or thoughts that you might have on any matter to the attention of your superiors, the Joint Chiefs of Staff.

General MacArthur: No restrictions whatsoever.

Senator McMahon: You see, General, what I was raising was the question of the advisability, if not the propriety, of any subordinate military officer to take his differences of opinion, on a governmental policy, when he is in the military command, and chain of command, to people in political life.

General MacArthur: I do not know what you mean by "people in political life," Senator.

Senator McMahon: We have your answer, General, in the letter to Mr. Martin.

General MacArthur: It seems to me that the American people are entitled to certain basic facts, when it involves the lives of their sons, and, perhaps, the future of our country.

I do not believe in the gag rule, if that is what you are talking about.

I am free to confess I do not quite follow what you are driving at, or how it appertains to this particular investigation.

Senator McMahon: General, you are not going to, by that statement, without a mild dissent from me, place in this record that I am in favor of what you choose to denominate as "the gag rule."

I am not an expert on military affairs. I was merely of the opinion, and always have been, from what I did know, that every officer and every man in the United States Army reported to his superiors, and fought out his differences with his superiors.

Now, General, you have stated that the issue that faces this Nation is global in nature.

As I see it, there are three questions, fundamentally, in global strategy.

Who is overwhelmingly the main enemy, in your opinion?

Senator [*Leverett*] *Saltonstall* [(R., Mass.)]: What was that question?

Senator McMahon: Who is overwhelmingly the main enemy—that we have to take into cognizance—take into consideration?

General MacArthur: Communism, in my opinion.

Senator McMahon: When you talk about communism, do you mean as evidenced in Red China, or the Kremlin?

General MacArthur: I mean all over the world, including the interior of many of the fine democratic countries of the world.

Senator McMahon: General, where is the source and brains of this conspiracy?

General MacArthur: How would I know?

Senator McMahon: Would you think that the Kremlin was the place that might be the loci?

General MacArthur: I might say that it is one of the loci.

Senator McMahon: Would you say it was one of the main loci, the main place?

General MacArthur: I think the world public opinion would so locate it.

Senator McMahon: Pardon me?

General MacArthur: I say, I should think that the world public opinion would so locate it.

Senator McMahon: You would not differ from that opinion, General?

General, if we were to fight a victorious war with China, will you tell this committee how the strength of the Soviet Union, the armed strength of the Soviet Union, would be impaired, assuming she does not come into the war? . . .

General MacArthur: As I have said so frequently, Senator, our purpose, as I see it in the Korean War, is to force China to stop her aggression in North Korea. It does not necessarily mean the overwhelming in China, it simply means that sufficient pressure be brought upon her to make her stop killing our boys by the thousands in Korea.

Just how that might impinge with reference to the Soviet forces, is purely speculative.

Senator McMahon: Well, General, you make a pretty good speculation if Russia does not come in, and we do go into China in a limited way for the further extension of a now limited war. Is it not true that it wouldn't impair the 175 divisions that the Soviets are reputed to have, or the 16,000 operational aircraft, nor her stockpile and growing stockpile of atomic weapons?

General MacArthur: If you mean to say . . . that the diminution of China's potential power doesn't diminish the total power of communism throughout the world, why, that would be fallacious, Senator.

Senator McMahon: I asked, General, about its diminution of their military striking power, and I listed their aircraft, their atomic weapons, and their 175 divisions. It is obvious that we agree they are our main enemy—that the Soviet Union is.

General MacArthur: I didn't agree to it.

Senator MacMahon: You do not agree?

General MacArthur: I said that communism throughout the world was our main enemy.

Senator McMahon: I see.

General MacArthur: It is your argument to confine it to one section of the world.

Senator McMahon: I see.

And you have the feeling that if we take over China, that we will have made——

General MacArthur: I didn't say we would ever take over China, Senator. I said to the contrary yesterday, that we had no objectives in China proper, except to put sufficient force on China so that she would stop her depredation in North Korea.

Senator McMahon: General, as I take it, you have no opinion to give us as to when we will be best prepared for a war that would include the Soviet Union, if one had to come?

General MacArthur: Such studies, as that, Senator, are made [by] higher authority than my own. They are available, I am sure, to you.

Senator McMahon: And, as a former Chief of Staff of the Army, you realize that those higher authorities have to take into account many factors which a theater commander cannot take into account?

General MacArthur: Unquestionably.

Senator McMahon: What are some of those factors, General?

General MacArthur: Some of those factors are the general resources that would be available to us and our allies; the strengths that would be available to the enemy, the disposition of the forces; the general political atmosphere that prevails; the controversial questions that might arise between the governments, and many other things which, of course would be much beyond any sector commander's responsibility.

Senator McMahon: That is very helpful, General; and those are the factors which you assumed that these men whom you believe to be competent have weighed, and must weigh, in relation to our global policy and our global defense.

General MacArthur: That is not only their responsibility, Senator, but it is their authority.

Senator McMahon: And, General——

General MacArthur: It is inherent in their command position.

Senator McMahon (continuing): If they show up here and say that they have weighed all of those factors, and they believe that the policy which we are pursuing in the east is the correct one, I assume that you would agree with them inasmuch as you have not studied those factors which will influence the opinion of these competent men?

General MacArthur: Any decisions they'd make, Senator, are like all other human decisions. They have to pass before the high court of public opinion.

The fact that any group in authority, in carrying out its responsibilities makes decisions, that when they make that decision every man accepts it as an infallibly correct one is absurd.

Senator McMahon: General, I hope I am a democrat, with a small "d" as well as a large one. I say I hope I am a democrat, with a small "d" as well as a large one, but I wonder if the logical extension of your last observation does not mean that we should take a national poll or referendum on how we should conduct the strategy of defending America. You do not wish to be put in that position, General, do you?

General MacArthur: Not at all, Senator. Every military man is subject to assignment. If he doesn't perform his duties satisfactorily, he is subject to removal. If an administration doesn't conduct its processes satisfactorily, every 4 years we have a referendum.

Our system of government is based upon that. . . .

Testimony by Secretary of Defense George C. Marshall

Secretary Marshall: I have a brief statement to make, but first I would like to observe that it is a very distressing necessity, a very distressing occasion, that compels me to appear here this morning and in effect in almost direct opposition to a great many of the views and actions of General MacArthur.

He is a brother Army officer, a man for whom I have tremendous respect as to his military capabilities and military performances and from all I can learn, as to his administration of Japan.

I am here primarily to answer whatever questions you and the members of the committees may care to ask me.

However, I think it may be helpful if, at the outset, I make a brief preliminary statement which I think will clarify some of the issues raised in the course of your hearings last week.

From the very beginning of the Korean conflict, down to the present moment, there has been no disagreement between the President, the Secretary of Defense, and the Joint Chiefs of Staff that I am aware of.

There have been, however, and continue to be basic differences of judgment between General MacArthur, on the one hand, and the President, the Secretary of Defense, and the Joint Chiefs of Staff, on the other hand.

Our objective in Korea continues to be the defeat of the aggression and the restoration of peace. We have persistently sought to confine the conflict to Korea and to prevent its spreading into a third world war. In this effort, we stand allied with the great majority of our fellow-members of the United Nations. Our efforts have succeeded in thwarting the aggressors, in Korea, and in stemming the tide of aggression in southeast Asia and elsewhere throughout the world. Our efforts in Korea have given us some sorely needed time and impetus to accelerate the building of our defenses and those of our allies against the threatened onslaught of Soviet imperialism.

General MacArthur, on the other hand, would have us, on our own initiative, carry the conflict beyond Korea against the mainland of Communist China, both from the sea and from the air. He would have us accept the risk [of] involvement not only in an extension of the war with Red China, but in an all-out war with the Soviet Union. He would have us do this even at the expense of losing our allies and wrecking the coalition of free peoples throughout the world. He would have us do this even though the effect of such action might expose Western Europe to attack by the millions of Soviet troops poised in Middle and Eastern Europe.

This fundamental divergence is one of judgment as to the proper course of action to be followed by the United States. This divergence arises from the inherent difference between the position of a field commander, whose mission is limited to a particular area and a particular antagonist, and the position of the Joint Chiefs of Staff, the Secretary of Defense, and the President, who are responsible for the total security of the United States, and who, to achieve and maintain this security, must weigh our interests and objectives in one part of the globe with those in other areas of the world so as to attain the best over-all balance.

It is their responsibility to determine where the main threat to our security lies, where we must fight holding actions, and where and how we must gain time to grow stronger. On the other hand, the responsibilities and the courses of action assigned to a theater commander necessarily apply to his own immediate area of responsibility. It is completely understandable and, in fact, at times commendable that a theater commander should become so wholly wrapped up in his own aims and responsibilities that some of the directives received by him from higher authority are not those that he would have written for himself. There is nothing new about this sort of thing in our military history. What is new, and what has brought about the necessity for General MacArthur's removal, is the wholly unprecedented situation of a local theater commander publicly expressing his displeasure at and his disagreement with the foreign and military policy of the United States.

It became apparent that General MacArthur had grown so far out of sympathy with the established policies of the United States that there was grave doubt as to whether he could any longer be permitted to exercise the authority in making decisions that normal command functions would assign to a theater commander. In this situation, there was no other recourse but to relieve him. . . .

Chairman [*Richard B.*] *Russell* [(D., Ga.)]: Now, General, as a military man with distinguished service to your country over a long period of years, I would like to get your professional opinion as well as your views as Secretary of Defense as to whether or not the Chinese Reds can be driven out of Korea and Korea pacified without the implementing General MacArthur recommends?

Secretary Marshall: When you use the expression "driven out of Korea" I assume you mean all of Korea, both north and south.

Chairman Russell: Yes, sir, I mean to carry out the original directive of the United Nations.

Secretary Marshall: I should say that if the Chinese Communists continue in force in North Korea with the potential of additional reinforcements that might be made available, and with our situation where we visualize no considerable reinforcement of the United Nations army, that they could not be driven out of North Korea, and I have my own doubts as to whether the actions recommended by General MacArthur would bring the conflict to a victorious end.

I am afraid, in my own opinion, it might result in a great increase in casualties without a decisive finish, but that is his view to the contrary as the theater commander.

[Deleted.]*

Chairman Russell: Wait a minute, do you mean to say in your opinion there is doubt even if we do bomb them whether they could be driven from there?

Secretary Marshall: I didn't hear the end of your question.

Chairman Russell: Did you say in your statement that you doubted whether they could be driven out even if we adopted these recommendations?

Secretary Marshall: Yes, sir.

Chairman Russell: Is that what you wanted to state?

Secretary Marshall: That is what I wanted to state. You can get into the details of this with the Chiefs of Staff, [deleted].

Senator [*Henry Cabot*] *Lodge* [(R., Mass.)]: But you have no objection

*[Where "[deleted]" occurs in the hearings, it is part of the printed text. Before being published, the hearings were censored to remove sensitive security information (*ed.*).]

to having your belief stated that in your judgment the bombing of the Chinese bases would not bring victory?

Secretary Marshall: That is correct, sir.

Chairman Russell: General, that brings me to the question that I think is plaguing the American people and is causing great indecision in the country, uncertainty and a certain depth of feeling. How will we ever bring the Korea episode to a conclusion?

Secretary Marshall: Now, what I am going to say now must not all be released because I can't advertise my conclusions as to that to the enemy.

[Deleted.]

They have had tremendous losses. We speak of their very large forces, but when you take the percentage of the losses that they have suffered, they are tremendous.

Now the question is how long can that go on unless they are assisted by the Soviet Government. If they renew the attack and they meet the same result that came from their attack of the last 2 weeks, we will have almost destroyed again or ruined the fighting power of some, I think it is, 34 new divisions. There were that number concentrated on what was the left of our line on the First Corps, and I know after the fourth day the report was that we had disposed of 26 of them up to that time.

Now on their part that cannot continue without wrecking them very seriously because they have troubles in China themselves. They had this threat they were carrying out against Indochina. That I am quite certain has been decidedly delayed by the effect of what is going on in Korea, and the same thing applies to any threats to Thailand or Siam.

[Deleted.]

When we turn to this country, I think we must keep in mind throughout that we had almost nothing in the summer of 1950 in the way of available troops in this country other than one airborne division, the eighty-second, and a part of a Marine division.

Everything else has been built up since that time [deleted].

You have the choice of employing all the means General MacArthur recommends, which would certainly enlarge the fighting—and whether it would bring victory is a matter of opinion. The Chiefs of Staff can give you their own views in regard to it, and in which I concur that it would not.

We have the choice then of what I have just described to you or we have the choice of withdrawing from Korea and leaving those people to assassination and virtual destruction. Those are your choices, and with our rather conspicuous successes recently as the command built up, as replacements are immediately available, and as the rotation starts, we will vitalize the command to a very considerable extent, and the efficiency of our Air Corps is increasing all the time.

Chairman Russell: Do I understand you to believe that that entire statement should be off of the record, Mr. Secretary?

Secretary Marshall: The first part of that should be off the record [deleted]. The next part where I spoke of what we were now struggling for should not be on the record. The generalization, I don't mind that being on the record.

Chairman Russell: I understand, then, that you recommend a continuation of the present policy in Korea rather than adopting General MacArthur's proposal?

General Marshall: That is correct, sir. I must add to that, of course, that if the Chinese Communists with at least equipment support from the Soviets and maybe more support carry the war to us outside of Korea. [Deleted] then we have to retaliate.

[Deleted.]

We have no choice then. The security of that command is our first consideration. . . .

Testimony of General of the Army Omar N. Bradley, Chairman of the Joint Chiefs of Staff

General Bradley: Mr. Chairman and members of the committees, at the very outset, I want to make it clear that I would not say anything to discredit the long and illustrious career of Gen. Douglas MacArthur. We may have different views on certain aspects of our Government's military policy, but that is not unusual.

Certainly there have been no personal considerations in our differences of opinion. In matters of such great scope and of such importance many people have different ideas and might consequently recommend different courses of action.

As Chairman of the Joint Chiefs of Staff, I am one of the military advisers to the President, the Secretary of Defense, and the National Security Council. I pass on to them the collective advice and recommendations of the Joint Chiefs. When the Joint Chiefs of Staff express their opinion on a subject, it is from the military point of view, and is given with a full realization that considerations other than military may be overriding in making the final decision. The relative importance of the military aspect varies. In some cases it is greatly overshadowed by other considerations. In other cases, the military aspects may be the decisive ones.

When all of these aspects are considered the Government's policy is determined. As military men we then abide by the decision.

Before your interrogation on the details of our Government's policies in Korea and the Far East, I would like to ask myself this question: What is the great issue at stake in this hearing?

Principally I would say that you are trying to determine the course we should follow as the best road to peace. There are military factors which must be evaluated before a sound decision can be made. At present the issue is obscured in the public mind by many details which do not relate to the task of keeping the peace and making America secure.

The fundamental military issue that has arisen is whether to increase the risk of a global war by taking additional measures that are open to the United States and its allies. We now have a localized conflict in Korea. Some of the military measures under discussion might well place the United States in the position of responsibility for broadening the war and at the same time losing most if not all of our allies.

General MacArthur has stated that there are certain additional measures which can and should be taken, and that by so doing no unacceptable increased risk of global war will result.

The Joint Chiefs of Staff believe that these same measures do increase the risk of global war and that such a risk should not be taken unnecessarily. At the same time we recognize the military advantages that might accrue to the United Nations' position in Korea and to the United States position in the Far East by these measures. While a field commander very properly estimates his needs from the viewpoint of operations in his own theater or sphere of action, those responsible for higher direction must necessarily base their actions on broader aspects, and on the needs, actual or prospective, of several theaters. The Joint Chiefs of Staff, in view of their global responsibilities and their perspective with respect to the world-wide strategic situation, are in a better position that is any single theater commander to assess the risk of general war. Moreover, the Joint Chiefs of Staff are best able to judge our own military resources with which to meet that risk.

In order that all may understand the strategy which the Joint Chiefs of Staff believe the United States must pursue, I would like to discuss in broad terms this perspective in which we view our security problems.

As a background to our consideration of global strategy, we must realize that human beings have invented a great variety of techniques designed to influence other nations. Right now, nations are being subjected to persuasion by propaganda and coercion by force of arms. It is my conviction that broad and comprehensive knowledge of the strength, aims, and the policies of nations is basic to understanding the problem of security in a world of tension.

We must understand—as we conduct our foreign affairs and our military affairs—that while power and nationalism prevail, it is up to us to gain strength through cooperative efforts with other nations which have common ideals and objectives with our own. At the same time, we must create and maintain the power essential to persuasion, and to our own security in such a world. We must understand the role and nature, including the limitations, of this power if we are to exercise it wisely.

One of the great power potentials of this world is the United States of America and her allies. The other great power in this world is Soviet Russia and her satellites. As much as we desire peace, we must realize that we have two centers of power supporting opposing ideologies.

From a global viewpoint—and with the security of our Nation of prime importance—our military mission is to support a policy of preventing communism from gaining the manpower, the resources, the raw materials, and the industrial capacity essential to world domination. If Soviet Russia ever controls the entire Eurasian land mass, then the Soviet-satellite imperialism may have the broad base upon which to build the military power to rule the world.

Three times in the past 5 years the Kremlin-inspired imperialism has been thwarted by direct action.

In Berlin, Greece, and Korea, the free nations have opposed Communist aggression with a different type of action. But each time the power of the United States has been called upon and we have become involved. Each incident has cost us money, resources, and some lives.

But in each instance we have prevented the domination of one more area, and the absorption of another source of manpower, raw materials, and resources.

Korea, in spite of the importance of the engagement, must be looked upon with proper perspective. It is just one engagement, just one phase of this battle that we are having with the other power center in the world which opposes us and all we stand for. For 5 years this "guerrilla diplomacy" has been going on. In each of the actions in which we have participated to oppose this gangster conduct, we have risked world war III. But each time we have used methods short of total war. As costly as Berlin and Greece and Korea may be, they are less expensive than the vast destruction which would be inflicted upon all sides if a total war were to be precipiated.

I am under no illusion that our present strategy of using means short of total war to achieve our ends and oppose communism is a guarantee that a world war will not be thrust upon us. But a policy of patience and determination without provoking a world war, while we improve our military power, is one which we believe we must continue to follow.

As long as we keep the conflict within its present scope, we are holding to a minimum the forces we must commit and tie down.

The strategic alternative, enlargement of the war in Korea to include Red China, would probably delight the Kremlin more than anything else we could do. It would necessarily tie down additional forces, especially our sea power and our air power, while the Soviet Union would not be obliged to put a single man into the conflict.

Under present circumstances, we have recommended against enlarging the war. The course of action often described as a "limited war" with Red China would increase the risk we are taking by engaging too much of our power in an area that is not the critical strategic prize.

Red China is not the powerful nation seeking to dominate the world. Frankly, in the opinion of the Joint Chiefs of Staff, this strategy would involve us in the wrong war, at the wrong place, at the wrong time, and with the wrong enemy.

There are some other considerations which have tended to obscure this main issue. Some critics have not hesitated to state that the policy our Government is following, and its included strategy, is not that which has been recommended by the Joint Chiefs of Staff.

Statements have been made that the President, as Commander in Chief, and the Secretary of State and the Secretary of Defense, have a policy all their own, and that the Joint Chiefs of Staff have been overridden.

This is just not so. The Joint Chiefs of Staff have continually given their considered opinion—always from a military viewpoint—concerning our global capabilities and responsibilities and have recommended our present strategy in and for Korea. This has been the course of action which the Secretary of Defense and the Commander in Chief have adopted as far as practicable.

I pointed out earlier that many times the international policy considerations, including the views of our allies, are also considered and in some instances modify the course of action.

In other instances, even after the international considerations and the views of our allies have been considered, the proposed military strategy has not been altered.

Our over-all policy has been one of steadfast patience and determination in opposing Communist aggression without provoking unnecessarily a total war.

There are many critics who have become impatient with this strategy and who would like to call for a show-down. From a purely military viewpoint, this is not desirable. We are not in the best military position to seek a show-down, even if it were the Nation's desire to forfeit the chances for peace by precipitating a total war.

Undoubtedly, this statement will be misconstrued by some critics who will say, "Why are the Joint Chiefs of Staff advertising the fact that we are not militarily in a position to have a show-down?"

I can assure those critics that with the methods we must pursue in a democracy in order to support a military establishment—including this present investigation of our strategy in the Far East—our capabilities are not unknown to the Communists.

They are apt students of military power, and fully realize that although we are not prepared to deliver any ultimatum, we could hurt them badly if they attacked us or our friends.

They also know that with our potential, and the strength of our allies, in the long run they could not win a war with a United States that is alert, and continuously prepared.

I would not be a proponent of any policy which would ignore the military facts and rush us headlong into a show-down before we are ready. It is true that this policy of armed resistance to aggression, which we pursue while we are getting stronger, often risks a world war. But so far we have taken these risks without disastrous results.

I think our global strategy is paying off and I see no reason to let impatience alter it in the Far East. Certainly the course of action we are pursuing has avoided a total war which could only bring death and destruction to millions of Americans, both in the United States and on the battlefield. Our present course of action has at the same time won us respect and admiration everywhere in the world, both inside and outside the iron curtain.

There are also those who deplore the present military situation in Korea and urge us to engage Red China in a larger war to solve this problem. Taking on Red China is not a decisive move, does not guarantee the end of the war in Korea, and may not bring China to her knees. We have only to look back to the five long years when the Japanese, one of the greatest military powers of that time, moved into China and had almost full control of a large part of China, and yet were never able to conclude that war successfully. I would say that from past history one would only jump from a smaller conflict to a larger deadlock at greater expense. My own feeling is to avoid such an engagement if possible because victory in Korea would not be assured and victory over Red China would be many years away. We believe that every effort should be made to settle the present conflict without extending it outside Korea. If this proves to be impossible, then other measures may have to be taken.

In my consideration of this viewpoint, I am going back to the basic objective of the American people—as much peace as we can gain without appeasement.

Some critics of our strategy say if we do not immediately bomb troop concentration points and airfields in Manchuria, it is "appeasement." If we do not immediately set up a blockade of Chinese ports—which to be successful would have to include British and Russian ports in Asia—it is "appeasement." These same critics would say that if we do not provide the logistical support and air and naval assistance to launch Chinese Nationalists troops into China it is "appeasement."

These critics ignore the vital questions:

Will these actions, if taken, actually assure victory in Korea?

Do these actions mean prolongation of the war by bringing Russia into the fight?

Will these actions strip us of our allies in Korea and in other parts of the world?

From a military viewpoint, appeasement occurs when you give up something, which is rightfully free, to an aggressor without putting up a struggle, or making him pay a price. Forsaking Korea—withdrawing from the fight unless we are forced out—would be an appeasement to aggression. Refusing to enlarge the quarrel to the point where our global capabilities are diminished, is certainly not appeasement but is a militarily sound course of action under the present circumstances.

It is my sincere hope that these hearings will encourage us as a Nation to follow a steadfast and determined course of action in this world, which would deny any free nation to Soviet imperialism, and at the same time preserve the peace for which so many men died in World War I, World War II, and in Greece, Indochina, Malaya, and Korea. . . .

Senator [*Styles*] *Bridges* [(R., N. H.)]: . . . . Suppose there is a basic conflict between the military authorities and the political authorities in this country on a military subject. Which, in your judgment, should prevail?

General Bradley: It depends on the subject, sir. In some cases I believe the military aspects should be guiding; in others, I admit that the political and the diplomatic considerations may be overriding the military aspects.

Senator Bridges: Well, now, in the case where the military should prevail, if the military is overriden, don't you think the American public are entitled to the best military judgment of our military leaders?

General Bradley: Yes, sir. We are supposed to be your military advisers, and we give you our honest opinion. Now if somebody overrules that we cannot help it.

Senator Bridges: But supposing General MacArthur—is not that the point at issue here? Was not his best military opinion the other way, and his head suffered at the block as the result?

General Bradley: Yes; but he had a responsibility for a theater only.

Senator Bridges: Well, I mean you put yourself in a different position from General MacArthur?

General Bradley: I have greater responsibilities and wider responsibilities, global. I must know more about the global situation than I think General MacArthur was required to know, and, furthermore, he did not have the responsibility.

Senator Bridges: If it reaches the time in this country where you think the political decision is affecting what you believe to be basically right militarily, what would you do?

General Bradley: Well, if after several instances in which the best military advice we could give was turned down for other reasons, I would decide that my advice was no longer of any help, why, I would quit. I feel that is the way you would have to do. Let them get some other military adviser whose advice apparently would be better or at least more acceptable.

Senator Bridges: Would you speak out, tell the American public?

General Bradley: No, sir.

Senator Bridges: Don't you think that is your duty, your loyalty to your country, to do that?

General Bradley: No, sir; I don't think so. I have been brought up a little differently.

Senator Bridges: Where does the loyalty to your country come in?

General Bradley: I am loyal to my country, but I am also loyal to the Constitution, and you have certain elected officials under the Constitution, and I wouldn't profess that my judgment was better than the President of the United States or the administration.

Senator Bridges: Would it not be on a military subject?

General Bradley: Yes.

Senator Bridges: Should not you speak out?

General Bradley: I would; yes, to the constituted authorities; yes.

Senator Bridges: But you would stop there?

General Bradley: Yes. . . .

Senator [*Lyndon B.*] *Johnson* [D., Tex.)]: . . . General Bradley, it has been stated that you personally recommended relieving General MacArthur. I should like for you to state for the record whether or not that is true and, if so, give the committee some details and elaborate on the reasons for your recommendation and the conclusions that you reached.

General Bradley: I think I could probably give a better answer to that if I would go back just a little bit to the meetings preceding the recommendation of the Joint Chiefs of Staff.

Senator Johnson: General, I purposely made my question as brief as possible in order that you could make your explanation as lengthy as you desire.

General Bradley: All right, sir.

The first meeting which I attended at the White House was on Friday, the 6th of April, in which the President called the four of us in—I believe that has been stated—Secretary Acheson, General Marshall, Mr. Harriman, and myself, and we discussed the various things involved in the matter.

He told us to go back, and the four of us to get together and discuss it further among ourselves, which we did that afternoon. At neither of these meetings were any decisions made.

Then when we went back to the White House on Saturday morning, we suggested to the President that he make no decision until he had studied it over the week end and other people had had a chance to study it, and he said he would discuss it with other Government leaders.

Who they were I do not know, but at that same meeting on Saturday he directed that we get an opinion of the Joint Chiefs of Staff in the matter, strictly from a military point of view. So I called such a meeting on Sunday afternoon with the three Chiefs, and we discussed the matter, and then we went up to General Marshall's office at 4 o'clock, and the Chiefs gave him their reasons why from a military point of view they thought that General MacArthur should be relieved, and they set forth these from a military point of view, as follows:

1. That by his public statements and by his official communications to us, he had indicated that he was not in sympathy with the decision to try to limit the conflict to Korea. This would make it difficult for him to carry out Joint Chiefs of Staff directives. Since we had decided to try to confine the conflict to Korea and avoid a third world war, it was necessary to have a commander more responsive to control from Washington.

The second reason advanced by the Chiefs was that General MacArthur had failed to comply with the Presidential directive to clear statements on policy before making such statements public. He had also taken independent action in proposing to negotiate directly with the enemy field commander for an armistice and had made that statement public despite the fact that he knew the President had such a proposal under consideration from a governmental level.

The third reason advanced by the Chiefs was that—

> they, the Joint Chiefs of Staff, have felt and feel now that the military must be controlled by civilian authority in this country.

They have always adhered to this principle and they felt that General MacArthur's actions were continuing to jeopardize the civilian control over the military authorities.

These reasons were given by the Chiefs to General Marshall on Sunday afternoon.

Senator Johnson: General, this paper that you just read, is that a paper that was concurred in by all three of the Joint Chiefs?

General Bradley: Yes, sir. We sat down afterward and wrote these up. First, they were given orally to General Marshall. We sat down afterward with the three Chiefs and they agreed that these were the reasons they gave to General Marshall on that Sunday afternoon.

Senator Johnson: Did you personally concur in those recommendations that you have just read or did you just transmit the recommendations of the various Chiefs?

General Bradley: I transmitted these to the President the next day as the three statements of the Joint Chiefs of Staff to General Marshall, and

General Marshall has stated that I would make these known, and since they were given to him as an adviser, I think that releases me to give these to you by his statement before this committee.

Senator Johnson: First, I want to ask you this: You told us about the position taken by Admiral Sherman, General Vandenberg, and General Collins.

Now, did you share the same views, and did you express those views to the President?

General Bradley: I expressed these to the President as the views of the Joint Chiefs of Staff.

Senator Johnson: Did you express any personal views to him?

General Bradley: I did not express any, one way or the other, because I pass on to him the opinions of the Joint Chiefs of Staff. If I had not concurred in them I would have said so.

Senator Johnson: But you did concur in the recommendations made by the Joint Chiefs of Staff?

General Bradley: I did.

Senator Johnson: Did you indicate to the President that you did concur?

General Bradley: No; except the fact that I did not state any non-concurrence. I transmit to him the views of the Joint Chiefs of Staff, and if I did not concur in them, I would have said so; that is according to the law.

Senator Johnson: So then, the President——

General Bradley: That is according to the law. You see, they have the vote, and I am their spokesman on certain occasions.

Senator Johnson: I am not asking about any votes. I am just asking about opinions. We know what that opinion was, and is it fair to state that you had the same opinion?

General Bradley: I did. . . .

PART 

Policies for the Long Pull

Containment

Deterrence

Aid to Developing Nations

Policies for the Long Pull: Containment

SELECTION **22**

The Doctrine: George F. Kennan, "The Sources of Soviet Conduct"

By the early 1950s, the United States and the Soviet Union were nearly at war. Through NATO, American forces were lodged on the frontier of the Soviet empire in Europe. Under the auspices of the United Nations, American armies were fighting in Korea against armies supported and equipped by the Soviet Union. From Southeast Asia across the Indian frontier to the Middle East lay a vast zone in which each nation had a watchful eye on the other.

For Americans the situation was an unfamiliar one. Through all their previous history, they had lived in comparative safety. In the two world wars, they had risen in fury and striven to destroy their enemy, expecting that afterward their lives would be tranquil again. Now, Americans found a contest that promised no quick, happy end—one that might go on nerve-rackingly for another generation, and another and another.

Many were slow to adjust to such an uncomfortable prospect. A large number reacted with enthusiasm to voices such as MacArthur's, speaking the old, familiar words—"showdown," "victory," and the like. As is illustrated later, many responded by listening to seductive voices that said all the trouble was at home, the fault of subversives in the State Department, the Army, or "the power elite." The 1950s were years in which Americans had to learn what terrifying and inescapable responsibilities went with being the foremost nation of the earth.

In the meantime, the men guiding the American government had to give thought to the long pull ahead. How was the cold war to be waged? With what objectives? With what prospect of preventing the world-wide catastrophe of nuclear war? With what hope of creating in some distant future a world in which Americans could live again in tranquility and unconcern?

Hard thinking within the government yielded three fundamental ideas: containment, deterrence, and aid to underdeveloped peoples. The documents in this part illustrate these ideas.

In 1947, with the Truman Doctrine and the Marshall Plan, the American government had moved to check Communist expansion. These steps were reactions to situations that required reactions of some kind. To an extent, however, these measures were also outgrowths of a developing doctrine about the long-term strategy required to cope with Communist expansionism. This doctrine, presently labeled "containment," was set forth most clearly in a staff paper prepared by one of the State Department's experts on Soviet affairs, George F. Kennan.

Anonymously, as "X," Kennan published a version of his staff paper. It appeared under the title "The Sources of Soviet Conduct," in the influential quarterly Foreign Affairs, *volume 25 (July, 1947), pages 566–582, and is reproduced below.*

The political personality of Soviet power as we know it today is the product of ideology and circumstances: ideology inherited by the present Soviet leaders from the movement in which they had their political origin, and circumstances of the power which they now have exercised for nearly three decades in Russia. There can be few tasks of psychological analysis more difficult than to try to trace the interaction of these two forces and the relative role of each in the determination of official Soviet conduct. Yet the attempt must be made if that conduct is to be understood and effectively countered.

It is difficult to summarize the set of ideological concepts with which the Soviet leaders came into power. Marxian ideology, in its Russian-Communist projection, has always been in process of subtle evolution. The materials on which it bases itself are extensive and complex. But the outstanding features of Communist thought as it existed in 1916 may perhaps be summarized as follows: *(a)* that the central factor in the life of man, the fact which determines the character of public life and the "physiognomy of society," is the system by which material goods are produced and exchanged; *(b)* that the capitalist system of production is a nefarious one which inevitably leads to the exploitation of the working class by the capital-owning class and is incapable of developing adequately the economic resources of society or of distributing fairly the material goods produced by human labor; *(c)* that capitalism contains the seeds of its own destruction and must, in view of the inability of the capital-owning class to adjust itself to economic change, result eventually and inescapably in a revolutionary transfer of power to the working class; and *(d)* that imperialism, the final phase of capitalism, leads directly to war and revolution.

The rest may be outlined in Lenin's own words: "Unevenness of economic and political development is the inflexible law of capitalism. It follows from this that the victory of Socialism may come originally in a few capitalist countries or even in a single capitalist country. The victorious proletariat of that country, having expropriated the capitalists and having organized Socialist production at home, would rise against the remaining capitalist world, drawing to itself in the process the oppressed classes of other countries." It must be noted that there was no assumption that capitalism would perish without proletarian revolution. A final push was needed from a revolutionary proletariat movement in order to tip over the tottering structure. But it was regarded as inevitable that sooner or later that push be given.

For fifty years prior to the outbreak of the Revolution, this pattern of thought had exercised great fascination for the members of the Russian revolutionary movement. Frustrated, discontented, hopeless of finding self-expression—or too impatient to seek it—in the confining limits of the Tsarist political system, yet lacking wide popular support for their choice of bloody revolution as a means of social betterment, these revolutionists found in Marxist theory a highly convenient rationalization for their own instinctive desires. It afforded pseudo-scientific justification for their impatience, for their categoric denial of all value in the Tsarist system, for their yearning for power and revenge and for their inclination to cut corners in the pursuit of it. It is therefore no wonder that they had come to believe implicitly in the truth and soundness of the Marxian-Leninist teachings, so congenial to their own impulses and emotions. Their sincerity need not be impugned. This is a phenomenon as old as human nature itself. It has never been more aptly described than by Edward Gibbon, who wrote in *The Decline and Fall of the Roman Empire:* "From enthusiasm to imposture the step is perilous and slippery; the demon of Socrates affords a memorable instance how a wise man may deceive himself; how a good man may deceive others, how the conscience may slumber in a mixed and middle state between self-illusion and voluntary fraud." And it was with this set of conceptions that the members of the Bolshevik Party entered into power.

Now it must be noted that through all the years of preparation for revolution, the attention of these men, as indeed of Marx himself, had been centered less on the future form which Socialism would take than on the necessary overthrow of rival power which, in their view, had to precede the introduction of Socialism. Their views, therefore, on the positive program to be put into effect, once power was attained, were for the most part nebulous, visionary and impractical. Beyond the nationalization of industry and the expropriation of large private capital holdings, there was no agreed program. The treatment of the peasantry, which according to the Marxist formulation was not of the proletariat, had always been a vague spot in the pattern of Communist thought; and it remained an object of controversy and vacillation for the first ten years of Communist power.

The circumstances of the immediate post-Revolution period—the existence in Russia of civil war and foreign intervention, together with the obvious fact that the Communists represented only a tiny minority of the Russian people—made the establishment of dictatorial power a necessity. The experiment with "war Communism" and the abrupt attempt to eliminate private production and trade had unfortunate economic consequences and caused further bitterness against the new revolutionary regime. While the temporary relaxation of the effort to communize Russia, represented by the New Economic Policy, alleviated some of this economic distress and thereby served its purpose, it also made it evident that the "capitalistic sector of society" was still prepared to profit at once from any relaxation of governmental pressure, and would, if permitted to continue to exist, always constitute a powerful opposing element to the Soviet regime and a serious rival for influence in the country. Somewhat the same situation prevailed with respect to the individual peasant who, in his own small way, was also a private producer.

Lenin, had he lived, might have proved a great enough man to reconcile these conflicting forces to the ultimate benefit of Russian society, though this is questionable. But be that as it may, Stalin, and those whom he led in the struggle for succession to Lenin's position of leadership, were not the men to tolerate rival political forces in the sphere of power which they coveted. Their sense of insecurity was too great. Their particular brand of fanaticism, unmodified by any of the Anglo-Saxon traditions of compromise, was too fierce and too jealous to envisage any permanent sharing of power. From the Russian-Asiatic world out of which they had emerged they carried with them a skepticism as to the possibilities of permanent and peaceful coexistence of rival forces. Easily persuaded of their own doctrinaire "rightness," they insisted on the submission or destruction of all competing power. Outside of the Communist Party, Russian society was to have no rigidity. There were to be no forms of collective human activity or association which would not be dominated by the Party. No other force in Russian society was to be permitted to achieve vitality or integrity. Only the Party was to have structure. All else was to be an amorphous mass.

And within the Party the same principle was to apply. The mass of Party members might go through the motions of election, deliberation, decision and action; but in these motions they were to be animated not by their own individual wills but by the awesome breath of the Party leadership and the overbrooding presence of "the world."

Let it be stressed again that subjectively these men probably did not seek absolutism for its own sake. They doubtless believed—and found it easy to believe—that they alone knew what was good for society and that they would accomplish that good once their power was secure and unchallengeable. But in seeking that security of their own rule they were prepared to recognize no restrictions, either of God or man, on the character of their methods. And until such time as that security might be achieved, they placed far down on their scale of operational priorities the comforts and happiness of the peoples entrusted to their care.

Now the outstanding circumstance concerning the Soviet regime is that down to the present day this process of political consolidation has never been completed and the men in the Kremlin have continued to be predominantly absorbed with the struggle to secure and make absolute the power which they seized in November 1917. They have endeavored to secure it primarily against forces at home, within Soviet society itself. But they have also endeavored to secure it against the outside world. For ideology, as we have seen, taught them that the outside world was hostile and that it was their duty eventually to overthrow the political forces beyond their borders. The powerful hands of Russian history and tradition reached up to sustain them in this feeling. Finally, their own aggressive intransigence with respect to the outside world began to find its own reaction; and they were soon forced, to use another Gibbonesque phrase, "to chastise the contumacy" which they themselves had provoked. It is an undeniable privilege of every man to prove himself right in the thesis that the world is his enemy; for if he reiterates it frequently enough and makes it the background of his conduct he is bound eventually to be right.

Now it lies in the nature of the mental world of the Soviet leaders, as well as in the character of their ideology, that no opposition to them can be officially recognized as having any merit or justification whatsoever. Such opposition can flow, in theory, only from the hostile and incorrigible forces of dying capitalism. As long as remnants of capitalism were officially recognized as existing in Russia, it was possible to place on them, as an internal element, part of the blame for the maintenance of a dictatorial form of society. But as these remnants were liquidated, little by little, this justification fell away; and when it was indicated officially that they had been finally destroyed, it disappeared altogether. And this fact created one of the most basic of the compulsions which came to act upon the Soviet regime: since capitalism no longer existed in Russia and since it could not be admitted that there could be serious or widespread opposition to the Kremlin springing spontaneously from the liberated masses under its authority, it became necessary to justify the retention of the dictatorship by stressing the menace of capitalism abroad.

This began at an early date. In 1924, Stalin specifically defended the retention of the "organs of suppression," meaning, among others, the army and the secret police, on the ground that "as long as there is a capitalist encirclement there will be danger of intervention with all the consequences that flow from that danger." In accordance with that theory, and from that time on, all internal opposition forces in Russia have consistently been portrayed as the agents of foreign forces of reaction antagonistic to Soviet power.

By the same token, tremendous emphasis has been placed on the original Communist thesis of a basic antagonism between the capitalist and Socialist worlds. It is clear, from many indications, that this emphasis is not founded in reality. The real facts concerning it have been confused by the existence abroad of genuine resentment provoked by Soviet philosophy and tactics and occasionally by the existence of great centers of military power, notably the Nazi regime in Germany and the Japanese government of the late 1930's, which did indeed have aggressive designs against the Soviet Union. But there is ample evidence that the stress laid in Moscow on the menace confronting Soviet society from the world outside its borders is founded not in the realities of foreign antagonism but in the necessity of explaining away the maintenance of dictatorial authority at home.

Now the maintenance of this pattern of Soviet power, namely, the pursuit of unlimited authority domestically, accompanied by the cultivation of the semi-myth of implacable foreign hostility, has gone far to shape the actual machinery of Soviet power as we know it today. Internal organs of administration which did not serve this purpose withered on the vine. Organs which did serve this purpose became vastly swollen. The security of Soviet power came to rest on the iron discipline of the Party, on the severity and ubiquity of the secret police, and on the uncompromising economic monopolism of the state. The "organs of suppression," in which the Soviet leaders had sought security from rival forces, became in large measure the masters of those whom they were designed to serve. Today the major part of the structure of Soviet power is committed to the perfection of the dictatorship and to the maintenance of the concept of Russia as in a state of siege, with the enemy lowering beyond the walls. And the millions of human beings who form that part of the structure of power must defend at all costs this concept of Russia's position, for without it they are themselves superfluous.

As things stand today, the rulers can no longer dream of parting with these organs of suppression. The quest for absolute power, pursued now for nearly three decades with a ruthlessness unparalleled (in scope at least) in modern times, has again produced internally, as it did externally, its own reaction. The excesses of the police apparatus have fanned the potential opposition to the regime into something far greater and more dangerous than it could have been before those excesses began.

But least of all can the rulers dispense with the fiction by which the maintenance of dictatorial power has been defended. For this fiction has been canonized in Soviet philosophy by the excesses already committed in its name; and it is now anchored in the Soviet structure of thought by bonds far greater than those of mere ideology.

II

So much for the historical background. What does it spell in terms of the political personality of Soviet power as we know it today?

Of the original ideology, nothing has been officially junked. Belief is maintained in the basic badness of capitalism, in the inevitability of its destruction, in the obligation of the proletariat to assist in that destruction and to take power into its own hands. But stress has come to be laid primarily on those concepts which relate most specifically to the Soviet regime itself: to its position as the sole truly Socialist regime in a dark and misguided world, and to the relationships of power within it.

The first of these concepts is that of the innate antagonism between capitalism and Socialism. We have seen how deeply that concept has become inbedded in foundations of Soviet power. It has profound implications for Russia's conduct as a member of international society. It means that there can never be on Moscow's side any sincere assumption of a community of aims between the Soviet Union and powers which are regarded as capitalism. It must invariably be assumed in Moscow that the aims of the capitalist world are antagonistic to the Soviet regime and, therefore, to the interests of the peoples it controls. If the Soviet government occasionally sets its signature to documents which would indicate the contrary, this is to be regarded as a tactical maneuver permissible in dealing with the enemy (who is without honor) and should be taken in the spirit of *caveat emptor*. Basically, the antagonism remains. It is postulated. And from it flow many of the phenomena which we find disturbing in the Kremlin's conduct of foreign policy: the secretiveness, the lack of frankness, the duplicity, the war suspiciousness, and the basic unfriendliness of purpose. These phenomena are there to stay, for the foreseeable future. There can be variations of degree and of emphasis. When there is something the Russians want from us, one or the other of these features of their policy may be thrust temporarily into the background; and when that happens there will always be Americans who will leap forward with gleeful announcements that "the Russians have changed," and some who will even try to take credit for having brought about such "changes." But we should not be misled by tactical maneuvers. These characteristics of Soviet policy, like the postulate from which they flow, are basic to the internal nature of Soviet power, and will be with us, whether in the foreground or the background, until the internal nature of Soviet power is changed.

This means that we are going to continue for a long time to find the Russians difficult to deal with. It does not mean that they should be considered as embarked upon a do-or-die program to overthrow our society by a given date. The theory of the inevitability of the eventual fall of capitalism has the fortunate connotation that there is no hurry about it. The forces of progress can take their time in preparing the final *coup de grâce*. Meanwhile, what is vital is that the "Socialist fatherland"—that oasis of power which has been already won for Socialism in the person of the Soviet Union—should be cherished and defended by all good Communists at home and abroad, its fortunes promoted, its enemies badgered and confounded. The promotion of premature, "adventuristic" revolutionary projects abroad which might embarrass Soviet power in any way would be an inexcusable, even a counter-revolutionary act. The cause of Socialism is the support and promotion of Soviet power, as defined in Moscow.

This brings us to the second of the concepts important to contemporary Soviet outlook. That is the infallibility of the Kremlin. The Soviet concept of power, which permits no focal points of organization outside the Party itself, requires that the Party leadership remain in theory the sole repository of truth. For if truth were to be found elsewhere, there would be justification for its expression in organized activity. But it is precisely that which the Kremlin cannot and will not permit.

The leadership of the Communist Party is therefore always right and has been always right ever since in 1929 Stalin formalized his personal power by announcing that decisions of the Politburo were being taken unanimously.

On the principle of infallibility there rests the iron discipline of the Communist Party. In fact, the two concepts are mutually self-supporting. Perfect discipline requires recognition of infallibility. Infallibility requires the observance of discipline. And the two together go far to determine the behaviorism of the entire Soviet apparatus of power. But their effect cannot be understood unless a third factor be taken into account: namely, the fact that the leadership is at liberty to put forward for tactical purposes any particular thesis which it finds useful to the cause at any particular moment and to require the faithful and unquestioning acceptance of that thesis by the members of the movement as a whole. This means that truth is not a constant but is actually created, for all intents and purposes, by the Soviet leaders themselves. It may vary from week to week, from month to month. It is nothing absolute and immutable—nothing which flows from objective reality. It is only the most recent manifestation of the wisdom of those in whom the ultimate wisdom is supposed to reside, because they represent the logic of history. The accumulative effect of these factors is to give to the whole subordinate apparatus of Soviet power an unshakeable stubbornness and steadfastness in its orientation. This orientation can be changed at will by the Kremlin but by no other power. Once a given party line has been laid down on a given issue of current policy, the whole Soviet governmental machine, including the mechanism of diplomacy, moves inexorably along the prescribed path, like a persistent toy automobile wound up and headed in a given direction, stopping only when it meets with some unanswerable force. The individuals who are the components of this machine are unamenable to argument or reason which comes to them from outside sources. Their whole training has taught them to mistrust and discount the glib persuasiveness of the outside world. Like the white dog before the phonograph, they hear only the "master's voice." And if they are to be called off from the purposes last dictated to them, it is the master who must call them off. Thus the foreign representative cannot hope that his words will make any impression on them. The most that he can hope is that they will be transmitted to those at the top, who are capable of changing the party line. But even those are not likely to be swayed by any normal logic in the words of the bourgeois representative. Since there can be no appeal to common purposes, there can be no appeal to common mental approaches. For this reason, facts speak louder than words to the ears of the Kremlin; and words carry the greatest weight when they have the ring of reflecting, or being backed up by, facts of unchallengeable validity.

But we have seen that the Kremlin is under no ideological compulsion to accomplish its purposes in a hurry. Like the Church, it is dealing in ideological concepts which are of long-term validity, and it can afford to be patient. It has no right to risk the existing achievements of the revolution for the sake of vain baubles of the future. The very teachings of Lenin himself require great caution and flexibility in the pursuit of Communist purposes. Again, these precepts are fortified by the lessons of Russian history: of centuries of obscure battles between nomadic forces over the stretches of a vast unfortified plain. Here caution, circumspection, flexibility and deception are the valuable qualities; and their value finds natural appreciation in the Russian or the oriental mind. Thus the Kremlin has no compunction about retreating in the face of superior force. And being under the compulsion of no timetable, it does not get panicky under the necessity for such retreat. Its political action is a fluid stream which moves constantly, wherever it is permitted to move, toward a given goal. Its main concern is to make sure that it has filled every nook and cranny available to it in the basin of world power. But if it finds unassailable barriers in its path, it accepts these philosophically and accommodates itself to them. The main thing is that there should always be pressure, increasing constant pressure, toward the desired goal. There is no trace of any feeling in Soviet psychology that that goal must be reached at any given time.

These considerations make Soviet diplomacy at once easier and more difficult to deal with than the diplomacy of individual aggressive leaders like Napoleon and Hitler. On the one hand it is more sensitive to contrary force, more ready to yield on individual sectors of the diplomatic front when that force is felt to be too strong, and thus more rational in the logic and rhetoric of power. On the other hand it cannot be easily defeated or discouraged by a single victory on the part of its opponents. And the patient persistence by which it is animated means that it can be effectively countered not by sporadic acts which represent the momentary whims of democratic opinion but only by intelligent long-range policies on the part of Russia's adversaries—policies no less steady in their purpose, and no less variegated and resourceful in their application, than those of the Soviet Union itself.

In these circumstances it is clear that the main element of any United States policy toward the Soviet Union must be that of a long-term, patient but firm and vigilant containment of Russian expansive tendencies. It is important to note, however, that such a policy has nothing to do with outward histrionics: with threats or blustering or superfluous gestures of outward "toughness." While the Kremlin is basically flexible in its reaction to political realities, it is by no means unamenable to considerations of prestige. Like almost any other government, it can be placed by tactless and threatening gestures in a position where it cannot afford to yield even though this might be dictated by its sense of realism. The Russian leaders are keen judges of human psychology, and as such they are highly conscious that loss of temper and of self-control is never a source of strength in political affairs. They are quick to exploit such evidences of weakness. For these reasons, it is a *sine qua non* of successful dealing with Russia that the foreign government in question should remain at all times cool and collected and that its demands on Russian policy should be put forward in such a manner as to leave the way open for a compliance not too detrimental to Russian prestige.

III

In the light of the above, it will be clearly seen that the Soviet pressure against the free institutions of the Western world is something that can be contained by the adroit and vigilant application of counter-force at a series of constantly shifting geographical and political points, corresponding to the shifts and maneuvers of Soviet policy, but which cannot be charmed or talked out of existence. The Russians look forward to a duel of infinite duration, and they see that already they have scored great successes. It must be borne in mind that there was a time when the Communist Party represented far more of a minority in the sphere of Russian national life than Soviet power today represents in the world community.

But if ideology convinces the rulers of Russia that truth is on their side and that they can therefore afford to wait, those of us on whom that ideology has no claim are free to examine objectively the validity of that premise. The Soviet thesis not only implies complete lack of control by the West over its own economic destiny, it likewise assumes Russian unity, discipline and patience over an infinite period. Let us bring this apocalyptic vision down to earth, and suppose that the Western world finds the strength and resourcefulness to contain Soviet power over a period of ten to fifteen years. What does that spell for Russia itself?

The Soviet leaders, taking advantage of the contributions of modern technique to the arts of despotism, have solved the question of obedience within the confines of their power. Few challenge their authority; and even those who do are unable to make that challenge valid as against the organs of suppression of the state.

The Kremlin has also proved able to accomplish its purpose of building up in Russia, regardless of the interests of the inhabitants, an industrial foundation of heavy metallurgy, which is, to be sure, not yet complete but which is nevertheless continuing to grow and is approaching those of the other major industrial countries. All of this, however, both the maintenance of internal political security and the building of heavy industry, has been carried out at a terrible cost in human life and in human hopes and energies. It has necessitated the use of forced labor on a scale unprecedented in modern times under conditions of peace. It has involved the neglect or abuse of other phases of Soviet economic life, particularly agriculture, consumers' goods production, housing and transportation.

To all that, the war has added its tremendous toll of destruction, death and human exhaustion. In consequence of this, we have in Russia today a population which is physically and spiritually tired. The mass of the people are disillusioned, skeptical and no longer as accessible as they once were to the magical attraction which Soviet power still radiates to its followers abroad. The avidity with which people seized upon the slightest respite accorded to the Church for tactical reasons during the war was eloquent testimony to the fact that their capacity for faith and devotion found little expression in the purposes of the regime.

In these circumstances, there are limits to the physical and nervous strength of people themselves. These limits are absolute ones, and are binding even for the cruelest dictatorship, because beyond them people cannot be driven. The forced labor camps and the other agencies of constraint provide temporary means of compelling people to work longer hours than their own volition or mere economic pressure would dictate; but if people survive them at all they become old before their time and must be considered as human casualties to the demands of dictatorship. In either case their best powers are no longer available to society and can no longer be enlisted in the service of the state.

Here only the younger generation can help. The younger generation, despite all vicissitudes and sufferings, is numerous and vigorous; and the Russians are a talented people. But it still remains to be seen what will be the effects on mature performance of the abnormal emotional strains of childhood which Soviet dictatorship created and which were enormously increased by the war. Such things as normal security and placidity of home environment have practically ceased to exist in the Soviet Union outside of the most remote farms and villages. And observers are not yet sure whether that is not going to leave its mark on the over-all capacity of the generation now coming into maturity.

In addition to this, we have the fact that Soviet economic development, while it can list certain formidable achievements, has been precariously spotty and uneven. Russian Communists who speak of the "uneven development of capitalism" should blush at the contemplation of their own national economy. Here certain branches of economic life, such as the metallurgical and machine industries, have been pushed out of all proportion to other sectors of economy. Here is a nation striving to become in a short period one of the great industrial nations of the world while it still has no highway network worthy of the name and only a relatively primitive network of railways. Much has been done to increase efficiency of labor and to teach primitive peasants something about the operation of machines. But maintenance is still a crying deficiency of all Soviet economy. Construction is hasty and poor in quality. Depreciation must be enormous. And in vast sectors of economic life it has not yet been possible to instill into labor anything like that general culture of production and technical self-respect which characterizes the skilled worker of the West.

It is difficult to see how these deficiencies can be corrected at an early date by a tired and dispirited population working largely under the shadow of fear and compulsion. And as long as they are not overcome, Russia will remain economically a vulnerable, and in a certain sense an impotent, nation, capable of exporting its enthusiasms and of radiating the strange charm of its primitive political vitality but unable to back up those articles of export by the real evidences of material power and prosperity.

Meanwhile, a great uncertainty hangs over the political life of the Soviet Union. That is the uncertainty involved in the transfer of power from one individual or group of individuals to others.

This is, of course, outstandingly the problem of the personal position of Stalin. We must remember that his succession to Lenin's pinnacle of preeminence in the Communist movement was the only such transfer of individual authority which the Soviet Union has experienced. That transfer took twelve years to consolidate. It cost the lives of millions of people and shook the state to its foundations, the attendant tremors were felt all through the international revolutionary movement, to the disadvantage of the Kremlin itself.

It is always possible that another transfer of preeminent power may take place quietly and inconspicuously, with no repercussions anywhere. But again, it is possible that the questions involved may unleash, to use some of Lenin's words, one of those "incredibly swift transitions" from "delicate deceit" to "wild violence" which characterize Russian history, and may shake Soviet power to its foundations.

But this is not only a question of Stalin himself. There has been, since 1938, a dangerous congealment of political life in the higher circles of Soviet power. The All-Union Party Congress, in theory the supreme body of the Party, is supposed to meet not less often than once in three years. It will soon be eight full years since its last meeting. During this period membership in the Party has numerically doubled. Party mortality during the war was enormous, and today well over half of the Party members are persons who have entered since the last Party congress was held. Meanwhile, the same small group of men has carried on at the top through an amazing series of national vicissitudes. Surely there is some reason why the experiences of the war brought basic political changes to every one of the great governments of the West. Surely the causes of that phenomenon are basic enough to be present somewhere in the obscurity of Soviet political life, as well. And yet no recognition has been given to these causes in Russia.

It must be surmised from this that even within so highly disciplined an organization as the Communist Party there must be a growing divergence in age, outlook and interest between the great mass of Party members, only so recently recruited into the movement, and the little self-perpetuating clique of men at the top, whom most of these Party members have never met, with whom they have never conversed, and with whom they can have no political intimacy.

Who can say whether, in these circumstances, the eventual rejuvenation of the higher spheres of authority (which can only be a matter of time) can take place smoothly and peacefully, or whether rivals in the quest for higher power will not eventually reach down into these politically immature and inexperienced masses in order to find support for their respective claims. If this were ever to happen, strange consequences could flow for the Communist Party: for the membership at large has been exercised only in the practices of iron discipline and obedience and not in the arts of compromise and accommodation. And if disunity were ever to seize and paralyze the Party, the chaos and weakness of Russian society would be revealed in forms beyond description. For we have seen that Soviet power is only a crust concealing an amorphous mass of human beings among whom no independent organizational structure is tolerated. In Russia there is not even such a thing as local government. The present generation of Russians have never known spontaneity of collective action. If, consequently, anything were ever to occur to disrupt the unity and efficacy of the Party as a political instrument, Soviet Russia might be changed overnight from one of the strongest to one of the weakest and most pitiable of national societies.

Thus the future of Soviet power may not be by any means as secure as Russian capacity for self-delusion would make it appear to the men in the Kremlin. That they can keep power themselves, they have demonstrated. That they can quietly and easily turn it over to others remains to be proved. Meanwhile, the hardships of their rule and the vicissitudes of international life have taken a heavy toll of the strength and hopes of the great people on whom their power rests. It is curious to note that the ideological power of Soviet authority is strongest today in areas beyond the frontiers of Russia, beyond the reach of its police power. This phenomenon brings to mind a comparison used by Thomas Mann in his great novel *Buddenbrooks*. Observing that human institutions often show the greatest outward brilliance at a moment when inner decay is in reality farthest advanced, he compared the Buddenbrook family, in the days of its greatest glamour to one of those stars whose light shines most brightly on this world when in reality it has long ceased to exist. And who can say with assurance that the strong light still cast by the Kremlin on the dissatisfied peoples of the Western world is not the powerful afterglow of a constellation which is in actuality on the wane? This cannot be proved. And it cannot be disproved. But the possibility remains (and in the opinion of this writer it is a strong one) that Soviet power, like the capitalist world of its conception, bears within it the seeds of its own decay, and that the sprouting of these seeds is well advanced.

IV

It is clear that the United States cannot expect in the foreseeable future to enjoy political intimacy with the Soviet regime. It must continue to regard the Soviet Union as a rival, not a partner, in the political arena. It must continue to expect that Soviet policies will reflect no abstract love of peace and stability, no real faith in the possibility of a permanent happy coexistence of the Socialist and capitalist worlds, but rather a cautious, persistent pressure toward the disruption and weakening of all rival influence and rival power.

Balanced against this are the facts that Russia, as opposed to the Western world in general, is still by far the weaker party, that Soviet policy is highly flexible, and that Soviet society may well contain deficiencies which will eventually weaken its own total potential. This would of itself warrant the United States entering with reasonable confidence upon a policy of firm containment, designed to confront the Russians with unalterable counter-force at every point where they show signs of encroaching upon the interests of a peaceful and stable world.

But in actuality the possibilities for American policy are by no means limited to holding the line and hoping for the best. It is entirely possible for the United States to influence by its actions the internal developments, both within Russia and throughout the international Communist movement, by which Russian policy is largely determined. This is not only a question of the modest measure of informational activity which this government can conduct in the Soviet Union and elsewhere, although that, too, is important. It is rather a question of the degree to which the United States can create among the peoples of the world generally the impression of a country which knows what it wants, which is coping successfully with the problems of its internal life and with the responsibilities of a World Power, and which has a spiritual vitality capable of holding its own among the major ideological currents of the time. To the extent that such an impression can be created and maintained, the aims of Russian Communism must appear sterile and quixotic, the hopes and enthusiasm of Moscow's supporters must wane, and added strain must be imposed on the Kremlin's foreign policies. For the palsied decrepitude of the capitalist world is the keystone of Communist philosophy. Even the failure of the United States to experience the early economic depression which the ravens of the Red Square have been predicting with such complacent confidence since hostilities ceased would have deep and important repercussions throughout the Communist world.

By the same token, exhibitions of indecision, disunity and internal disintegration within this country have an exhilarating effect on the whole Communist movement. At each evidence of these tendencies, a thrill of hope and excitement goes through the Communist world; a new jauntiness can be noted in the Moscow tread; new groups of foreign supporters climb on to what they can only view as the band wagon of international politics; and Russian pressure increases all along the line in international affairs.

It would be an exaggeration to say that American behavior unassisted and alone could exercise a power of life and death over the Communist movement and bring about the early fall of Soviet power in Russia. But the United States has it in its power to increase enormously the strains under which Soviet policy must operate, to force upon the Kremlin a far greater degree of moderation and circumspection than it has had to observe in recent years, and in this way to promote tendencies which must eventually find their outlet in either the break-up or the gradual mellowing of Soviet power. For no mystical, Messianic movement—and particularly not that of the Kremlin—can face frustration indefinitely without eventually adjusting itself in one way or another to the logic of that state of affairs.

Thus the decision will really fall in large measure in this country itself. The issue of Soviet-American relations is in essence a test of the over-all worth of the United States as a nation among nations. To avoid destruction the United States need only measure up to its own best traditions and prove itself worthy of preservation as a great nation.

Surely, there was never a fairer test of national quality than this. In the light of these circumstances, the thoughtful observer of Russian-American relations will find no cause for complaint in the Kremlin's challenge to American society. He will rather experience a certain gratitude to a Providence which, by providing the American people with this implacable challenge, has made their entire security as a nation dependent on their pulling themselves together and accepting the responsibilities of moral and political leadership that history plainly intended them to bear.

The Line in Asia: The Southeast Asia Treaty, September 8, 1954

The doctrine of containment did not go uncriticized. Followers of Henry Wallace condemned it for assuming antagonism instead of potential friendship. Larger groups at the other end of the political spectrum attacked it on other grounds. They declared that, instead of just responding to Soviet moves, the United States should take positive action to liberate areas under Soviet control and to overthrow communism in the Soviet Union itself.

During the presidential campaign of 1952, some Republican spokesmen addressed appeals to right-wing critics of containment. John Foster Dulles, who was to become President Eisenhower's Secretary of State, proclaimed that a Republican administration would actively seek "liberation of captive peoples."

In practice, however, the Republican administration was faithful to the doctrine Kennan had enunciated. In 1954, it faced a crisis in Southeast Asia. The French, after battling Communist-led guerrillas for eight bloody years, had to confess that, alone, they could no longer hold the northern part of Indochina. The French requested aid from American air, naval, and ground forces.

After anxious debate, the American government decided not to enter the Indochinese war. Some details on this debate are revealed in the memoirs of participants, particularly Dwight D. Eisenhower, Mandate for Change *(1963), Sherman Adams,* Firsthand Report *(1961), Richard M. Nixon,* Six Decisions *(1962), and M. B. Ridgway,* Soldier *(1956). The background of the problem is sketched in Ellen Hammer,* The Struggle for Indo China *(1954) and Donald Lancaster,* The Emancipation of French Indo-China *(1961).*

The decision of the Eisenhower administration was to draw a line in Southeast Asia and attempt to contain Communist expansion behind that line. At Geneva, agreements were negotiated by which Indochina gained independence, dividing into three states, Vietnam, Laos, and Cambodia. Vietnam, the largest of the three, was further divided, with Communists in control north of 17° and non-Communists in control south of that boundary. The object of subsequent American policy was to prevent Communist expansion into Laos, Cambodia, or South Vietnam.

The mechanism for containment in Southeast Asia was a treaty patterned on the North Atlantic Treaty. It was signed at Manila on September 8, 1954, by the United States, Britain, France, Australia, New Zealand, Thailand, the Philippines, and Pakistan. Although its wording was somewhat ambiguous, the treaty was intended to give a military guarantee to Laos, Cambodia, and South Vietnam. A Southeast Asia Treaty Organization (SEATO), modeled on NATO, was afterward set up.

Containment did not work as well in Southeast Asia as in Europe. Laos was repeatedly a scene of warfare between government forces and Communist guerrillas. With backing from North Vietnam, guerrilla forces south of 17° waged campaigns that increasingly threatened the existence of the non-Communist regime in Saigon. American military forces were sent to South Vietnam. At first their role was simply that of advisers. In time they became engaged in active combat not only against the guerrillas in the south but also against the North Vietnamese themselves.

The document below is the text of the Southeast Asia Treaty. It is taken from United States Department of State, Publication number 6446, American Foreign Policy, 1950–1955: Basic Documents *(two volumes, Government Printing Office, 1957), pages 912–916.*

The Parties to this Treaty,

Recognizing the sovereign equality of all the Parties,

Reiterating their faith in the purposes and principles set forth in the Charter of the United Nations and their desire to live in peace with all peoples and all governments,

Reaffirming that, in accordance with the Charter of the United Nations, they uphold the principle of equal rights and self-determination of peoples, and declaring that they will earnestly strive by every peaceful means to promote self-government and to secure the independence of all countries whose peoples desire it and are able to undertake its responsibilities,

Desiring to strengthen the fabric of peace and freedom and to uphold the principles of democracy, individual liberty and the rule of law, and to promote the economic well-being and development of all peoples in the treaty area,

Intending to declare publicly and formally their sense of unity, so that any potential aggressor will appreciate that the Parties stand together in the area, and

Desiring further to coordinate their efforts for collective defense for the preservation of peace and security,

Therefore agree as follows:

Article I

The Parties undertake, as set forth in the Charter of the United Nations, to settle any international disputes in which they may be involved by peaceful means in such a manner that international peace and security and justice are not endangered, and to refrain in their international relations from the threat or use of force in any manner inconsistent with the purposes of the United Nations.

Article II

In order more effectively to achieve the objectives of this Treaty, the Parties, separately and jointly, by means of continuous and effective self-help and mutual aid will maintain and develop their individual and collective capacity to resist armed attack and to prevent and counter subversive activities directed from without against their territorial integrity and political stability.

Article III

The Parties undertake to strengthen their free institutions and to cooperate with one another in the further development of economic measures, including technical assistance, designed both to promote economic progress and social well-being and to further the individual and collective efforts of governments toward these ends.

Article IV

1. Each Party recognizes that aggression by means of armed attack in the treaty area against any of the Parties or against any State or territory which the Parties by unanimous agreement may hereafter designate, would endanger its own peace and safety, and agrees that it will in that event act to meet the common danger in accordance with its constitutional processes. Measures taken under this paragraph shall be immediately reported to the Security Council of the United Nations.

2. If, in the opinion of any of the Parties, the inviolability or the integrity of the territory or the sovereignty or political independence of any Party in the treaty area or of any other State or territory to which the provisions of paragraph 1 of this Article from time to time apply is threat-

ened in any way other than by armed attack or is affected or threatened by any fact or situation which might endanger the peace of the area, the Parties shall consult immediately in order to agree on the measures which should be taken for the common defense.

3. It is understood that no action on the territory of any State designated by unanimous agreement under paragraph 1 of this Article or on any territory so designated shall be taken except at the invitation or with the consent of the government concerned.

Article V

The Parties hereby establish a Council, on which each of them shall be represented, to consider matters concerning the implementation of this Treaty. The Council shall provide for consultation with regard to military and any other planning as the situation obtaining in the treaty area may from time to time require. The Council shall be so organized as to be able to meet at any time.

Article VI

This Treaty does not affect and shall not be interpreted as affecting in any way the rights and obligations of any of the Parties under the Charter of the United Nations or the responsibility of the United Nations for the maintenance of international peace and security. Each Party declares that none of the international engagements now in force between it and any other of the Parties or any third party is in conflict with the provisions of this Treaty, and undertakes not to enter into any international engagement in conflict with this Treaty.

Article VII

Any other State in a position to further the objectives of this Treaty and to contribute to the security of the area may, by unanimous agreement of the Parties, be invited to accede to this Treaty. Any State so invited may become a Party to the Treaty by depositing its instrument of accession with the Government of the Republic of the Philippines. The Government of the Republic of the Philippines shall inform each of the Parties of the deposit of each such instrument of accession.

Article VIII

As used in this Treaty, the "treaty area" is the general area of Southeast Asia, including also the entire territories of the Asian Parties, and the general area of the Southwest Pacific not including the Pacific area north of 21 degrees 30 minutes north latitude. The Parties may, by unanimous agreement, amend this Article to include within the treaty area the territory of any State acceding to this Treaty in accordance with Article VII or otherwise to change the treaty area.

Article IX

1. This Treaty shall be deposited in the archives of the Government of the Republic of the Philippines. Duly certified copies thereof shall be transmitted by that government to the other signatories.
2. The Treaty shall be ratified and its provisions carried out by the Parties in accordance with their respective constitutional processes. The instruments of ratification shall be deposited as soon as possible with the Government of the Republic of the Philippines, which shall notify all of the other signatories of such deposit.
3. The Treaty shall enter into force between the States which have ratified it as soon as the instruments of ratification of a majority of the signatories shall have been deposited, and shall come into effect with respect to each other State on the date of the deposit of its instrument of ratification.

Article X

This Treaty shall remain in force indefinitely, but any Party may cease to be a Party one year after its notice of denunciation has been given to the Government of the Republic of the Philippines, which shall inform the Governments of the other Parties of the deposit of each notice of denunciation.

Article XI

The English text of this Treaty is binding on the Parties, but when the Parties have agreed to the French text thereof and have so notified the Government of the Republic of the Philippines, the French text shall be equally authentic and binding on the Parties.

UNDERSTANDING OF THE UNITED STATES OF AMERICA

The United States of America in executing the present Treaty does so with the understanding that its recognition of the effect of aggression and armed attack and its agreement with reference thereto in Article IV, paragraph 1, apply only to communist aggression but affirms that in the event of other aggression or armed attack it will consult under the provisions of Article IV, paragraph 2.

In witness whereof, the undersigned Plenipotentiaries have signed this Treaty.

Done at Manila, this eighth day of September, 1954.

PROTOCOL TO THE TREATY

Designation of States and Territory as to Which Provisions of Article IV and Article III Are to Be Applicable

The Parties to the Southeast Asia Collective Defense Treaty unanimously designate for the purposes of Article IV of the Treaty the States of Cambodia and Laos and the free territory under the jurisdiction of the State of Vietnam.

The Parties further agree that the above mentioned states and territory shall be eligible in respect of the economic measures contemplated by Article III.

This Protocol shall enter into force simultaneously with the coming into force of the Treaty.

IN WITNESS WHEREOF, the undersigned Plenipotentiaries have signed this Protocol to the Southeast Asia Collective Defense Treaty.

Done at Manila, this eight day of September, 1954.

The Line in the Middle East—The Eisenhower Doctrine: Dwight D. Eisenhower, Special Message to Congress, January 5, 1957

In the Far East, the Eisenhower administration applied the doctrine of containment rigorously. Its attitude with regard to Quemoy and Matsu is an illustration. These tiny islands, just off the coast of China, were held by Chinese Nationalists. From the shore, the Chinese Communists began to bombard them with gunfire. It seemed as if the Communists would soon attempt seizure. Although Eisenhower did not declare explicitly that the United States would defend these offshore islands, he issued a solemn warning that the United States would respond with force to any move that it interpreted as a threat to Taiwan. He obtained from Congress a resolution backing up his stand. In the upshot, the offshore islands were spared capture by the Communists.

In 1956, there developed an apparent menace of Communist expansion in the Middle East. Ardently nationalistic army officers had seized power in Egypt. They opened a crash campaign to modernize their country and expand its influence in the Arab world. Their leader was Colonel Gamal Abdel Nasser. In order both to obtain outside capital and to enhance Egypt's prestige, Nasser attempted to get the United States and the Soviet Union to bid against one another for influence. He succeeded in obtaining from the United States and its associates a promise of large-scale aid for construction of a dam and hydroelectric facility at Aswân on the Nile. With the Soviet Union and its satellites, Nasser then made a deal to exchange cotton for arms and modern military aircraft.

Outraged by Nasser's deal with the Communists, Eisenhower and Secretary of State Dulles announced abruptly that the Aswân dam project would be canceled. Nasser retaliated by seizing the British- and French-owned Suez Canal. He would build the dam, he declared, with tolls collected from traffic through the canal.

Months went by in negotiations, with Nasser not budging an inch. Finally, in October, without warning Washington, the British, French, and Israeli governments acted in concert to retake the canal zone by force.

The Soviet government demanded that the British, French, and Israeli forces withdraw. Moscow communiqués spoke of the possible use of missiles and nuclear weapons.

The American government was caught in a dilemma. If it supported Britain, France, and Israel, the result might be a third world war. At best, the outcome would be a situation in which Egypt and most of the Arab world was aligned with the Soviet Union. On the other hand, if the United States joined the Soviets in condemning the attack on Egypt, the result would be a severe blow to the prestige of America's most important allies and perhaps even a rupture of the North Atlantic Treaty system.

After anguished debate, the Eisenhower administration elected to oppose its allies. The President appealed to the UN for a resolution in favor of a cease-fire and the withdrawal of British, French, and Israeli forces. The UN promptly passed the requested resolution.

Menaced by the Soviet Union and opposed by the United States, London, Paris, and Tel Aviv had no choice but to comply. Peace was restored with Nasser firmly in control of Suez. Although there followed a period of troubled relations between the United States, Britain, France, and Israel, amity and cooperation were, in the end, restored.

Coincidentally, the United States had faced a simultaneous crisis elsewhere. An uprising in Hungary in October overthrew the Soviet-backed regime. The Hungarian rebels appealed for support from Washington. It was not forthcoming. The American government stood regretfully by while Soviet troops marched across the Hungarian border, suppressed the revolt, and reinstated a Communist government. In this episode, the Eisenhower administration opted decisively for the doctrine of containment over the more risky doctrine of liberation.

The Suez and Hungarian crises of 1956 set the stage for an explicit extension to the Middle East of the doctrine of containment. On January 5, 1957, President Eisenhower went before Congress to ask for a resolution empowering him to use economic aid and, if necessary, military forces to block Communist expansion into the Middle East. His pronouncement was popularly labeled the "Eisenhower Doctrine."

Subsequently, aid was in fact extended to Egypt and other Middle Eastern states. On more than one occasion, most notably in Lebanon in 1958, American forces were landed to support governments in seeming danger of overthrow through a Communist coup. A judicious survey of the problems arising in the region is J. C: Campbell, Defense of the Middle East *(1960).*

The document that follows is the Presidential message embodying the Eisenhower Doctrine. It is taken from The Public Papers of the Presidents: Dwight D. Eisenhower, 1957 *(Government Printing Office, 1958), pages 6–16.*

First may I express to you my deep appreciation of your courtesy in giving me, at some inconvenience to yourselves, this early opportunity of addressing you on a matter I deem to be of grave importance to our country.

In my forthcoming State of the Union Message, I shall review the international situation generally. There are worldwide hopes which we can reasonably entertain, and there are worldwide responsibilities which we must carry to make certain that freedom—including our own—may be secure.

There is, however, a special situation in the Middle East which I feel I should, even now, lay before you.

Before doing so it is well to remind ourselves that our basic national objective in international affairs remains peace—a world peace based on justice. Such a peace must include all areas, all peoples of the world if it is to be enduring. There is no nation, great or small, with which we would refuse to negotiate, in mutual good faith, with patience and in the determination to secure a better understanding between us. Out of such understandings must, and eventually will, grow confidence and trust, indispensable ingredients to a program of peace and to plans for lifting from us all the burdens of expensive armaments. To promote these objectives, our government works tirelessly, day by day, month by month, year by year. But until a degree of success crowns our efforts that will assure to all nations peaceful existence, we must, in the interests of peace itself, remain vigilant, alert and strong.

I

The Middle East has abruptly reached a new and critical stage in its long and important history. In past decades many of the countries in that area were not fully self-governing. Other nations exercised considerable authority in the area and the security of the region was largely built around their power. But since the First World War there has been a steady evolution toward self-government and independence. This development the United States has welcomed and has encouraged. Our country supports without reservation the full sovereignty and independence of each and every nation of the Middle East.

The evolution to independence has in the main been a peaceful process. But the area has been often troubled. Persistent cross-currents of distrust and fear with raids back and forth across national boundaries have brought about a high degree of instability in much of the Mid East. Just recently there have been hostilities involving Western European nations that once exercised much influence in the area. Also the relatively large attack by

Israel in October has intensified the basic differences between that nation and its Arab neighbors. All this instability has been heightened and, at times, manipulated by International Communism.

II

Russia's rulers have long sought to dominate the Middle East. That was true of the Czars and it is true of the Bolsheviks. The reasons are not hard to find. They do not affect Russia's security, for no one plans to use the Middle East as a base for aggression against Russia. Never for a moment has the United States entertained such a thought.

The Soviet Union has nothing whatsoever to fear from the United States in the Middle East, or anywhere else in the world, so long as its rulers do not themselves first resort to aggression.

That statement I make solemnly and emphatically.

Neither does Russia's desire to dominate the Middle East spring from its own economic interest in the area. Russia does not appreciably use or depend upon the Suez Canal. In 1955 Soviet traffic through the Canal represented only about three fourths of 1% of the total. The Soviets have no need for, and could provide no market for, the petroleum resources which constitute the principal natural wealth of the area. Indeed, the Soviet Union is a substantial exporter of petroleum products.

The reason for Russia's interest in the Middle East is solely that of power politics. Considering her announced purpose of Communizing the world, it is easy to understand her hope of dominating the Middle East.

This region has always been the crossroads of the continents of the Eastern Hemisphere. The Suez Canal enables the nations of Asia and Europe to carry on the commerce that is essential if these countries are to maintain well-rounded and prosperous economies. The Middle East provides a gateway between Eurasia and Africa.

It contains about two thirds of the presently known oil deposits of the world and it normally supplies the petroleum needs of many nations of Europe, Asia and Africa. The nations of Europe are peculiarly dependent upon this supply, and this dependency relates to transportation as well as to production! This has been vividly demonstrated since the closing of the Suez Canal and some of the pipelines. Alternate ways of transportation and, indeed, alternate sources of power can, if necessary, be developed. But these cannot be considered as early prospects.

These things stress the immense importance of the Middle East. If the nations of that area should lose their independence, if they were dominated by alien forces hostile to freedom, that would be both a tragedy for the area and for many other free nations whose economic life would be subject to near strangulation. Western Europe would be endangered just as though there had been no Marshall Plan, no North Atlantic Treaty Organization. The free nations of Asia and Africa, too, would be placed in serious jeopardy. And the countries of the Middle East would lose the markets upon which their economies depend. All this would have the most adverse, if not disastrous, effect upon our own nation's economic life and political prospects.

Then there are other factors which transcend the material. The Middle East is the birthplace of three great religions—Moslem, Christian and Hebrew. Mecca and Jerusalem are more than places on the map. They symbolize religions which teach that the spirit has supremacy over matter and that the individual has a dignity and rights of which no despotic government can rightfully deprive him. It would be intolerable if the holy places of the Middle East should be subjected to a rule that glorifies atheistic materialism.

International Communism, of course, seeks to mask its purposes of domination by expressions of good will and by superficially attractive offers of political, economic and military aid. But any free nation, which is the subject of Soviet enticement, ought, in elementary wisdom, to look behind the mask.

Remember Estonia, Latvia and Lithuania! In 1939 the Soviet Union entered into mutual assistance pacts with these then independent countries; and the Soviet Foreign Minister, addressing the Extraordinary Fifth Session of the Supreme Soviet in October 1939, solemnly and publicly declared that "we stand for the scrupulous and punctilious observance of the pacts on the basis of complete reciprocity, and we declare that all the nonsensical talk about the Sovietization of the Baltic countries is only to the interest of our common enemies and of all anti-Soviet provocateurs." Yet in 1940, Estonia, Latvia and Lithuania were forcibly incorporated into the Soviet Union.

Soviet control of the satellite nations of Eastern Europe has been forcibly maintained in spite of solemn promises of a contrary intent, made during World War II.

Stalin's death [in 1953 (*ed.*)] brought hope that this pattern would change. And we read the pledge of the Warsaw Treaty of 1955 that the Soviet Union would follow in satellite countries "the principles of mutual respect for their independence and sovereignty and non-interference in domestic affairs." But we have just seen the subjugation of Hungary by naked armed force. In the aftermath of this Hungarian tragedy, world respect for and belief in Soviet promises have sunk to a new low. International Communism needs and seeks a recognizable success.

Thus, we have these simple and indisputable facts:

1. The Middle East, which has always been coveted by Russia, would today be prized more than ever by International Communism.
2. The Soviet rulers continue to show that they do not scruple to use any means to gain their ends.
3. The free nations of the Mid East need, and for the most part want, added strength to assure their continued independence.

III

Our thoughts naturally turn to the United Nations as a protector of small nations. Its charter gives it primary responsibility for the maintenance of international peace and security. Our country has given the United Nations its full support in relation to the hostilities in Hungary and in Egypt. The United Nations was able to bring about a cease-fire and withdrawal of hostile forces from Egypt because it was dealing with governments and peoples who had a decent respect for the opinions of mankind as reflected in the United Nations General Assembly. But in the case of Hungary, the situation was different. The Soviet Union vetoed action by the Security Council to require the withdrawal of Soviet armed forces from Hungary. And it has shown callous indifference to the recommendations, even the censure, of the General Assembly. The United Nations can always be helpful, but it cannot be a wholly dependable protector of freedom when the ambitions of the Soviet Union are involved.

IV

Under all the circumstances I have laid before you, a greater responsibility now devolves upon the United States. We have shown, so that none can doubt, our dedication to the principle that force shall not be used internationally for any aggressive purpose and that the integrity and independence of the nations of the Middle East should be inviolate. Seldom in history has a nation's dedication to principle been tested as severely as ours during recent weeks.

There is general recognition in the Middle East, as elsewhere, that the United States does not seek either political or economic domination over any other people. Our desire is a world environment of freedom, not servitude. On the other hand many, if not all, of the nations of the Middle East are aware of the danger that stems from International Communism and welcome closer cooperation with the United States to realize for themselves the United Nations goals of independence, economic well-being and spiritual growth.

If the Middle East is to continue its geographic role of uniting rather than separating East and West; if its vast economic resources are to serve the well-being of the peoples there, as well as that of others; and if its cultures and religions and their shrines are to be preserved for the uplifting of the spirits of the peoples, then the United States must make more evident its willingness to support the independence of the freedom-loving nations of the area.

V

Under these circumstances I deem it necessary to seek the cooperation of the Congress. Only with that cooperation can we give the reassurance needed to deter aggression, to give courage and confidence to those who are dedicated to freedom and thus prevent a chain of events which would gravely endanger all of the free world. . . .

VI

It is nothing new for the President and the Congress to join to recognize that the national integrity of other free nations is directly related to our own security.

We have joined to create and support the security system of the United Nations. We have reinforced the collective security system of the United Nations by a series of collective defense arrangements. Today we have security treaties with 42 other nations which recognize that our peace and security are intertwined. We have joined to take decisive action in relation to Greece and Turkey and in relation to Taiwan.

Thus, the United States through the joint action of the President and the Congress, or, in the case of treaties, the Senate, has manifested in many endangered areas its purpose to support free and independent governments—and peace—against external menace, notably the menace of International Communism. Thereby we have helped to maintain peace and security during a period of great danger. It is now essential that the United States should manifest through joint action of the President and the Congress our determination to assist those nations of the Mid East area, which desire that assistance.

The action which I propose would have the following features.

It would, first of all authorize the United States to cooperate with and assist any nation or group of nations in the general area of the Middle East in the development of economic strength dedicated to the maintenance of national independence.

It would, in the second place, authorize the Executive to undertake in the same region programs of military assistance and cooperation with any nation or group of nations which desires such aid.

It would, in the third place, authorize such assistance and cooperation to include the employment of the armed forces of the United States to secure and protect the territorial integrity and political independence of such nations, requesting such aid, against overt armed aggression from any nation controlled by International Communism. . . .

VII

This program will not solve all the problems of the Middle East. Neither does it represent the totality of our policies for the area. There are the problems of Palestine and relations between Israel and the Arab States, and the future of the Arab refugees. There is the problem of the future status of the Suez Canal. These difficulties are aggravated by International Communism, but they would exist quite apart from that threat. It is not the purpose of the legislation I propose to deal directly with these problems. The United Nations is actively concerning itself with all these matters, and we are supporting the United Nations. The United States has made clear, notably by Secretary Dulles' address of August 26, 1955, that we are willing to do much to assist the United Nations in solving the basic problems of Palestine.

The proposed legislation is primarily designed to deal with the possibility of Communist aggression, direct and indirect. There is imperative need that any lack of power in the area should be made good, not by external or alien force, but by the increased vigor and security of the independent nations of the area.

Experience shows that indirect aggression rarely if ever succeeds where there is reasonable security against direct aggression; where the government disposes of loyal security forces, and where economic conditions are such as not to make Communism seem an attractive alternative. The program I suggest deals with all three aspects of this matter and thus with the problem of indirect aggression.

It is my hope and belief that if our purpose be proclaimed, as proposed by the requested legislation, that very fact will serve to halt any contemplated aggression. We shall have heartened the patriots who are dedicated to the independence of their nations. They will not feel that they stand alone, under the menace of great power. And I should add that patriotism is, throughout this area, a powerful sentiment. It is true that fear sometimes perverts true patriotism into fanaticism and to the acceptance of dangerous enticements from without. But if that fear can be allayed, then the climate will be more favorable to the attainment of worthy national ambitions.

And as I have indicated, it will also be necessary for us to contribute economically to strengthen those countries, or groups of countries, which have governments manifestly dedicated to the preservation of independence and resistance to subversion. Such measures will provide the greatest insurance against Communist inroads. Words alone are not enough.

VIII

Let me refer again to the requested authority to employ the armed forces of the United States to assist to defend the territorial integrity and the political independence of any nation in the area against Communist armed aggression. Such authority would not be exercised except at the desire of the nation attacked. Beyond this it is my profound hope that this authority would never have to be exercised at all.

Nothing is more necessary to assure this than that our policy with respect to the defense of the area be promptly and clearly determined and declared. Thus the United Nations and all friendly governments, and indeed governments which are not friendly, will know where we stand.

If, contrary to my hope and expectation, a situation arose which called for the military application of the policy which I ask the Congress to join me in proclaiming, I would of course maintain hour-by-hour contact with the Congress if it were in session. And if the Congress were not in session, and if the situation had grave implications, I would, of course, at once call the Congress into special session.

In the situation now existing, the greatest risk, as is often the case, is that ambitious despots may miscalculate. If power-hungry Communists should either falsely or correctly estimate that the Middle East is inadequately defended, they might be tempted to use open measures of armed attack. If so, that would start a chain of circumstances which would almost surely involve the United States in military action. I am convinced that the best insurance against this dangerous contingency is to make clear now our readiness to cooperate fully and freely with our friends of the

Middle East in ways consonant with the purposes and principles of the United Nations. I intend promptly to send a special mission to the Middle East to explain the cooperation we are prepared to give.

IX

The policy which I outline involves certain burdens and indeed risks for the United States. Those who covet the area will not like what is proposed. Already, they are grossly distorting our purpose. However, before this Americans have seen our nation's vital interests and human freedom in jeopardy, and their fortitude and resolution have been equal to the crisis, regardless of hostile distortion of our words, motives and actions.

Indeed, the sacrifices of the American people in the cause of freedom have, even since the close of World War II, been measured in many billions of dollars and in thousands of the precious lives of our youth. These sacrifices, by which great areas of the world have been preserved to freedom, must not be thrown away.

In those momentous periods of the past, the President and the Congress have united, without partisanship, to serve the vital interests of the United States and of the free world.

The occasion has come for us to manifest again our national unity in support of freedom and to show our deep respect for the rights and independence of every nation—however great, however small. We seek not violence, but peace. To this purpose we must now devote our energies, our determination, ourselves.

SELECTION 25

The Decision to Build a Hydrogen Bomb: From United States Atomic Energy Commission "In the Matter of J. Robert Oppenheimer"

The second American policy designed for a long cold war was deterrence. In part, this policy was a companion of containment, inseparable from it. To block Communist expansion, the United States had to have the military power with which to react to any aggressive moves by the foe. Words alone would not suffice.

The aim of the United States was, however, to forestall seizures of territory. It was not, as in Korea, to force aggressors to give up what they had already seized. It followed, therefore, that the United States needed ready military power of such formidable proportions as to discourage, or deter, any attempt by the Communists to take territory by force.

By the 1950s, there was still another danger to be deterred. The Soviets, in 1949, had perfected an atomic bomb. They were hard at work on high-speed, long-range missiles which could carry nuclear warheads. Once these missiles existed, the Soviet Union would have the capacity to stage a surprise attack on the continental United States, causing horrendous destruction and loss of life. It was obviously not inconceivable that the Soviets would be tempted to launch such an attack. If it put the United States out of action, the whole world would be open to conquest. The United States needed retaliatory power of such proportions and character as to deter the Soviet government from chancing a surprise attack.

All this was evident. Well before the Korean conflict, American officials began to discuss means of building up the military power of the United States.

The issue that developed had to do with types of forces. To deter small grabs of territory, the United States would, it seemed, need ground forces with naval and air support. To deter a surprise attack, the nation would need large stockpiles of nuclear weapons, missiles, and missile defenses, if such could be developed. It would also need underground shelters and other provisions for civil defense. All these items were expensive—so expensive that they could not all be paid for. Choices had to be made.

One school in Washington held that emphasis should go to conventional forces and to research on missiles, missile defenses, and civil defense. A second school favored emphasis on development of the biggest possible bombs. The view of this second school was not only that the threat of surprise attack was greater than the threat of small-scale aggressions but that the ability of the United States to threaten obliteration of the Soviet homeland was the key to deterring aggressions of all kinds. Faced with such a threat, this second school held, the Kremlin would take no gambles.

Controversy between these two schools became acute late in 1949, just after the Soviet Union tested its first atomic bomb. A group of scientists led by Dr. Edward Teller became champions of a crash program to produce a bomb much more powerful than the atomic bomb—a hydrogen bomb, or H-bomb, also known as "the super." These scientists mobilized support in the armed forces and among members of the Joint Congressional Committee on Atomic Energy. Because of the expense of developing a hydrogen bomb, a decision in favor of this program would be a decision to give such a bomb priority over all other weapons and forces.

Those who preferred a different order of priority naturally opposed the proposal to develop the H-bomb. The leader of this group was another physicist, J. Robert Oppenheimer, the Chairman of the United States Atomic Energy Commission's General Advisory Committee. With support from other scientists and the Chairman of the AEC, David E. Lilienthal, Oppenheimer worked for a decision either not to build an H-bomb or to proceed slowly with it.

An additional consideration for Oppenheimer, and even more for some other scientists, was a moral question as to whether the United States should create a weapon of such awesome destructive power that it could conceivably wipe out all life on the planet.

In the end, in January, 1950, the President's decision was to proceed with a crash program for a hydrogen bomb. The new bomb was perfected in 1952. Only a year later, the Soviet Union revealed that it, too, had developed such a bomb.

Late in 1953, a brusque announcement was made from the White House that Oppenheimer's security clearance had been revoked. The reason was that Oppenheimer had been charged, on various counts, with being a "security risk."

Most of the counts had to do with incidents dating back to World War II, when Oppenheimer had been in charge of work on the original atomic bomb. At that time, he had continued social contacts with former university friends who were members of the Communist party. To shield one of them, he lied to a security officer. The friend had made a tentative approach about slipping classified information to the Russians, and Oppenheimer, though reporting the incident, minimized its significance and concealed the name of the individual.

It was clear, however, that the central charge against Oppenheimer was that he had opposed the H-bomb. Contesting the revocation of his clearance, Oppenheimer insisted on a full hearing before a Personnel Security Board. In the course of this extended hearing, a great deal was revealed about the concept of deterrence and about the debate within the government over the priorities to be assigned to nuclear and conventional weapons. The published transcript of the hearing, containing over a million words, is the most important single source presently available on the development of United States foreign and defense policy in the late 1940s. The material below is extracted from it.

On the Oppenheimer case, there are two lengthy studies: Joseph and Stewart Alsop, We Accuse *(1954) and C. P. Curtis,* The Oppenheimer Case *(1955). On the concept of deterrence and the issues involved in the Oppenheimer hearing, the best general study is S. P. Huntington,* The Common Defense *(1961). Other important or useful works are W. R. Schilling, P. Y. Hammond, and G. H. Snyder,* Strategy, Politics, and Defense Budgets *(1962); H. A. Kissinger's influential* Nuclear Weapons and Foreign Policy *(1957) and* The Necessity for Choice *(1961); Bernard Brodie,* Strategy in the Missile Age *(1959); W. W. Kaufmann (ed.),* Military Policy and National Security *(1956); C. J. Hitch and R. N. McKean,* The Economics of Defense in the Nuclear Age *(1960); and Walter Millis, H. C. Mansfield, and Harold Stein,* Arms and the State *(1958).*

The extracts below are from United States Atomic Energy Commission, Personnel Security Board, In the Matter of J. Robert Oppenheimer *(Government Printing Office, 1954), pages 17–19, 69–81, 242–243, 360–361, 399–404, 682–685, 714–717.*

LETTER FROM J. ROBERT OPPENHEIMER TO THE LOYALTY AND SECURITY REVIEW BOARD

. . . I need to turn now to an account of some of the measures which, as Chairman of the General Advisory Committee, and in other capacities, I advocated in the years since the war to increase the power of the United States and its allies to resist and defeat aggression.

The initial members of the General Advisory Committee were Conant, then president of Harvard, DuBridge, president of the California Institute of Technology, Fermi of the University of Chicago, Rabi of Columbia University, Rowe, vice president of the United Fruit Co., Seaborg of the University of California, Cyril Smith of the University of Chicago, and Worthington of the duPont Co. In 1948 Buckley, president of the Bell Telephone Laboratories, replaced Worthington; in the summer of 1950, Fermi, Rowe, and Seaborg were replaced by Libby of the University of Chicago, Murphree, president of Standard Oil Development Co., and Whitman of the Massachusetts Institute of Technology. Later Smith resigned and was succeeded by von Neumann of the Institute for Advanced Study.

In these years from early 1947 to mid-1952 the Committee met some 30 times and transmitted perhaps as many reports to the Commission. Formulation of policy and the management of the vast atomic-energy enterprises were responsibilities vested in the Commission itself. The General Advisory Committee had the role, which was fixed for it by statute, to advise the Commission. In that capacity we gave the Commission our views on questions which the Commission put before us, brought to the Commission's attention on our initiative technical matters of importance, and encouraged and supported the work of the several major installations of the Commission.

At one of our first meetings in 1947 we settled down to the job of forming our own views of the priorities. And while we agreed that the development of atomic power and the support and maintenance of a strong basic scientific activity in the fields relevant to it were important, we assigned top priority to the problem of atomic weapons. At that time we advised the Commission that one of its first jobs would be to convert Los Alamos into an active center for the development and improvement of atomic weapons. In 1945–46 during the period immediately following the war, the purposes of Los Alamos were multiple. It was the only laboratory in the United States that worked on atomic weapons. Los Alamos also had wide interests in scientific matters only indirectly related to the weapons program. We suggested that the Commission recognize as the laboratory's central and primary program the improvement and diversification of atomic weapons, and that this undertaking have a priority second to none. We suggested further that the Commission adopt administrative measures to make work at Los Alamos attractive, to assist the laboratory in recruiting, to help build up a strong theoretical division for guidance in atomic-weapons design, and to take advantage of the availability of the talented and brilliant consultants who had been members of the laboratory during the war. In close consultation with the director of the Los Alamos Laboratory, we encouraged and supported courses of development which would markedly increase the value of our stockpile in terms of the destructive power of our weapons, which would make the best use of existing stockpiles and those anticipated, which would provide weapons suitable for modern combat conditions and for varied forms of delivery and which in their cumulative effect would provide us with the great arsenal we now have.

We encouraged and supported the building up of the laboratory at Sandia whose principal purpose is the integration of the atomic warhead with the weapons system in which it is to be used. In agreement with the Los Alamos staff we took from the very first the view that no radical improvement in weapons development would be feasible without a program of weapons testing. We strongly supported such a program, helped Los Alamos to obtain authorization for conducting the tests it wished, and encouraged the establishment of a permanent weapons testing station and the adoption of a continental test station to facilitate this work. As time went on and the development of atomic weapons progressed, we stressed the importance of integrating our atomic warheads and the development of the carriers, aircraft, missiles, etc., which could make them of maximum effectiveness.

We observed that there were opportunities which needed to be explored for significantly increasing our arsenal of weapons both in numbers and in capabilities by means of production plant expansion and by ambitious programs to enlarge the sources of raw materials. It was not our function to formulate military requirements. We did regard it as our function to indicate that neither the magnitude of existing plant nor the mode of operation of existing plant which the Commission inherited, nor the limitation of raw materials to relatively well known and high-grade sources of ore, need limit the atomic-weapons program.

The four major expansion programs which were authorized during the 6 years 1946 to 1952 reflect the decision of the Commission, the Military Establishment, the Joint Congressional Committee and other agencies of the Government to go far beyond the production program that was inherited in 1946. And the powerful arsenal of atomic weapons and the variety of their forms adaptable to a diversity of military uses which is today a major source of our military strength in turn reflect the results of these decisions. The record of minutes, reports and other activities of the

General Advisory Committee will show that that body within the limits of its role as an advisory group played a significant, consistent, and unanimous part in encouraging and supporting and sometimes initiating the measures which are responsible for these results. . . .

During all the years that I served on the General Advisory Committee, however, its major preoccupation was with the production and perfection of atomic weapons. On the various recommendations which I have described, there were never, so far as I can remember, any significant divergences of opinion among the members of the committee. These recommendations, of course, constitute a very small sample of the committee's work, but a typical one.

In view of the controversies that have developed I have left the subject of the super and thermonuclear weapons for separate discussion—although our committee regarded this as a phase of the entire problem of weapons.

The super itself had a long history of consideration, beginning . . . with our initial studies in 1942 before Los Alamos was established. It continued to be the subject of study and research at Los Alamos throughout the war. After the war, Los Alamos itself was inevitably handicapped pending the enactment of necessary legislation for the atomic energy enterprise. With the MacMahon Act, the appointment of the Atomic Energy Commission and the General Advisory Committee, we in the committee had occasion at our early meetings in 1947 as well as in 1948 to discuss the subject. In that period the General Advisory Committee pointed out the still extremely unclear status of the problem from the technical standpoint, and urged encouragement of Los Alamos' efforts which were then directed toward modest exploration of the super and of thermonuclear systems. No serious controversy arose about the super until the Soviet explosion of an atomic bomb in the autumn of 1949.

Shortly after that event, in October 1949, the Atomic Energy Commission called a special session of the General Advisory Committee and asked us to consider and advise on two related questions: First, whether in view of the Soviet success the Commission's program was adequate, and if not, in what way it should be altered or increased; second, whether a crash program for the development of the super should be a part of any new program. The committee considered both questions, consulting various officials from the civil and military branches of the executive departments who would have been concerned, and reached conclusions which were communicated in a report to the Atomic Energy Commission in October 1949.

This report, in response to the first question that had been put to us, recommended a great number of measures that the Commission should take the increase in many ways our overall potential in weapons.

As to the super itself, the General Advisory Committee stated its unanimous opposition to the initiation by the United States of a crash program of the kind we had been asked to advise on. The report of that meeting, and the Secretary's notes, reflect the reasons which moved us to this conclusion. The annexes, in particular, which dealt more with political and policy considerations—the report proper was essentially technical in character—indicated differences in the views of members of the committee.

There were two annexes, one signed by Rabi and Fermi, the other by Conant, DuBridge, Smith, Rowe, Buckley and myself. (The ninth member of the committee, Seaborg, was abroad at the time.)

It would have been surprising if eight men considering a problem of extreme difficulty had each had precisely the same reasons for the conclusion in which we joined. But I think I am correct in asserting that the unanimous opposition we expressed to the crash program was based on the conviction, to which technical considerations as well as others contributed, that because of our overall situation at that time such a program might weaken rather than strengthen the position of the United States.

After the report was submitted to the Commission, it fell to me as chairman of the committee to explain our position on several occasions, once at a meeting of the Joint Congressional Committee on Atomic Energy. All this, however, took place prior to the decision by the President to proceed with the thermonuclear program.

This is the full story of my "opposition to the hydrogen bomb." It can be read in the records of the general transcript of my testimony before the joint congressional committee. It is a story which ended once and for all when in January 1950 the President announced his decision to proceed with the program. . . .

INTERROGATION OF DR. J. ROBERT OPPENHEIMER

Q: Now, would you tell the board something about what the committee actually did and begin with the first meeting?

A: My recollection is not clear as to what happened at the first and what happened at the second meeting, but I think this is perhaps not too important.

Very early in the game we thought it important to see whether we agreed or had any views at all about what the job of the Commission was. That, of course, was the Commission's business to determine, but the nature of the advice we gave would be dependent on that.

Without debate—I suppose with some melancholy—we concluded that the principal job of the Commission was to provide atomic weapons and good atomic weapons and many atomic weapons. This referred to atomic explosives. There are other things, like the atomic submarine that you can call an atomic weapon, but that is not what we had in mind.

We thought it had three other undertakings. We thought from the first that however remote civil power might be, the Commission had an absolute mandate to do everything it could economically and fruitfully to get on with the exploration of it. We thought that the Commission needed to respond to requests from the military and needed to alert the military establishment as to other applications of atomic energy of military use, of which propulsion, radiological warfare may be two examples. I won't attempt to evaluate them at this moment. . . .

I ought to say that, at our first meeting or two—I don't remember which—we brooded to a very considerable length about the thermonuclear program. I think the state of affairs was that not much was known about it; it had not been pursued very vigorously, and the unknowns overwhelmed the knowns.

Q: Just to recapitulate, the work in the thermonuclear field began when at Los Alamos?

A: The theoretical work began in Berkeley in the summer of 1942. The thermonuclear work was pursued merely as a theoretical job and not a development job. I think it would naturally have been somewhat intensified after the war with the view of making better measurements and better calculations because it was one of the interesting things to do.

The question we tried to ask ourselves was, Is there enough in this so that it ought to be pushed, or is it something that will be a distraction from the very immediate job of getting some weapons into the places where they are needed? Our answer was, I think, the following: That it was a very interesting problem or set of problems; that if work were going on at Los Alamos it would attract first-rate theoretical physicists and that the probability was that if people studied the thermonuclear problems at Los Alamos this would help the other program rather than hurt it because it would have the effect of increasing the brains and resources of the laboratory.

I will have to give you a complete review of the thermonuclear thing, but this was our initial recommendation.

We made a number of other observations relevant to the weapons program. I think one of the important ones—I am not sure we were the first to do it—was to keep asking the Commission not how many bombs should they make, because that was not our job—that was the job of the Military Establishment—but what were the real limits on how many they could make. How much material could be made available? Because, even though very great strides were made between 1947 and 1949 in the effectiveness with which material was used, there was still the question, Is the plant we have being used in the best possible way? Is there any inherent limitation on the plant? Is there enough raw material to sustain more plant? Is there any way in which you can relieve the limitation on raw material? Does this come back to a dollar limitation?

We addressed to the Commission from time to time questions intended to make clear to the Military Establishment that the requirements they were placing for atomic weapons were perhaps all that could be done right then with existing plant, raw material, operation, and bomb design, but by no means all that you could do if you really set to work on it.

The very large expansion programs which, of course, were not approved or formulated by us were certainly in part stimulated by the set of questions. There have been several expansion programs, and the whole atomic-weapons capacity has risen enormously. It took quite a while for this to take hold, but I think we started on it fairly early.

We were very concerned—I think probably this concern reached its maximum during the Korean war but started earlier and continued later—to adapting atomic warheads so that they could be used by a variety of carriers. This sometimes meant developing designs which were not, from the point of view of nuclear physics, the most perfect design, because you had to make a compromise in order to get the thing light or small or thin or whatever else it was that the carrier required. But experience showed that almost every improvement that you made in trying to make, let us say, a physically smaller atomic bomb was reflected in an improvement in the performance of the larger ones.

So, as this thing began to unroll, you could not really tell whether an effort aimed at making an atomic bomb that you could shoot out of a machinegun—to take an obviously unclassified example—would not also help the very large bombs which are the most efficient.

This had something to do with trying to bring together the enormous program . . . of missiles and the adaptation of weapons plans and missile plans. In this connection we welcomed the building up of Sandia . . . and tried generally to get as much coordination between the hardware side, the military application side, and the development of the atomic explosives themselves. I believe we were rather early in this preoccupation, which later became quite general.

We were concerned with flexibility and made a number of recommendations to the Commission which I need not spell out, the purpose of which was to be sure that if, during a war, you found out bombs you had were not exactly the one you wanted, you could do something about it. We felt that no amount of crystal-balling would make it certain that your stockpile corresponded to what you really needed in combat.

We suggested a variety of devices by which you could take advantage of what you learned in combat and come up quickly with what you needed.

I have listed these as some of the things about weapons. I have obviously left the hydrogen bomb for a separate item. . . .

Q: This brings us logically to the report on the H-bomb in the fall of 1949. . . . The story begins, I take it, with the Russian explosion of an atomic bomb on September 23, 1949?

A: I don't think the story begins there. I will go back a little bit. We can begin in the middle and go both backward and forward.

In September of 1949, I had a call from either General Nelson or Mr. Northrop. * * * [*sic*]

A little later I came down to Washington and met with a panel. I see it says in my summary that this was advisory to General Vandenberg.* I never was entirely clear as to who the panel was supposed to advise. . . . I think I had seen a good deal of the evidence before the panel was convened. In any case, we went over it very carefully and it was very clear to us that this was the real thing, and there was not any doubt about it. We so reported to whomever we were reporting. I think it was General Vandenberg. This was an atomic bomb, * * * [*sic*]

Yesterday you read evidence that in 1948 I was not thinking it would come so soon. * * * [*sic*]

I went over to the State Department where the question was being discussed—I was asked to go over by the Under Secretary—should this be

*[General Hoyt S. Vandenberg, Chief of Staff of the United States Air Force (*ed.*).]

publicly announced by the President and I gave some arguments in favor of that.

I don't know who finally resolved the matter, but the President did make a public statement. I was taken up to hearings before the Joint Congressional Committee. General Vandenberg certainly appeared and probably Admiral Hillenkoetter and other people whom I have forgotten. The committee was quite skeptical as to whether this was the real thing.

*Mr. Gray:** Is this the GAC?

The Witness: No, the Joint Congressional Committee. They were quite skeptical and I was not allowed to tell them the evidence. It was understood that this was to be kept secret. All I could do was just sound as serious and convinced and certain about it as I knew how. I think by the time we left the Joint Congressional Committee understood that this event had been real. I do remember Senator Vandenberg's asking me, and it was the last time I met with him—he became ill not long thereafter—"Doctor, what do we do now?" I should have said I don't know. I did say we should stay strong and healthy, and we make sure of our friends. This was immediately before the General Advisory Committee meeting.

The Committee had a whole lot of stuff on its docket. I have forgotten the details. There was a docket for us. We disposed of that business, and we talked about this event. At that point Dr. Rabi returned. He had been in Europe on the UNESCO Mission. He read about this in the newspapers. The President had announced it. He said very naturally, "I think we ought to decide what to do. I think we ought to advise the Commission." I opposed that. I think most all other members of the Committee did on the ground that it might take a little while to think what to do and also on the ground that many of the things to do would be done against a framework of governmental decision as to which at that point we could only speculate.

During October or late September, I think October, a good many people came to see me or called me or wrote me letters about the super program. I remember three things. Dr. Teller arrived. He told me that he thought this was the moment to go all out on the hydrogen-bomb program.

Mr. Gray: May I interrupt? I am sorry. This is following——

The Witness: Following the GAC meeting of September and prior to the meeting in October.

Mr. Gray: Yes.

The Witness: Dr. Bethe arrived. I think they were there together or their visits partly overlapped, although I am not sure. He was very worried about it. He will testify.

Q: About what?

A: About the thermonuclear program, whether it was right or wrong; what his relations to it should be. I assume he will testify to that better than I can. It was not clear to me what the right thing to do was.

Mr. Robb: †You say to you or to him?

*[Gordon Gray, Chairman of the AEC Personnel Security Board (*ed.*).]
†[Roger Robb, Counsel for the AEC (*ed.*).]

The Witness: To me. I had a communication. I can't find it as a letter, and I don't know whether it was a letter or phone call. It was from Dr. Conant. He said that this would be a very great mistake.

Q: What would be a great mistake?

A: To go all out with the super. Presumably he also will testify to this. He did not go into detail, but said if it ever came before the General Advisory Committee, he would certainly oppose it as folly.

The General Advisory Committee was called to meet in Washington, and met on two questions which were obviously related. The first was, was the Commission doing what it ought to be doing. Were there other things which it should now be undertaking in the light of the Soviet explosion.

The second was the special case of this; was it crash development, the most rapid possible development and construction of a super among the things that the Commission ought to be doing.

Now I have reviewed for you in other connections some of the earlier hydrogen-bomb tale. The work on it in the summer of 1942, when we were quite enthusiastic about the possibility, my report on this work to Bush, the wartime work in which there were 2 discoveries. 1 was very much casting doubt on the feasibility, and 1 which had a more encouraging quality with regard to the feasibility. Of the talks with General Groves in which he had indicated that this was not something to rush into after the war. Of the early postwar work, prior to the establishment of the Commission. Of our encouragement to the Commission and thus to Los Alamos and also directly to Los Alamos to study the problem and get on with it in 1947 and 1948.

The GAC record shows I think that there were some thermonuclear devices that we felt were feasible and sensible and encouraged. I believe this was in 1948. But that we made a technically disparaging remark about the super in 1948. This was the judgment we then had. I remember that before 1949 and the bomb, Dr. Teller had discussed with me the desirability of his going to Los Alamos and devoting himself to this problem. I encouraged him to do this. In fact, he later reminded me of that, that I encouraged him in strong terms to do it.

Now, the meetings on——

Q: The meeting of October 19?

A: The meeting of October 19, 1949. Have we the date right?

Mr. Robb: October 29.

The Witness: October 29. I think what we did was the following. We had a first meeting with the Commission at which they explained to us the double problem: What should they do and should they do this? We then consulted a number of people. * * * [*sic*]

We had consultations not with the Secretary of State, but with the head of the policy planning staff, who represented him, George Kennan, as to what he thought the Russians might be up to, and where our principal problems lay from the point of view of assessment of Russian behavior and Russian motives. We had consultations with the Military Establishment, General Bradley was there, Admiral Parsons, I think General Hull or General Kyes, head of the Weapons Systems Evaluation Committee, General Nichols, probably. I won't try to recall all. Also Mr. LeBaron.

Prior to this meeting there had been no great expression of interest on the part of the military in more powerful weapons. The atomic bomb had of course been stepped up some, but we had not been pressed to push that development as fast as possible. There had been no suggestion that very large weapons would be very useful. The pressure was all the other way; get as many as you can.

We discussed General Bradley's analysis of the effects of the Russian explosion, and what problems he faced and with the staff, of course.

Then we went into executive session. I believe I opened the session by asking Fermi to give an account of the technical state of affairs. He has always been interested in this possibility. I think it occurred to him very early that the high temperatures of a fission bomb might be usable in igniting lighter materials. He has also an extremely critical and clear head. I asked others to add to this. Then we went around the table and everybody said what he thought the issues were that were involved. There was a surprising unanimity—to me very surprising—that the United States ought not to take the initiative at that time in an all out program for the development of thermonuclear weapons.

Different people spoke in different ways. I don't know how available to you the actual record of this conversation is or even whether it fully exists. But there was not any difference of opinion in the final finding. I don't know whether this is the first thing we considered or whether we considered the Commission's other question first. I imagine we went back and forth between the two of them.

To the Commission's other question, were they doing enough, we answered no. Have you read this report, because if you have, my testimony about it will add nothing. . . .

Q: I think you better say what you recollect of it.

A: I recollect of it that the first part of the report contained a series of affirmative recommendations about what the Commission should do. I believe all of them were directed toward weapons expansion, weapons improvement and weapons diversification. Some of them involved the building of new types of plant which would give a freedom of choice with regard to weapons. Some of them involved just a stepping up of the amount. I don't think that this expressed satisfaction with the current level of the Commission effort.

On the super program itself, I attempted to give a description of what this weapon was, of what would have to go into it, and what we thought the design would be. I explained that the uncertainties in this game were very great, that one would not know whether one had it or not unless one had built it and tested it, and that realistically one would have to expect not one test, but perhaps more than one test. That this would have to be a program of design and testing. . . .

The first page of the page-and-a-half of the report on the super bomb is an account of what it is supposed to be, what has to be done in order to bring it about, and some semiquantitative notions of what it would take, what kind of damage it would do, and what kind of a program would be required. The essential point there is that as we then saw it, it was a weapon that you could not be sure of until you tried it out, and it is a problem of calculation and study, and then you went out in the proper place in the Pacific and found out whether it went bang and found out to what extent your ideas had been right and to what extent they had been wrong.

It is on the second page that we start talking about the extent of damage and the first paragraph is just a factual account of the kind of damage, the kind of carrier, and I believe I should not give it—I believe it is classified, even if it is not possibly entirely accurate.

I would like to state one conclusion which is that for anything but very large targets, this was not economical in terms of damage per dollar, and then even for large targets it was uncertain whether it would be economical in terms of damage per dollar. I am not claiming that this was good foresight, but I am just telling you what it says in here.

I am going to read two sentences:

> We all hope that by one means or another, the development of these weapons can be avoided. We are all reluctant to see the United States take the initiative in precipitating this development. We are all agreed that it would be wrong at the present moment to commit ourselves to an all-out effort towards its development.

This is the crux of it and it is a strong negative statement. We added to this some comments as to what might be declassified and what ought not to be declassified and held secret if any sort of a public statement were contemplated. If the President were going to say anything about it, there were some things we thought obvious and there would be no harm in mentioning them. Actually, the secret ones were out in the press before very long.

The phrase that you heard this morning, "We believe that the imaginative and concerted attack on the problem has a better than even chance of producing the weapon * * *"—I find that in this report, and in this report there is, therefore, no statement that it is unfeasible. There is a statement of uncertainty which I believed at the time was a good assessment. You would have found people who would have said this was too conservative, it could be done faster and more certainly, and you would find other people who would say that it could not be done at all; but the statement as read here, no member of the General Advisory Committee objected to, and I have heard very little objection to that as an assessment of the feasibility at that time.

This is the report itself, and there are parts of it which I think you should read but, for the record, there are parts that I cannot get into here. . . .

One important point to make is that lack of feasibility is not the ground on which we made our recommendations.

Another point I ought to make is that lack of economy, although alleged, is not the primary or only ground, the competition with fission weapons is obviously in our minds. The real reason, the weight, behind the report is, in my opinion, a failing of the existence of these weapons would be a disadvantageous thing. It says this over and over again.

I may read, which I am sure has no security value, from the so-called minority report, Fermi and Rabi.

> The fact that no limits exist to the destructiveness of this weapon makes it[s] very existence and the knowledge of its construction a danger to humanity as a whole. It is necessarily an evil thing considered in any light. For these reasons, we believe it important for the President of the United States to tell the American public and the world that we think it wrong on fundamental ethical principles to initiate the development of such a weapon.

In the report which got to be known as the majority report, which Conant wrote, DuBridge, Buckley and I signed, things are not quite so ethical and fundamental, but it says in the final paragraph: "In determining not to proceed to develop the super bomb, we see a unique opportunity of providing by example some limitations on the totality of war and thus of eliminating the fear and arousing the hope of mankind."

I think it is very clear that the objection was that we did not like the weapon, not that it couldn't be made.

Now, it is a matter of speculation whether, if we had before us at that time, if we had had the technical knowledge and inventiveness which we did have somewhat later, we would have taken a view of this kind. These are total views where you try to take into account how good the thing is, what the enemy is likely to do, what you can do with it, what the competition is, and the extent to which this is an inevitable step anyway.

My feeling about the delay in the hydrogen bomb, and I imagine you want to question me about it, is that if we had had good ideas in 1945, and had we wanted to, this object might have been in existence in 1947 or 1948, perhaps 1948. If we had had all of the good ideas in 1949, I suppose some little time might have been shaved off the development as it actually occurred. If we had not had good ideas in 1951, I do not think we would have it today. In other words, the question of delay is keyed in this case to the question of invention, and I think the record should show—it is known to you—that the principal inventor in all of this business was Teller, with many important contributions * * * [*sic*] other people, * * * [*sic*] It has not been quite a one-man show, but he has had some very, very good ideas, and they have kept coming. It is probably true that an idea of mine is embodied in all of these things. It is not very ingenious but it turned out to be very useful, and it was not enough to establish feasibility or have a decisive bearing on their feasibility.

The notion that the thermonuclear arms race was something that was in the interests of this country to avoid if it could was very clear to us in 1949. We may have been wrong. We thought it was something to avoid even if we could jump the gun by a couple of years, or even if we could outproduce the enemy, because we were infinitely more vulnerable and infinitely less likely to initiate the use of these weapons, and because the world in which great destruction has been done in all civilized parts of the world is a harder world for America to live with than it is for the Communists to live with. This is an idea which I believe is still right, but I think what was not clear to us then and what is clearer to me now is that it probably lay wholly beyond our power to prevent the Russians somehow from getting ahead with it. I think if we could have taken any action at that time which would have precluded their development of this weapon, it would have been a very good bet to take that, I am sure. I do not know enough about contemporary intelligence to say whether or not our actions have had any effect on theirs but you have ways of finding out about that.

I believe that their atomic effort was quite imitative and that made it quite natural for us to think that their thermonuclear work would be quite imitative and that we should not set the pace in this development. I am trying to explain what I thought and what I believe my friends thought. I am not arguing that this is right, but I am clear about one thing: if this affair could have been averted on the part of the Russians, I am quite clear that we would be in a safer world today by far.

Mr. Gray: Would you repeat that last sentence. I didn't quite get it.

The Witness: If the development by the enemy as well as by us of thermonuclear weapons could have been averted, I think we would be in a somewhat safer world today than we are. God knows, not entirely safe because atomic bombs are not jolly either. . . .

I think we have to keep strictly away from the technical questions. I do not think we want to argue technical questions here, and I do not think it is very meaningful for me to speculate as to how we would have responded had the technical picture at that time been more as it was later.

However, it is my judgment in these things that when you see something that is technically sweet, you go ahead and do it and you argue about what to do about it only after you have had your technical success. That is the way it was with the atomic bomb. I do not think anybody opposed making it; there were some debates about what to do with it after it was made. I cannot very well imagine if we had known in late 1949 what we got to know by early 1951 that the tone of our report would have been the same. You may ask other people how they feel about that. I am not at all sure they will concur; some will and some will not. . . .

Q: I hand you a copy of a letter dated October 21, 1949, bearing the typewritten signature Robert Oppenheimer, addressed to Dr. James B. Conant, president, Harvard University: "Dear Uncle Jim:" I ask you if you write that letter.

A: October 21, 1949?

Q: Yes, sir.

A: I would like to look it over.

Q: Certainly. That is why I handed it to you, Doctor. I want you to look it over carefully. Take your time.

A: I wrote this letter.

Q: You wrote that letter.

A: Can we read it in full?

Q: I am going to. You sent this letter on or about October 21, 1949.

A: I have no reason to doubt it.

Q: Doctor, in this letter as in the other, the classification officer has expurgated a few words which are indicated by brackets. Will you look at them now so you will know what they are when I read it?

A: Yes. Could we paraphrase this by saying for a number of applications of military importance?

Q: I will tell you what, Doctor. When I get to that point, I will stop and you paraphrase it, because you can paraphrase that sort of stuff better than I can.

> Dear Uncle Jim:
>
> We are exploring the possibilities for our talk with the President on October 30th. All members of the advisory committee will come to the meeting Saturday except Seaborg, who must be in Sweden, and whose general views we have in written form. Many of us will do some preliminary palavering on the 28th.
>
> There is one bit of background which I would like you to have before we meet. When we last spoke, you thought perhaps the reactor program offered the most decisive example of the need for policy clarification. I was inclined to think that the super might also be relevant. On the technical side, as far as I can tell, the super is not very different from what it was when we first spoke of it more than 7 years ago: a weapon of unknown design, cost, deliverability and military value. But a very great change has taken place in the climate of opinion. On the one hand, two experienced promoters have been at work, i.e., Ernest Lawrence and Edward Teller. The project has long been dear to Teller's heart; and Ernest has convinced himself that we must learn from Operation Joe that the Russians will soon do the super, and that we had better beat them to it.

What was Operation Joe, the Russian explosion?

A: Right. . . .

Q: Of September 1949?

A: Right.

Q: Continuing your letter: "On the technical side, he proposes to get some neutron producing heavy water reactors built; and to this, for a variety of reasons, I think we must say amen since"—now would you paraphrase?

A: There were three military applications other than the super which these reactors would serve.

Q: * * * [*sic*] and many other things will all profit by the availability of neutrons.

> But the real development has not been of a technical nature. Ernest spoke to Knowland and McMahon,* and to some at least of the joint chiefs. The joint congressional committee, having tried to find something tangible to chew on ever since September 23d, has at last found its answer. We must have a super, and we must have it fast. A subcommittee is heading west to investigate this problem at Los Alamos, and in Berkeley. The joint chiefs appear informally to have decided to give the development of the super over-

*[Senators William F. Knowland (R., Calif.) and Brien McMahon (D., Conn.) (*ed.*).]

riding priority, though no formal request has come through. The climate of opinion among the competent physicists also shows signs of shifting. Bethe, for instance, is seriously considering return on a full time basis; and so surely are some others. I have had long talks with Bradbury and Manley, and with Von Neumann. Bethe, Teller, McCormack, and LeBaron are all scheduled to turn up within the next 36 hours. I have agreed that if there is a conference on the super program at Los Alamos, I will make it my business to attend.

What concerns me is really not the technical problem. I am not sure the miserable thing will work, nor that it can be gotten to a target except by ox-cart. It seems likely to me even further to worsen the unbalance of our present war plans. What does worry me is that this thing appears to have caught the imagination, both of the congressional and of military people, as the answer to the problem posed by the Russian advance. It would be folly to oppose the exploration of this weapon. We have always known it had to be done; and it does have to be done, though it appears to be singularly proof against any form of experimental approach. But that we become committed to it as the way to save the country and the peace appears to me full of dangers.

We will be faced with all this at our meeting; and anything that we do or do not say to the President, will have to take it into consideration. I shall feel far more secure if you have had an opportunity to think about it. . . .

Q: Would you agree, Doctor, that your references to Dr. Lawrence and Dr. Teller and their enthusiasm for the super bomb, their work on the super bomb, that your references in this letter are a little bit belittling?

A: Dr. Lawrence came to Washington. He did not talk to the Commission. He went and talked to the joint congressional committee and to members of the Military Establishment. I think that deserves some belittling.

Q: So you would agree that your references to those men in this letter were belittling?

A: No. I pay my great respects to them as promoters. I don't think I did them justice.

Q: You used the word "promoters" in an invidious sense, didn't you?

A: I promoted lots of things in my time.

Q: Doctor, would you answer my question? When you use the word "promoters" you meant it to be in a slightly invidious sense, didn't you?

A: I have no idea.

Q: When you use the word now with reference to Lawrence and Teller, don't you intend it to be invidious?

A: No.

Q: You think that their work of promotion was admirable, is that right?

A: I think they did an admirable job of promotion.

Q: Do you think it was admirable that they were promoting this project?

A: I told you that I think that the methods—I don't believe Teller was involved, Lawrence promoted it—were not proper.

Q: You objected to them going to Knowland and McMahon?

A: I objected to their not going to the Commission.

Q: Knowland and McMahon, by that you meant Senator Knowland and Senator McMahon.

A: Of course. . . .

INTERROGATION OF GEORGE F. KENNAN

Q: When it came time for you to give the Secretary of State your views or your analysis of the problem, what did you report to him, and when was it approximately?

A: I reported to him approximately in the month of January, I would think around the middle of the month or shortly after.

Mr. Robb: 1950?

The Witness: 1950, yes. The gist of my own views was simply this: I felt that this Government was in no way in good position to make any great decisions with regard to either the international control of atomic energy or actually with regard to its own weapons program before it gained greater clarity in its own mind as to the purposes for which it was holding what were sometimes called the A, B, C, weapons in general. By that I am thinking of the weapons of mass destruction, the atomic, chemical, and so forth. It seemed to me that there was unclarity in the councils of our Government as to the reasons why we were cultivating and holding these weapons. The unclarity revolved around this question. Were we holding them only as a means of deterring other people from using them against us and retaliating against any such use of these weapons against us, or were we building them into our military establishment in such a way that we would indicate that we were going to be dependent upon them in any future war, and would have to use them, regardless of whether they were used against us first.

Q: Have we not taken the position that we would only use them for purposes of retaliation?

A: It is not my impression that we have, and it was not my impression at that time that there was any such determination in the councils of the United States Government.

On the other hand, if I remember correctly, I was able to cite statements that had been made by some of our high military leaders—I think both in the councils of this Government and in the NATO councils of Europe—which indicated very strongly that we were getting ourselves into a position where we would have to use these weapons as forward military weapons, regardless of whether they were used against us.

The point that I tried to emphasize to the Secretary of State related, of course, directly to the question of international control about which I had been asked. I told him that I thought we ought first to face this problem. It was my belief that we should hold these weapons only for purposes of retaliation and as a deterrent to their use against us. That anything else would get us into a race with these mass destruction weapons to which I could see no end, which I was afraid would distort the thinking of the public mind about problems of foreign policy and military policy in this country if it were permitted to proceed. So as I say, I favored the holding of these weapons only for purposes of retaliation and as a deterrent.

Whether that came out clearly in my report to the Secretary of State, I do not know, because that was not actually the question that was asked me. But I am sure it was implicit in what I said to the Secretary, and by the same token I think it was implicit that we ought really to make this other decision before we made decisions about the hydrogen bomb.

Q: Mr. Kennan, you will have to explain a little more to me at least what you conceived to be the relevance of clarification of this question to the question of whether or not we ought to proceed with making hydrogen bombs.

A: Yes. As I saw it, the relevance was this. If you were asked, should we or should we not proceed to the development of a whole new range of more powerful atomic weapons which was involved in the hydrogen bomb decision, you had to ask yourself how much do we need the weapons of mass destruction in general. That is the first question that had to be faced, because if you already had enough, perhaps you didn't need the hydrogen bomb at all. I could not see how you could answer the question of how much do we need until you had answered the question of why are we holding these weapons anyway, and what do we expect to accomplish with them.

If you were holding them as deterrents and for purposes of retaliation, really for purposes in order that they might not be used against you, then what you needed was merely enough to make it an unprofitable and unpromising undertaking on the part of anyone else, the Russians in particular, to use these weapons against us.

If on the other hand you were going to regard them as an integral part of forward American military planning and something on which we would be dependent in a future war, regardless of the circumstances of the origin of that war, then you came up with a different answer or you might come up with a different one in regard to the hydrogen bomb.

Q: So the point you are making is not that you were opposed to the hydrogen bomb necessarily, but only it seemed to you that it was essential first that this other subsidiary question should be clarified?

A: That is correct. I must say that personally while I was not competent to form a finished opinion on this and was never called upon to do so, I had not at that time seen the evidence that what we already held in the old and regular atomic bomb, if I may speak of it that way, was not enough to make it a fruitless undertaking from the standpoint of Soviet policy to launch a war on us with these weapons.

In other words, I considered the burden of proof to rest on that point. It seemed to me you would have to prove that we could not do the job with the weapons we already had, and to my knowledge that was never demonstrated to me at the time. Perhaps the answer might have been one thing or the other, but I had never seen the proof. . . .

INTERROGATION OF DAVID E. LILIENTHAL

Q: . . . I want to turn . . . to the situation as it existed after the Soviet atomic explosion, I think, of September 23, 1949. Would you tell us very briefly what our defense posture was as far as you can in unclassified terms with respect to the AEC's function and responsibility?

A: I will try to summarize this. The details of course are available to the board. . . .

The situation on September 23, which I believe is the date which President Truman announced the atomic explosion in Russia, as far as the AEC's program for weapons was concerned was something like this:

A program for the expansion of weapon production had been under study by the Military Establishment and the AEC over a period of months, probably beginning in February, and continuing through October 19, when President Truman formally approved this expansion program. This was encouraged by the GAC, and it was certainly a program that included additions to Oak Ridge and elsewhere, additions to Los Alamos and so on.

As to the improvement of weapons, here too there was a program which had been recommended by our Division of Military Application, had been approved and amended in some ways by the General Advisory Committee, by Los Alamos Laboratory, and it had a number of parts. These are rather important. These are found in these records, but I think it might serve to spell it out a little in lay terms. . . .

This weapons improvement program which was in effect—that is, the program had been approved or was actually in operation at Los Alamos and Sandia—was of several parts. Among these parts were a program for an increase in the numbers of atomic weapons through new design, an increase in the numbers of weapons through greater material production, an increase in the numbers of weapons through programs relating to raw materials, a program for increasing the destructive power of the weapons over those at Hiroshima and Nagasaki by a substantial factor, an improvement in the combat usefulness of the weapons by reengineering these weapons.

This led to the establishment of the Sandia operation and my soliciting the aid of the Bell Laboratories and the Western Electric on behalf of the Commission and the President to take over that operation in order that we might have weapons that had field usefulness, as distinguished from weapons that it almost took a Ph.D. in physics to handle, instead of a sergeant.

This is an important story and I only refer to it. The details, I am sure, are in the file.

An improvement in problems associated with delivery. This concerns size and weight and other matters of that kind of great importance. And finally, plans for greatly stepped up power of weapons by a very large factor, by certain innovations of design that had been worked on for some time, but were at the point where a program for building such weapons was just around the corner.

The product of this stepped up program for this greatly heightened destructive power of weapons would produce a weapon which was so much larger than the original weapons that we were advised that one such bomb would take out almost any target in the world, and two would take out any target.

. . . President Eisenhower in his United Nations speech on December 8 spoke of an attainment of a fission bomb—an A-bomb type—of 25 times the power of the original bombs with an energy release of the order of 500,000 tons of TNT equivalent. Whether that bomb is the bomb that was recommended by the GAC and the Division of Military Applications, and was part of the program at the time of the Russian A-bomb, I don't know. I state these facts, and I am assuming that this must be the fission bomb that was planned at that time.

That was the program roughly that we had at the time of September 23. I ought also to say that to the best of my knowledge the Commission had not received, nor had any of the divisions any request from the Defense Establishment for a weapon of unlimited size or destructive power, nor any request for a weapon of greater destructive power than the stepped up fission bomb to which I have just referred. That the Commission did not have a military evaluation at that time of the military value of a hydrogen bomb or a bomb of size without definite limit. That it had not before it no diplomatic or political evaluation of the effect of such a weapon pro or con, on such matters of the cold war, or the effect on our alliances and other diplomatic and international relations.

The board is familiar with the fact, and the records are here that the Commission asked the GAC to assemble, especially to consider certain questions affecting the Commission's duties that grew out of the announcement about the Russians' success with an A-bomb. Those questions roughly seemed to me something like this:

Is this program that we now have and have under way adequate to fulfill our duties? If not, what modification or what alternative course or alternative courses should be pursued? Among those alternative courses, should an all-out H-bomb program be instituted in order that we should adequately and properly fulfill our duty? . . .

Q: Will you tell us what happened thereafter?

A: There was one other thing. It is known to the board, but I want to make sure that in my remarks I take full cognizance of it, that the occasion for the precise occasion for considering the H-bomb either as a part of the program or a supplement to the existing program was a memorandum from our fellow Commissioner, Mr. Strauss,* dated about October 5 or 6, which is in the record. All of these documents added together represented the frame of the Commission's thinking at the time of the meeting on October 29th and 30th.

Q: Now, what happened at that meeting, as far as you can recall, or whatever impressed you about it.

A: Some of the Commissioners, perhaps all, but certainly I, attended the opening meeting or part of the opening meeting of the GAC. It was their meeting. Their practice was to ask us in as observers or to ask us questions. If we wanted to meet with them as our meeting, we would ask them to come to the Commission's room. In this way it preserved the identity of the meeting being as either a GAC meeting or AEC meeting. This was a GAC meeting.

I opened the conference by repeating as well as I can recall the substance of the paragraph in the letter that has been read into the record indicating

*[Lewis L. Strauss, Chairman of the AEC under Eisenhower and reportedly the man who initiated the move to revoke Oppenheimer's clearance (*ed.*).]

that we wanted their advice on whether our program as it had been approved, the present program, the program in planning to which I referred, met the requirements of our duty, and if not, how it should be supplemented and in particular should it be supplemented by an all-out program on the H-bomb as proposed by Commissioner Strauss.

The GAC's report is in your record. The points that most impressed me were two. One, the technical considerations that were discussed in the time while I was in their meeting which did not by any means include the whole meeting. Most of their meeting was in executive session, but there were considerations of diversions of materials to another program, the H-bomb program, which was problematical, discussion of whether such a weapon as the hydrogen, deuterium, tritium, et cetera, weapon that was then under consideration would improve our retaliatory strength sufficiently to justify the risks involved in diversion of materials and other related points.

There was discussion of whether a weapon larger than the 500,000 tons fission weapon that was in the works, half a million tons of TNT equivalent, whether a weapon larger than that didn't go beyond the point of diminishing returns in terms of the destruction it would effect.

There was a consideration of whether our program then was not the best way to use the materials and the manpower that we had. These technical considerations impressed me very much.

The second point that impressed me a good deal was one I had thought about myself and others, of course, and that was a consensus among a number of GAC members that launching of a weapon larger than the stepped up weapon would not give us a false impression of security and illusion of security that we had gained a decisive or absolute weapon, an illusion of security which a number of the GAC members attributed to our possession of the A-bomb, an overvaluation of the security that could be secured from large bombs alone as distinguished from a balanced military establishment.

In any case the GAC's views and the AEC's views were submitted to the President in writing on November 9. They are of course in this record.

Q: They may be in the files and not in this record.

A: Yes, they are in the files. In this report we tried to make the President's job as easy as possible by agreeing on as many things as we could about the facts. This was largely a staff paper prepared which we approved. There is agreement in this report which you will find that went to the President on a number of things——

Mr. Robb: This is the report that went to the President from the Commission?

The Witness: Yes.

Mr. Robb: Not the GAC report.

The Witness: No. The GAC report was included in it. The Commission's report began with an agreement, "Mr. President, we are in agreement completely on a number of the basic facts about this situation."

Mr. Robb: Excuse me for interrupting.

The Witness: I am sure this is a document if it is relevant is not so long that the board may not read it. It is a classified report, of course.

Then we recognize, that is, the AEC, that this is not a question which the AEC could decide. This is a question for the President. But we do indicate what our views are. Mr. Strauss indicated, as indicated earlier, for an all out program. Three of us, Commissioners Pike, Smyth, and myself, said in one sentence we are not for this program—we are not at this time, I think are the words that are used—and Mr. Dean had a position which I think might be described as not quite at this time.

There was a preliminary thing that ought to be gone through. This is spelled out in his own words in the report, and I won't take the time to review it if you wish me to.

Just as an individual, if I may say so, I don't conceive that the question to which I am to address myself is the wisdom or unwisdom of either of these courses. At that time this represented the best judgment that each of us could summon to this question prior to the consultations which took after this at which time I had another chance to look at the problem in the light of the State and Defense Department views.

Q: I think it might be of some interest to know to what extent the Commissioners and the Commission were relying on the GAC report. Also I am going to ask you about the National Security Council, or perhaps you will come to that in your testimony directly, to what extent that relied on the GAC report.

A: In this case I can only speak for myself. The other Commissioners either have or will indicate the extent to which they relied on the GAC. It was my view that technical considerations advanced by the GAC in the first part of the report which deals with technical matters was very persuasive. I recognized I was a layman but these were men of great competence, and the things that they said were most persuasive to me. They included in their report statements about matters that were not technical but which they asserted were related to technical considerations, strongly planted, or expressions of that kind.

Some of these impressed me, one of them particularly, that there was a point of diminishing returns, that to announce publicly as apparently it was necessary, the building of a weapon of almost unlimited size would be in conflict—would put us in the eyes of our friends and potential friends in an unfavorable light without compensating advantages to us, and similar considerations of that kind.

Some of the members expressed themselves in various ways and which seemed to me to have some validity. In my first report of views to the President I laid considerable stress on that. Also on the concern I had then which was increased a great deal after I served on the committee with the State Department and Defense Department to which we were relying almost entirely upon atomic weapons, upon large weapons.

That brings me then to the final stage in my own participation in this.

On November 19, that is 10 days after this report of the AEC and the views of its individual Commissioners, the GAC report, and the views of its members, went to the President, the President created a subcommittee of the National Security Council to advise him further on this matter. That committee consisted of the Secretary of State, Mr. Acheson, the Secretary of Defense, Mr. Johnson, and myself. I would say that I had resigned and my resignation had been approved by the President early in November to be effective, I think, the first of December, but he asked me to stay on until this particular chore was finished.

May I interrupt to say that the report of November 9 as the record will show or the file will show did not contain as of that date I think the views of Mr. Smyth and Mr. Strauss, except as to their conclusions. They sent their memoranda a few days later or some time later, in any case. I consider that the November 9 report supplemented by these subsequently filed statements as the views of the AEC.

Returning then to the National Security Council subcommittee, this subcommittee was set up by a letter from the President to the members of the subcommittee, which is in the file, that I examined yesterday, and therefore is available to the members of the board. It set up the considerations the President wanted weighed. It began a series of staff studies and consultations, recognizing that the issue was not really an AEC issue but a broad issue, as broad as the powers and the functions of the Chief Magistrate himself.

We had meetings of this kind. I met along with Commissioner Smyth, whom I asked to accompany me, because he was a scientist, and a technical man, as well as a member of the Commission, and we met with General Bradley and others of the Military Establishment. I should say that what impressed me most in this consultation was later set out in the argument I sought to make to the National Security Council and that was that General Bradley stated rather flatly that they had no reserve except the A-bomb in the event of aggression against us any place in the world. Later General Bradley stated this publicly in a speech in Chicago in November before the Executives Club, I believe. It was harrowing experience to me to be told this, and it made a great impression on me in this respect. Right or wrong, this was the reaction I had. We had, it seemed to me, falsely relied upon the security of simply a stockpile of A-bombs, that we had impoverished our Military Establishment—this was the period of an economy drive—we were closing military establishments. Instead of drafting boys, we were reversing the process. We were bringing our national budget away down. This seemed to me really quite harassing in the light of the fact that trouble might break out anywhere and as indeed it did break out in June in Korea at which time, of course, our reliance on the atomic bomb was certainly not a sufficient one. . . .

INTERROGATION OF MAJOR GENERAL ROSCOE C. WILSON, USAF

Q: General, I think it would be helpful to the board if you could give us in your own way something of the history of the position of the military and the Air Force on this matter. You may of course refer to notes to refresh your recollection.

A: I find it a little difficult to pinpoint some of these things. For instance, I am aware of a meeting at Los Alamos which had been requested by the scientists to discuss matters of military interest. I remember at that meeting General LeMay was asked what size bomb do you want. There had been a great deal of discussion about smaller bombs.

* * * * * * * [*sic*]

I have a lot of this sort of information in my hand, and I am embarrassed that I can't put dates to it. But I do have a few dates.

I have a statement that I found in a document marked top secret, sir, but the statement itself is not top secret. This is a little confusing to me, but it does indicate—I think it is safe to say it—that in 1948 both the Research and Development Board, and the Joint Chiefs of Staff had expressed an interest in continuing research on the thermonuclear weapon. This is the first written statement I can find in my own records—in 1948.

On September 23, 1949, we had the announcement of the Russian A-bomb, and that I really think sparked off the military interest in this larger weapon.

In the early part of October, Drs. Bradbury and Lawrence visited the Armed Forces Special Weapons project, where they talked to General Nichols and at the same time Dr. Edward Teller visited the Air Force, where they talked to a group at which I was present on the possibilities of a thermonuclear weapon. They urged that the military express its interest in the development of this weapon. . . .

On October 13 of 1949—and I am sure as a result of the urging of Dr. Bradbury and Dr. Lawrence—General Nichols, who was of course the subordinate of General Vandenberg, went to General Vandenberg with General Everest of the Air Force, and urged General Vandenberg as the No. 1 bomber man to express again the military's interest in a large weapon.

General Vandenberg directed Nichols and Everest to express his point of view to the Joint Chiefs of Staff that afternoon, since Vandenberg was not going to be present at that meeting. This they did.

On October 14, 1949, the Joint Chiefs met with the joint congressional committee on Atomic Energy, where General Vandenberg, speaking for the Joint Chiefs, strongly urged the development of this thermonuclear weapon. I have a copy of the excerpts of the notes of the meeting covering General Vandenberg's statement if the committee wishes it to be read.

Mr. Robb: I might say, Mr. Chairman, that has been released by formal action of the joint committee, confirmed to General Nichols by letter which we received this morning.

Mr. Gray: You may read it.

The Witness:

> Page 1792. One of the things which the military is preeminently concerned with as the result of the early acquisition of the bomb by Russia is its great desire that the Commission reemphasize and even accentuate the development work on the so-called super bomb. General Vandenberg discussed this subject briefly and stated that it was the military point of view that the super bomb should be pushed to completion as soon as possible, and that the General Staff had so recommended. In fact, his words were, "We have built a fire under the proper parties," which immediately brought forth the comment, who are the right parties? General Vandenberg replied that it was being handled through the Military Liaison Committee. He further stated

that having the super weapon would place the United States in the superior position that it had enjoyed up to the end of September 1949 by having exclusive possession of the weapon. There followed a series of questions, somewhat of a technical nature about the super weapon, which General Nichols answered for the Chiefs of Staff. He stated that it was the opinion of the scientists that the possibility of a successful super weapon is about the same as was the possibility of developing the first atomic weapon at the 1941–42 stage of development. He stated that the military fears that now the Russians have a regular atomic weapon, they may be pushing for the super weapon, and conceivably might succeed prior to success in this country of the same project. . . .

On October 27, there was a joint meeting of the Atomic Energy Commission and the Military Liaison Committee, at which the Commission announced that it had asked the General Advisory Committee to consider the super weapon in the light of recent developments. Then of course on the 28th and 29th of October was the meeting of the GAC.

On November 8, 1949, the MLC at its meeting heard a report from the Secretary that in accordance with the directive to reconvene the long-range objectives panel, he had been determining the availability of membership of the panel, and that he had discussed the panel with Dr. Oppenheimer on the 29th of October, and that Dr. Oppenheimer agreed that the panel should meet but "felt strongly that this should not be done until a great deal more information was available, probably not before February of 1950."

November 9, 1949, is the letter from the AEC to the President. . . .

November 19 was the letter from the President to Admiral Souers of the National Security Council, and during this period a military committee or subcommittee was set up to advise Admiral Souers in determining the position on the thermonuclear development. This was a committee composed of General Nichols, Admiral Hill, and General Norstad of the Air Force.

On the 13th of January 1950 there is a letter to the Secretary of Defense from General Bradley in which the military views are set out. I do not have that document. I have a hazy recollection of what might have been in it, sir. I do know that it expressed concern lest the Russians come up with this bomb before the United States did, and the feeling that this situation would be intolerable, since it would reverse the advantage we had had in this country prior to the Russian A-bomb explosion.

The rest of my notes are to the effect that in February the Air Force announced that it had undertaken the development of an aircraft to carry a weapon of this sort, and a program which it was coordinating with the AEC.

On February 18—and I would like to say that my memory of this date is not certain—I have noted February 18, 1950, to the best of my knowledge, the long-range objectives panel was completed and submitted to the Committee on Atomic Energy.

Q: Can you tell us about that report, General?

A: This panel was composed of a group of military people, of which I was one, and the chairman was Dr. Oppenheimer. Another member was

Dr. Bacher, and another Dr. Luis Alvarez. The panel contained some conservative statements on the possibility or the feasibility of an early production of a thermonuclear weapon. These reservations were made on technical grounds. They were simply not challengeable by the military. They did, however, cause some concern in the military.

It is hard for me to explain this, except to say that most of us have an almost extravagant admiration for Dr. Oppenheimer and Dr. Bacher as physicists, and we simply would not challenge any technical judgment that they might make. But I must confess, and I find this exceedingly embarrassing, sir, that as a result of this panel and other actions that had taken place in the Committee on Atomic Energy, that I felt compelled to go the Director of Intelligence to express my concern over what I felt was a pattern of action that was simply not helpful to national defense.

Q: Action by whom?

A: By Dr. Oppenheimer.

Q: Would you explain what that pattern was?

A: I would like first to say that I am not talking about loyalty. I want this clearly understood. If I may, I would like to say that this is a matter of my judgment versus Dr. Oppenheimer's judgment. This is a little embarrassing to me, too. But Dr. Oppenheimer was dealing in technical fields and I was dealing in other fields, and I am talking about an overall result of these actions.

First, I would like to say, sir, that I am a dedicated airman. I believe in a concept which I am going to have to tell you or my testimony doesn't make sense.

The U. S. S. R. in the airman's view is a land power. It is practically independent of the rest of the world. I feel that it could exist for a long time without sea communications. Therefore, it is really not vulnerable to attack by sea. Furthermore, it has a tremendous store of manpower. If you can imagine such a force, it could probably put 300 to 500 divisions in the field, certainly far more than this country could put into the field. It is bordered by satellite countries upon whom would be expended the first fury of any land assault that would be launched against Russia, and it has its historical distance and climate. So my feeling is that it is relatively invulnerable to land attack.

Russia is the base of international communism. My feeling is that the masters in the Kremlin cannot risk the loss of their base. This base is vulnerable only to attack by air power. I don't propose for a moment to say that only air power should be employed in case of a war with Russia, but I say what strategy is established should be centered around air power.

I further believe that whereas air power might be effective with ordinary weapons, that the chances of success against Russia with atomic weapons or nuclear weapons are far, far greater.

It is against this thinking that I have to judge Dr. Oppenheimer's judgments. Once again, his judgments were based upon technical matters. It is the pattern I am talking about.

I have jotted down from my own memory some of these things that worried me.

First was my awareness of the fact that Dr. Oppenheimer was interested in what I call the internationalizing of atomic energy, this at a time when the United States had a monopoly, and in which many people, including myself, believed that the A-bomb in the hands of the United States with an Air Force capable of using it was probably the greatest deterrent to further Russian aggression. This was a concern.

* * * * * * * [*sic*]

To do this the Air Force felt that it required quite an elaborate system of devices. Some were relatively simple to produce, some of them were exceedingly difficult to produce, and some of them were very costly. Dr. Oppenheimer was not enthusiastic about 2 out of 3 of these devices or systems. I do not challenge his technical judgment in these matters, but the overall effect was to deny to the Air Force the mechanism which we felt was essential to determine when this bomb went off. In our judgment, this was one of the critical dates, or would be at that time, for developing our national-defense policy.

Dr. Oppenheimer also opposed the nuclear-powered aircraft. His opposition was based on technical judgment. I don't challenge his technical judgment, but at the same time he felt less strongly opposed to the nuclear-powered ships. The Air Force feeling was that at least the same energy should be devoted to both projects.

* * * * * * * [*sic*]

The approach to the thermonuclear weapons also caused some concern. Dr. Oppenheimer, as far as I know, had technical objections, or, let me say, approached this conservatism for technical reasons, more conservatism than the Air Force would have liked.

The sum total of this, to my mind, was adding up that we were not exploiting the full military potential in this field. Once again it was a matter of judgment. I would like to say that the fact that I admire Dr. Oppenheimer so much, the fact that he is such a brilliant man, the fact that he has such a command of the English language, has such national prestige, and such power of persuasion, only made me nervous, because I felt if this was so it would not be to the interest of the United States, in my judgment. It was for that reason that I went to the Director of Intelligence to say that I felt unhappy.

Mr. Robb: That is all I care to ask. Thank you, General. . . .

INTERROGATION OF DR. EDWARD TELLER

Q: Doctor, it has been suggested here that the ultimate success on the thermonuclear was the result of a brilliant discovery or invention by you, and that might or might not have taken 5 or 10 years. What can you say about that?

A: I can say about it this. If I want to walk from here to that corner of the room, and you ask me how long it takes to get there, it depends all on what speed I am walking with and in what direction. If I start in that direction I will never get there, probably. It so happened that very few people gave any serious thought in this country to the development of the thermonuclear bomb. This was due to the fact that during the war we were much too busy with things that had to be done immediately in order that it should be effective during the war, and therefore not much time was left over.

After the war the people who stayed in Los Alamos, few and discouraged as they were, had their hands full in keeping the laboratory alive, keeping up even the knowledge of how to work on the simple fission weapons. The rest of the scientists were, I think, equally much too busy trying to be very sure not to get into an armament race, and arguing why to continue the direction in which we had been going due to the war would be completely wrong. I think that it was neither a great achievement nor a brilliant one. It just had to be done. I must say it was not completely easy. There were some pitfalls. But I do believe that if the original plan in Los Alamos, namely, that the laboratory with such excellent people like Fermi and Bethe and others, would have gone after the problem, probably some of these people would have had either the same brilliant idea or another one much sooner.

In that case I think we would have had the bomb in 1947. I do not believe that it was a particularly difficult thing as scientific discoveries go. I do not think that we should now feel that we have a safety as compared to the Russians, and think it was just necessary that somebody should be looking and looking with some intensity and some conviction that there is also something there.

Q: Is this a fair summary——

A: May I perhaps say that this again is an attempt at appreciating or evaluating a situation, and I may be of course quite wrong, because this is clearly not a matter of fact but a matter of opinion.

Q: Is this a fair summary of your opinion, Doctor, that if you don't seek, you don't find?

A: Certainly.

Q: Do you recall when the Russians exploded their first bomb in September 1949? Do you recall that event?

A: Certainly.

Q: Will you tell the board whether or not shortly thereafter you had a conversation with Dr. Oppenheimer about the thermonuclear or about what activity should be undertaken to meet the Russian advance?

A: I remember two such conversations. One was in the fall and necessarily superficial. That was just a very few hours after I heard, returning from a trip abroad, that the Russians had exploded an A-bomb. I called up Oppenheimer who happened to be in Washington, as I was at that time, and I asked him for advice, and this time I remember his advice literally. It was, "Keep your shirt on."

Perhaps I might mention that my mind did not immediately turn in the direction of working on the thermonuclear bomb. I had by that time quite thoroughly accepted the idea that with the reduced personnel it was much too difficult an undertaking. I perhaps should mention, and I think it will clear the picture, that a few months before the Russian explosion I agreed to rejoin Los Alamos for the period of 1 year on leave of absence from the University of Chicago.

I should also mention that prior to that Oppenheimer had talked to me and encouraged me to go back to Los Alamos, and help in the work there. I also went back to Los Alamos with the understanding and with the expectation that I shall just help along in their normal program in which some very incipient phases of the thermonuclear work was included, but nothing on a very serious scale.

I was quite prepared to contribute mostly in the direction of the fission weapons. At the time when I returned from this short trip abroad, and was very much disturbed about the Russian bomb, I was looking around for ways in which we could more successfully speed up our work and only after several weeks of discussion did I come to the conclusion that no matter what the odds seemed to be, we must at this time—I at least must at this time—put my full attention to the thermonuclear program.

I also felt that this was much too big an undertaking and I was just very scared of it. I was looking around for some of the old crew to come out and participate in this work. Actually if anyone wanted to head this enterprise, one of the people whom I went to visit, in fact the only one where I had very strong hopes, was Hans Bethe.

Q: About when was this, Doctor?

A: To the best of my recollection it was the end of October.

Q: 1949?

A: Right. Again I am not absolutely certain of my dates, but that is the best of my memory. I can tie it down a little bit better with respect to other dates. It was a short time before the GAC meeting in which that committee made a decision against the thermonuclear program.

After a somewhat strenuous discussion, Bethe, to the best of my understanding, decided that he would come to Los Alamos and help us. During this discussion, Oppenheimer called up and invited Bethe and me to come and discuss this matter with him in Princeton. This we did do, and visited Oppenheimer in his office.

When we arrived, I remember that Oppenheimer showed us a letter on his desk which he said he had just received. This letter was from Conant. I do not know whether he showed us the whole letter or whether he showed us a short section of it, or whether he only read to us a short section. Whichever it was, and I cannot say which it was, one phrase of Conant's sticks in my mind, and that phrase was "over my dead body," referring to a decision to go ahead with a crash program on the thermonuclear bomb.

Apart from showing us this letter, or reading it to us, whichever it was, Oppenheimer to the best of my recollection did not argue against any crash program. We did talk for quite awhile and could not possibly reproduce the whole argument but at least one important trend in this discussion—and I do not know how relevant this is—was that Oppenheimer argued that some phases of exaggerated secrecy in connection with the A-bomb was perhaps not to the best interests of the country, and that if he undertook the thermonuclear development, this should be done right from the first and should be done more openly.

I remembered that Bethe reacted to that quite violently, because he thought that if we proceeded with thermonuclear development, then both

—not only our methods of work—but even the fact that we were working and if possible the results of our work should be most definitely kept from any public knowledge or any public announcement.

To the best of my recollection, no agreement came out of this, but when Bethe and I left Oppenheimer's office, Bethe was still intending to come to Los Alamos. Actually, I had been under the impression that Oppenheimer is opposed to the thermonuclear bomb or to a development of the thermonuclear bomb, and I don't think there was terribly much direct evidence to base this impression on. I am pretty sure that I expressed to Bethe the worry, we are going to talk with Oppenheimer now, and after that you will not come. When we left the office, Bethe turned to me and smiled and he said, "You see, you can be quite satisfied. I am still coming."

I do not know whether Bethe has talked again with Oppenheimer about that or not. I have some sort of a general understanding that he did not, but I am not at all sure that this is true.

Two days later I called up Bethe in New York, and he was in New York at that time, and Bethe then said that he thought it over, and he had changed his mind, and he was not coming.

I regretted this very much, and Bethe actually did not join work on the thermonuclear development until quite late in the game, essentially to put on the finishing touches.

I do not know whether this sufficiently answers your question.

Q: Yes, sir. Then, Doctor, the record here shows that on October 29 and 30, 1949, the GAC held its meeting, and thereafter reported its views on the thermonuclear program. Did you later see a copy of the report of the GAC?

A: I did. . . .

Q: Doctor, in what way did you think that the work would be affected by the report?

A: I would say that when I saw the report, I thought that this definitely was the end of any thermonuclear effort in Los Alamos. Actually I was completely mistaken. The report produced precisely the opposite effect.

Q: Why?

A: Immediately, of course, it stopped work because we were instructed not to work, but it gave people in Los Alamos much greater eagerness to proceed in this direction and from discussions I had in Los Alamos in the following days, I gathered the following psychological reaction:

First of all, people were interested in going on with the thermonuclear device because during the war it had been generally understood that this was one of the things that the laboratory was to find out at some time or other. It was a sort of promise in all of our minds.

Another thing was that the people there were a little bit tired—at least many, particularly of the younger ones—of going ahead with minor improvements and wanted to in sort of an adventurous spirit go into a new field. However, I think the strongest point and the one which was a reaction to this report was this: Not only to me, but to very many others who said this to me spontaneously, the report meant this. As long as you people go ahead and make minor improvements and work very hard and diligently at it, you are doing a fine job, but if you succeed in making a really great piece of progress, then you are doing something that is immoral. This kind of statement stated so bluntly was not of course made in the report. But this kind of an implication is something which I think a human being can support in an abstract sense. But if it refers to his own work, then I think almost anybody would become indignant, and this is what happened in Los Alamos, and the result was that I think the feelings of people in consequence of this report turned more toward the thermonuclear development than away from it.

Q: You mean it made them mad.

A: Yes.

Q: Doctor, in the absence of the President's decision of January, would that anger have been effective?

A: No. . . .

Massive Retaliation: John Foster Dulles, Address to the Council on Foreign Relations, January 12, 1954

When the Eisenhower administration took office in 1953, hydrogen bombs were in production. The costs were high. The ancillary costs were even higher, for work also had to progress on new types of bombers and long-, medium-, and short-range missiles. Determined to balance the budget and reduce Federal expenditures, the new administration eyed these mounting military costs with horror.

The decision made was to depend almost altogether on weapons of mass destruction. Announcing that a "new look" was being taken at defense expenditures, the Eisenhower administration pared outlays on conventional ground, air, and naval forces. When necessity to use such forces arose, as in Lebanon in 1958, the administration could scarcely put together a single division, and six weeks were required to gather it at the scene of crisis. The administration counted on deterring the Soviets from any and all kinds of adventure by possessing the ability to inflict massive destruction on their homeland.

The defense policy of the Eisenhower administration was outlined in 1954 by Secretary of State John Foster Dulles, in a speech before the Council on Foreign Relations. In that speech, Dulles developed what became known as the doctrine of "massive retaliation." The text of his speech follows. It is taken from the State Department Bulletin, *volume 30 (Jan. 25, 1954), pages 107–110.*

It is now nearly a year since the Eisenhower administration took office. During that year I have often spoken of various parts of our foreign policies. Tonight I should like to present an overall view of those policies which relate to our security.

First of all, let us recognize that many of the preceding foreign policies were good. Aid to Greece and Turkey had checked the Communist drive to the Mediterranean. The European Recovery Program had helped the peoples of Western Europe to pull out of the postwar morass. The Western powers were steadfast in Berlin and overcame the blockade with their airlift. As a loyal member of the United Nations, we had reacted with force to repel the Communist attack in Korea. When that effort exposed our military weakness, we rebuilt rapidly our military establishment. We also sought a quick buildup of armed strength in Western Europe.

These were the acts of a nation which saw the danger of Soviet communism; which realized that its own safety was tied up with that of others; which was capable of responding boldly and promptly to emergencies. These are precious values to be acclaimed. Also, we can pay tribute to congressional bipartisanship which puts the nation above politics.

But we need to recall that what we did was in the main emergency action, imposed on us by our enemies.

Let me illustrate.

1. We did not send our army into Korea because we judged in advance that it was sound military strategy to commit our Army to fight land battles in Asia. Our decision had been to pull out of Korea. It was Soviet-inspired action that pulled us back.

2. We did not decide in advance that it was wise to grant billions annually as foreign economic aid. We adopted that policy in response to the Communist efforts to sabotage the free economies of Western Europe.

3. We did not build up our military establishment at a rate which involved huge budget deficits, a depreciating currency, and a feverish economy because this seemed, in advance, a good policy. Indeed, we decided otherwise until the Soviet military threat was clearly revealed.

We live in a world where emergencies are always possible and our survival may depend upon our capacity to meet emergencies. Let us pray that we shall always have that capacity. But, having said that, it is necessary also to say that emergency measures—however good for the emergency—do not necessarily make good permanent policies. Emergency measures are costly; they are superficial; and they imply that the enemy has the initiative. They cannot be depended on to serve our long-time interests.

This "long time" factor is of critical importance.

The Soviet Communists are planning for what they call "an entire historical era," and we should do the same. They seek, through many types of maneuvers, gradually to divide and weaken the free nations by overextending them in efforts which, as Lenin put it, are "beyond their strength, so that they come to practical bankruptcy." Then, said Lenin, "our victory is assured." Then, said Stalin, will be "the moment for the decisive blow."

In the face of this strategy, measures cannot be judged adequate merely because they ward off an immediate danger. It is essential to do this, but it is also essential to do so without exhausting ourselves.

When the Eisenhower administration applied this test, we felt that some transformations were needed.

It is not sound military strategy permanently to commit U.S. land forces to Asia to a degree that leaves us no strategic reserves.

It is not sound economics, or good foreign policy, to support permanently other countries; for in the long run, that creates as much ill will as good will.

Also, it is not sound to become permanently committed to military expenditures so vast that they lead to "practical bankruptcy."

Change was imperative to assure the stamina needed for permanent security. But it was equally imperative that change should be accompanied by understanding of our true purposes. Sudden and spectacular change had to be avoided. Otherwise, there might have been a panic among our friends and miscalculated aggression by our enemies. We can, I believe, make a good report in these respects.

We need allies and collective security. Our purpose is to make these relations more effective, less costly. This can be done by placing more reliance on deterrent power and less dependence on local defensive power.

This is accepted practice so far as local communities are concerned. We keep locks on our doors, but we do not have an armed guard in every home. We rely principally on a community security system so well equipped to punish any who break in and steal that, in fact, would-be aggressors are generally deterred. That is the modern way of getting maximum protection at a bearable cost.

What the Eisenhower administration seeks is a similar international security system. We want, for ourselves and the other free nations, a maximum deterrent at a bearable cost.

Local defense will always be important. But there is no local defense which alone will contain the mighty landpower of the Communist world. Local defenses must be reinforced by the further deterrent of massive retaliatory power. A potential aggressor must know that he cannot always prescribe battle conditions that suit him. Otherwise, for example, a potential aggressor, who is glutted with manpower, might be tempted to attack in confidence that resistance would be confined to manpower. He might be tempted to attack in places where his superiority was decisive.

The way to deter aggression is for the free community to be willing and able to respond vigorously at places and with means of its own choosing.

So long as our basic policy concepts were unclear, our military leaders could not be selective in building our military power. If an enemy could pick his time and place and method of warfare—and if our policy was to remain the traditional one of meeting aggression by direct and local opposition—then we needed to be ready to fight in the Arctic and in the Tropics; in Asia, the Near East, and in Europe; by sea, by land, and by air; with old weapons and with new weapons.

The total cost of our security efforts, at home and abroad, was over $50 billion per annum, and involved, for 1953, a projected budgetary deficit of $9 billion; and $11 billion for 1954. This was on top of taxes comparable to wartime taxes; and the dollar was depreciating in effective value. Our allies were similarly weighed down. This could not be continued for long without grave budgetary, economic, and social consequences.

But before military planning could be changed, the President and his advisers, as represented by the National Security Council, had to take some basic policy decisions. This has been done. The basic decision was to depend primarily upon a great capacity to retaliate, instantly, by means and at places of our choosing. Now the Department of Defense and the Joint Chiefs of Staff can shape our military establishment to fit what is *our* policy, instead of having to try to be ready to meet the enemy's many choices. That permits of a selection of military means instead of a multiplication of means. As a result, it is now possible to get, and share, more basic security at less cost.

Let us now see how this concept has been applied to foreign policy, taking first the Far East.

In Korea this administration effected a major transformation. The fighting has been stopped on honorable terms. That was possible because the aggressor, already thrown back to and behind his place of beginning, was faced with the possibility that the fighting might, to his own great peril, soon spread beyond the limits and methods which he had selected.

The cruel toll of American youth and the non-productive expenditure of many billions have been stopped. Also our armed forces are no longer largely committed to the Asian mainland. We can begin to create a strategic reserve which greatly improves our defensive posture.

This change gives added authority to the warning of the members of the United Nations which fought in Korea that, if the Communists renewed the aggression, the United Nations response would not necessarily be confined to Korea.

I have said in relation to Indochina that, if there were open Red Chinese army aggression there, that would have "grave consequences which might not be confined to Indochina."

I expressed last month the intention of the United States to maintain its position in Okinawa. This is needed to insure adequate striking power to implement the collective security concept which I describe.

All of this is summed up in President Eisenhower's important statement of December 26. He announced the progressive reduction of the U.S. ground forces in Korea. He pointed out that U.S. military forces in the Far East will now feature "highly mobile naval, air and amphibious units"; and he said in this way, despite some withdrawal of land forces, the United States will have a capacity to oppose aggression "with even greater effect than heretofore."

The bringing home of some of our land forces also provides a most eloquent rebuttal to the Communist charge of "imperialism."

If we turn to Europe, we see readjustments in the NATO collective security effort. Senator Vandenberg called the North Atlantic Treaty pledges "the most practical deterrent and discouragement to war which the wit of man has yet devised." But he said also that "if the concept and objective are to build sufficient forces in being to hold the Russian line . . . it presents ruinous corollaries both at home and abroad."

In the first years of the North Atlantic Treaty Organization, after the aggression in Korea, its members made an emergency buildup of military strength. I do not question the judgment of that time. The strength thus built has served well the cause of peace. But the pace originally set could not be maintained indefinitely.

At the April meeting of the NATO Council, the United States put forward a new concept, now known as that of the "long haul." That meant a steady development of defensive strength at a rate which will preserve and not exhaust the economic strength of our allies and ourselves. This would be reinforced by the striking power of a strategic air force based on internationally agreed positions.

We found, at the Council of last December, that there was general acceptance of the "long haul" concept and recognition that it better served the probable needs than an effort to create full defensive land strength at a ruinous price. . . .

New collective security concepts reduce nonproductive military expenses of our allies to a point where it is desirable and practicable also to reduce economic aid. There was need of a more self-respecting relationship, and that, indeed, is what our allies wanted. Trade, broader markets, and a flow of investments are far more healthy than intergovernmental grants-in-aid.

There are still some strategic spots where the local governments cannot maintain adequate armed forces without some financial support from us. In these cases, we take the judgment of our military advisers as to how to proceed in the common interest. For example, we have contributed largely, ungrudgingly, and I hope constructively, to end aggression and advance freedom in Indochina.

The technical assistance program is being continued, and we stand ready to meet nonrecurrent needs due to crop failures or like disasters.

But, broadly speaking, foreign budgetary aid is being limited to situations where it clearly contributes to military strength.

In the ways I outlined we gather strength for the long-term defense of freedom.

We do not, of course, claim to have found some magic formula that insures against all forms of Communist successes. It is normal that at some times and at some places there may be setbacks to the cause of freedom. What we do expect to insure is that any setbacks will have only temporary and local significance, because they will leave unimpaired those free world assets which in the long run will prevail.

If we can deter such aggression as would mean general war, and that is our confident resolve, then we can let time and fundamentals work for us. We do not need self-imposed policies which sap our strength.

The fundamental, on our side, is the richness—spiritual, intellectual, and material—that freedom can produce and the irresistible attraction it then sets up. That is why we do not plan ourselves to shackle freedom to preserve freedom. We intend that our conduct and example shall continue, as in the past, to show all men how good can be the fruits of freedom.

If we rely on freedom, then it follows that we must abstain from diplomatic moves which would seem to endorse captivity. That would, in effect, be a conspiracy against freedom. I can assure you that we shall never seek illusory security for ourselves by such a "deal."

We do negotiate about specific matters but only to advance the cause of human welfare.

President Eisenhower electrified the world with his proposal to lift a great weight of fear by turning atomic energy from a means of death into a source of life. Yesterday, I started procedural talks with the Soviet Government on that topic.

We have persisted, with our allies, in seeking the unification of Germany and the liberation of Austria. Now the Soviet rulers have agreed to discuss these questions. We expect to meet them soon in Berlin. I hope they will come with a sincerity which will equal our own.

We have sought a conference to unify Korea and relieve it of foreign troops. So far, our persistence is unrewarded; but we have not given up.

These efforts at negotiation are normal initiatives that breathe the spirit of freedom. They involve no plan for a partnership division of world power with those who suppress freedom.

If we persist in the courses I outline we shall confront dictatorship with a task that is, in the long run, beyond its strength. For unless it changes, it must suppress the human desires that freedom satisfies—as we shall be demonstrating.

If the dictators persist in their present course, then it is they who will be limited to superficial successes, while their foundation crumbles under the tread of their iron boots.

Human beings, for the most part, want simple things.

They want to worship God in accordance with the dictates of their conscience. But that is not easily granted by those who promote an atheistic creed.

They want to think in accordance with the dictates of their reason. But that is not easily granted by those who represent an authoritarian system.

They want to exchange views with others and to persuade and to be persuaded by what appeals to their reason and their conscience. But that is not easily granted by those who believe in a society of conformity.

They want to live in their homes without fear. But that is not easily granted by those who believe in a police state system.

They want to be able to work productively and creatively and to enjoy the fruits of their labor. But that is not easily granted by those who look upon human beings as a means to create a powerhouse to dominate the world.

We can be sure that there is going on, even within Russia, a silent test of strength between the powerful rulers and the multitudes of human beings. Each individual no doubt seems by himself to be helpless in this struggle. But their aspirations in the aggregate make up a mighty force.

There are signs that the rulers are bending to some of the human desires of their people. There are promises of more food, more household goods, more economic freedom.

That does not prove that the Soviet rulers have themselves been converted. It is rather that they may be dimly perceiving a basic fact, that is that there are limits to the power of any rulers indefinitely to suppress the human spirit.

In that God-given fact lies our greatest hope. It is a hope that can sustain us. For even if the path ahead be long and hard, it need not be a warlike path; and we can know that at the end may be found the blessedness of peace.

Balanced Forces: Testimony by Secretary of Defense Robert S. McNamara, 1962

By 1960 many people were concerned about American defense policy. Two chiefs of staff of the Army, Matthew B. Ridgway and Maxwell Taylor, had resigned and afterward published books criticizing the administration's excessive reliance on weapons of mass destruction. Ridgway's book was Soldier *(1956), Taylor's* The Uncertain Trumpet *(1960). Various Democratic senators echoed these criticisms. Among them were John F. Kennedy of Massachusetts and Lyndon B. Johnson of Texas. In 1960 Kennedy was elected President and Johnson Vice President.*

As his Secretary of Defense, Kennedy selected Robert McNamara, the president of the Ford Motor Company. The general instructions that Kennedy gave McNamara were to redress the imbalance between conventional and nuclear forces in America's arsenal. Among accounts of what McNamara achieved, the most comprehensive is W. W. Kaufmann, The McNamara Strategy *(1964). The following is Secretary McNamara's second annual review of the defense posture of the United States. It is taken from Eighty-seventh Congress, second session, Armed Services Committee, House of Representatives,* Hearings on Military Posture, *pages 3162–3167.*

When I took office in January 1961, President Kennedy instructed me to—

1. Develop the force structure necessary to our military requirements without regard to arbitrary or predetermined budget ceilings. And secondly, having determined that force structure, to procure and operate it at the lowest possible cost.

I followed this guidance in all of the three amendments to the fiscal year 1962 program and budget, and I have applied it to the development of the fiscal year 1963–67 force programs and to the fiscal year 1963 budget.

Our first step in the formulation of the fiscal year 1963 budget was to initiate a series of studies dealing with what we judged to be the most critical requirements problems in the Department. At the same time we began a detailed review and analysis of the Communist threat, now and in the future, based on the latest and best intelligence information available.

While this work was underway, we requested the military departments, last May, to submit their program proposals for the period 1963 through 1967. No dollar ceilings were assigned or indicated to the military departments. Instead, the military departments were instructed to submit proposals for such forces and such new programs as, in their judgment, were required to support our basic national security objectives. The departments were particularly encouraged to submit alternative forces and programs so that we would have before us in reaching our decisions the principal choices available.

The service proposals were received during July and August. Including civil defense and the military assistance program, they aggregated over $63 billion in obligational authority for fiscal year 1963 and more than $67 billion for fiscal year 1966, which was one of the program years. And since these submissions were prepared unilaterally by each service, it is understandable that duplication and overlapping occurred in certain areas, particularly the Strategic Retaliatory Forces.

The service proposals were consolidated and subjected to a systematic analysis by the OSD* staff. With the assistance of our principal military and civilian advisers, Mr. Gilpatric† and I then reviewed in great detail each of the programs in the light of—

First, the mission to be accomplished.

Second, the cost-effectiveness relationships among the various alternative means of performing the mission, and

Third, the latest intelligence data on the capabilities of the Soviet Union and its satellites. This took the majority of the summer. And by September, upon completion of this review, my tentative program decisions were forwarded to the military departments and the Chairman of the Joint Chiefs of Staff to serve as the basis for the preparation of the detailed budget requests for fiscal year 1963. In order to assist the services in their forward planning, this guidance, in most cases, was projected through fiscal year 1967.

In my memorandum forwarding the guidance, I sent them this set of instructions:

1. The services should feel free, in preparing their fiscal year 1963 budget requests, to change details of the guidance wherever they felt such changes essential to meet military requirements.

2. I expected to continue discussing the tentative program decisions which I had already made, with the service Secretaries and the Chiefs until the final fiscal year 1963 budget decisions were made later in the year.

3. Our major objective would be to increase combat power and, therefore, nonessentials and expensive programs that contribute only marginally to our combat strength must be eliminated. . . .

*[Office of the Secretary of Defense (*ed.*).]

†[Roswell Gilpatric, Deputy Secretary of Defense (*ed.*).]

And fourth, the cost estimates associated with the tentatively approved programs projected in the guidance were approximate and, in many cases, I felt they were much too high, and would be subject to detailed scrutiny by me during the budget review.

No attempt was made to preclude the services from recommending programs over and above those contained in these instructions. In effect, this arrangement provided the services with an opportunity to reclaim my tentative program decisions. We did this to insure that all reasonable alternatives would be thoroughly considered before the final 1963 budget decisions were made.

The last step in the process involved the formulation and review of the fiscal year 1963 budget request. The military departments submitted their requests beginning on October 23. As has been the custom in past years, the requests were reviewed jointly by the budget examiners of my office and the Bureau of the Budget. The findings and analyses developed in this examination and review were forwarded to me for decision.

Again, in consultation with our principal advisers, Mr. Gilpatric and I reviewed and decided some 560 individual items ranging in value from several hundred thousand dollars of cuts to several hundred million dollars of cuts or increases. Those decisions were transmitted to the respective services, and in the final step of the review outstanding differences that remained between the service Secretaries or Chiefs and myself were resolved.

Throughout the program and budget review phases, discussions were held with the service Secretaries, the Chiefs of Staff, and the Director of the Bureau of the Budget. Progressively, during these discussions, outstanding differences were isolated and finally resolved. I believe it is fair to say that the defense budget recommended to the Congress by President Kennedy is the product of the best thought available in the Department of Defense and the executive branch of the Government.

Throughout our collective efforts, we were able to provide a balanced program adequate to our needs and at the same time to reduce the budget, in terms of new obligational authority, first from the 63 billion level down to 54.2 billion which was subsequently requested by the services and then to 51.6 billion which was proposed by the President. . . .

Serious instability in other parts of the world may provide the Communists . . . opportunities to enlarge the area of the struggle. As we have seen in the past, the Communists are quick to take advantage of a breakdown of law and order in any part of the world. They are quick to identify themselves with any change in the status quo, and with any emerging threat to existing authority.

One has only to contemplate the ferment which exists in many countries around the globe, including the Western Hemisphere, to appreciate the potential for new crises. Clearly, one of the major problems confronting this Nation and its allies is how to help safeguard freedom during a period of rapid and often drastic change in many parts of the world. The problem is particularly acute in the emerging nations of Africa, the relatively new sovereignties in southeast Asia, and in those nations in South and Central America which are now and will be going through a period of great social reform. . . .

Obviously, military power alone cannot solve all of these problems. Diplomacy, economic assistance, and ideological conviction all have their roles to play in the struggle to safeguard freedom. The principal purpose of our military programs, including military assistance, is to deter the Communists from resorting to the use of armed force in seeking to achieve their objectives. Even here, the line of demarcation is far from clear. As we have seen in recent months, the Communists have stepped up what Mr. Khrushchev* called, in his January 6 speech of last year, wars of national liberation, or popular revolts, and which we know as covert armed aggression, guerrilla warfare, and subversion. To meet this form of the Communist threat, new means must be devised.

Meanwhile, we must continue to guard against general nuclear war and local wars which may escalate into general war. These continue to be the most acute dangers to our national security and, indeed, to the security of the entire free world.

But our policy is not merely defensive. We need not and are not merely reacting to the Communist initiative. Our ultimate objective is a peaceful world in which every nation large and small is free to determine its own destiny. To this end we shall continue our efforts to achieve a safeguarded system of disarmament or arms reduction. But, we shall not hesitate to take up arms to defend freedom and our own vital interests. We are resolved to continue the struggle in all its forms until such time as the Communist leaders, both Soviet and Chinese, are convinced that their aggressive policies, motivated by their drive to communize the world, endanger their security as well as ours. . . .

Our military policy, as in the past, continues to be firmly based on the principle of the collective defense of the free world. Aside from the obvious fact that we are stronger united than alone, any loss in the free world position is a loss to the security of the United States. . . .

For the sake of our own safety we must be prepared to defend the outposts of freedom around the world. We must be ready to meet the Communist challenge in its various forms using whatever means—military, economic, political or ideological—best serves the purpose. We cannot, and need not, do this job alone. Our allies around the world have great and growing economic and military strength. What is needed is a unity of purpose—a common determination to use this strength effectively in the collective defense of the free world alliance.

In this alliance, NATO plays a very special role. Not only do our NATO partners represent, after the United States, the greatest source of economic, political, military, and ideological strength opposing the Communist camp; they also constitute the bastion of free world power closest to the center of Communist military strength. There is no question but that [deleted] [*sic*] NATO represents the balance of power in the struggle against communism. The loss or neutralization of this area would

*[N. S. Khrushchev, Chairman of the Council of Ministers of the U.S.S.R., 1955–1964 (*ed.*).]

be a disastrous blow to our own security. Therefore, if for no other reason than our own self-interest, we must maintain within the NATO alliance the closest kind of cooperation at all levels and in all spheres; we must concert our efforts no matter how great the difficulties. And, indeed, the difficulties or existence of difficulties should not dismay us. After all, we are dealing with sovereign nations whose history extends back far beyond our own, nations with their own particular devotion to [deleted] [*sic*] freedom. They clearly are entitled to their own views and their views are entitled to the most careful consideration by us.

Thus, in planning our own military forces we must take into account the plans of the other free world nations, particularly our NATO partners. We must continue to plan for the collective defense, with each member of the alliance providing the forces best suited to its capabilities and talents. Collectively, particularly within NATO, these forces should be brought into better balance with the changing character of the threat.

After long and intensive study, we have reached the conclusion that, while our own nuclear forces are increasing, greater emphasis than in the past must be given, both by ourselves and our NATO allies, to our non-nuclear forces. This does not mean that we would hesitate to use nuclear weapons even in a limited war situation, if needed. As I stated in my appearance before the Congress last spring:

> * * * Even in limited war situations we should not preclude the use of tactical nuclear weapons, for no one can foresee how such situations might develop. But the decision to employ tactical nuclear weapons in limited conflicts should not be forced upon us simply because we have no other means to cope with them. There are many possible situations in which it would not be advisable or feasible to use such weapons. What is being proposed today, as it was then, is not a reversal of our existing national policy but an increase in our nonnuclear capabilities to provide a greater degree of versatility to our limited war forces.

That was then our policy and it is still our policy.

With the help and support of the Congress, I believe we have made a good start in adding to our conventional forces. But much more needs to be done, as you will see. We must not only raise the general level of our nonnuclear forces, but we must also bring the various elements into proper balance. And this problem of balance is one that I will stress frequently during the review of our program.

If we are to have the capacity to respond promptly to limited wars in any part of the globe, and possibly in more than one place at the same time, we must have—

(*a*) Adequate combat-ready conventional forces.

(*b*) Airlift and sealift to move these forces promptly to wherever they may be needed.

(*c*) Tactical air support for the ground forces.

(*d*) Sea forces to insure control of the seas.

(*e*) Along with balanced and properly positioned inventories of weapons, equipment, and combat consumables to insure that these forces have what they need to fight effectively.

We have also made a good start on building up the specialized forces required to cope with covert military aggression, guerrilla warfare, and so forth, and we are pressing forward with the development of the specialized equipment and weapons required by such forces.

But, even more importantly, we must help the less developed and less stable nations of the free world to develop these same capabilities. This is the primary need in such countries as South Vietnam. We must help them, not only with the specialized weapons and equipment required, but also with training and on-the-spot advice. All of us in the free world have much to learn about counterinsurgency and guerrilla warfare operations, but learn we must if we are to meet successfully this particular aspect of the Communist threat.

Admittedly, it will take much more than military force alone to stamp out communism permanently in such places as South Vietnam. We must help these people to provide a more desirable alternative to communism, and to do this will require all the means at our disposal—political, ideological, technical, scientific, and economic, as well as military. . . .

SELECTION 28

Truman on Point Four

The third American policy for the long pull was aid to underdeveloped areas. Underlying the Truman Doctrine and the Marshall Plan had been an assumption that the people most easily prey to communism were the poor, the hungry, and the hopeless. Since people in most parts of the globe were so conditioned, it seemed logical that one way of combating communism was, as in Europe, to use America's wealth in order to give people in non-Communist lands food, clothing, shelter, and hope of a better life.

Checking communism was not, of course, the only motive. It had not been the only motive for the Marshall Plan. Humanitarianism played a part. So did a sense of long-range self-interest. Economic development in poverty-stricken areas of the world would mean more markets for American products and more abundant goods for everyone. It might also mean one day, when the policy of containment had worked its objective and the Communist bloc had lost or outgrown its expansive tendencies, that there would be a world in which all nations could live in comfort and tranquility.

The logic of foreign aid, and the practical effects of America's programs, have been the subjects of innumerable books. The best two have identical titles, Foreign Aid and Foreign Policy. *One is by Herbert Feis (1964), the other by Edward S. Mason (1964). Other useful works are J. B. Bingham,* Shirt-sleeve Diplomacy: Point Four in Action *(1953); E. R. Black,* The Diplomacy of Economic Development *(1960); P. M. Glick,* The Administration of Technical Assistance *(1957); and H. M. Teaf, Jr., and P. G. Franck,* Hands across Frontiers: Case Studies in Technical Cooperation *(1956).*

The first move of the United States toward a world-wide aid program came when President Truman made a general proposal to this effect as the fourth point in his inaugural address of January 20, 1949. Thereafter, technical assistance to underdeveloped areas was often labeled "Point Four" aid. The first document below is the revelant portion of Truman's address. It is taken from the State Department Bulletin, *volume 20 (Jan. 30, 1949), page 125.*

The second document is a message that Truman delivered to Congress on June 24, 1949, elaborating his proposal. Truman asked an appropriation for aid and technical assistance. He also asked legislation authorizing the Export-Import Bank to guarantee, or insure, private investments in underdeveloped nations. Although Congress put up less money than the President requested, it voted both of the requested measures. The second document is from the State Department Bulletin, *volume 20 (July 4, 1949), pages 862–865.*

INAUGURAL ADDRESS, 1949

Fourth, we must embark on a bold new program for making the benefits of our scientific advances and industrial progress available for the improvement and growth of underdeveloped areas.

More than half the people of the world are living in conditions approaching misery. Their food is inadequate. They are victims of disease. Their economic life is primitive and stagnant. Their poverty is a handicap and a threat both to them and to more prosperous areas.

For the first time in history, humanity possesses the knowledge and the skill to relieve the suffering of these people.

The United States is preeminent among nations in the development of industrial and scientific techniques. The material resources which we can afford to use for the assistance of other peoples are limited. But our imponderable resources in technical knowledge are constantly growing and are inexhaustible.

I believe that we should make available to peace-loving peoples the benefits of our store of technical knowledge in order to help them realize their aspirations for a better life. And, in cooperation with other nations, we should foster capital investment in areas needing development.

Our aim should be to help the free peoples of the world, through their own efforts, to produce more food, more clothing, more materials for housing, and more mechanical power to lighten their burdens.

We invite other countries to pool their technological resources in this undertaking. Their contributions will be warmly welcomed. This should be a cooperative enterprise in which all nations work together through the United Nations and its specialized agencies wherever practicable. It must be a world-wide effort for the achievement of peace, plenty, and freedom.

With the cooperation of business, private capital, agriculture, and labor in this country, this program can greatly increase the industrial activity in other nations and can raise substantially their standards of living.

Such new economic developments must be devised and controlled to benefit the peoples of the areas in which they are established. Guaranties to the investor must be balanced by guaranties in the interest of the people whose resources and whose labor go into these developments.

The old imperialism—exploitation for foreign profit—has no place in our plans. What we envisage is a program of development based on the concepts of democratic fair-dealing.

All countries, including our own, will greatly benefit from a constructive program for the better use of the world's human and natural resources. Experience shows that our commerce with other countries expands as they progress industrially and economically.

Greater production is the key to prosperity and peace. And the key to greater production is a wider and more vigorous application of modern scientific and technical knowledge.

Only by helping the least fortunate of its members to help themselves can the human family achieve the decent, satisfying life that is the right of all people.

Democracy alone can supply the vitalizing force to stir the peoples of the world into triumphant action, not only against their human oppressors, but also against their ancient enemies—hunger, misery, and despair.

SPECIAL MESSAGE TO CONGRESS, JUNE 24, 1949

In order to enable the United States, in cooperation with other countries, to assist the peoples of economically underdeveloped areas to raise their standards of living, I recommend the enactment of legislation to authorize an expanded program of technical assistance for such areas, and an experimental program for encouraging the outflow of private investment beneficial to their economic development. These measures are the essential first steps in an undertaking which will call upon private enterprise and voluntary organizations in the United States, as well as the government, to take part in a constantly growing effort to improve economic conditions in the less developed regions of the world.

The grinding poverty and the lack of economic opportunity for many millions of people in the economically underdeveloped parts of Africa, the Near and Far East, and certain regions of Central and South America, constitute one of the greatest challenges of the world today. In spite of their age-old economic and social handicaps, the peoples in these areas have, in recent decades, been stirred and awakened. The spread of industrial civilization, the growing understanding of modern concepts of government, and the impact of two World Wars have changed their lives and their outlook. They are eager to play a greater part in the community of nations.

All these areas have a common problem. They must create a firm economic base for the democratic aspirations of their citizens. Without such an economic base, they will be unable to meet the expectations which the modern world has aroused in their peoples. If they are frustrated and disappointed, they may turn to false doctrines which hold that the way of progress lies through tyranny.

For the United States the great awakening of these peoples holds tremendous promise. It is not only a promise that new and stronger nations will be associated with us in the cause of human freedom, it is also a promise of new economic strength and growth for ourselves.

With many of the economically underdeveloped areas of the world, we have long had ties of trade and commerce. In many instances today we greatly need the products of their labor and their resources. If the productivity and the purchasing power of these countries are expanded, our own industry and agriculture will benefit. Our experience shows that the volume of our foreign trade is far greater with highly developed countries than it is with countries having a low standard of living and inadequate industry. To increase the output and the national income of the less developed regions is to increase our own economic stability.

In addition, the development of these areas is of utmost importance to our efforts to restore the economies of the free European nations. As the economies of the underdeveloped areas expand, they will provide needed products for Europe and will offer a better market for European goods. Such expansion is an essential part of the growing system of world trade which is necessary for European recovery.

Furthermore, the development of these areas will strengthen the United Nations and the fabric of world peace. The preamble to the Charter of the United Nations states that the economic and social advancement of all people is an essential bulwark of peace. Under article 56 of the Charter, we have promised to take separate action and to act jointly with other nations "to promote higher standards of living, full employment, and conditions of economic and social progress and development."

For these various reasons, assistance in the development of the economically underdeveloped areas has become one of the major elements of our foreign policy. In my inaugural address, I outlined a program to help the peoples of these areas to attain greater production as a way to prosperity and peace.

The major effort in such a program must be local in character; it must be made by the people of the underdeveloped areas themselves. It is essential, however, to the success of their effort that there be help from abroad. In some cases, the peoples of these areas will be unable to begin their part of this great enterprise without initial aid from other countries.

The aid that is needed falls roughly into two categories. The first is the technical, scientific, and managerial knowledge necessary to economic development. This category includes not only medical and educational knowledge, and assistance and advice in such basic fields as sanitation, communications, road building, and governmental services, but also, and perhaps most important, assistance in the survey of resources and in planning for long-range economic development.

The second category is production goods—machinery and equipment—and financial assistance in the creation of productive enterprises. The underdeveloped areas need capital for port and habor development, roads and communications, irrigation and drainage projects, as well as for public utilities and the whole range of extractive, processing, and manufacturing industries. Much of the capital required can be provided by these areas themselves, in spite of their low standards of living. But much must come from abroad.

The two categories of aid are closely related. Technical assistance is necessary to lay the ground-work for productive investment. Investment, in turn, brings with it technical assistance. In general, however, technical surveys of resources and of the possibilities of economic development must precede substantial capital investment. Furthermore, in many of the areas concerned, technical assistance in improving sanitation, communications, or education is required to create conditions in which capital investment can be fruitful.

This country, in recent years, has conducted relatively modest programs of technical cooperation with other countries. In the field of education, channels of exchange and communication have been opened between our citizens and those of other countries. To some extent, the expert assistance of a number of Federal agencies, such as the Public Health Service and the Department of Agriculture, has been made available to other countries.

We have also participated in the activities of the United Nations, its specialized agencies, and other international organizations to disseminate useful techniques among nations.

Through these various activities, we have gained considerable experience in rendering technical assistance to other countries. What is needed now is to expand and integrate these activities and to concentrate them particularly on the economic development of underdeveloped areas.

Much of the aid that is needed can be provided most effectively through the United Nations. Shortly after my inaugural address, this government asked the Economic and Social Council of the United Nations to consider what the United Nations and the specialized international agencies could do in this program.

The Secretary-General of the United Nations thereupon asked the United Nations Secretariat and the Secretariats of the specialized international agencies to draw up cooperative plans for technical assistance to underdeveloped areas. As a result, a survey was made of technical projects suitable for these agencies in such fields as industry, labor, agriculture, scientific research with respect to natural resources, and fiscal management. The total cost of the program submitted as a result of this survey was estimated to be about 35 million dollars for the first year. It is expected that the United Nations and the specialized international agencies will shortly adopt programs for carrying out projects of the type included in this survey.

In addition to our participation in this work of the United Nations, much of the technical assistance required can be provided directly by the United States to countries needing it. A careful examination of the existing information concerning the underdeveloped countries shows particular need for technicians and experts with United States training in plant and animal diseases, malaria and typhus control, water supply and sewer systems, metallurgy and mining, and nearly all phases of industry.

It has already been shown that experts in these fields can bring about tremendous improvements. For example, the health of the people of many foreign communities has been greatly improved by the work of United States sanitary engineers in setting up modern water supply systems. The food supply of many areas has been increased as the result of the advice of United States agricultural experts in the control of animal diseases and the improvement of crops. These are only examples of the wide range of benefits resulting from the careful application of modern techniques to local problems. The benefits which a comprehensive program of expert assistance will make possible can only be revealed by studies and surveys undertaken as a part of the program itself.

To inaugurate the program, I recommend a first year appropriation of not to exceed 45 million dollars. This includes 10 million dollars already requested in the 1950 Budget for activities of this character. The sum recommended will cover both our participation in the programs of the international agencies and the assistance to be provided directly by the United States.

In every case, whether the operation is conducted through the United Nations, the other international agencies, or directly by the United States, the country receiving the benefit of the aid will be required to bear a substantial portion of the expense.

The activities necessary to carry out our program of technical aid will be diverse in character and will have to be performed by a number of different government agencies and private instrumentalities. It will be necessary to utilize not only the resources of international agencies and the United States Government, but also the facilities and the experience of the private business and nonprofit organizations that have long been active in this work.

Since a number of Federal agencies will be involved in the program, I recommend that the administration of the program be vested in the President, with authority to delegate to the Secretary of State and to other government officers, as may be appropriate. With such administrative flexibility, it will be possible to modify the management of the program as it expands and to meet the practical problems that will arise in its administration in the future.

The second category of outside aid needed by the underdeveloped areas is the provision of capital for the creation of productive enterprises. The International Bank for Reconstruction and Development and the Export-Import Bank have provided some capital for underdeveloped areas, and, as the economic growth of these areas progresses, should be expected to provide a great deal more. In addition, private sources of funds must be encouraged to provide a major part of the capital required.

In view of the present troubled condition of the world—the distortion of world trade, the shortage of dollars, and other aftereffects of the war—the problem of substantially increasing the flow of American capital abroad presents serious difficulties. In all probability novel devices will have to be employed if the investment from this country is to reach proportions sufficient to carry out the objectives of our program.

All countries concerned with the program should work together to bring about conditions favorable to the flow of private capital. To this end we are negotiating agreements with other countries to protect the American investor from unwarranted or discriminatory treatment under the laws of the country in which he makes his investment.

In negotiating such treaties we do not, of course, ask privileges for American capital greater than those granted to other investors in underdeveloped countries or greater than we ourselves grant in this country. We believe that American enterprise should not waste local resources, should provide adequate wages and working conditions for local labor, and should bear an equitable share of the burden of local taxes. At the same time, we believe that investors will send their capital abroad on an increasing scale only if they are given assurance against risk of loss through expropriation without compensation, unfair or discriminatory treatment, destruction through war or rebellion, or the inability to convert their earnings into dollars.

Although our investment treaties will be directed at mitigating such risks, they cannot eliminate them entirely. With the best will in the world a foreign country, particularly an underdeveloped country, may not be able to obtain the dollar exchange necessary for the prompt remittance of earnings on dollar capital. Damage or loss resulting from internal and international violence may be beyond the power of our treaty signatories to control.

Many of these conditions of instability in underdeveloped areas which deter foreign investment are themselves a consequence of the lack of economic development which only foreign investment can cure. Therefore, to wait until stable conditions are assured before encouraging the outflow of capital to underdeveloped areas would defer the attainment of our objectives indefinitely. It is necessary to take vigorous action now to break out of this vicious circle.

Since the development of underdeveloped economic areas is of major importance in our foreign policy, it is appropriate to use the resources of the government to accelerate private efforts toward that end. I recommend, therefore, that the Export-Import Bank be authorized to guarantee United States private capital, invested in productive enterprises abroad which contribute to economic development in underdeveloped areas, against the risks peculiar to those investments.

This guarantee activity will at the outset be largely experimental. Some investments may require only a guarantee against the danger of inconvertibility, others may need protection against the danger of expropriation and other dangers as well. It is impossible at this time to write a standard guarantee. The Bank will, of course, be able to require the payment of premiums for such protection, but there is no way now to determine what premium rates will be most appropriate in the long run. Only experience can provide answers to these questions.

The Bank has sufficient resources at the present time to begin the guarantee program and to carry on its lending activities as well without any increase in its authorized funds. If the demand for guarantees should prove large, and lending activities continue on the scale expected, it will be necessary to request the Congress at a later date to increase the authorized funds of the Bank.

The enactment of these two legislative proposals, the first pertaining to technical assistance and the second to the encouragement of foreign investment, will constitute a national endorsement of a program of major importance in our efforts for world peace and economic stability. Nevertheless, these measures are only the first steps. We are here embarking on a venture that extends far into the future. We are at the beginning of a rising curve of activity, private, governmental, and international, that will continue for many years to come. It is all the more important, therefore, that we start promptly.

In the economically underdeveloped areas of the world today there are new creative energies. We look forward to the time when these countries will be stronger and more independent than they are now, and yet more closely bound to us and to other nations by ties of friendship and commerce, and by kindred ideals. On the other hand, unless we aid the newly awakened spirit in these peoples to find the course of fruitful development, they may fall under the control of those whose philosophy is hostile to human freedom, thereby prolonging the unsettled state of the world and postponing the achievement of permanent peace.

Before the peoples of these areas we hold out the promise of a better future through the democratic way of life. It is vital that we move quickly to bring the meaning of that promise home to them in their daily lives.

SELECTION 29

An Appeal to Public Opinion by President Eisenhower, May 21, 1957

After 1949, foreign aid was a permanent feature of American foreign policy. It took many forms. In addition to technical assistance, or Point Four aid, there were direct grants of funds for economic development, grants of food from the surpluses accumulated by the Commodity Credit Corporation, and special grants designed to build up military strength in nations menaced by communism.

Of all these programs, the one that commanded the most support in Congress and the country was the last—military aid. There was a tendency to label all the others "giveaways," and Congress usually pared away large sums before grudgingly approving nonmilitary aid programs.

In 1957, President Eisenhower appealed to public opinion to take a more generous view of foreign aid and to recognize that aid programs, whether military or not, contributed to the security and well-being of the United States. His address, delivered over radio and television on the evening of May 21, 1957, had no lasting effects. Congress's handling of his requests was no different from its handling of earlier requests. But Eisenhower's address stands as a significant reflection of the fact that foreign aid was a cardinal feature of Republican as well as Democratic foreign policy. The text of the address is taken from the Public Papers of the Presidents: Dwight D. Eisenhower, 1957 *(Government Printing Office, 1958), pages 385–396.*

My Fellow Citizens:

Just one week ago I talked with you about our Federal budget as a whole. Tonight I want to talk with you about one part of it: our Mutual Security programs. These programs are the source of military and economic strength for our alliances throughout the free world. They form, in fact, a saving shield of freedom.

Although the cost of these programs amounts to only 5 percent of the budget, I am talking exclusively about them tonight for two simple reasons.

First: In my judgment these programs do more than any other—dollar for dollar—in securing the safety of our country and the peaceful lives of all of us.

Second: They are the most misunderstood of any of the Federal Government's activities. Their nature, their purposes, their results are vitally important to all of us—but little known to many of us.

The common label of "foreign aid" is gravely misleading—for it inspires a picture of bounty for foreign countries at the expense of our own. No misconception could be further from reality. These programs serve our own basic national and personal interests.

They do this both immediately and lastingly.

In the long term, the ending or the weakening of these programs would vastly increase the risk of future war.

And—in the immediate sense—it would impose upon us additional defense expenditures many times greater than the cost of mutual security today.

This evening it is my purpose to give you incontestable proof of these assertions.

We have, during this century, twice spent our blood and our treasure fighting in Europe—and twice in Asia. We fought because we saw—too late to prevent war—that our own peace and security were imperilled, by the urgent danger—or the ruthless conquest—of other lands.

We have gained wisdom from that suffering. We know, and the world knows, that the American people will fight hostile and aggressive despotisms when their force is thrown against the barriers of freedom, when they seek to gain the high ground of power from which to destroy us. But we also know that to fight is the most costly way to keep America secure and free. Even an America victorious in atomic war could scarcely escape disastrous destruction of her cities and a fearful loss of life. Victory itself could be agony.

Plainly, we must seek less tragic, less costly ways to defend ourselves. We must recognize that whenever any country falls under the domination of Communism, the strength of the Free World—and of America—is by that amount weakened and Communism strengthened. If this process, through our neglect or indifference, should proceed unchecked, our continent would be gradually encircled. Our safety depends upon recognition of the fact that the Communist design for such encirclement must be stopped before it gains momentum—before it is again too late to save the peace.

This recognition dictates two tasks. We must maintain a common worldwide defense against the menace of International Communism. And we must demonstrate and spread the blessings of liberty—to be cherished by those who enjoy these blessings, to be sought by those now denied them.

This is not a new policy nor a partisan policy.

This is a policy for America that began ten years ago when a Democratic President and a Republican Congress united in an historic declaration. They then declared that the independence and survival of two countries menaced by Communist aggression—Greece and Turkey—were so important to the security of America that we would give them military and economic aid.

That policy saved those nations. And it did so without the cost of American lives.

That policy has since been extended to all critical areas of the world. It recognizes that America cannot exist as an island of freedom in a surrounding sea of Communism. It is expressed concretely by mutual security treaties embracing 42 other nations. And these treaties reflect a solemn finding by the President and by the Senate that our own peace would be endangered if any of these countries were conquered by International Communism.

The lesson of the defense of Greece and Turkey ten years ago has since been repeated in the saving of other lands and peoples. A recent example is the Southeast Asian country of Viet-Nam, whose President has just visited us as our honored guest.

Two years ago it appeared that all Southeast Asia might be over-run by the forces of International Communism. The freedom and security of nations for which we had fought throughout World War II and the Korean War again stood in danger. The people of Viet-Nam responded bravely—under steadfast leadership.

But bravery alone could not have prevailed.

We gave military and economic assistance to the Republic of Viet-Nam. We entered into a treaty—the Southeast Asia Security Treaty—which plainly warned that an armed attack against this area would endanger our own peace and safety, and that we would act accordingly. Thus Viet-Nam has been saved for freedom.

This is one of the nations where we have been spending the largest amounts of so-called "foreign aid." What could be plainer than the fact that this aid has served not only the safety of another nation—but also the security of our own.

The issue, then, is solemn and serious and clear.

When our young men were dying in the Argonne in 1918 and on the beaches of Normandy and in the Western Pacific in 1944 and at Pusan in 1950—and when the battlefields of Europe and Africa and Asia were strewn with billions of dollars worth of American military equipment, representing the toil and the skills of millions of workers—no one for an instant doubted the need and the rightness of this sacrifice of blood and labor and treasure.

Precisely the same needs and purposes are served by our Mutual Security programs today—whether these operate on a military or an economic front. For on both fronts they are truly defense programs.

To the truth of this, a number of thoughtful and qualified Americans have recently testified.

When the Congress last year approved the Mutual Security programs, I believed—as did many others—that it was time to review their whole concept. Since then, careful studies have been completed by Committees of the Congress, by competent private groups and by two public groups of leading citizens from all walks of life.

All these studies unanimously agreed that these programs are vital to our national interest and must be continued.

Some important revisions in the structure of our programs were recommended by these various studies. And with the benefit of these recommendations, my Message to the Congress today has proposed certain changes.

The whole design of this defense against Communist conspiracy and encirclement cannot be with guns alone. For the freedom of nations can be menaced not only by guns—but by the poverty that Communism can exploit.

You cannot fight poverty with guns.

You cannot satisfy hunger with deadly ammunition.

Economic stability and progress—essential to any nation's peace and well-being—cannot be assured merely by the firepower of artillery or the speed of jets.

And so our Mutual Security programs today—at a cost of some 4 billion dollars—are designed to meet dangers in whatever form they may appear. Thus, their key purposes are three.

First: To help friendly nations equip and support armed forces for their own and our defense.

Second: To help, in a sustained effort, less advanced countries grow in the strength that can sustain freedom as their way of life.

And third: To meet emergencies and special needs affecting our own national interest.

II

Examining each of these purposes briefly, I first speak of the military aspect of these programs.

This accounts for about three-fourths of their total cost—just under 3 billion dollars. This sum serves—indeed it belongs to—our own national defense. And to recognize that plain fact, I have today requested the Congress henceforth to appropriate funds for military assistance as part of the regular budget of our Department of Defense.

Our system of collective defense unites us with all those 42 countries with whom we have defense treaties. It embraces the Organization of American States in this Western Hemisphere, and defense arrangements with many Far Eastern countries like Korea and the Republic of China. It includes our readiness to cooperate in the Middle East with any free country threatened by Communist aggression and seeking our aid.

In Europe this collective effort is symbolized by NATO—the 15 countries of the North Atlantic Treaty alliance. And NATO's strength involves much more than symbols. In addition to our forces, NATO has more than 80 trained divisions, active and reserve, some 5 thousand modern aircraft, 600 major naval vessels. Here—as elsewhere throughout the world—our allies provide manpower, resources, and bases, while we help with weapons and military training.

Here again we see in the most concrete and practical way how collective effort and collective security serve our own national good. For our nation to try, completely alone, to counter the Communist military threat would be not only more hazardous strategy; it would also be far more costly.

It would demand many billions of dollars more in defense expenditures.

It would mean raising the draft calls throughout our land. It would mean more of our sons in uniform. It would mean longer service for them.

And even if we did all these things—and I do not hear the critics of Mutual Security publicly proposing such alternatives—even then we would finally provide a defense inferior in strength to the collective defense we share with our allies today.

Around the world we have provided our allies, over the past 7 years, some 17 billion dollars in direct military assistance. Over the same period, the defense budgets of our allies have totalled some 107 billion dollars.

Let us see what this united effort has achieved in 8 years.

In 1950, the strength of our allies totalled 1,000 combat vessels, 3.5 million men in their ground forces, and 500 jet aircraft.

Now, in 1957, they have: 2,500 combat vessels, 5 million men, and 13 thousand jets.

Within this world-wide program, our own contribution is vital. There are free countries in danger which—if thrown back completely on their own resources—would have to cut their armed forces. They would at once become targets for renewed Communist pressures. We would have to increase our own military strength—and in the process we would suffer in terms of both cost and security. And the endangered nations would suffer a slow strangulation quite as fateful as sudden aggression.

These are the harsh and inescapable facts of international life in this mid-twentieth century. We must face these facts and act accordingly—or face, instead, ultimate disaster as a people.

III

Now let us look at Mutual Security on the economic front.

The peril here can be just as great to us as in the military arena.

Today in many countries one billion free people—across three continents—live in lands where the average yearly income of each man is one hundred dollars or less. These lands include the 19 nations that have won their independence since World War II. Most of them are on the frontier of the Communist world, close to the pressure of Communist power. For centuries the peoples of these countries have borne a burden of poverty. Now they are resolved to hold on to political independence—to achieve the economic strength to sustain that independence, and to support rising standards of living.

In these lands no government can justly rule, or even survive, which does not reflect this resolve, which does not offer its people hope of progress. And wherever moderate government disappears, Communist extremists will extend their brand of despotic imperialism.

Our own strength would suffer severely from the loss of these lands—their people and their resources—to Communist domination. As these lands improve their own standards of living they will be stronger allies in defense of freedom. And there will be widening opportunity for trade with them.

We seek to help these people to help themselves.

We cannot export progress and security to them.

Essentially, they must achieve these for themselves. But there are practical ways by which we can help—especially in the early struggles of these young nations to survive.

For one thing, they need the knowledge of skilled people—farm experts, doctors, engineers—to teach new techniques to their people. Our program of technical cooperation aims to do this. It will cost 150 million dollars next year.

At the same time—because their inherited poverty leaves these peoples so little for saving—they need the help of some capital to begin essential investment in roads, dams, railroads, utilities—the sinews of economic strength.

Already many of these countries, like India and Pakistan, are with great difficulty devoting substantial amounts of their limited resources to this kind of long-range investment. But at this critical moment of their economic growth a relatively small amount of outside capital can fatefully decide the difference between success and failure. What is critical now is to start and to maintain momentum.

While we want and intend to see that private investors and other lending agencies supply as much as possible of this outside capital, our Development Assistance Program under Mutual Security has a vital role to play.

Here I am convinced that we should rely more upon loans than upon gifts. This is the sound and proper way for free allies to work together—to respect and to encourage the pride of each nation, to inspire in each nation greater zeal and sense of responsibility, to encourage throughtful long-term planning rather than frantic emergency action.

This outlook signifies a fundamental shift of emphasis from the practice of past years.

I have accordingly asked the Congress to create a Development Loan Fund with enough capital to allow orderly and continuing operations. Only this kind of sustained operations will allow for the prudent and thoughtful use of money. Only such operations will assure priority to the most sound and necessary projects.

To assure this continuity and coherence of action, I have specifically requested for the first year 500 million dollars already in the budget, and authority for 750 million dollars for each of the two succeeding years.

In this whole program, we do not seek to buy friends.

We do not seek to make satellites.

We do seek to help other peoples to become strong and stay free—and learn, through living in freedom, how to conquer poverty, how to know the blessings of peace and progress.

This purpose—I repeat—serves our own national interest.

It also reflects our own national character. We are stirred not only by calculations of self-interest but also by decent regard for the needs and the hopes of all our fellowmen. I am proud of this fact, as you are. None of us would wish it to be otherwise.

This is not mere sentimentality. This is the very nature of America—realistically understood and applied.

If ever we were to lose our sense of brotherhood, of kinship with all free men, we would have entered upon our nation's period of decline. Without vision—without a quick sense of justice and compassion—no people can claim greatness.

IV

There remains—in addition to continuing defense and economic aid—a final aspect to our Mutual Security programs. This entails assistance to meet various special needs, including sudden crises against which prior planning is impossible. Such crises generally demand the swiftest action.

We have seen several such examples in recent years.

In the Middle East, the freedom of Iran only 4 years ago was threatened by the rule of a Government inclined toward Communism. Under the courageous leadership of the Shah, the people of Iran met that danger. In their effort to restore economic stability, they received indispensable help from us. Iran remains free. And its freedom continues to prove of vital importance to our own freedom.

In our own hemisphere, Guatemala not long ago faced a similar peril, with heavy Communist infiltration into the Government. Here, too, the people rose to repel this threat, but they needed—and they received—the help without which their efforts could have been in vain.

Most recently, we have witnessed a like instance in the Middle East. The Kingdom of Jordan came under the sway of a succession of Cabinets, each one seemingly more tolerant of Communist infiltration and subversion. King Hussein has acted swiftly and resolutely to forestall disaster, and the peril now seems checked.

Yet this victory would surely be lost without economic aid from outside Jordan. Jordan's armed forces must be paid. The nation's utilities must function. And, above all, the people must have hope.

Some necessary aid can come from neighboring Arab countries, such as Saudi Arabia, but some also must come from the United States. For the security of Jordan means strength for all the forces of freedom in the Middle East.

Now, you have undoubtedly heard charges of waste and inefficiency in some of these programs of assistance such as that in Iran. I do not doubt that isolated incidents could be cited to support such charges.

On this I have two convictions.

First: the remarkable truth is not that a few Americans working abroad may have been inefficient, but that so many thousands of patriotic Americans have willingly and competently done their jobs in distant lands, under the most difficult conditions, often in the presence of real danger.

And second: when we speak of waste, let none of us forget that there is no waste so colossal as war itself—and these programs are totally dedicated to the prevention of that most appalling kind of waste.

All such situations—as in Iran, Guatemala, Jordan—have been tense moments in the world struggle. Each such moment has vitally touched our own national interest.

I have asked the Congress for the sum of 300 million dollars to enable us to act—and to act swiftly—in any such moment as it may strike.

Only such part of that sum will be used as is clearly needed to serve our national interest. But the history of these years surely means one thing: to give saving help at such moments is true economy on a world scale—for it can mean the saving of whole nations and the promotion of peace.

V

These, then, are the kinds of help and action that make up our Mutual Security programs, for which I have asked the Congress to appropriate less than 4 billion dollars—one-twentieth of our national budget. This is not a mathematical guess or an arbitrary sum. It reflects economies already achieved in some aspects of military aid.

It is a reasoned figure.

And, considering the issues at stake, it is a minimum figure.

I know of no more sound or necessary investment that our Nation can make. I know of no expenditure that can contribute so much—in the words of the Constitution—to our "common defense" and to securing the blessings of liberty for ourselves and our posterity.

To see all the day-to-day results of these programs in concrete terms is not always easy. They operate in distant lands whose histories, even their names, seem remote. Often the results are not swift and dramatic, but gradual and steady. They operate in a way rather like police or fire protection in our own cities. When they are least in the news, they are really doing the most effective work.

We live at a time when our plainest task is to put first things first. Of all our current domestic concerns—lower taxes, bigger dams, deeper harbors, higher pensions, better housing—not one of these will matter if our nation is put in peril. For all that we cherish and justly desire—for ourselves or for our children—the securing of peace is the first requisite.

We live in a time when the cost of peace is high.

Yet the price of war is higher and is paid in different coin—with the lives of our youth and the devastation of our cities.

The road to this disaster could easily be paved with the good intentions of those blindly striving to save the money that must be spent as the price of peace.

It is no accident that those who have most intimately lived with the horrors of war are generally the most earnest supporters of these programs to secure peace.

To cripple our programs for Mutual Security in the false name of "economy" can mean nothing less than a weakening of our nation.

To try to save money at the risk of such damage is neither conservative nor constructive.

It is reckless.

It could mean the loss of peace. It could mean the loss of freedom. It could mean the loss of both.

I know that you would not wish your government to take such a reckless gamble.

I do not intend that your government take that gamble.

I am convinced of the necessity of these programs of Mutual Security—for the very safety of our nation. For upon them critically depends all that we hold most dear—the heritage of freedom from our fathers, the peace and well-being of the sons who will come after us.

Thank you—and good night.

The Alliance for Progress

Eisenhower mentioned in his 1957 address that, at one time, Guatemala had seemed in danger of turning Communist. It had had a short-lived regime that seemed pro-Soviet. Rebels, with some assistance from outside, overthrew this regime.

Then, in 1959, communism gained a foothold in the Americas. A bearded young revolutionary, Fidel Castro, seized power in Cuba. At first, Castro appeared to be merely a reform leader. From his conduct, it soon became apparent that he was more than that. By late 1960 he had disclosed publicly that he and his associates were Communists and that Cuba now belonged to the bloc of Communist nations.

The takeover of Cuba caused more dismay than any event since the fall of China. It awakened the public, the press, and Congress to the fact that most of the Western Hemisphere was ripe for revolutions such as Castro's.

The Eisenhower administration moved to step up economic and military aid to American republics. Subscribing to the Act of Bogotá of 1960, the American government pledged larger contributions to a Social Progress Fund on which Latin American nations could draw to finance land reform and other such projects.

Campaigning for the presidency in 1960, John F. Kennedy called for a still larger and bolder program. Kennedy spoke of an "Alliance for Progress."

After Kennedy's election, steps were promptly taken to forge such an alliance. The United States promised to provide, partly through encouraging private investment, a billion dollars a year for ten years. Cooperative planning was to enable the American republics to undertake badly needed reform in land distribution, taxation, and public welfare.

Two works discussing the development and aim of this program are John S. Dreier, The Alliance for Progress *(1962) and Lincoln Gordon,* A New Deal for Latin America *(1962). A sketch of the background is E. R. May, "The Alliance for Progress in Historical Perspective,"* Foreign Affairs *(July, 1963), pages 757–774.*

The first document below is President Kennedy's message to the Inter-American Economic and Social Council, meeting at Punta del Este, Uruguay. It is from the State Department Bulletin, *volume 45 (Aug. 28, 1961), pages 355–356. The second is the Charter of Punta del Este, which states the aims of the Alliance for Progress. It is from* ibid. *(Sept. 11, 1961), pages 462–469.*

JOHN F. KENNEDY, MESSAGE TO THE INTER-AMERICAN ECONOMIC AND SOCIAL COUNCIL, AUGUST 5, 1961

Fellow citizens of the Americas: Twenty-five years ago one of the greatest of my predecessors, Franklin Roosevelt, addressed the Inter-American Conference for the Maintenance of Peace, meeting at Buenos Aires—a conference called to protect the peace and freedom of the hemisphere.

That conference was a great success. Its accomplishments were, in Roosevelt's words, "far-reaching and historic." New molds of friendship and cooperation were forged. A new day in the history of the Americas had begun.

Yet, on his return from the conference, President Roosevelt stopped in Montevideo just a few miles from your meeting place to warn that "We have not completed our task. . . . That task is a continuing one. We seek new remedies for new conditions; new conditions will continue to arise. . . . But the net result is that we move forward."

Today, a quarter century later, we meet to carry on that task to demonstrate anew that freedom is not merely a word or an abstract theory but the most effective instrument for advancing the welfare of man. We face new conditions and we must devise new remedies to meet them, and we are confident that we will move forward.

Those of you at this conference are present at an historic moment in the life of this hemisphere. For this is far more than an economic discussion or a technical conference on development. In a very real sense it is a demonstration of the capacity of free nations to meet the human and material problems of the modern world. It is a test of the values of our own society, a proving ground for the vitality of freedom in the affairs of man.

The views of the United States on the important social and economic questions encompassed by the agenda will be fully explained by Secretary [of the Treasury *(ed.)*] C. Douglas Dillon. Underlying those views are the simple and basic principles of the Alliance for Progress.

We live in a hemisphere whose own revolution has given birth to the most powerful forces of the modern age—the search for the freedom and self-fulfillment of man. We meet to carry on that revolution to shape the future as we have the past.

This means that all of our countries—nations of the north and nations of the south—must make new efforts of unparalleled magnitude.

Self-fulfillment for the developing nations means careful national planning, the orderly establishment of goals, priorities, and long-range programs.

It means expanded export markets, closer economic integration within Latin America, and greater market stability for the major primary products.

It means the dedication of a greatly increased proportion of national resources and capital to the cause of development.

And it means full recognition of the right of all the people to share fully in our progress. For there is no place in democratic life for institutions which benefit the few while denying the needs of the many even though the elimination of such institutions may require far-reaching and difficult changes such as land reform and tax reform and a vastly increased emphasis on education and health and housing. Without these changes our common effort cannot succeed.

The Alliance for Progress also means a greatly increased effort by the United States both in terms of material resources and deeper comprehension of the basic needs of Latin America. My country has already begun its contribution. During the year which began on March 13 with the announcement of the Alliance for Progress the United States will allocate more than $1 billion in development assistance to Latin America. This amount is more than three times that made available last year. It includes less than half of the $500 million appropriated under the Act of Bogotá. It does not include the additional resources which will be made available through the World Bank, other international institutions, and private sources.

This rapid increase in the level of our assistance is only the first step in our continuing and expanding effort to help build a better life for the people of the hemisphere, an effort to which I am devoting my personal attention. And as the nations of Latin America take the necessary steps, as they formulate the plans, mobilize the internal resources, make the difficult and necessary social reforms, and accept the sacrifice necessary if their national energy is to be fully directed to economic development—then I believe that the United States should supplement this effort by helping to provide resources of a scope and magnitude adequate to realize the bold and elevated goals envisaged by the Alliance for Progress. For, as I have said before, only an effort of towering dimension—an effort similar to that which was needed to rebuild the economies of Western Europe—can insure fulfillment of our Alliance for Progress.

This heroic effort is not for governments alone. Its success demands the participation of all our people—of workers and farmers, businessmen and intellectuals, and, above all, of the young people of the Americas. For to them and to their children belongs the new world we are resolved to create.

The tasks before us are vast, the problems difficult, the challenges unparalleled. But we carry with us the vision of a new and better world and the unlimited power of free men guided by free governments. And I believe that our ultimate success will make us proud to have lived and worked at this historic moment in the life of our hemisphere.

THE CHARTER OF PUNTA DEL ESTE, AUGUST 17, 1961: ESTABLISHING THE ALLIANCE FOR PROGRESS WITHIN THE FRAMEWORK OF OPERATION PAN AMERICA

Preamble

We, the American Republics, hereby proclaim our decision to unite in a common effort to bring our people accelerated economic progress and broader social justice within the framework of personal dignity and political liberty.

Almost two hundred years ago we began in this Hemisphere the long struggle for freedom which now inspires people in all parts of the world. Today, in ancient lands, men moved to hope by the revolutions of our young nations search for liberty. Now we must give a new meaning to that revolutionary heritage. For America stands at a turning point in history. The men and women of our Hemisphere are reaching for the better life which today's skills have placed within their grasp. They are determined for themselves and their children to have decent and ever more abundant lives, to gain access to knowledge and equal opportunity for all, to end those conditions which benefit the few at the expense of the needs and dignity of the many. It is our inescapable task to fulfill these just desires—to demonstrate to the poor and forsaken of our countries, and of all lands, that the creative powers of free men hold the key to their progress and to the progress of future generations. And our certainty of ultimate success rests not alone on our faith in ourselves and in our nations but on the indomitable spirit of free man which has been the heritage of American civilization.

Inspired by these principles, and by the principles of Operation Pan America and the Act of Bogotá, the American Republics hereby resolve to adopt the following program of action to establish and carry forward an Alliance for Progress.

Title I. Objectives of the Alliance for Progress

It is the purpose of the Alliance for Progress to enlist the full energies of the peoples and governments of the American republics in a great cooperative effort to accelerate the economic and social development of the participating countries of Latin America, so that they may achieve maximum levels of well-being, with equal opportunities for all, in democratic societies adapted to their own needs and desires.

The American republics agree to work toward the achievement of the following fundamental goals in the present decade:

1. To achieve in the participating Latin American countries a substantial and sustained growth of per capita incomes at a rate designed to attain, at the earliest possible date, levels of income capable of assuring self-sustaining development, and sufficient to make Latin American income levels constantly larger in relation to the levels of the more industrialized nations. In this way the gap between the living standards of Latin America and those of the more developed countries can be narrowed. Similarly, presently existing differences in income levels among the Latin American countries will be reduced by accelerating the development of the relatively less developed countries and granting them maximum priority in the distribution of resources and in international cooperation in general. In evaluating the degree of relative development, account will be taken not only of average levels of real income and gross product per capita, but also of indices of infant mortality, illiteracy, and per capita daily caloric intake.

It is recognized that, in order to reach these objectives within a reasonable time, the rate of economic growth in any country of Latin America should be not less than 2.5 per cent per capita per year, and that each participating country should determine its own growth target in the light of its stage of social and economic evolution, resource endowment, and ability to mobilize national efforts for development.

2. To make the benefits of economic progress available to all citizens of all economic and social groups through a more equitable distribution of national income, raising more rapidly the income and standard of living of the needier sectors of the population, at the same time that a higher proportion of the national product is devoted to investment.

3. To achieve balanced diversification in national economic structures, both regional and functional, making them increasingly free from dependence on the export of a limited number of primary products and the importation of capital goods while seeking to attain stability in the prices of exports or in income derived from exports.

4. To accelerate the process of rational industrialization so as to increase the productivity of the economy as a whole, taking full advantage of the talents and energies of both the private and public sectors, utilizing the natural resources of the country and providing productive and remunerative employment for unemployed or part-time workers. Within this

process of industrialization, special attention should be given to the establishment and development of capital-goods industries.

5. To raise greatly the level of agricultural productivity and output and to improve related storage, transportation, and marketing services.

6. To encourage, in accordance with the characteristics of each country, programs of comprehensive agrarian reform leading to the effective transformation, where required, of unjust structures and systems of land tenure and use, with a view to replacing latifundia and dwarf-holdings by an equitable system of land tenure so that, with the help of timely and adequate credit, technical assistance and facilities for the marketing and distribution of products, the land will become for the man who works it the basis of his economic stability, the foundation of his increasing welfare, and the guarantee of his freedom and dignity.

7. To eliminate adult illiteracy and by 1970 to assure, as a minimum, access to six years of primary education for each school-age child in Latin America; to modernize and expand vocational, secondary and higher educational and training facilities, to strengthen the capacity for basic and applied research, and to provide the competent personnel required in rapidly-growing societies.

8. To increase life expectancy at birth by a minimum of five years, and to increase the ability to learn and produce, by improving individual and public health. To attain this goal it will be necessary, among other measures, to provide adequate potable water supply and drainage to not less than 70 per cent of the urban and 50 per cent of the rural population; to reduce the mortality rate of children less than five years of age to at least one-half of the present rate; to control the more serious transmissible diseases, according to their importance as a cause of sickness and death; to eradicate those illnesses, especially malaria, for which effective cures are known; to improve nutrition; to train medical and health personnel to meet at least minimum standards of competence; to improve basic health services at national and local levels; to intensify scientific research and apply its results more fully and effectively to the prevention and cure of illness.

9. To increase the construction of low-cost houses for low-income families in order to replace inadequate and deficient housing and to reduce housing shortages; and to provide necessary public services to both urban and rural centers of population.

10. To maintain stable price levels, avoiding inflation or deflation and the consequent social hardships and maldistribution of resources, bearing always in mind the necessity of maintaining an adequate rate of economic growth.

11. To strengthen existing agreements on economic integration, with a view to the ultimate fulfillment of aspirations for a Latin American common market that will expand and diversify trade among the Latin American countries and thus contribute to the economic growth of the region.

12. To develop cooperative programs designed to prevent the harmful effects of excessive fluctuations in the foreign exchange earnings derived from exports of primary products, which are of vital importance to economic and social development; and to adopt the measures necessary to facilitate the access of Latin American exports to international markets.

Title II. Economic and Social Development

Chapter I. Basic Requirements for Economic and Social Development. The American republics recognize that to achieve the foregoing goals it will be necessary:

1. That comprehensive and well-conceived national programs of economic and social development, aimed at the achievement of self-sustaining growth, be carried out in accordance with democratic principles.
2. That national programs of economic and social development be based on the principle of self-help—as established in the Act of Bogotá—and the maximum use of domestic resources, taking into account the special conditions of each country.
3. That in the preparation and execution of plans for economic and social development, women should be placed on an equal footing with men.
4. That the Latin American countries obtain sufficient external financial assistance, a substantial portion of which should be extended on flexible conditions with respect to periods and terms of repayment and forms of utilization, in order to supplement domestic capital formation and reinforce their import capacity; and that in support of well-conceived programs, including the necessary structural reforms and measures for the mobilization of internal resources, a supply of capital from all external sources during the coming ten years of at least 20 billion dollars be made available to the Latin American countries, with priority to the relatively less developed countries. The greater part of this sum should be in public funds.
5. That institutions in both the public and private sectors, including labor, cooperative, commercial, industrial and financial institutions, be strengthened and improved for increasingly effective use of domestic resources, and that the necessary social reforms be effected to permit a fair distribution of the fruits of economic and social progress.

Chapter II. National Development Programs. 1. Participating Latin American countries agree to introduce or strengthen systems for the preparation, execution and periodic revision of national programs for economic and social development consistent with the principles, objectives and requirements contained in this document. Participating Latin American countries should formulate, if possible within the next eighteen months, long-term development programs. Such programs should embrace, according to the characteristics of each country, the elements outlined in the Appendix.

2. National development programs should incorporate self-help efforts directed to:

a. The improvement of human resources and widening of opportunities through raising general standards of education and health; improving and extending technical education and the training of professionals, with emphasis on science and technology; providing adequate remuneration for work performed; encouraging managerial, entrepreneurial, and salaried talent; providing more productive employment for underemployed manpower; establishing effective systems of labor relations, and procedures for consultation and collaboration among public authorities, employer associations, and labor organizations; promoting local institutions for basic and applied research; and improving the standards of public administration.

b. The wider development and more efficient use of natural resources, especially those which are now idle or underutilized, including measures for the processing of raw materials.

c. The strengthening of the agricultural base, progressively extending the benefits of the land to those who work it, and ensuring in countries with Indian populations the integration of these populations into the economic, social, and cultural processes of modern life. To carry out these aims, measures should be adopted, among others, to establish or improve, as the case may be, the following services: extension, credit, technical assistance, agricultural research and mechanization; health and education; storage and distribution; cooperatives and farmers' associations; and community development.

d. The more effective, rational and equitable mobilization and use of financial resources through the reform of tax structures, including fair and adequate taxation of large incomes and real estate, and the strict application of measures to improve fiscal administration. Development programs should include the adaptation of budget expenditures to development needs, measures for the maintenance of price stability, the creation of essential credit facilities at reasonable rates of interest, and the encouragement of private savings.

e. The promotion through appropriate measures, including the signing of agreements for the purpose of reducing or eliminating double taxation, of conditions that will encourage the flow of foreign investments and help to increase the capital resources of participating countries in need of capital.

f. The improvement of systems of distribution and sales in order to make markets more competitive and prevent monopolistic practices.

Chapter III. Immediate and Short-term Action Measures. 1. Recognizing that a number of Latin American countries, despite their best efforts, may require emergency financial assistance, the United States will provide assistance from the funds which are or may be established for such purposes. The United States stands ready to take prompt action on applications for such assistance. Applications relating to existing situations should be submitted within the next 60 days.

2. Participating Latin American countries should immediately increase their efforts to accelerate their development, giving special emphasis (in addition to the creation or strengthening of machinery for long-term development programming) to the following objectives:

a. The completion of projects already under way and the initiation of projects for which the basic studies have been made in order to accelerate their financing and execution.

b. The implementation of new projects which are designed:

i. To meet the most pressing social needs and benefit directly the greatest number of people;

ii. To concentrate efforts within each country in the less developed or more depressed areas in which particularly serious social problems exist;

iii. To utilize idle capacity or resources, particularly underemployed manpower;

iv. To survey and assess natural resources.

c. The facilitation of the preparation and execution of long-term programs through measures designed:

i. To train teachers, technicians, and specialists;

ii. To provide accelerated training to workers and farmers;

iii. To improve basic statistics;
iv. To establish needed credit and marketing facilities;
v. To improve services and administration.

3. The United States will assist in the realization of these short-term measures with a view to achieving concrete results from the Alliance for Progress at the earliest possible moment. In connection with the measures set forth above, and in accordance with the statement of President Kennedy, the United States will provide assistance under the Alliance, including assistance for the financing of short-term measures, totalling more than one billion dollars in the year ending March 1962.

Chapter IV. External Assistance in Support of National Development Programs. 1. The economic and social development of Latin America will require large public and private financial assistance on the part of capital-exporting countries, including the members of the Development Assistance Group and international lending agencies. The measures provided for in the Act of Bogotá and the new measures provided for in this Charter are designed to create a framework within which such additional assistance can be provided and effectively utilized.

2. The United States will assist those participating countries whose Development Programs establish self-help measures, economic policies and programs consistent with the goals and principles of this Charter. To supplement the domestic efforts of such countries, the United States is prepared to allocate resources which, along with those anticipated from other external sources, will be of a scope and magnitude adequate to realize the goals envisaged in this Charter. Such assistance will be allocated to both social and economic development, and where appropriate, will take the form of grants or loans on flexible terms and conditions. The participating countries will request the assistance of other capital-exporting countries and international institutions so that they may provide assistance for the attainment of these objectives.

3. The United States will assist in the financing of technical assistance projects proposed by a participating country or by the Secretariat of the Organization of American States for the purpose of; a) contracting, in agreement with governments, for experts to assist the governments, including the preparation of specific investment projects and the strengthening of national mechanisms for preparing projects, using specialized engineering firms where appropriate; b) carrying out, pursuant to cooperative agreements existing among the Secretariat of the Organization of American States, the Economic Commission for Latin America, and the Inter-American Development Bank, field investigations and studies, including those relating to development problems, the organization of national planning agencies and the preparation of development programs, agrarian reform and rural development, health, cooperatives, housing, education and professional training, and taxation and tax administration; and c) convening meetings of experts and officials on development and related problems.

The governments or above-mentioned organizations should, when appropriate, seek the cooperation of the United Nations and its Specialized Agencies in the execution of these activities.

4. The participating Latin American countries recognize that each has in varying degree a capacity to assist fellow republics by providing external technical and financial assistance. They recognize that this capacity will increase as their economies grow. They therefore affirm their intention to assist fellow republics increasingly as their individual circumstances permit.

Chapter V. Organization and Procedures. 1. In order to provide technical assistance for the formulation of development programs, as may be requested by participating nations, the Organization of American States, the Economic Commission for Latin America, and the Inter-American Development Bank will continue and strengthen their agreements for coordination in this field, in order to have available a group of programming experts whose service can be used to facilitate the implementation of this Charter. The participating countries will also seek an intensification of technical assistance from the Specialized Agencies of the United Nations for the same purpose.

2. The Inter-American Economic and Social Council, on the joint nomination of the Secretary General of the Organization of American States, the President of the Inter-American Development Bank, and the Executive Secretary of the United Nations Economic Commission for Latin America, will appoint a panel of nine high-level experts, exclusively on the basis of their experience, technical ability, and competence in the various aspects of economic and social development. The experts may be of any nationality, though if of Latin American origin an appropriate geographical distribution will be sought. They will be attached to the Inter-American Economic and Social Council, but will nevertheless enjoy complete autonomy in the performance of their duties. They may not hold any other remunerative position. The appointment of these experts will be for a period of three years, and may be renewed.

3. Each government, if it so wishes, may present its program for economic and social development for consideration by an ad hoc committee, composed of no more than three members drawn from the panel of experts referred to in the preceding paragraph together with an equal number of experts not on the panel. The experts who compose the ad hoc Committee will be appointed by the Secretary General of the Organization of American States at the request of the interested government and with its consent.

4. The Committee will study the development program, exchange opinions with the interested government as to possible modifications and, with the consent of the government, report its conclusions to the Inter-American Development Bank and to other governments and institutions that may be prepared to extend external financial and technical assistance in connection with the execution of the program.

5. In considering a development program presented to it, the ad hoc Committee will examine the consistency of the program with the principles of the Act of Bogotá and of this Charter, taking into account the elements in the Appendix.

6. The General Secretariat of the Organization of American States will provide the personnel needed by the experts referred to in paragraphs 2 and 3 of this Chapter in order to fulfill their tasks. Such personnel may be employed specifically for this purpose or may be made available from the

permanent staffs of the Organization of American States, the Economic Commission for Latin America, and the Inter-American Development Bank, in accordance with the present liaison arrangements between the three organizations. The General Secretariat of the Organization of American States may seek arrangements with the United Nations Secretariat, its Specialized Agencies and the Inter-American Specialized Organizations, for the temporary assignment of necessary personnel.

7. A government whose development program has been the object of recommendations made by the ad hoc Committee with respect to external financing requirements may submit the program to the Inter-American Development Bank so that the Bank may undertake the negotiations required to obtain such financing, including the organization of a consortium of credit institutions and governments disposed to contribute to the continuing and systematic financing, on appropriate terms, of the development program. However, the government will have full freedom to resort through any other channels to all sources of financing, for the purpose of obtaining, in full or in part, the required resources.

The ad hoc Committee shall not interfere with the right of each government to formulate its own goals, priorities, and reforms in its national development programs.

The recommendations of the ad hoc Committee will be of great importance in determining the distribution of public funds under the Alliance for Progress which contribute to the external financing of such programs. These recommendations shall give special consideration to Title I. 1.

The participating governments will also use their good offices to the end that these recommendations may be accepted as a factor of great importance in the decisions taken, for the same purpose, by inter-American credit institutions, other international credit agencies, and other friendly governments which may be potential sources of capital.

8. The Inter-American Economic and Social Council will review annually the progress achieved in the formulation, national implementation, and international financing of development programs; and will submit to the Council of the Organization of American States such recommendations as it deems pertinent.

Appendix

Elements of National Development Programs. 1. The establishment of mutually consistent targets to be sought over the program period in expanding productive capacity in industry, agriculture, mining, transport, power and communications, and in improving conditions of urban and rural life, including better housing, education and health.

2. The assignment of priorities and the description of methods to achieve the targets, including specific measures and major projects. Specific development projects should be justified in terms of their relative costs and benefits, including their contribution to social productivity.

3. The measures which will be adopted to direct the operations of the public sector and to encourage private action in support of the development program.

4. The estimated cost, in national and foreign currency, of major projects and of the development program as a whole, year by year over the program period.

5. The internal resources, public and private, estimated to become available for the execution of the program.

6. The direct and indirect effects of the program on the balance of payments, and the external financing, public and private, estimated to be required for the execution of the program.

7. The basic fiscal and monetary policies to be followed in order to permit implementation of the program within a framework of price stability.

8. The machinery of public administration—including relationships with local governments, decentralized agencies and non-governmental organizations, such as labor organizations, cooperatives, business and industrial organizations—to be used in carrying out the program, adapting it to changing circumstances and evaluating the progress made.

Title III. Economic Integration of Latin America

The American republics consider that the broadening of present national markets in Latin America is essential to accelerate the process of economic development in the Hemisphere. It is also an appropriate means for obtaining greater productivity through specialized and complementary industrial production which will, in turn, facilitate the attainment of greater social benefits for the inhabitants of the various regions of Latin America. The broadening of markets will also make possible the better use of resources under the Alliance for Progress. Consequently, the American Republics recognize that:

1. The Montevideo Treaty (because of its flexibility and because adherence to it is available to all of the Latin American nations) and the Central American Treaty on Economic Integration are appropriate instruments for the attainment of these objectives, as was recognized in Resolution No. 11 (III) of the Ninth Session of the Economic Commission for Latin America.

2. The integration process can be intensified and accelerated not only by the specialization resulting from the broadening of markets through the liberalization of trade but also through the use of such instruments as the agreements for complementary production within economic sectors provided for in the Montevideo Treaty.

3. In order to insure the balanced and complementary economic expansion of all of the countries involved, the integration process should take into account, on a flexible basis, the condition of countries at a relatively less advanced stage of economic development, permitting them to be granted special, fair, and equitable treatment.

4. In order to facilitate economic integration in Latin America, it is advisable to establish effective relationships between the Latin American Free Trade Association and the group of countries adhering to the Central American Economic Integration Treaty, as well as between either of these groups and other Latin American countries. These arrangements should be established within the limits determined by these instruments.

5. The Latin American countries should coordinate their actions to meet the unfavorable treatment accorded to their foreign trade in world markets, particularly that resulting from certain restrictive and discriminatory policies of extra-continental countries and economic groups.

6. In the application of resources under the Alliance for Progress, special attention should be given not only to investments for multinational projects that will contribute to strengthening the integration process in all its aspects, but also to the indispensable financing of industrial production, and to the growing expansion of trade in industrial products within Latin America.

7. In order to facilitate the participation of countries at a relatively lower stage of economic development in multinational Latin American economic cooperation programs, and in order to promote the balanced and harmonious development of the Latin American integration process, special attention should be given to the needs of these countries in the administration of financial resources provided under the Alliance for Progress, particularly in connection with infrastructure programs and the promotion of new lines of production.

8. The economic integration process implies a need for additional investment in various fields of economic activity and funds provided under the Alliance for Progress should cover these needs as well as those required for the financing of national development programs.

9. When groups of Latin American countries have their own institutions for financing economic integration, the financing referred to in the preceding paragraph should preferably be channeled through these institutions. With respect to regional financing designed to further the purposes of existing regional integration instruments, the cooperation of the Inter-American Development Bank should be sought in channeling extra-regional contributions which may be granted for these purposes.

10. One of the possible means for making effective a policy for the financing of Latin American integration would be to approach the International Monetary Fund and other financial sources with a view to providing a means for solving temporary balance-of-payments problems that may occur in countries participating in economic integration arrangements.

11. The promotion and coordination of transportation and communications systems is an effective way to accelerate the integration process. In order to counteract abusive practices in relation to freight rates and tariffs, it is advisable to encourage the establishment of multinational transport and communication enterprises in the Latin American countries, or to find other appropriate solutions.

12. In working toward economic integration and complementary economies, efforts should be made to achieve an appropriate coordination of national plans, or to engage in joint planning for various economies through the existing regional integration organizations. Efforts should also be made to promote an investment policy directed to the progressive elimination of unequal growth rates in the different geographic areas, particularly in the case of countries which are relatively less developed.

13. It is necessary to promote the development of national Latin American enterprises, in order that they may compete on an equal footing with foreign enterprises.

14. The active participation of the private sector is essential to economic

integration and development, and except in those countries in which free enterprise does not exist, development planning by the pertinent national public agencies, far from hindering such participation, can facilitate and guide it, thus opening new perspectives for the benefit of the community.

15. As the countries of the Hemisphere still under colonial domination achieve their independence, they should be invited to participate in Latin American economic integration programs.

Title IV. Basic Export Commodities

The American Republics recognize that the economic development of Latin America requires expansion of its trade, a simultaneous and corresponding increase in foreign exchange incomes received from exports, a lessening of cyclical or seasonal fluctuations in the incomes of those countries that still depend heavily on the export of raw materials, and the correction of the secular deterioration in their terms of trade.

They therefore agree that the following measures should be taken:

I. National Measures. National measures affecting commerce in primary products should be directed and applied in order to:

1. Avoid undue obstacles to the expansion of trade in these products;
2. Avoid market instability;
3. Improve the efficiency of international plans and mechanisms for stabilization;
4. Increase their present markets and expand their area of trade at a rate compatible with rapid development.

Therefore:

A. Importing member countries should reduce and if possible eliminate, as soon as feasible, all restrictions and discriminatory practices affecting the consumption and importation of primary products, including those with the highest possible degree of processing in the country of origin, except when these restrictions are imposed temporarily for purposes of economic diversification, to hasten the economic development of less developed nations or to establish basic national reserves. Importing countries should also be ready to support, by adequate regulations, stabilization programs for primary products that may be agreed upon with producing countries.

B. Industrialized countries should give special attention to the need for hastening economic development of less developed countries. Therefore, they should make maximum efforts to create conditions, compatible with their international obligations, through which they may extend advantages to less developed countries so as to permit the rapid expansion of their markets. In view of the great need for this rapid development, industrialized countries should also study ways in which to modify, wherever possible, international commitments which prevent the achievement of this objective.

C. Producing member countries should formulate their plans for production and export, taking account of their effect on world markets and of the necessity of supporting and improving the effectiveness of international stabilization programs and mechanisms. Similarly they should try to avoid increasing the uneconomic production of goods which can be obtained under better conditions in the less developed countries of the Continent and which are an important source of employment.

D. Member countries should adopt all necessary measures to direct technological studies toward finding new uses and by-products of those primary commodities that are most important to their economies.

E. Member countries should try to reduce, and, if possible, eliminate within a reasonable time export subsidies and other measures which cause instability in the markets for basic commodities and excessive fluctuations in prices and income.

II. International Cooperation Measures. 1. Member countries should make coordinated, and if possible, joint, efforts designed:

a. To eliminate as soon as possible undue protection of the production of primary products;

b. To eliminate internal taxes and reduce excessive domestic prices which discourage the consumption of imported primary products;

c. To seek to end preferential agreements and other measures which limit world consumption of Latin American primary products and their access to international markets, especially the markets of Western European countries in process of economic integration, and of countries with centrally planned economies.

d. To adopt the necessary consultation mechanisms so that their marketing policies will not have damaging effects on the stability of the markets of basic commodities.

2. Industrialized countries should give maximum cooperation to less developed countries so that their raw material exports will have the greatest degree of processing that is economic.

3. Through their representation in international financial organizations, member countries should suggest that these organizations, when considering loans for the promotion of production for export, take into account the effect of such loans on products which are in surplus in world markets.

4. Member countries should support the efforts being made by international commodity study groups and by the Commission on International Commodity Trade of the United Nations. In this connection, it should be considered that producing and consuming nations bear a joint responsibility for taking national and international steps to reduce market instability.

5. The Secretary General of the Organization of American States shall convene a group of experts appointed by their respective Governments to meet before November 30, 1961 and to report, not later than March 31, 1962 on measures to provide an adequate and effective means of offsetting the effects of fluctuations in the volume and prices of exports of basic products. The Government experts shall:

a. Consider the questions regarding compensatory financing raised during the present meeting;

b. Analyze the proposal for establishing an international fund for the stabilization of export receipts submitted in the Report of the Group of Experts to the Special Meeting of the IA–ECOSOC as well as any other alternative proposals;

c. Prepare a draft plan for the creation of mechanisms for compensatory financing. This draft plan should be circulated among the member Governments and their opinions obtained well in advance of the next meeting of the Commission on International Commodity Trade.

6. Member countries should support the efforts under way to improve and strengthen international commodity agreements and should be prepared to cooperate in the solution of specific commodity problems. Furthermore, they should endeavor to adopt adequate solutions for the short- and long-term problems affecting markets for primary products so that the economic interests of producers and consumers are equally safeguarded.

7. Member countries should request the cooperation of other producer and consumer countries in stabilization programs, bearing in mind that the raw materials of the Western Hemisphere are also produced and consumed in other parts of the world.

8. Member countries recognize that the disposal of accumulated reserves and surpluses can be a source for achieving the goals outlined in the first part of this Title, so that, together with the generation of local resources, the consumption of essential products in the receiving countries may be simultaneously increased. The disposal of surpluses and reserves should be carried out in an orderly manner, in order to:

a. Avoid disturbing existing commercial markets in member countries, and

b. Expand the sale of their products to other markets.

However, it is recognized that:

a. The disposal of surpluses should not displace commercial sales of identical products traditionally carried out by other countries; and

b. Such sales should not substitute for large scale financial and technical assistance programs.

IN WITNESS WHEREOF this Charter is signed, in Punta del Este, Uruguay, on the seventeenth day of August, nineteen hundred sixty-one.

The original texts shall be deposited in the archives of the Pan American Union, through the Secretary General of the Special Meeting, in order that certified copies may be sent to the Governments of the Member States of the Organization of American States.

The records of the Conference include a statement that the only authoritative text of agreements reached during the Conference is contained in the Charter of Punta del Este and in the specific resolutions passed by the Conference.

PART SEVEN

Traces of a Mild Thaw

SELECTION 31

The Spirit of Camp David

In 1953, Soviet Premier Stalin died. In the competition for power that ensued, the man who eventually emerged triumphant was Nikita Sergeevich Khrushchev.

Many Americans hoped that the change in the Soviet Union might lead to a lessening of tensions. Though holding firm the line against Communist expansion and continuing work on nuclear missiles, the Eisenhower administration made several overtures to the Kremlin. Eisenhower made a speech suggesting possible Soviet-American cooperation in developing the peaceful uses of atomic energy. He initiated negotiations for an end to the nuclear arms race and announced that the United States would unilaterally suspend tests of nuclear weapons. Previous tests by both sides had increased atmospheric radioactivity to near-perilous levels.

For a long time, there was no positive Soviet response. In fact, Soviet behavior indicated that Khrushchev interpreted Eisenhower's overtures as signs of weakness. In 1958, the Soviet Premier threatened to remove restraints from East Germany and allow that Communist regime to attempt the conquest of Berlin. The American government answered this threat with threats of its own, the implication being that a move against Berlin would provoke the "massive retaliation" of which Secretary of State Dulles had warned.

Khrushchev backed away. He had earlier spoken of a deadline for signing a separate peace treaty with East Germany. Now he said that there was no deadline.

In September, 1959, after long preparation, Khrushchev paid a visit to the United States. Unlike his cold and suspicious predecessor, Khrushchev had an outgoing personality. Shaking hands and cracking jokes, he reminded Americans of their own politicians. Public antagonism toward the Soviet Union diminished. Then Khrushchev met with President Eisenhower at Camp David, a Presidential retreat in the Catoctins. Although no specific agreements resulted, the talks seemed to go harmoniously. Afterward, the press spoke of a "spirit of Camp David." There was optimistic speculation about a possible end of the cold war.

The first document below is the official communiqué following the Camp David meeting between Eisenhower and Khrushchev. It is dated September 27, 1959. The second is an excerpt from a Presidential press conference held on September 28. One noteworthy element in the press conference is Eisenhower's use of the term "abnormal" with reference to the situation in Berlin. Afterward, some observers speculated that the Soviet Premier had been misled by Eisenhower's use of this term and expected wrongly that the American government would offer to compromise on the Berlin question.

The texts are from Public Papers of the Presidents: Dwight D. Eisenhower, 1959 *(Government Printing Office, 1960), pages 692, 694–702.*

COMMUNIQUÉ AFTER TALKS BETWEEN PRESIDENT EISENHOWER AND CHAIRMAN OF THE COUNCIL OF MINISTERS OF THE U.S.S.R. N. S. KHRUSHCHEV, SEPTEMBER 27, 1959

The Chairman of the Council of Ministers of the USSR, N. S. Khrushchev, and President Eisenhower have had a frank exchange of opinions at Camp David. In some of these conversations United States Secretary of State Herter and Soviet Foreign Minister Gromyko, as well as other officials from both countries, participated.

Chairman Khrushchev and the President have agreed that these discussions have been useful in clarifying each other's position on a number of subjects. The talks were not undertaken to negotiate issues. It is hoped, however, that their exchanges of view will contribute to a better understanding of the motives and position of each and thus to the achievement of a just and lasting peace.

The Chairman of the Council of Ministers of the USSR and the President of the United States agreed that the question of general disarmament is the most important one facing the world today. Both governments will make every effort to achieve a constructive solution of this problem.

In the course of the conversations an exchange of views took place on the question of Germany including the question of a peace treaty with Germany, in which the positions of both sides were expounded.

With respect to the specific Berlin question, an understanding was reached, subject to the approval of the other parties directly concerned, that negotiations would be reopened with a view to achieving a solution which would be in accordance with the interests of all concerned and in the interest of the maintenance of peace.

In addition to these matters useful conversations were held on a number of questions affecting the relations between the Union of Soviet Socialist Republics and the United States. These subjects included the question of trade between the two countries. With respect to an increase in exchanges of persons and ideas, substantial progress was made in discussions between officials and it is expected that certain agreements will be reached in the near future.

The Chairman of the Council of Ministers of the USSR and the President of the United States agreed that all outstanding international questions should be settled not by the application of force but by peaceful means through negotiation.

Finally it was agreed that an exact date for the return visit of the President to the Soviet Union next spring would be arranged through diplomatic channels.

PRESS CONFERENCE REMARKS BY PRESIDENT EISENHOWER, SEPTEMBER 28, 1959

Q. Marvin L. Arrowsmith, Associated Press: Mr. President, could you give us a general evaluation of your talks with Mr. Khrushchev, and tell us specifically whether the renunciation of force mentioned in the communique means that Mr. Khrushchev now has withdrawn any Soviet threats or ultimatums with respect to Berlin?

The President: Well, to have a little bit of outline, because this is a very involved subject, I think I had better try to keep straight on the track in this way:

First of all, I want to thank the American people. I think their restraint and their conduct on the whole was a credit to them. And if there is a better understanding on the part of Mr. Khrushchev of our people, of their aspirations, of their general attitudes about international questions, and particularly about their desire for peace, then that has been done by the American people.

I invited Mr. Khrushchev, as you know, to come here so that we might have a chance to discuss some of the obvious reasons for tensions in the world, and particularly between our two countries, because of the outstanding unsettled matters.

I did not ask him here for substantive negotiations, because those are impossible without the presence of our associates. But I thought that, through this visit of his and through these conversations, possibly I think as I have said to you before, some of the ice might be melted.

Now, if any of this has been done, again it's due to the American people; and I make special acknowledgements to the Mayors, Governors, the local officials who carried so much of the responsibility for making these visits possible, and for directing so many of the activities necessarily involved.

With respect to one other point, I think this: I think the American people have proved that they have an enlightened outlook toward these international problems; that they have got the strength in their own beliefs and convictions to listen to the other man politely, attentively, although reserving to themselves a right to oppose bitterly any imposition upon themselves of some of the practices, the beliefs, and convictions that are proposed and supported by another ideology; that they came through this with a very much better understanding, and proving that they themselves are very sophisticated, and if not sophisticated, let us say enlightened and understanding in these matters.

Now, the Chairman and I discussed the Berlin question at length. As you know, no specific negotiations can be carried out in such question as this without our allies, but you will have read the communique which brings up this point and says that negotiations are to be reundertaken, after making proper arrangements, in the aim to get a solution that will protect the legitimate interests of the Soviets, the East Germans, the West Germans, and above all, the Western people.

Over and above this, we agreed, in addition to what the communique said, that these negotiations should not be prolonged indefinitely but there could be no fixed time limit on them. I think that's perfectly clear and plain; and since it was the agreement of two individuals, I think that I should not attempt to go further in expounding on that point. . . .

Q. Felix Belair, New York Times: Mr. President, can you tell us if the general subject of China arose during the talks and in what context?

The President: To this extent, yes: it was raised, but the discussion was largely confined to this: a statement of our respective views which, you know, are diametrically opposed on almost every point; and it was agreed that it would be unprofitable to try to raise the China question in the matter of, you might say, the philosophy of action. . . .

Q. Charles H. Mohr, Time Magazine: Can we take it, sir, that your agreement that there is to be no fixed time limit on the negotiations over Berlin also means that there can be no fixed time limit on our occupation rights there, and our access rights to that city?

The President: Well, of course there can be no fixed limit. We do say this, all of us agree that this is an abnormal situation, all the world does.

Here is a free city, sitting inside a Communist country, and a hundred and ten miles from the Western Germany of which it feels it is a part. Therefore, the only way you can get a solution is by negotiations that will probably take some time. We agree that these would not be unnecessarily or unduly extended, but we did say there is no fixed time to which they are limited. . . .

Q. Andrew F. Tully, Jr., Scripps-Howard: Sir, what did you think of Mr. Khrushchev?

The President: Well, he is a dynamic and arresting personality. He is a man that uses every possible debating method available to him. He is capable of great flights, you might say, of mannerism and almost disposition, from one of almost negative, difficult attitude, to the most easy, affable, genial type of discussion.

I think that the American people sensed as they went around that they were seeing some man who is an extraordinary personality, there is no question about it.

Now, I thoroughly believe that he is sure that the basic tenets of the socialistic, or communistic, doctrine are correct. He has made great dents into the original concept of this doctrine. For example, he very definitely stated that he had made much better use of the incentive system in the Soviet economy than we. He knows all about our taxes and all the rest of it, but he talks in terms that if you do a better job you get a better house. He talked about some of the things they are providing for their people who really perform. So, in a number of ways, he shows how the application of the doctrine has been changed very greatly in modern usage in the Soviet region.

Q. Edward T. Folliard, Washington Post: Mr. President, to use your phrase, do you think that you and Mr. Khrushchev did melt some of the ice around East-West relations and if so, how much?

The President: Well, I'd say this: the most that could be done here, Mr. Folliard, is a beginning.

I think that there are a number of people close to him that are quite aware of some of the problems that come about unless we do melt some ice. For example, he himself deplored the need for spending so much money on defenses. We tried, between ourselves, to talk for a little bit about our comparative costs, therefore how we could calculate just exactly how much of our wealth is going into these things that are, after all, negative and sterile and purely defensive. Well, this was an interesting exercise, but of course we got nowhere except his continued insistence they're just too expensive, we must find better ways.

The same way with the individual whose name I forget exactly, the man who was talking to Mr. McCone—well, Mr. McCone's opposite number.* He pointed out their effort to develop this program of peaceful use of atomic energy; he said we must do it together because it is just too expensive for one country alone.

So, in a number of ways you find, if the ice isn't melted, an awareness on their part; not only the one that great wars are unthinkable, that's in the background, but in many ways, detailed ways, they are finding out we just have to do something that's a little bit more reasonable than what we have been doing.

Q. Charles W. Roberts, Newsweek: Sir, the most important of the three preconditions for a summit that we've made now seems to be the removal of threats to Berlin. I know you touched on that in the first question, but I wonder if you could indicate to us whether the Chairman did promise to ease the pressure or remove pressure somewhat.

The President: I think the statement I have read answers your question; the reason that I don't want to say any more, we agreed exactly on that statement and I'm sure that he himself will make it, corroborate it. But to go further can be putting words in somebody else's mouth, that I don't think is fair.

I personally think that the question is answered right there: there is no fixed time on this. No one is under duress, no one is under any kind of threat. As a matter of fact, he stated emphatically that never had he an intention to give anything that was to be interpreted as duress or compulsion.

Q. Warren Rogers, New York Herald Tribune: When Mr. Khrushchev talked to your grandchildren, sir, did he tell them that one day they might live under communism?

The President: Well, I don't think—no, I know he didn't. I think one of them might have thought he's old enough to know what he might have been saying. But he didn't; no, as a matter of fact, on the contrary, this was the kind of heartwarming family scene that any American would like to see taking place between his grandchildren and a stranger. . . .

Q. John Scali, Associated Press: Mr. President, when we move into these new negotiations on Berlin, could you tell us whether we will be guided by the same standards and principles that we had before, namely, that any solution must guarantee allied rights there, and protect the freedom of the West Berliners?

The President: I can't guarantee anything of this kind, for the simple reason I don't know what kind of a solution may finally prove acceptable.

But you must start out with this: the situation is abnormal; it was

*[The reference is to John A. McCone, then Chairman of the Atomic Energy Commission (*ed.*).]

brought about by a truce, a military truce, after the end of the war—an armistice—and it put strangely a number of free people in a very awkward position.

Now, we've got to find a system that will be really acceptable to all the people in that region, including those most concerned, the West Berliners.

Marvin L. Arrowsmith, Associated Press: Thank you, Mr. President.

SELECTION 32

The Berlin Crisis of 1961: John F. Kennedy, Address to the Nation, July 25, 1961

The optimism generated by the Camp David talks was short-lived. In 1960, Eisenhower was to repay Khrushchev's visit. First, the two leaders were to meet in Paris with the British and French Premiers. On the eve of this conference, Khrushchev announced that an American U-2 reconnaissance plane had been shot down over the Soviet Union. He demanded a formal apology for the violation of Soviet airspace. Eisenhower refused. The U-2 flights, said the President, were justified by America's need to protect herself against surprise attack. At the Paris Conference, the Soviet Premier did little besides denounce Eisenhower's stand, and the President's projected trip to the Soviet Union was canceled. The cold war seemed as cold as ever.

In January, 1961, Kennedy replaced Eisenhower. In foreign affairs, the new administration made a bad start. It inherited a Central Intelligence Agency plan for a coup to overthrow the Communist regime in Cuba. A force of about 1,400 Cuban exiles, trained by the CIA, was to stage a surprise landing at the Bahia de Cochinos, or Bay of Pigs, on the southern shore of Cuba. The expectation was that this attack would set off uprisings elsewhere on the island. It did not. On the contrary, the exile force was rapidly overwhelmed by Castro's troops. The fact that the American government had sponsored the landing quickly leaked out. The Kennedy administration thus bore the onus not only of having contrived a sneak attack but of having failed at it.

Evidently believing that the Kennedy administration lacked strength of will, the Soviet government revived the Berlin issue. Again, as in 1958, Khrushchev threatened to make East Germany independent and let it shut off access to the city, including access by air.

Kennedy arranged to meet Khrushchev on neutral ground, in Vienna. He warned the Soviet Premier that the Western powers would not yield up Berlin. But Khrushchev, unimpressed, continued to utter threats. Tension mounted.

On July 25, 1961, Kennedy appropriated time for a radio and television address to the American people. He announced the steps he was taking in response to Soviet pressure. This address is significant not only as a clear statement of the American position on the Berlin issue but also as a reflection of Kennedy's views on containment and deterrence.

The text is from the State Department Bulletin, *volume 45 (Aug. 14, 1961). pages 267–273.*

Seven weeks ago tonight I returned from Europe to report on my meeting with Premier Khrushchev and the others. His grim warnings about the future of the world, his aide memoire on Berlin, his subsequent speeches and threats which he and his agents have launched, and the increase in the Soviet military budget that he has announced have all prompted a series of decisions by the administration and a series of consultations with the members of the NATO organization. In Berlin, as you recall, he intends to bring to an end, through a stroke of the pen, first, our legal rights to be in West Berlin and, secondly, our ability to make good on our commitment to the 2 million free people of that city. That we cannot permit.

We are clear about what must be done—and we intend to do it. I want to talk frankly with you tonight about the first steps that we shall take. These actions will require sacrifice on the part of many of our citizens. More will be required in the future. They will require, from all of us, courage and preseverance in the years to come. But if we and our allies act out of strength and unity of purpose—with calm determination and steady nerves, using restraint in our words as well as our weapons—I am hopeful that both peace and freedom will be sustained.

The immediate threat to free men is in West Berlin. But that isolated outpost is not an isolated problem. The threat is worldwide. Our effort must be equally wide and strong and not be obsessed by any single manufactured crisis. We face a challenge in Berlin, but there is also a challenge in southeast Asia, where the borders are less guarded, the enemy harder to find, and the danger of communism less apparent to those who have so little. We face a challenge in our own hemisphere and indeed wherever else the freedom of human beings is at stake.

Let me remind you that the fortunes of war and diplomacy left the free people of West Berlin in 1945 110 miles behind the Iron Curtain. This map [visible to the television audience (*ed.*)] makes very clear the problem that we face. The white is West Germany, the East is the area controlled by the Soviet Union; and as you can see from the chart, West Berlin is 110 miles within the area which the Soviets now dominate—which is immediately controlled by the so-called East German regime.

We are there as a result of our victory over Nazi Germany, and our basic rights to be there deriving from that victory include both our presence in West Berlin and the enjoyment of access across East Germany. These rights have been repeatedly confirmed and recognized in special agreements with the Soviet Union. Berlin is not a part of East Germany, but a separate territory under the control of the allied powers. Thus our rights there are clear and deep-rooted. But in addition to those rights is our commitment to sustain—and defend, if need be—the opportunity for more than 2 million people to determine their own future and choose their own way of life.

Thus our presence in West Berlin, and our access thereto, cannot be ended by any act of the Soviet Government. The NATO shield was long ago extended to cover West Berlin, and we have given our word that an attack in that city will be regarded as an attack upon us all.

For West Berlin, lying exposed 110 miles inside East Germany, surrounded by Soviet troops and close to Soviet supply lines, has many roles. It is more than a showcase of liberty, a symbol, an island of freedom in a Communist sea. It is even more than a link with the free world, a beacon of hope behind the Iron Curtain, an escape hatch for refugees.

West Berlin is all of that. But above all it has now become, as never before, the great testing place of Western courage and will, a focal point where our solemn commitments, stretching back over the years since 1945, and Soviet ambitions now meet in basic confrontation.

It would be a mistake for others to look upon Berlin, because of its location, as a tempting target. The United States is there, the United Kingdom and France are there, the pledge of NATO is there, and the people of Berlin are there. It is as secure, in that sense, as the rest of us, for we cannot separate its safety from our own.

I hear it said that West Berlin is militarily untenable. And so was Bastogne. And so, in fact, was Stalingrad. Any dangerous spot is tenable if men—brave men—will make it so.

We do not want to fight, but we have fought before. And others in earlier times have made the same dangerous mistake of assuming that the West was too selfish and too soft and too divided to resist invasions of freedom in other lands. Those who threaten to unleash the forces of war on a dispute over West Berlin should recall the words of the ancient philosopher: "A man who causes fear cannot be free from fear."

We cannot and will not permit the Communists to drive us out of Berlin, either gradually or by force. For the fulfillment of our pledge to that city is essential to the morale and security of Western Germany, to the unity of Western Europe, and to the faith of the entire free world. Soviet strategy has long been aimed not merely at Berlin but at dividing and neutralizing all of Europe, forcing us back to our own shores. We must meet our oft-stated pledge to the free peoples of West Berlin—and maintain our rights and their safety, even in the face of force—in order to maintain the confidence of other free peoples in our word and our resolve. The strength of the alliance on which our security depends in dependent in turn on our willingness to meet our commitments to them.

So long as the Communists insist that they are preparing to end by themselves unilaterally our rights in West Berlin and our commitments to its people, we must be prepared to defend those rights and those commitments. We will at all times be ready to talk, if talk will help. But we must also be ready to resist with force, if force is used upon us. Either alone would fail. Together, they can serve the cause of freedom and peace.

The new preparations that we shall make to defend the peace are part of the long-term buildup in our strength which has been under way since January. They are based on our needs to meet a worldwide threat, on a basis which stretches far beyond the present Berlin crisis. Our primary purpose is neither propaganda nor provocation—but preparation.

A first need is to hasten progress toward the military goals which the North Atlantic allies have set for themselves. In Europe today nothing less will suffice. We will put even greater resources into fulfilling those goals, and we look to our allies to do the same.

The supplementary defense buildups that I asked from the Congress in March and May have already started moving us toward these and our other defense goals. They included an increase in the size of the Marine Corps, improved readiness of our reserves, expansion of our air- and sealift, and stepped-up procurement of needed weapons, ammunition, and other items. To insure a continuing invulnerable capacity to deter or destroy any aggressor, they provided for the strengthening of our missile power and for putting 50 percent of our B–52 and B–47 bombers on a ground alert which would send them on their way with 15 minutes' warning.

These measures must be speeded up, and still others must now be taken. We must have sea- and airlift capable of moving our forces quickly and in large numbers to any part of the world.

But even more importantly, we need the capability of placing in any critical area at the appropriate time a force which, combined with those of our allies, is large enough to make clear our determination and our ability to defend our rights at all costs and to meet all levels of aggressor pressure with whatever levels of force are required. We intend to have a wider choice than humiliation or all-out nuclear action.

While it is unwise at this time either to call up or send abroad excessive numbers of these troops before they are needed, let me make it clear that I intend to take, as time goes on, whatever steps are necessary to make certain that such forces can be deployed at the appropriate time without lessening our ability to meet our commitments elsewhere.

Thus, in the days and months ahead, I shall not hesitate to ask the Congress for additional measures or exercise any of the Executive powers that I possess to meet this threat to peace. Everything essential to the security of freedom must be done; and if that should require more men, or more taxes, or more controls, or other new powers, I shall not hesitate to ask them. The measures proposed today will be constantly studied, and altered as necessary. But while we will not let panic shape our policy, neither will we permit timidity to direct our program.

Accordingly I am now taking the following steps:

1. I am tomorrow requesting of the Congress for the current fiscal year an additional $3,247,000,000 of appropriations for the Armed Forces.

2. To fill out our present Army divisions and to make more men available for prompt deployment, I am requesting an increase in the Army's total authorized strength from 875,000 to approximately 1 million men.

3. I am requesting an increase of 29,000 and 63,000 men, respectively, in the active-duty strength of the Navy and the Air Force.

4. To fulfill these manpower needs, I am ordering that our draft calls be doubled and tripled in the coming months; I am asking the Congress for authority to order to active duty certain ready reserve units and individual reservists and to extend tours of duty; and, under that authority, I am planning to order to active duty a number of air transport squadrons and Air National Guard tactical air squadrons to give us the airlift capacity and protection that we need. Other reserve forces will be called up when needed.

5. Many ships and planes once headed for retirement are to be retained or reactivated, increasing our airpower tactically and our sealift, airlift, and

antisubmarine warfare capability. In addition, our strategic air power will be increased by delaying the deactivation of B–47 bombers.

6. Finally, some $1.8 billion—about half of the total sum—is needed for the procurement of nonnuclear weapons, ammunition, and equipment.

The details on all these requests will be presented to the Congress tomorrow. Subsequent steps will be taken to suit subsequent needs. Comparable efforts for the common defense are being discussed with our NATO allies. For their commitment and interest are as precise as our own.

And let me add that I am well aware of the fact that many American families will bear the burden of these requests. Studies or careers will be interrupted; husbands and sons will be called away; incomes in some cases will be reduced. But these are burdens which must be borne if freedom is to be defended. Americans have willingly borne them before, and they will not flinch from the task now.

We have another sober responsibility. To recognize the possibilities of nuclear war in the missile age without our citizens' knowing what they should do and where they should go if bombs begin to fall would be a failure of responsibility. In May I pledged a new start on civil defense. Last week I assigned, on the recommendation of the Civil Defense Director, basic responsibility for this program to the Secretary of Defense, to make certain it is administered and coordinated with our continental defense efforts at the highest civilian level. Tomorrow I am requesting of the Congress new funds for the following immediate objectives: to identify and mark space in existing structures—public and private—that could be used for fallout shelters in case of attack; to stock those shelters with food, water, first-aid kits, and other minimum essentials for survival; to increase their capacity; to improve our air-raid warning and fallout detection systems, including a new household warning system which is now under development; and to take other measures that will be effective at an early date to save millions of lives if needed.

In the event of an attack, the lives of those families which are not hit in a nuclear blast and fire can still be saved—*if* they can be warned to take shelter and *if* that shelter is available. We owe that kind of insurance to our families—and to our country. In contrast to our friends in Europe, the need for this kind of protection is new to our shores. But the time to start is now. In the coming months I hope to let every citizen know what steps he can take without delay to protect his family in case of attack. I know that you will want to do no less. . . .

But I must emphasize again that the choice is not merely between resistance and retreat, between atomic holocaust and surrender. Our peacetime military posture is traditionally defensive; but our diplomatic posture need not be. Our response to the Berlin crisis will not be merely military or negative. It will be more than merely standing firm. For we do not intend to leave it to others to choose and monopolize the forum and the framework of discussion. We do not intend to abandon our duty to mankind to seek a peaceful solution.

As signers of the U.N. Charter we shall always be prepared to discuss international problems with any and all nations that are willing to talk—and listen—with reason. If they have proposals, not demands, we shall hear them. If they seek genuine understanding, not concessions of our rights, we shall meet with them. We have previously indicated our readiness to remove any actual irritants in West Berlin, but the freedom of that city is not negotiable. We cannot negotiate with those who say, "What's mine is mine and what's yours is negotiable." But we are willing to consider any arrangement or treaty in Germany consistent with the maintenance of peace and freedom and with the legitimate security interests of all nations.

We recognize the Soviet Union's historical concerns about their security in central and eastern Europe after a series of ravaging invasions, and we believe arrangements can be worked out which will help to meet those concerns and make it possible for both security and freedom to exist in this troubled area.

For it is not the freedom of West Berlin which is "abnormal" in Germany today but the situation in that entire divided country. If anyone doubts the legality of our rights in Berlin, we are ready to have it submitted to international adjudication. If anyone doubts the extent to which our presence is desired by the people of West Berlin, compared to East German feelings about their regime, we are ready to have that question submitted to a free vote in Berlin and, if possible, among all the German people. And let us hear at that time from the 2½ million refugees who have fled the Communist regime in East Germany—voting for Western-type freedom with their feet.

The world is not deceived by the Communist attempt to label Berlin as a hotbed of war. There is peace in Berlin today. The source of world trouble and tension is Moscow, not Berlin. And if war begins, it will have begun in Moscow and not Berlin.

For the choice of peace or war is largely theirs, not ours. It is the Soviets who have stirred up this crisis. It is they who are trying to force a change. It is they who have opposed free elections. It is they who have rejected an all-German peace treaty and the rulings of international law. And as Americans know from our history on our own old frontier, gun battles are caused by outlaws and not by officers of the peace.

In short, while we are ready to defend our interests, we shall also be ready to search for peace—in quiet exploratory talks, in formal or informal meetings. We do not want military considerations to dominate the thinking of either East or West. And Mr. Khrushchev may find that his invitation to other nations to join in a meaningless treaty may lead to *their* inviting *him* to join in the community of peaceful men, in abandoning the use of force, and in respecting the sanctity of agreements.

While all of these efforts go on, we must not be diverted from our total responsibilities, from other dangers, from other tasks. If new threats in Berlin or elsewhere should cause us to weaken our program of assistance to the developing nations who are also under heavy pressure from the same source, or to halt our efforts for realistic disarmament, or to disrupt or slow down our economy, or to neglect the education of our children, then those threats will surely be the most successful and least costly maneuver in Communist history. For we can afford all these efforts, and more—but we cannot afford *not* to meet this challenge.

And the challenge is not to us alone. It is a challenge to every nation which asserts its sovereignty under a system of liberty. It is a challenge to all who want a world of free choice. It is a special challenge to the Atlantic Community, the heartland of human freedom.

We in the West must move together in building military strength. We must consult one another more closely than ever before. We must together design our proposals for peace and labor together as they are pressed at the conference table. And together we must share the burdens and the risks of this effort.

The Atlantic Community, as we know it, has been built in response to challenge: the challenge of European chaos in 1947, of the Berlin blockade in 1948, the challenge of Communist aggression in Korea in 1950. Now, standing strong and prosperous after an unprecedented decade of progress, the Atlantic Community will not forget either its history or the principles which gave it meaning.

The solemn vow each of us gave to West Berlin in time of peace will not be broken in time of danger. If we do not meet our commitments to Berlin, where will we later stand? If we are not true to our word there, all that we have achieved in collective security, which relies on these words, will mean nothing. And if there is one path above all others to war, it is the path of weakness and disunity.

Today the endangered frontier of freedom runs through divided Berlin. We want it to remain a frontier of peace. This is the hope of every citizen of the Atlantic Community, every citizen of Eastern Europe, and, I am confident, every citizen of the Soviet Union. For I cannot believe that the Russian people, who bravely suffered enormous losses in the Second World War, would now wish to see the peace upset once more in Germany. The Soviet Government alone can convert Berlin's frontier of peace into a pretext for war.

The steps I have indicated tonight are aimed at avoiding that war. To sum it all up: We seek peace, but we shall not surrender. That is the central meaning of this crisis—and the meaning of your Government's policy.

With your help, and the help of other free men, this crisis can be surmounted. Freedom can prevail, and peace can endure.

I would like to close with a personal word. When I ran for the Presidency of the United States, I knew that this country faced serious challenges, but I could not realize—nor could any man realize who does not bear the burdens of this office—how heavy and constant would be those burdens.

Three times in my lifetime our country and Europe have been involved in major wars. In each case serious misjudgments were made on both sides of the intentions of others, which brought about great devastation. Now, in the thermonuclear age, any misjudgment on either side about the intentions of the other could rain more devastation in several hours than has been wrought in all the wars of human history.

Therefore I, as President and Commander in Chief, and all of us as Americans are moving through serious days. I shall bear this responsibility under our Constitution for the next 3½ years, but I am sure that we all, regardless of our occupations, will do our very best for our country and for our cause. For all of us want to see our children grow up in a country at peace and in a world where freedom endures.

I know that sometimes we get impatient; we wish for some immediate action that would end our perils. But I must tell you that there is no quick and easy solution. The Communists control over a billion people, and they recognize that if we should falter their success would be imminent.

We must look to long days ahead which, if we are courageous and presevering, can bring us what we all desire. In these days and weeks I ask for your help and your advice. I ask for your suggestions, when you think we could do better.

All of us, I know, love our country, and we shall all do our best to serve it.

In meeting my responsibilities in these coming months as President, I need your good will and your support—and above all, your prayers.

Kennedy on the Cuban Missiles Crisis of 1962

In the Berlin crisis, Kennedy acted swiftly and forcefully. The Soviet government backed down. Premier Khrushchev indicated that he would not in the immediate future make East Germany independent or interfere with Western access to Berlin.

Khrushchev did not, however, retreat into the amiableness of 1959. His attitude remained menacing. Since 1958, both the United States and the Soviet Union had voluntarily refrained from testing nuclear weapons above ground. Without warning, Khrushchev announced that the Soviet Union intended to resume such tests. He claimed that Soviet scientists had developed an H-bomb with an explosive power of 100 megatons, or the equivalent of 100 million tons of TNT.

The United States, too, resumed testing. The amount of poisonous radioactivity in the atmosphere steadily increased.

Then, in the autumn of 1962, the Soviet Union took a still more menacing step. It installed missile launching sites in Castro's Cuba. At these sites were medium-range missiles capable of raining nuclear destruction on most of the Eastern seaboard of the United States.

When Kennedy learned what was going on in Cuba, his reactions were quick and stern. He adopted countermeasures, demanded that the Soviet Union immediately dismantle the missile bases in Cuba, and warned that failure to comply with the demand could have the gravest consequences.

The nation and the world looked on in terrified suspense. Messages shot back and forth between the White House, the Kremlin, and the UN Secretariat General in New York. Finally, a communication came from Khrushchev which, though tough in tone, hinted at a possible compromise. After reading it, one of

Kennedy's advisers reportedly said, "We are eyeball to eyeball, and I think the other fellow just blinked."

In the end, Khrushchev agreed to dismantle the bases and remove the missiles from Cuba. He exacted in return a promise by Kennedy that the United States would not invade Cuba. But this did not suffice to mar the fact that the Soviet leader had been forced to retreat. Khrushchev had gambled that the United States would not face up to the danger of a nuclear clash, and his gamble had failed.

The following documents illustrate the crisis. The first is the text of Kennedy's radio and television address to the American public on October 22, 1962. The second is Kennedy's reply to the message from Khrushchev hinting at a compromise. The third is the President's communication to Khrushchev after the announcement that the Soviet Union would remove the missiles from Cuba. They are taken from Public Papers of the Presidents: John F. Kennedy, 1962 *(Government Printing Office, 1963), pages 806–809, 813–814, 814–815.*

ADDRESS TO THE NATION, OCTOBER 22, 1962

Good evening, my fellow citizens:

This Government, as promised, has maintained the closest surveillance of the Soviet military buildup on the island of Cuba. Within the past week, unmistakable evidence has established the fact that a series of offensive missile sites is now in preparation on that imprisoned island. The purpose of these bases can be none other than to provide a nuclear strike capability against the Western Hemisphere.

Upon receiving the first preliminary hard information of this nature last Tuesday morning at 9 a.m., I directed that our surveillance be stepped up. And having now confirmed and completed our evaluation of the evidence and our decision on a course of action, this Government feels obliged to report this new crisis to you in fullest detail.

The characteristics of these new missile sites indicate two distinct types of installations. Several of them include medium range ballistic missiles, capable of carrying a nuclear warhead for a distance of more than 1,000 nautical miles. Each of these missiles, in short, is capable of striking Washington, D.C., the Panama Canal, Cape Canaveral, Mexico City, or any other city in the southeastern part of the United States in Central America, or in the Caribbean area.

Additional sites not yet completed appear to be designed for intermediate range ballistic missiles—capable of traveling more than twice as far—and thus capable of striking most of the major cities in the Western Hemisphere, ranging as far north as Hudson Bay, Canada, and as far south as Lima, Peru. In addition, jet bombers, capable of carrying nuclear weapons, are now being uncrated and assembled in Cuba, while the necessary air bases are being prepared.

This urgent transformation of Cuba into an important strategic base—by the presence of these large, long-range, and clearly offensive weapons of sudden mass destruction—constitutes an explicit threat to the peace and security of all the Americas, in flagrant and deliberate defiance of the Rio Pact of 1947, the traditions of this Nation and hemisphere, the joint resolution of the 87th Congress, the Charter of the United Nations, and my own public warnings to the Soviets on September 4 and 13. This action also contradicts the repeated assurances of Soviet spokesmen, both publicly and privately delivered, that the arms buildup in Cuba would retain its original defensive character, and that the Soviet Union had no need or desire to station strategic missiles on the territory of any other nation.

The size of this undertaking makes clear that it has been planned for some months. Yet only last month, after I had made clear the distinction between any introduction of ground-to-ground missiles and the existence of defensive antiaircraft missiles, the Soviet Government publicly stated on September 11 that, and I quote, "the armaments and military equipment sent to Cuba are designed exclusively for defensive purposes," that, and I quote the Soviet Government, "there is no need for the Soviet Government to shift its weapons . . . for a retaliatory blow to any other country, for instance Cuba," and that, and I quote their government, "the Soviet Union has so powerful rockets to carry these nuclear warheads that there is no need to search for sites for them beyond the boundaries of the Soviet Union." That statement was false.

Only last Thursday, as evidence of this rapid offensive buildup was already in my hand, Soviet Foreign Minister Gromyko told me in my office that he was instructed to make it clear once again, as he said his government had already done, that Soviet assistance to Cuba, and I quote, "pursued solely the purpose of contributing to the defense capabilities of Cuba," that, and I quote him, "training by Soviet specialists of Cuban nationals in handling defensive armaments was by no means offensive, and if it were otherwise," Mr. Gromyko went on, "the Soviet Government would never become involved in rendering such assistance." That statement also was false.

Neither the United States of America nor the world community of nations can tolerate deliberate deception and offensive threats on the part of any nation, large or small. We no longer live in a world where only the actual firing of weapons represents a sufficient challenge to a nation's security to constitute maximum peril. Nuclear weapons are so destructive and ballistic missiles are so swift, that any substantially increased possibility of their use or any sudden change in their deployment may well be regarded as a definite threat to peace.

For many years, both the Soviet Union and the United States, recognizing this fact, have deployed strategic nuclear weapons with great care, never upsetting the precarious status quo which insured that these weapons would not be used in the absence of some vital challenge. Our own strategic missiles have never been transferred to the territory of any other nation under a cloak of secrecy and deception; and our history—unlike that of the Soviets since the end of World War II—demonstrates that we have no desire to dominate or conquer any other nation or impose our system upon its people. Nevertheless, American citizens have become adjusted to living daily on the bull's-eye of Soviet missiles located inside the U.S.S.R. or in submarines.

In that sense, missiles in Cuba add to an already clear and present danger—although it should be noted the nations of Latin America have never previously been subjected to a potential nuclear threat.

But this secret, swift, and extraordinary buildup of Communist missiles

—in an area well known to have a special and historical relationship to the United States and the nations of the Western Hemisphere, in violation of Soviet assurances, and in defiance of American and hemispheric policy—this sudden, clandestine decision to station strategic weapons for the first time outside of Soviet soil—is a deliberately provocative and unjustified change in the status quo which cannot be accepted by this country, if our courage and our commitments are ever to be trusted again by either friend or foe.

The 1930's taught us a clear lesson: aggressive conduct, if allowed to go unchecked and unchallenged, ultimately leads to war. This nation is opposed to war. We are also true to our word. Our unswerving objective, therefore, must be to prevent the use of these missiles against this or any other country, and to secure their withdrawal or elimination from the Western Hemisphere.

Our policy has been one of patience and restraint, as befits a peaceful and powerful nation, which leads a worldwide alliance. We have been determined not to be diverted from our central concerns by mere irritants and fanatics. But now further action is required—and it is under way; and these actions may only be the beginning. We will not prematurely or unnecessarily risk the costs of worldwide nuclear war in which even the fruits of victory would be ashes in our mouth—but neither will we shrink from that risk at any time it must be faced.

Acting, therefore, in the defense of our own security and of the entire Western Hemisphere, and under the authority entrusted to me by the Constitution as endorsed by the resolution of the Congress, I have directed that the following *initial* steps be taken immediately:*

First; to halt this offensive buildup, a strict quarantine on all offensive military equipment under shipment to Cuba is being initiated. All ships of any kind bound for Cuba from whatever nation or port will, if found to contain cargoes of offensive weapons, be turned back. This quarantine will be extended, if needed, to other types of cargo and carriers. We are not at this time, however, denying the necessities of life as the Soviets attempted to do in their Berlin blockade of 1948.

Second; I have directed the continued and increased close surveillance of Cuba and its military buildup. The foreign ministers of OAS,† in their communiqué of October 6, rejected secrecy on such matters in this hemisphere. Should these offensive military preparations continue, thus increasing the threat to the hemisphere, further action will be justified. I have directed the Armed Forces to prepare for any eventualities; and I trust that in the interest of both the Cuban people and the Soviet technicians at the sites, the hazards to all concerned of continuing this threat will be recognized.

Third; it shall be the policy of this Nation to regard any nuclear missile launched from Cuba against any nation in the Western Hemisphere as an attack by the Soviet Union on the United States, requiring a full retaliatory response upon the Soviet Union.

Fourth; as a necessary military precaution, I have reinforced our base at Guantanamo, evacuated today the dependents of our personnel there, and ordered additional military units to be on a standby alert basis.

Fifth; we are calling tonight for an immediate meeting of the Organ of Con-

* [Italics in the original (*ed.*).]
† [Organization of American States (*ed.*).]

sultation under the Organization of American States, to consider this threat to hemispheric security and to invoke articles 6 and 8 of the Rio Treaty in support of all necessary action. The United Nations Charter allows for regional security arrangements—and the nations of this hemisphere decided long ago against the military presence of outside powers. Our other allies around the world have also been alerted.

Sixth; under the Charter of the United Nations, we are asking tonight that an emergency meeting of the Security Council be convoked without delay to take action against this latest Soviet threat to world peace. Our resolution will call for the prompt dismantling and withdrawal of all offensive weapons in Cuba, under the supervision of U.N. observers, before the quarantine can be lifted.

Seventh and finally; I call upon Chairman Khrushchev to halt and eliminate this clandestine, reckless, and provocative threat to world peace and to stable relations between our two nations. I call upon him further to abandon this course of world domination, and to join in an historic effort to end the perilous arms race and to transform the history of man. He has an opportunity now to move the world back from the abyss of destruction—by returning to his government's own words that it had no need to station missiles outside its own territory, and withdrawing these weapons from Cuba—by refraining from any action which will widen or deepen the present crisis—and then by participating in a search for peaceful and permanent solutions.

This Nation is prepared to present its case against the Soviet threat to peace, and our own proposals for a peaceful world, at any time and in any forum—in the OAS, in the United Nations, or in any other meeting that could be useful—without limiting our freedom of action. We have in the past made strenuous efforts to limit the spread of nuclear weapons. We have proposed the elimination of all arms and military bases in a fair and effective disarmament treaty. We are prepared to discuss new proposals for the removal of tensions on both sides—including the possibilities of a genuinely independent Cuba, free to determine its own destiny. We have no wish to war with the Soviet Union—for we are a peaceful people who desire to live in peace with all other peoples.

But it is difficult to settle or even discuss these problems in an atmosphere of intimidation. That is why this latest Soviet threat—or any other threat which is made either independently or in response to our actions this week—must and will be met with determination. Any hostile move anywhere in the world against the safety and freedom of peoples to whom we are committed—including in particular the brave people of West Berlin—will be met by whatever action is needed.

Finally, I want to say a few words to the captive people of Cuba, to whom this speech is being directly carried by special radio facilities. I speak to you as a friend, as one who knows of your deep attachment to your fatherland, as one who shares your aspirations for liberty and justice for all. And I have watched and the American people have watched with deep sorrow how your nationalist revolution was betrayed—and how your fatherland fell under foreign domination. Now your leaders are no longer Cuban leaders inspired by Cuban ideals. They are puppets and agents of an international conspiracy which has turned Cuba against your friends and neighbors in the Americas—and turned it into the first Latin American country to become a target for nuclear war—the first Latin American country to have these weapons on its soil.

These new weapons are not in your interest. They contribute nothing to your peace and well-being. They can only undermine it. But this country has no wish to cause you to suffer or to impose any system upon you. We know that your lives and land are being used as pawns by those who deny your freedom.

Many times in the past, the Cuban people have risen to throw out tyrants who destroyed their liberty. And I have no doubt that most Cubans today look forward to the time when they will be truly free—free from foreign domination, free to choose their own leaders, free to select their own system, free to own their own land, free to speak and write and worship without fear or degradation. And then shall Cuba be welcomed back to the society of free nations and to the associations of this hemisphere.

My fellow citizens: let no one doubt that this is a difficult and dangerous effort on which we have set out. No one can foresee precisely what course it will take or what costs or casualties will be incurred. Many months of sacrifice and self-discipline lie ahead—months in which both our patience and our will will be tested—months in which many threats and denunciations will keep us aware of our dangers. But the greatest danger of all would be to do nothing.

The path we have chosen for the present is full of hazards, as all paths are—but it is the one most consistent with our character and courage as a nation and our commitments around the world. The cost of freedom is always high—but Americans have always paid it. And one path we shall never choose, and that is the path of surrender or submission.

Our goal is not the victory of might, but the vindication of right—not peace at the expense of freedom, but both peace *and* freedom, here in this hemisphere, and, we hope, around the world. God willing, that goal will be achieved.

Thank you and good night.

MESSAGE TO CHAIRMAN KHRUSHCHEV, OCTOBER 27, 1962

Dear Mr. Chairman:

I have read your letter of October 26th with great care and welcomed the statement of your desire to seek a prompt solution to the problem. The first thing that needs to be done, however, is for work to cease on offensive missile bases in Cuba and for all weapons systems in Cuba capable of offensive use to be rendered inoperable, under effective United Nations arrangements.

Assuming this is done promptly, I have given my representatives in New York instructions that will permit them to work out this weekend—in cooperation with the Acting Secretary General and your representative—an arrangement for a permanent solution to the Cuban problem along the lines suggested in your letter of October 26th. As I read your letter, the key elements of your proposals—which seem generally acceptable as I understand them—are as follows:

1. You would agree to remove these weapons systems from Cuba under appropriate United Nations observation and supervision; and undertake, with

suitable safeguards, to halt the further introduction of such weapons systems into Cuba.

2. We, on our part, would agree—upon the establishment of adequate arrangements through the United Nations to ensure the carrying out and continuation of these commitments—(a) to remove promptly the quarantine measures now in effect and (b) to give assurances against an invasion of Cuba. I am confident that other nations of the Western Hemisphere would be prepared to do likewise.

If you will give your representative similar instructions, there is no reason why we should not be able to complete these arrangements and announce them to the world within a couple of days. The effect of such a settlement on easing world tensions would enable us to work toward a more general arrangement regarding "other armaments," as proposed in your second letter which you made public. I would like to say again that the United States is very much interested in reducing tensions and halting the arms race; and if your letter signifies that you are prepared to discuss a detente affecting NATO and the Warsaw Pact, we are quite prepared to consider with our allies any useful proposals.

But the first ingredient, let me emphasize, is the cessation of work on missile sites in Cuba and measures to render such weapons inoperable, under effective international guarantees. The continuation of this threat, or a prolonging of this discussion concerning Cuba by linking these problems to the broader questions of European and world security, would surely lead to an intensification of the Cuban crisis and a grave risk to the peace of the world. For this reason I hope we can quickly agree along the lines outlined in this letter and in your letter of October 26th.

JOHN F. KENNEDY

MESSAGE IN REPLY TO A BROADCAST BY CHAIRMAN KHRUSHCHEV, OCTOBER 28, 1962

Dear Mr. Chairman:

I am replying at once to your broadcast message of October twenty-eight, even though the official text has not yet reached me, because of the great importance I attach to moving forward promptly to the settlement of the Cuban crisis. I think that you and I, with our heavy responsibilities for the maintenance of peace, were aware that developments were approaching a point where events could have become unmanageable. So I welcome this message and consider it an important contribution to peace. . . .

Mr. Chairman, both of our countries have great unfinished tasks and I know that your people as well as those of the United States can ask for nothing better than to pursue them free from the fear of war. Modern science and technology have given us the possibility of making labor fruitful beyond anything that could have been dreamed of a few decades ago.

I agree with you that we must devote urgent attention to the problem of disarmament, as it relates to the whole world and also to critical areas. Perhaps now, as we step back from danger, we can together make real progress in this vital field. I think we should give priority to questions relating to the proliferation of nuclear weapons, on earth and in outer space, and to the great effort for a nuclear test ban. But we should also work hard to see if wider measures of disarmament can be agreed and put into operation at an early date. The United States Government will be prepared to discuss these questions urgently, and in a constructive spirit, at Geneva or elsewhere.

JOHN F. KENNEDY

The Test-Ban Agreement

During 1962, President Kennedy spoke time and again of the urgency of an American-Soviet agreement to suspend above-ground nuclear tests. The American decision to resume such tests had been due entirely, he said, to the Soviet resumption of testing. The United States could not afford to let the Soviet Union gain an edge in nuclear weaponry. But the common interest of both nations, and of the world, Kennedy declared, was to end all tests so as to halt the poisoning of the air.

After the Cuban missiles crisis of 1962, the Soviet government began for the first time to display interest in a test-ban agreement. Negotiations proceeded. At length, on July 25, 1963, a limited test-ban treaty was signed in Moscow.

The treaty seemed an indication that tensions were easing. No one could be sure that this was not an illusion, as it had been at the time of the Camp David meetings. But the treaty gave at least a glimmer of hope, and, in itself, the treaty was both useful and durable.

The first document below is President Kennedy's address to the nation reporting the signing of the treaty. The second is the text of the treaty. Both documents come from the State Department Bulletin, *volume 47 (Aug. 12, 1963), pages 234–240.*

JOHN F. KENNEDY, ADDRESS TO THE NATION, JULY 26, 1963

Good evening, my fellow citizens: I speak to you tonight in a spirit of hope. Eighteen years ago the advent of nuclear weapons changed the course of the world as well as the war. Since that time, all mankind has been struggling to escape from the darkening prospect of mass destruction on earth. In an age when both sides have come to possess enough nuclear power to destroy the human race several times over, the world of communism and the world of free choice have been caught up in a vicious circle of conflicting ideology and interest. Each increase of tension has produced an increase of arms; each increase of arms has produced an increase of tension.

In these years the United States and the Soviet Union have frequently communicated suspicion and warnings to each other, but very rarely hope. Our representatives have met at the summit and at the brink; they have met in Washington and in Moscow, in Geneva and at the United Nations. But too often these meetings have produced only darkness, discord, or disillusion.

Yesterday a shaft of light cut into the darkness. Negotiations were concluded in Moscow on a treaty to ban all nuclear tests in the atmosphere, in outer space, and under water. For the first time, an agreement has been reached on bringing the forces of nuclear destruction under international control—a goal first sought in 1946, when Bernard Baruch presented a comprehensive control plan to the United Nations.

That plan and many subsequent disarmament plans, large and small, have all been blocked by those opposed to international inspection. A ban on nuclear tests, however, requires on-the-spot inspection only for underground tests. This nation now possesses a variety of techniques to detect the nuclear tests of other nations which are conducted in the air or under water. For such tests produce unmistakable signs which our modern instruments can pick up.

The treaty initialed yesterday, therefore, is a limited treaty which permits continued underground testing and prohibits only those tests that we ourselves can police. It requires no control posts, no on-site inspection, no international body.

We should also understand that it has other limits as well. Any nation which signs the treaty will have an opportunity to withdraw if it finds that extraordinary events related to the subject matter of the treaty have jeopardized its supreme interests; and no nation's right of self-defense will in any way be impaired. Nor does this treaty mean an end to the threat of nuclear war. It will not reduce nuclear stockpiles; it will not halt the production of nuclear weapons; it will not restrict their use in time of war.

Nevertheless, this limited treaty will radically reduce the nuclear testing which would otherwise be conducted on both sides; it will prohibit the United States, the United Kingdom, the Soviet Union, and all others who sign it from engaging in the atmospheric tests which have so alarmed mankind; and it offers to all the world a welcome sign of hope.

For this is not a unilateral moratorium, but a specific and solemn legal obligation. While it will not prevent this nation from testing underground, or from being ready to conduct atmospheric tests if the acts of others so require, it gives us a concrete opportunity to extend its coverage to other nations and later to other forms of nuclear tests.

This treaty is in part the product of Western patience and vigilance. We have made clear—most recently in Berlin and Cuba—our deep resolve to protect our security and our freedom against any form of aggression. We have also made clear our steadfast determination to limit the arms race. In three administrations our soldiers and diplomats have worked together to this end, always supported by Great Britain. Prime Minister Macmillan joined with President Eisenhower in proposing a limited test ban in 1959, and again with me in 1961 and 1962.

But the achievement of this goal is not a victory for one side—it is a victory for mankind. It reflects no concessions either to or by the Soviet Union. It reflects simply our common recognition of the dangers in further testing.

This treaty is not the millennium. It will not resolve all conflicts, or cause the Communists to forgo their ambitions, or eliminate the dangers of war. It will not reduce our need for arms or allies or programs of assistance to others. But it is an important first step—a step toward peace—a step toward reason—a step away from war.

Here is what this step can mean to you and to your children and your neighbors.

First, this treaty can be a step toward reduced world tension and broader areas of agreement. The Moscow talks have reached no agreement on any other subject, nor is this treaty conditioned on any other matter. Under Secretary Harriman made it clear that any nonaggression arrangements across the division in Europe would require full consultation with our allies and full attention to their interests. He also made clear our strong preference for a more comprehensive treaty banning all tests everywhere and our ultimate hope for general and complete disarmament. The Soviet Government, however, is still unwilling to accept the inspection such goals require.

No one can predict with certainty, therefore, what further agreements, if any, can be built on the foundations of this one. They could include controls on preparations for surprise attack, or on numbers and type of armaments. There could be further limitations on the spread of nuclear weapons. The important point is that efforts to seek new agreements will go forward.

But the difficulty of predicting the next step is no reason to be reluctant about this step. Nuclear test ban negotiations have long been a symbol of East-West disagreement. If this treaty can also be a symbol—if it can symbolize the end of one era and the beginning of another—if both sides can by this treaty gain confidence and experience in peaceful collaboration—then this short and simple treaty may well become an historic mark in man's age-old pursuit of peace.

Western policies have long been designed to persuade the Soviet Union to renounce aggression, direct or indirect, so that their people and all people may live and let live in peace. The unlimited testing of new weapons of war cannot lead toward that end, but this treaty, if it can be followed by further progress, can clearly move in that direction.

I do not say that a world without aggression or threats of war would be an easy world. It will bring new problems, new challenges from the Communists, new dangers of relaxing our vigilance or of mistaking their intent.

But those dangers pale in comparison to those of the spiraling arms race and a collision course toward war. Since the beginning of history, war has been mankind's constant companion. It has been the rule, not the exception. Even a nation as young and as peace-loving as our own has fought through eight wars. And three times in the last two years and a half I have been required to report to you as President that this nation and the Soviet Union stood on the verge of direct military confrontation—in Laos, in Berlin, and in Cuba.

A war today or tomorrow, if it led to nuclear war, would not be like any war in history. A full-scale nuclear exchange, lasting less than 60 minutes, with the weapons now in existence, could wipe out more than 300 million Americans, Europeans, and Russians, as well as untold numbers elsewhere. And the survivors—as Chairman Khrushchev warned the

Communist Chinese, "The survivors would envy the dead." For they would inherit a world so devastated by explosions and poison and fire that today we cannot even conceive of its horrors. So let us try to turn the world from war. Let us make the most of this opportunity, and every opportunity, to reduce tension, to slow down the perilous nuclear arms race, and to check the world's slide toward final annihilation.

Second, this treaty can be a step toward freeing the world from the fears and dangers of radioactive fallout. Our own atmospheric tests last year were conducted under conditions which restricted such fallout to an absolute minimum. But over the years the number and the yield of weapons tested have rapidly increased and so have the radioactive hazards from such testing. Continued unrestricted testing by the nuclear powers, joined in time by other nations which may be less adept in limiting pollution, will increasingly contaminate the air that all of us must breathe.

Even then, the number of children and grandchildren with cancer in their bones, with leukemia in their blood, or with poison in their lungs might seem statistically small to some, in comparison with natural health hazards. But this is not a natural health hazard, and it is not a statistical issue. The loss of even one human life or the malformation of even one baby—who may be born long after we are gone—should be of concern to us all. Our children and grandchildren are not merely statistics toward which we can be indifferent.

Nor does this affect the nuclear powers alone. These tests befoul the air of all men and all nations, the committed and the uncommitted alike, without their knowledge and without their consent. That is why the continuation of atmospheric testing causes so many countries to regard all nuclear powers as equally evil; and we can hope that its prevention will enable those countries to see the world more clearly, while enabling all the world to breathe more easily.

Third, this treaty can be a step toward preventing the spread of nuclear weapons to nations not now possessing them. During the next several years, in addition to the four current nuclear powers, a small but significant number of nations will have the intellectual, physical, and financial resources to produce both nuclear weapons and the means of delivering them. In time, it is estimated, many other nations will have either this capacity or other ways of obtaining nuclear warheads, even as missiles can be commercially purchased today.

I ask you to stop and think for a moment what it would mean to have nuclear weapons in so many hands, in the hands of countries, large and small, stable and unstable, responsible and irresponsible, scattered throughout the world. There would be no rest for anyone then, no stability, no real security, and no chance of effective disarmament. There would only be the increased chance of accidental war and an increased necessity for the great powers to involve themselves in what otherwise would be local conflicts.

If only one thermonuclear bomb were to be dropped on any American, Russian, or any other city, whether it was launched by accident or design, by a madman or by an enemy, by a large nation or by a small, from any corner of the world, that one bomb could release more destructive power on the inhabitants of that one helpless city than all the bombs dropped in the Second World War.

Neither the United States nor the Soviet Union nor the United Kingdom nor France can look forward to that day with equanimity. We have a great obligation—all four nuclear powers have a great obligation—to use whatever time remains to prevent the spread of nuclear weapons, to persuade other countries not to test, transfer, acquire, possess, or produce such weapons.

This treaty can be the opening wedge in that campaign. It provides that none of the parties will assist other nations to test in the forbidden environments. It opens the door for further agreements on the control of nuclear weapons, and it is open for all nations to sign; for it is in the interest of all nations, and already we have heard from a number of countries who wish to join with us promptly.

Fourth and finally, this treaty can limit the nuclear arms race in ways which, on balance, will strengthen our nation's security far more than the continuation of unrestricted testing. For, in today's world, a nation's security does not always increase as its arms increase when its adversary is doing the same, and unlimited competition in the testing and development of new types of destructive nuclear weapons will not make the world safer for either side. Under this limited treaty, on the other hand, the testing of other nations could never be sufficient to offset the ability of our strategic forces to deter or survive a nuclear attack and to penetrate and destroy an aggressor's homeland.

We have, and under this treaty we will continue to have, the nuclear strength that we need. It is true that the Soviets have tested nuclear weapons of a yield higher than that which we thought to be necessary, but the hundred-megaton bomb of which they spoke 2 years ago does not and will not change the balance of strategic power. The United States has chosen, deliberately, to concentrate on more mobile and more efficient weapons, with lower but entirely sufficient yield, and our security is, therefore, not impaired by the treaty I am discussing.

It is also true, as Mr. Khrushchev would agree, that nations cannot afford in these matters to rely simply on the good faith of their adversaries. We have not, therefore, overlooked the risk of secret violations. There is at present a possibility that deep in outer space, hundreds and thousands and millions of miles away from the earth, illegal tests might go undetected. But we already have the capability to construct a system of observation that would make such tests almost impossible to conceal, and we can decide at any time whether such a system is needed in the light of the limited risk to us and the limited reward to others of violations attempted that range. For any tests which might be conducted so far out in space, which cannot be conducted more easily and efficiently and legally underground, would necessarily be of such a magnitude that they would be extremely difficult to conceal. We can also employ new devices to check on the testing of smaller weapons in the lower atmosphere. Any violation, moreover, involves, along with the risk of detection, the end of the treaty and the worldwide consequences for the violator.

Secret violations are possible and secret preparations for a sudden withdrawal are possible, and thus our own vigilance and strength must be maintained, as we remain ready to withdraw and to resume all forms of testing if we must. But it would be a mistake to assume that this treaty will be quickly broken. The gains of illegal testing are obviously slight compared to their cost and the hazard of discovery, and the nations which have initialed and will sign this treaty prefer it, in my judgment, to unrestricted testing as a matter of their own self-interest, for these nations, too, and all nations, have a stake in limiting the arms race, in holding the spread of nuclear weapons, and in breathing air that is not radioactive. While it may be theoretically possible to demonstrate the risks inherent in any treaty—and such risks in this treaty are small—the far greater risks to our security are the risks of unrestricted testing, the risk of a nuclear arms race, the risk of new nuclear powers, nuclear pollution, and nuclear war.

This limited test ban, in our most careful judgment, is safer by far for the United States than an unlimited nuclear arms race. For all these reasons, I am hopeful that this nation will promptly approve the limited test ban treaty. There will, of course, be debate in the country and in the Senate. The Constitution wisely requires the advice and consent of the Senate to all treaties, and that consultation has already begun. All this is as it should be. A document which may mark an historic and constructive opportunity for the world deserves an historic and constructive debate.

It is my hope that all of you will take part in that debate, for this treaty is for all of us. It is particularly for our children and our grandchildren, and they have no lobby here in Washington. This debate will involve military, scientific, and political experts, but it must be not left to them alone. The right and the responsibility are yours.

If we are to open new doorways to peace, if we are to seize this rare opportunity for progress, if we are to be as bold and farsighted in our control of weapons as we have been in their invention, then let us now show all the world on this side of the wall and the other that a strong America also stands for peace.

There is no cause for complacency. We have learned in times past that the spirit of one moment or place can be gone in the next. We have been disappointed more than once, and we have no illusions now that there are shortcuts on the road to peace. At many points around the globe the Communists are continuing their efforts to exploit weakness and poverty. Their concentration of nuclear and conventional arms must still be deterred.

The familiar contest between choice and coercion, the familiar places of danger and conflict, are still there, in Cuba, in Southeast Asia, in Berlin, and all around the globe, still requiring all the strength and the vigilance that we can muster. Nothing could more greatly damage our cause than if we and our allies were to believe that peace has already been achieved and that our strength and unity were no longer required.

But now, for the first time in many years, the path of peace may be open. No one can be certain what the future will bring. No one can say whether the time has come for an easing of the struggle. But history and our own conscience will judge us harsher if we do not now make every effort to test our hopes by action, and this is the place to begin. According to the ancient Chinese proverb, "A journey of a thousand miles must begin with a single step."

My fellow Americans, let us take that first step. Let us, if we can, get back from the shadows of war and seek out the way of peace. And if that journey is one thousand miles, or even more, let history record that we, in this land, at this time, took the first step.

Thank you and good night.

THE TEST-BAN TREATY, JULY 25, 1963

Treaty Banning Nuclear Weapons Tests in the Atmosphere, in Outer Space and under Water

The Governments of the United States of America, the United Kingdom of Great Britain and Northern Ireland, and the Union of Soviet Socialist Republics, hereinafter referred to as the "Original Parties,"

Proclaiming as their principal aim the speediest possible achievement of an agreement on general and complete disarmament under strict international control in accordance with the objectives of the United Nations which would put an end to the armaments race and eliminate the incentive to the production and testing of all kinds of weapons, including nuclear weapons,

Seeking to achieve the discontinuance of all test explosions of nuclear weapons for all time, determined to continue negotiations to this end, and desiring to put an end to the contamination of man's environment by radioactive substances,

Have agreed as follows:

Article I

1. Each of the Parties to this Treaty undertakes to prohibit, to prevent, and not to carry out any nuclear weapon test explosion, or any other nuclear explosion, at any place under its jurisdiction or control:

(*a*) in the atmosphere; beyond its limits, including outer space; or underwater, including territorial waters or high seas; or

(*b*) in any other environment if such explosion causes radioactive debris to be present outside the territorial limits of the State under whose jurisdiction or control such explosion is conducted. It is understood in this connection that the provisions of this subparagraph are without prejudice to the conclusion of a treaty resulting in the permanent banning of all nuclear test explosions, including all such explosions underground, the conclusion of which, as the Parties have stated in the Preamble to this Treaty, they seek to achieve.

2. Each of the Parties to this Treaty undertakes furthermore to refrain from causing, encouraging, or in any way participating in, the carrying out of any nuclear weapon test explosion, or any other nuclear explosion, anywhere which would take place in any of the environments described, or have the effect referred to, in paragraph 1 of this Article.

Article II

1. Any Party may propose amendments to this Treaty. The text of any proposed amendment shall be submitted to the Depositary Governments which shall circulate it to all Parties to this Treaty. Thereafter, if requested to do so by one-third or more of the Parties, the Depositary Governments shall convene a conference, to which they shall invite all the Parties, to consider such amendment.

2. Any amendment to this Treaty must be approved by a majority of the votes of all the Parties to this Treaty, including the votes of all of the Original Parties. The amendment shall enter into force for all Parties upon the deposit of instruments of ratification by a majority of all the Parties, including the instruments of ratification of all of the Original Parties.

Article III

1. This Treaty shall be open to all States for signature. Any State which does not sign this Treaty before its entry into force in accordance with paragraph 3 of this Article may accede to it at any time.

2. This Treaty shall be subject to ratification by signatory States. Instruments of ratification and instruments of accession shall be deposited with the Governments of the Original Parties—the United States of America, the United Kingdom of Great Britain and Northern Ireland, and the Union of Soviet Socialist Republics—which are hereby designated the Depositary Governments.

3. This Treaty shall enter into force after its ratification by all the Original Parties and the deposit of their instruments of ratification.

4. For States whose instruments of ratification or accession are deposited subsequent to the entry into force of this Treaty, it shall enter into force on the date of the deposit of their instruments of ratification or accession.

5. The Depositary Governments shall promptly inform all signatory and acceding States of the date of each signature, the date of deposit of each instrument of ratification of and accession to this Treaty, the date of its entry into force, and the date of receipt of any requests for conferences or other notices.

6. This Treaty shall be registered by the Depositary Governments pursuant to Article 102 of the Charter of the United Nations.

Article IV

This Treaty shall be of unlimited duration.

Each Party shall in exercising its national sovereignty have the right to withdraw from the Treaty if it decides that extraordinary events, related to the subject matter of this Treaty, have jeopardized the supreme interests of its country. It shall give notice of such withdrawal to all other Parties to the Treaty three months in advance.

Article V

This Treaty, of which the English and Russian texts are equally authentic, shall be deposited in the archives of the Depositary Governments. Duly certified copies of this Treaty shall be transmitted by the Depositary Governments to the Governments of the signatory and acceding States.

IN WITNESS WHEREOF the undersigned, duly authorized, have signed this Treaty.

PART EIGHT

The Great Red Scare

Onset

Ebb

The Great Red Scare: Onset

SELECTION **35**

The Hiss Case: Testimony by Alger Hiss and Whittaker Chambers before the House Committee on Un-American Activities, August, 5, 7, 16, 17, 1948

The tensions of the cold war bred hysteria. There had been a Red Scare after World War I. In the cold war, with Communists an actual enemy, a second Red Scare developed. It was to make the earlier one seem tame by comparison.

The Red Scare after World War II ran through the better part of a decade. It had roots not only in the cold war but in long-buried currents of anti-intellectualism and in the rapid social changes attendant on the shift from depression to prosperity. The background of the scare is sketched in Richard Hofstadter, Anti-Intellectualism in American Life *(1963) and in Daniel Bell (ed.),* The New American Right *(1955).*

Much of what was widely believed during the scare was nonsense. There was a notion, for example, that large numbers of Communists had infiltrated the American government. Their influence, it was held, had caused the Yalta agreements, prevented America, in 1945, from pushing the Soviet Union back to its prewar frontiers, and led to the failure to support Chiang Kai-shek which, in turn, led to the Communist seizure of power in China. There was another notion that large numbers of Communists had infiltrated the news media, the motion picture industry, and the clergy, so that news, movies, and sermons had gulled the public into approving pro-Communist policies. These beliefs rested on the fantasy that the United States, if it chose, could shape the world to its will and that, whenever anything went wrong, the fault had to lie at home.

But, unfortunately, the Red Scare rested on something other than sheer fantasy. During the depressed 1930s, communism had had a certain allure. Some individual Communists had achieved standing in the arts and the labor movement. Some intellectuals and reformers had become Communists. Some had gone so far as to adopt communism as a religion and to put loyalty to this creed above loyalty to country.

The Soviet Union exploited American Communists and fellow travelers. It used them to champion its causes during the 1930s; to fight against American intervention during the period of the Nazi-Soviet pact and to fight for intervention after the German invasion of 1941; to bellow for a second front during the war; and to battle the anti-Soviet policies of the Truman administration after the war. Worst of all, the Soviet Union enlisted some Americans as spies.

In the immediate aftermath of World War II, some politicians began to sound the refrain that Communists in America were a menace. The leaders were members of the House Un-American Activities Committee. A prewar creation, this committee had developed a shabby reputation under the chairmanship of an anti-Semitic, anti-Negro, antilabor Representative from Texas, Martin Dies. At first, its postwar din seemed to have little effect. An investigation of communism in Hollywood, for example, generated headlines but little else. There seemed a possibility that the committee's parent, the House of Representatives, might cut off its funds.

In 1948, an election year, the Un-American Activities Committee turned its attention to Communists in government. With fanfare, it took testimony from Elizabeth Bentley, an ex-Communist, and Whittaker Chambers, a chubby senior editor of Time. *Both claimed to have once worked with underground Communists who held high posts in Washington. These two witnesses provided the committee with names.*

Among the names supplied by Chambers was that of Alger Hiss, a former official of the State Department who, among other things, had been in Roosevelt's entourage at Yalta. Hiss voluntarily presented himself to the committee and not only denied Chambers's charges but denied that he had ever even known Chambers.

Most members of the committee were impressed with Hiss's testimony and felt that a mistake had been made. One member was doubtful. Richard M. Nixon (R., Calif.) insisted that Chambers and Hiss be interrogated further.

As the questioning progressed, it developed that Hiss had known Chambers. He identified Chambers as "Frank Crosley," a journalist to whom he had sublet an apartment in the 1930s. He had met Crosley, he said, while serving as committee counsel for Senator Gerald Nye in the celebrated 1934–1935 investigation of the munitions industry. Chambers continued to insist that he and Hiss had known one another as Communists, and, when he repeated the charge outside the committee room, Hiss sued for libel.

Before the libel suit came to trial, Chambers produced a sheaf of faded documents. They were, he said, confidential State Department documents that Hiss had passed on to him during 1938. Later, at his farm in Maryland, Chambers produced microfilm copies of still more documents. The rolls of film had been concealed inside a hollowed-out pumpkin.

The accusation against Hiss was no longer simply that of having been a Communist. Chambers now said that Hiss had acted as a Soviet spy.

Hiss was called before a grand jury in New York. Placed under oath, he was asked, "At any time did you, or Mrs. Hiss in your presence, turn any documents of the State Department or of any other government organization over to Whittaker Chambers?"

Hiss replied, "Never."

Another question put to him was, "Can you say definitely that you did not see Chambers after January 1, 1937?"

Hiss answered, "Yes, I think I can definitely say that."

Because of the statute of limitations, the government could not try Hiss for espionage. What it did instead was to put him on trial on two counts of perjury. He was charged with lying to the grand jury in declaring that he had not passed documents to Chambers. He was charged, in a second count, with lying in declaring that he had not seen Chambers after the beginning of 1937.

At Hiss's trial, the government introduced expert testimony that some of Chambers's "pumpkin papers" had been typed on a Woodstock typewriter that had been in the Hisses' possession in 1938. Others were identified by experts as being in Hiss's handwriting. Although unable to explain how these documents had come into Chambers's hands, Hiss stood by his guns. He denied having given material to Chambers. He denied having seen Chambers after knowing him as Frank Crosley. A long roster of witnesses testified to Hiss's upright character and to the untrustworthiness and emotional instability of Chambers.

The jury found itself unable to reach a decision. It divided 8 to 4 for conviction. Hiss was then tried again. This time, he was found guilty on both counts and sentenced to five years in the penitentiary.

Hiss's conviction produced serious repercussions. Afterward, many Americans were prepared to believe the worst of intellectuals who had had left-wing tendencies during the thirties. The best narrative of the hearings and trial is Alistair Cooke, Generation on Trial *(1950), and its title captures the significance of the case. In a sense, a whole generation was convicted by the jury that found Hiss guilty.*

Besides Cooke's book, there are firsthand accounts: Hiss, In the Court of Public Opinion *(1957); Chambers,* Witness *(1952); and Nixon,* Six Crises *(1962). There is also an English jurist's analysis of the trial, arguing that Hiss was denied due process—Earl Jowett,* The Strange Case of Alger Hiss *(1953), and a narrative by two newspapermen arguing that Hiss was unquestionably a spy—Ralph de Toledano and Victor Lasky,* The True Story of the Hiss-Chambers Tragedy *(1950).*

There follow excerpts from the original interrogations of Hiss and Chambers before the House Un-American Activities Committee. Besides Nixon, others asking questions are the chairman of the committee, Karl E. Mundt (R., S. Dak.); members of the committee: F. Edward Hébert (D., La.), John McDowell (R., Pa.), and John Rankin (D., Miss.); and Robert Stripling, the committee's chief counsel. The excerpts are from Eightieth Congress, second session, Hearings before the Committee on Un-American Activities, House of Representatives, Communist Espionage, *pages 642–647, 661–667, 669–670, 940–942, 944–951, 955–964, 977–986, 988.*

TESTIMONY OF ALGER HISS, AUGUST 5, 1948

Mr. Hiss: Mr. Chairman, may I be permitted to make a brief statement to the committee?

Mr. Mundt: You may.

Mr. Stripling: Before you proceed, I want you to give the committee your full name and your present address.

Mr. Hiss: My name is Alger Hiss. My residence is 22 East Eighth Street, New York City.

Mr. Rankin: Will you please give your age and place of birth?

Mr. Hiss: I was born in Baltimore, Md., on November 11, 1904. I am here at my own request to deny unqualifiedly various statements about me which were made before this committee by one Whittaker Chambers the day before yesterday. I appreciate the committee's having promptly granted my request. I welcome the opportunity to answer to the best of my ability any inquiries the members of this committee may wish to ask me.

I am not and never have been a member of the Communist Party. I do not and never have adhered to the tenets of the Communist Party. I am not and never have been a member of any Communist-front organization. I have never followed the Communist Party line, directly or indirectly. To the best of my knowledge, none of my friends is a Communist.

As a State Department official, I have had contacts with representatives of foreign governments, some of whom have undoubtedly been members of the Communist Party, as, for example, representatives of the Soviet Government. My contacts with any foreign representative who could possibly have been a Communist have been strictly official.

To the best of my knowledge, I never heard of Whittaker Chambers until in 1947, when two representatives of the Federal Bureau of Investigation asked me if I knew him and various other people, some of whom I knew and some of whom I did not know. I said I did not know Chambers. So far as I know, I have never laid eyes on him, and I should like to have the opportunity to do so. . . .

Except as I have indicated, the statements made about me by Mr. Chambers are complete fabrications. I think my record in the Government service speaks for itself. . . .

Mr. Mundt: . . . I want to say for one member of the committee that it is extremely puzzling that a man who is senior editor of Time Magazine, by the name of Whittaker Chambers, whom I had never seen until a day or two ago, and whom you say you have never seen——

Mr. Hiss: As far as I know, I have never seen him.

Mr. Mundt: Should come before this committee and discuss the Communist apparatus working in Washington, which he says is transmitting secrets to the Russian Government, and he lists a group of seven people—Nathan Witt, Lee Pressman, Victor Perlo, Charles Kramer, John Abt, Harold Ware, Alger Hiss, and Donald Hiss——

Mr. Hiss: That is eight.

Mr. Mundt: There seems to be no question about the subversive connections of the six other than the Hiss brothers, and I wonder what possible motive a man who edits Time magazine would have for mentioning Donald Hiss and Alger Hiss in connection with those other six.

Mr. Hiss: So do I, Mr. Chairman. I have no possible understanding of what could have motivated him. There are many possible motives, I assume, but I am unable to understand it. . . .

Mr. Stripling: You say you have never seen Mr. Chambers?

Mr. Hiss: The name means absolutely nothing to me, Mr. Stripling.

Mr. Stripling: I have here, Mr. Chairman, a picture which was made last Monday by the Associated Press. I understand from people who knew Mr. Chambers during 1934 and '35 that he is much heavier today than he was at that time, but I show you this picture, Mr. Hiss, and ask you if you have ever known an individual who resembles this picture.

Mr. Hiss: I would much rather see the individual. I have looked at all the pictures I was able to get hold of in, I think it was, yesterday's paper which had the pictures. If this is a picture of Mr. Chambers, he is not particularly unusual looking. He looks like a lot of people. I might even mistake him for the chairman of this committee. [Laughter.]

Mr. Mundt: I hope you are wrong in that.

Mr. Hiss: I didn't mean to be facetious but very seriously. I would not want to take oath that I have never seen that man. I would like to see him and then I think I would be better able to tell whether I had ever seen him. Is he here today?

Mr. Mundt: Not to my knowledge.

Mr. Hiss: I hoped he would be.

Mr. Mundt: You realize that this man whose picture you have just looked at, under sworn testimony before this committee, where all the laws of perjury apply, testified that he called at your home, conferred at great length, saw your wife pick up the telephone and call somebody whom he said must have been a Communist, plead with you to divert yourself from Communist activities, and left you with tears in your eyes, saying, "I simply can't make the sacrifice."

Mr. Hiss: I do know that he said that. I also know that I am testifying under those same laws to the direct contrary. . . .

TESTIMONY OF WHITTAKER CHAMBERS, AUGUST 7, 1948

Mr. Nixon: Mr. Chambers, you are aware of the fact that Mr. Alger Hiss appeared before this committee, before the Un-American Activities Committee, in public session and swore that the testimony which had been given by you under oath before this committee was false. The committee is now interested in questioning you further concerning your alleged acquaintanceship with Mr. Alger Hiss so that we can determine what course of action should be followed in this matter in the future.

Mr. Hiss in his testimony was asked on several occasions whether or not he had ever known or knew a man by the name of Whittaker Chambers. In each instance he categorically said "No."

At what period did you know Mr. Hiss? What time?

Mr. Chambers: I knew Mr. Hiss, roughly, between the years 1935 to 1937. . . .

Mr. Nixon: During the time that you knew Mr. Hiss, did he know you as Whittaker Chambers?

Mr. Chambers: No, he did not.

Mr. Nixon: By what name did he know you?

Mr. Chambers: He knew me by the party name of Carl.

Mr. Nixon: Did he ever question the fact that he did not know your last name?

Mr. Chambers: Not to me.

Mr. Nixon: Why not?

Mr. Chambers: Because in the underground Communist Party the principle of organization is that functionaries and heads of the group, in other words, shall not be known by their right names but by pseudonyms or party names.

Mr. Nixon: Were you a party functionary?

Mr. Chambers: I was a functionary.

Mr. Nixon: This entire group with which you worked in Washington did not know you by your real name?

Mr. Chambers: No member of that group knew me by my real name.

Mr. Nixon: All knew you as Carl?

Mr. Chambers: That is right.

Mr. Nixon: No member of that group ever inquired of you as to your real name?

Mr. Chambers: To have questioned me would have been a breach of party discipline, Communist Party discipline.

Mr. Nixon: I understood you to say that Mr. Hiss was a member of the party.

Mr. Chambers: Mr. Hiss was a member of the Communist Party. . . .

Mr. Nixon: Did Mr. Hiss have any children?

Mr. Chambers: Mr. Hiss had no children of his own.

Mr. Nixon: Were there any children living in his home?

Mr. Chambers: Mrs. Hiss had a son.

Mr. Nixon: Do you know the son's name?

Mr. Chambers: Timothy Hobson.

Mr. Nixon: Approximately how old was he at the time you knew him?

Mr. Chambers: It seems to me he was about 10 years old.

Mr. Nixon: What did you call him?

Mr. Chambers: Timmie.

Mr. Nixon: Did Mr. Hiss call him Timmie also?

Mr. Chambers: I think so. . . .

Mr. Nixon: What name did Mrs. Hiss use in addressing Mr. Hiss?

Mr. Chambers: Usually "Hilly."

Mr. Nixon: "Hilly"?

Mr. Chambers: Yes.

Mr. Nixon: Quite often?

Mr. Chambers: Yes.

Mr. Nixon: In your presence?

Mr. Chambers: Yes.

Mr. Nixon: Not "Alger"?

Mr. Chambers: Not "Alger."

Mr. Nixon: What nickname, if any, did Mr. Hiss use in addressing his wife?

Mr. Chambers: More often "Dilly" and sometimes "Pross." Her name was Priscilla. They were commonly referred to as "Hilly" and "Dilly."

Mr. Nixon: They were commonly referred to as "Hilly" and "Dilly"?

Mr. Chambers: By other members of the group.

Mr. Nixon: You don't mean to indicate that was simply the nicknames used by the Communist group?

Mr. Chambers: This was a family matter.

Mr. Nixon: In other words, other friends and acquaintances of theirs would possibly have used these names?

Did you ever spend any time in Hiss' home?

Mr. Chambers: Yes.

Mr. Nixon: Did you stay overnight?

Mr. Chambers: Yes; I stayed overnight for a number of days.

Mr. Nixon: You mean from time to time?
Mr. Chambers: From time to time.
Mr. Nixon: Did you ever stay longer than 1 day?
Mr. Chambers: I have stayed there as long as a week.
Mr. Nixon: A week one time. What would you be doing during that time?
Mr. Chambers: Most of the time reading.
Mr. Nixon: What arrangement was made for taking care of your lodging at that time? Were you there as a guest?
Mr. Chambers: I made that a kind of informal headquarters.
Mr. Nixon: I understand that, but what was the financial arrangement?
Mr. Chambers: There was no financial arrangement.
Mr. Nixon: You were a guest?
Mr. Chambers: Part of the Communist pattern. . . .
Mr. Nixon: Did the Hisses have any pets?
Mr. Chambers: They had, I believe, a cocker spaniel. I have a bad memory for dogs, but as nearly as I can remember it was a cocker spaniel.
Mr. Nixon: Do you remember the dog's name?
Mr. Chambers: No. I remember they used to take it up to some kennel. I think out Wisconsin Avenue.
Mr. Nixon: They took it to board it there?
Mr. Chambers: Yes. They made one or two vacation trips to the Eastern Shore of Maryland.
Mr. Nixon: They made some vacation trips to the Eastern Shore of Maryland?
Mr. Chambers: Yes, and at those times the dog was kept at the kennel.
Mr. Nixon: You state the Hisses had several different houses when you knew them? Could you describe any one of those houses to us?
Mr. Chambers: I think so. It seems to me when I first knew him he was living on 28th Street in an apartment house. There were two almost identical apartment houses. It seems to me that is a dead-end street and this was right at the dead end and certainly it is on the right-hand side as you go up.
It also seems to me that apartment was on the top floor. Now, what was it like inside, the furniture? I can't remember.
Mr. Mandel: What was Mr. Hiss' library devoted to?
Mr. Chambers: Very nondescript, as I recall.
Mr. Nixon: Do you recall what floor the apartment was on?
Mr. Chambers: I think it was on the top floor.
Mr. Nixon: The fourth?
Mr. Chambers: It was a walk-up. I think the fourth.
Mr. Nixon: It could have been the third, of course?
Mr. Chambers: It might have been.
Mr. Nixon: But you think it was the top, as well as you can recall?
Mr. Chambers: I think it was the top.
Mr. Nixon: Understand, I am not trying to hold you to absolute accuracy.
Mr. Chambers: I am trying to recall.
Mr. Nixon: Was there any special dish they served?
Mr. Chambers: No. I think you get here into something else. Hiss is a man of great simplicity and a great gentleness and sweetness of character,

and they lived with extreme simplicity. I had the impression that the furniture in that house was kind of pulled together from here or there, maybe got it from their mother or something like that, nothing lavish about it whatsoever, quite simple.

Their food was in the same pattern and they cared nothing about food. It was not a primary interest in their lives.

Mr. Mandel: Did Mr. Hiss have any hobbies?

Mr. Chambers: Yes; he did. They both had the same hobby—amateur ornithologists, bird observers. They used to get up early in the morning and go to Glen Echo, out the canal, to observe birds.

I recall once they saw, to their great excitement, a prothonotary warbler.

Mr. McDowell: A very rare specimen?

Mr. Chambers: I never saw one. I am also fond of birds.

Mr. Nixon: Did they have a car?

Mr. Chambers: Yes; they did. When I first knew them they had a car. Again I am reasonably sure—I am almost certain—it was a Ford and that it was a roadster. It was black and it was very dilapidated. There is no question about that.

I remember very clearly that it had hand windshield wipers. I remember that because I drove it one rainy day and had to work those windshield wipers by hand.

Mr. Nixon: Do you recall any other car?

Mr. Chambers: It seems to me in 1936, probably, he got a new Plymouth.

Mr. Nixon: Do you recall its type?

Mr. Chambers: It was a sedan, a two-seated car.

Mr. Mandel: What did he do with the old car?

Mr. Chambers: The Communist Party had in Washington a service station—that is, the man in charge or owner of this station was a Communist—or it may have been a car lot.

Mr. Nixon: But the owner was a Communist?

Mr. Chambers: The owner was a Communist. I never knew who this was or where it was. It was against all the rules of underground organization for Hiss to do anything with his old car but trade it in, and I think this investigation has proved how right the Communists are in such matters, but Hiss insisted that he wanted that car turned over to the open party so it could be of use to some poor organizer in the West or somewhere.

Much against my better judgment and much against Peters' better judgment, he finally got us to permit him to do this thing. Peters knew where this lot was and he either took Hiss there, or he gave Hiss the address and Hiss went there, and to the best of my recollection of his description of that happening, he left the car there and simply went away and the man in charge of the station took care of the rest of it for him. I should think the records of that transfer would be traceable.

Mr. Nixon: Where was that?

Mr. Chambers: In Washington, D. C., I believe; certainly somewhere in the District.

Mr. Nixon: You don't know where?

Mr. Chambers: No; never asked.

Mr. Nixon: Do you recall any other cars besides those two?

Mr. Chambers: No, I think he had the Plymouth when I broke with the whole business. . . .

Mr. Stripling: Do you know whether he was a member of a church?

Mr. Chambers: I don't know.

Mr. Stripling: Do you know if his wife was a member of a church?

Mr. Chambers: She came from a Quaker family. Her maiden name was Priscilla Fansler before she was married. She came from the Great Valley near Paoli, Pa.

Mr. Nixon: Did she tell you anything about her family?

Mr. Chambers: No; but she once showed me while we were driving beyond Paoli the road down which their farm lay.

Mr. Nixon: You drove with them?

Mr. Chambers: Yes.

Mr. Nixon: Did you ever go on a trip with them other than by automobile?

Mr. Chambers: No.

Mr. Nixon: Did you stay overnight on any of these trips?

Mr. Chambers: No. . . .

TESTIMONY OF ALGER HISS, AUGUST 16, 1948

Mr. Nixon: I am now showing you two pictures of Mr. Whittaker Chambers, also known as Carl, who testified that he knew you between the years 1934–37, and that he saw you in 1939.

I ask you now, after looking at those pictures, if you can remember that person either as Whittaker Chambers or as Carl or as any other individual you have met.

Mr. Hiss: May I recall to the committee the testimony I gave in the public session when I was shown another photograph of Mr. Whittaker Chambers, and I had prior to taking the stand tried to get as many newspapers that had photographs of Mr. Chambers as I could. I testified then that I could not swear that I had never seen the man whose picture was shown me. Actually the face has a certain familiarity. I think I also testified to that.

It is not according to the photograph a very distinctive or unusual face. I would like very much to see the individual face to face. I had hoped that would happen before. I still hope it will happen today.

I am not prepared to say that I have never seen the man whose pictures are now shown me. I said that when I was on the stand when a different picture was shown me. I cannot recall any person with distinctness and definiteness whose picture this is, but it is not completely unfamiliar.

Whether I am imagining that or not I don't know, but I certainly wouldn't want to testify without seeing the man, hearing him talk, getting some much more tangible basis for judging the person and the personality.

Mr. Nixon: Would your answer be any different if this individual were described to you as one who had stayed overnight in your house on several occasions?

Mr. Hiss: I think, Mr. Nixon, let me say this: In the course of my service in Government from 1933 to 1947 and the previous year 1929–30, and as a lawyer I have had a great many people who have visited in my house.

I have tried to recall in the last week or so anyone who would know my house whom I wouldn't know very well. There are many people that have come to my house on social occasions or on semibusiness occasions whom I probably wouldn't recall at all.

As far as staying overnight in my house is concerned———

Mr. Nixon: On several occasions.

Mr. Hiss: On several occasions?

Mr. Nixon: On several occasions.

Mr. Hiss: I can't believe, Mr. Nixon, that anyone could have stayed in my house when I was there———

Mr. Nixon: When you were there.

Mr. Hiss: ———Overnight on several occasions without my being able to recall the individual; and if this is a picture of anyone, I would find it very difficult to believe that that individual could have stayed in my house when I was there on several occasions overnight and his face not be more familiar than it is.

Mr. Nixon———

Mr. Nixon: Yes.

Mr. Hiss: I don't want to suggest any innovations in your procedure, but I do want to say specifically that I do hope I will have an opportunity actually to see the individual. . . .

Mr. Nixon: Your testimony now is that you are not a member of the Communist Party?

Mr. Hiss: That is correct.

Mr. Nixon: Never been a member of the Communist Party?

Mr. Hiss: Never been a member of the Communist Party.

Mr. Nixon: Or of any underground organization connected with the Communist Party?

Mr. Hiss: Not any underground organizations connected with the Communist Party.

Mr. Nixon: Do you have any children, Mr. Hiss?

Mr. Hiss: I have two children.

Mr. Nixon: You have two children. Could you give us their ages?

Mr. Hiss: One will be 22—he is my stepson—will be 22 September 19 next. His name is Timothy Hobson. He has been my stepson since he was 3 years old. I was married in 1929.

I have one other son who is now 7. . . .

Mr. Nixon: Did you testify before what your wife's name was?

Mr. Hiss: Her name was Priscilla Fansler, her maiden name. Her first marriage was to a Mr. Hobson, H-o-b-s-o-n.

Mr. Nixon: Where did she come from? What town?

Mr. Hiss: She was born in Evanston, Ill., but spent most of her early life outside of Philadelphia.

Mr. Nixon: In Paoli?

Mr. Hiss: Frazer.

Mr. Nixon: Is that near Paoli?

Mr. Hiss: It is on the main line not far from there. She went to school there and she went to school actually, I think, in Bryn Mawr, as well as to college in Bryn Mawr.

Mr. McDowell: Frazer and Paoli are a few miles apart?

Mr. Hiss: Yes.

Mr. Nixon: Did she live there on a farm?

Mr. Hiss: Her father was in the insurance business, and he acquired a small place—I suppose it could be called a farm—from which he commuted to his insurance business. . . .

Mr. Nixon, may I raise a question at this point?

Mr. Nixon: Certainly.

Mr. Hiss: I have been angered and hurt by one thing in the course of this committee testimony, and that was by the attitude which I think Mr. Mundt took when I was testifying publicly and which, it seems to me, you have been taking today, that you have a conflict of testimony between two witnesses—I restrained myself with some difficulty from commenting on this at the public hearing, and I would like to say it on this occasion, which isn't a public hearing.

Mr. Nixon: Say anything you like.

Mr. Hiss: It seems there is no impropriety in saying it. You today and the acting chairman publicly have taken the attitude when you have two witnesses, one of whom is a confessed former Communist, the other is me, that you simply have two witnesses saying contradictory things as between whom you find it most difficult to decide on credibility.

Mr. Nixon, I do not know what Mr. Whittaker Chambers testified to your committee last Saturday. It is necessarily my opinion of him from what he has already said that I do know that he is not capable of telling the truth or does not desire to, and I honestly have the feeling that details of my personal life which I give honestly can be used to my disadvantage by Chambers then ex post facto knowing those facts.

I would request that I hear Mr. Chambers' story of his alleged knowledge of me. I have seen newspaper accounts, Mr. Nixon, that you spent the week end—whether correct or not, I do not know—at Mr. Chambers' farm in New Jersey.

Mr. Nixon: That is quite incorrect.

Mr. Hiss: It is incorrect.

Mr. Nixon: Yes, sir. I can say, as you did a moment ago, that I have never spent the night with Mr. Chambers.

Mr. Hiss: Now, I have been cudgeling my brains, particularly on the train coming down this morning, and I had 3 or 4 hours on the train between New York and Washington, as to who could have various details about my family. Many people could.

Mr. Nixon, I do not wish to make it easier for anyone who, for whatever motive I cannot understand, is apparently endeavoring to destroy me, to make that man's endeavors any easier. I think in common fairness to my own self-protection and that of my family and my family's good name and my own, I should not be asked to give details which somehow he may hear and then may be able to use as if he knew them before. I would like him to say all he knows about me now. What I have done is public record, where I have lived is public record. Let him tell you all he knows, let that be made public, and then let my record be checked against those facts instead of my being asked, Mr. Nixon, to tell you personal facts about myself which, if they come to his ears, could sound very persuasive to other people that he had known me at some prior time.

Mr. Nixon: The questions I have asked you to date, Mr. Hiss, if you will recall them, have all been facts that could be corroborated by third parties. . . .

Mr. Stripling: . . . I listened to his testimony in New York and I can assure you that there was no prearrangement or anything else with Mr. Chambers, but here is what he did. He sat there and testified for hours. He said he spent a week in your house and he just rattled off details like that. He has either made a study of your life in great detail or he knows you, one or the other, or he is incorrect.

Mr. Hiss: Could I ask you to ask him some questions?

Mr. Stripling: Here is a larger picture. Let the record show this larger picture taken by the Associated Press photo on August 3, 1948, of Mr. Mundt and Mr. Whittaker Chambers and, as the record previously stated, Mr. Chambers is much heavier now than he was in 1937 or 1938.

Does this picture refresh your memory in any way, Mr. Hiss?

Mr. Hiss: It looks like the very same man I had seen in the other pictures of, and I see Mr. Mundt and him in the same picture. The face is definitely not an unfamiliar face. Whether I am imagining it, whether it is because he looks like a lot of other people, I don't know, but I have never known anyone who had the relationship with me that this man has testified to and that, I think, is the important thing here, gentlemen. This man may have known me, he may have been in my house. I have had literally hundreds of people in my house in the course of the time I lived in Washington.

The issue is not whether this man knew me and I don't remember him. The issue is whether he had a particular conversation that he has said he had with me and which I have denied and whether I am a member of the Communist Party or ever was, which he has said and which I have denied.

If I could see the man face to face, I would perhaps have some inkling as to whether he ever had known me personally.

I have met within the past week a man who said he worked on the same staff in a confidential relationship at San Francisco that I did who definitely knew me, and I have no recollection of ever having seen that man.

The Chairman: May I ask a few questions?

Mr. Nixon: Certainly.

The Chairman: Mr. Hiss, would you be able to recall a person if that person positively had been in your house three or four times, we will say, in the last 10 years?

Mr. Hiss: I would say that if he had spent the night———

Mr. Stripling: Ten years?

Mr. Nixon: Fifteen years.

The Chairman: All right.

Mr. Hiss: I would say if he had spent the night—how many times did you say?

Mr. Stripling: He spent a week there.

Mr. Hiss: A whole week at a time continuously?

Mr. Stripling: Yes.

Mr. Hiss: And I was there at the same time?

Mr. Stripling: Yes.

Mr. Hiss: Mr. Chairman, I could not fail to recall such a man if he were now in my presence.

The Chairman: Wait a minute. You are positive then that if Mr. X spent a week in your house in the past 15 years you would recognize him today, assuming that Mr. X looks today something like what he looked then?

Mr. Hiss: Exactly, if he hadn't had a face lifting.

The Chairman: No doubt in your mind?

Mr. Hiss: I have no doubt whatsoever.

The Chairman: Now, here is a man who says he spent a week in your house in the last 15 years. Do you recognize him?

Mr. Hiss: I do not recognize him from that picture.

Mr. Nixon: Did that man spend a week in your house in the last 15 years?

Mr. Hiss: I cannot say that man did, but I would like to see him.

The Chairman: You say you cannot believe, but I would like to have a little more definite answer if you could make it more definite. Would you say he did or did not spend a week in your house?

Mr. Hiss: Mr. Chairman, I hope you will not think I am being unreasonable when I say I am not prepared to testify on the basis of a photograph. On the train coming down this morning I searched my recollection of any possible person that this man could be confused with or could have got information from about me.

The Chairman: Then you are not prepared to testify on this subject from a photograph?

Mr. Hiss: I am not prepared to testify on the basis of a photograph. I would want to hear the man's voice.

The Chairman: If the man himself came in here, you would be able to say yes or no?

Mr. Hiss: I think I would, sir.

The Chairman: You think you would.

Mr. Hiss: I can't believe a man would have changed as much as that, and I am absolutely prepared to testify that nobody, that man or any other man, had any such conversation with me in my house or anywhere else as he has testified to.

Mr. Stripling: What conversations did he testify he had with you in your house?

Mr. Hiss: Mr. Chambers, according to the record that I read, he said that he came to my house and pled with me to break with the Communist Party, and that I refused, and that I had tears in my eyes, and that the reason I gave was something about the Communist Party line.

Mr. Nixon: Mr. Hiss, let me explain this. Mr. Chambers, as indicated, did testify that he spent a week in your house. He also testified to other facts concerning his acquaintanceship with you—alleged facts, I should say—and I want to point out that the committee by getting answers to completely objective questions from you will be in a position to go certainly to third parties and to find out whether or not Mr. Chambers has committed perjury.

Now, on one point it is pretty clear that you have indicated that Mr. Chambers must have committed perjury because he said he spent a week in your house.

Now, these other matters to which Mr. Chambers has testified involve the same type of testimony. I want to say when Mr. Chambers appeared, he was instructed that every answer he gave to every question would be material and he was instructed off the record before that that a material question would subject him to perjury. So consequently, as you see, a matter of membership in the Communist Party is one thing because that is a matter which might be and probably would be concealed, but a matter of objective items concerning his relationship with you, his alleged relationship with you, can be confirmed in some cases by third parties and that, frankly, is the purpose of these questions.

Mr. Hiss: May I say one thing for the record?

Mr. Nixon: Certainly.

Mr. Hiss: I have written a name on this pad in front of me of a person whom I knew in 1933 and 1934 who not only spent some time in my house but sublet my apartment. That man certainly spent more than a week, not while I was in the same apartment. I do not recognize the photographs as possibly being this man. If I hadn't seen the morning papers with an account of statements that he knew the inside of my house, I don't think I would even have thought of this name. I want to see Chambers face to face and see if he can be this individual. I do not want and I don't think I ought to be asked to testify now that man's name and everything I can remember about him. I have written the name on this piece of paper. . . .

Mr. Hébert: Mr. Hiss, let me say this to you now—and this is removed of all technicalities, it is just a man-to-man impression of the whole situation. I think it is pertinent. . . .

We did not know anything Mr. Chambers was going to say. I did not hear your name mentioned until it was mentioned in open hearing.

Mr. Hiss: I didn't know that.

Mr. Hébert: As I say, I am not trying to be cagey or anything, but trying to put it on the line as certainly one member of this committee who has an open mind and up to this point don't know which one of the two is lying, but I will tell you right now and I will tell you exactly what I told Mr. Chambers so that will be a matter of record, too: Either you or Mr. Chambers is lying.

Mr. Hiss: That is certainly true.

Mr. Hébert: And whichever one of you is lying is the greatest actor that America has ever produced. Now, I have not come to the conclusion yet which one of you is lying and I am trying to find the facts. Up to a few moments ago you have been very open, very cooperative. Now, you have hedged. You may be standing on what you consider your right and I am not objecting to that. I am not pressing you to identify a picture when you should be faced with the man. That is your right.

Now, as to this inquiry which you make much over, and not without cause, perhaps, we met Mr. Chambers 48 hours after you testified in open session. Mr. Chambers did not know or have any inclination of any indication as to the questions that we were going to ask him, and we probed him, as Mr. Stripling says, for hours and the committee, the three of us—Mr. Nixon, Mr. McDowell, Mr. Stripling, and myself—and we literally ran out of questions. There wasn't a thing that came to our minds that we didn't ask him about, these little details, to probe his own testimony or rather to test his own credibility.

There couldn't have been a possible inkling as to what we were going to say about minor details, and he could not have possibly by the farthest stretch of the imagination prepared himself to answer because he didn't know where the questions were coming from and neither did we because we questioned him progressively; so how he could have prepared himself to answer these details which we now, and Mr. Nixon has indicated, we are now checking and for the sake of corroboration—for my own part I can well appreciate the position you are in, but if I were in your position, I would do everything I humanly could to prove that Chambers is a liar instead of me.

Mr. Hiss: I intend to. . . .

The name of the man I brought in—and he may have no relation to this whole nightmare—is a man named George Crosley. I met him when I was working for the Nye committee. He was a writer. He hoped to sell articles to magazines about the munitions industry.

I saw him, as I say, in my office over in the Senate Office Building, dozens of representatives of the press, students, people writing books, research people. It was our job to give them appropriate information out of the record, show them what had been put in the record. This fellow was writing a series of articles, according to my best recollection, free lancing, which he hoped to sell to one of the magazines.

He was pretty obviously not successful in financial terms, but as far as I know, wasn't actually hard up.

Mr. Stripling: What color was his hair?

Mr. Hiss: Rather blondish, blonder than any of us here.

Mr. Stripling: Was he married?

Mr. Hiss: Yes, sir.

Mr. Stripling: Any children?

Mr. Hiss: One little baby, as I remember it, and the way I know that was the subleasing point. After we had taken the house on P Street and had the apartment on our hands, he one day in the course of casual conversation said he was going to specialize all summer in getting his articles done here in Washington, didn't know what he was going to do, and was thinking of bringing his family.

I said, "You can have my apartment. It is not terribly cool, but it is up in the air near the Wardman Park." He said he had a wife and little baby. The apartment wasn't very expensive, and I think I let him have it at exact cost. My recollection is that he spent several nights in my house because his furniture van was delayed. We left several pieces of furniture behind.

The P Street house belonged to a naval officer overseas and was partly furnished, so we didn't need all our furniture, particularly during the summer months, and my recollection is that definitely, as one does with a tenant trying to make him agreeable and comfortable, we left several pieces of furniture behind until the fall, his van was delayed, wasn't going to bring all the furniture because he was going to be there just during the summer, and we put them up 2 or 3 nights in a row, his wife and little baby.

Mr. Nixon: His wife and he and little baby did spend several nights in the house with you?

Mr. Hiss: This man Crosley; yes.

Mr. Nixon: Can you describe his wife?

Mr. Hiss: Yes; she was a rather strikingly dark person, very strikingly dark. I don't know whether I would recognize her again because I didn't see very much of her.

Mr. Nixon: How tall was this man, approximately?

Mr. Hiss: Shortish.

Mr. Nixon: Heavy?

Mr. Hiss: Not noticeably. That is why I don't believe it has any direct, but it could have an indirect, bearing.

Mr. Nixon: How about his teeth?

Mr. Hiss: Very bad teeth. That is one of the things I particularly want to see Chambers about. This man had very bad teeth, did not take care of his teeth.

Mr. Stripling: Did he have most of his teeth or just weren't well cared for?

Mr. Hiss: I don't think he had gapped teeth, but they were badly taken care of. They were stained and I would say obviously not attended to.

Mr. Nixon: Can you state again just when he first rented the apartment?

Mr. Hiss: I think it was about June of 1935. . . .

Mr. Stripling: What kind of automobile did that fellow have?

Mr. Hiss: No kind of automobile. I sold him an automobile. I had an old Ford that I threw in with the apartment and had been trying to trade it in and get rid of it. I had an old, old Ford we had kept for sentimental reasons. We got it just before we were married in 1929.

Mr. Stripling: Was it a model A or model T?

Mr. Hiss: Early A model with a trunk on the back, a slightly collegiate model.

Mr. Stripling: What color?

Mr. Hiss: Dark blue. It wasn't very fancy but it had a sassy little trunk on the back.

Mr. Nixon: You sold that car?

Mr. Hiss: I threw it in. He wanted a way to get around and I said, "Fine, I want to get rid of it. I have another car, and we kept it for sentimental reasons, not worth a damn." I let him have it along with the rent. . . .

Mr. Nixon: Going back to this man, do you know how many days approximately he stayed with you?

Mr. Hiss: I don't think more than a couple of times. He may have come back. I can't remember when it was I finally decided it wasn't any use expecting to collect from him, that I had been a sucker and he was a sort of deadbeat; not a bad character, but I think he just was using me for a soft touch.

Mr. Nixon: You said before he moved in your apartment he stayed in your house with you and your wife about how many days?

Mr. Hiss: I would say a couple of nights. I don't think it was longer than that.

Mr. Nixon: A couple of nights?

Mr. Hiss: During the delay of the van arriving.

Mr. Nixon: Wouldn't that be longer than 2 nights?

Mr. Hiss: I don't think so. I wouldn't swear that he didn't come back again some later time after the lease and say, "I can't find a hotel. Put me up overnight," or something of that sort. I wouldn't swear Crosley wasn't in my house maybe a total of 3 or 4 nights altogether. . . .

Mr. Nixon: You gave this Ford car to Crosley?

Mr. Hiss: Threw it in along with the apartment and charged the rent and threw the car in at the same time.

Mr. Nixon: In other words, added a little to the rent to cover the car?

Mr. Hiss: No; I think I charged him exactly what I was paying for the rent and threw the car in in addition. I don't think I got any compensation.

Mr. Stripling: You just gave him the car?

Mr. Hiss: I think the car just went right in with it. I don't remember whether we had settled on the terms of the rent before the car question came up, or whether it came up and then on the basis of the car and the apartment I said, "Well, you ought to pay the full rent." . . .

Mr. Stripling: What kind of car did you get?

Mr. Hiss: A Plymouth.

Mr. Stripling: A Plymouth?

Mr. Hiss: Plymouth sedan.

Mr. Stripling: Four-door?

Mr. Hiss: I think I have always had only two-door.

Mr. Stripling: What kind of a bill of sale did you give Crosley?

Mr. Hiss: I think I just turned over—in the District you get a certificate of title, I think it is. I think I just simply turned it over to him.

Mr. Stripling: Handed it to him?

Mr. Hiss: Yes.

Mr. Stripling: No evidence of any transfer. Did he record the title?

Mr. Hiss: That I haven't any idea. This is a car which had been sitting on the streets in snows for a year or two. I once got a parking fine because I forgot where it was parked. We were using the other car.

Mr. Stripling: Do those model Fords have windshield wipers?

Mr. Hiss: You had to work them yourself.

Mr. Stripling: Hand operated?

Mr. Hiss: I think that is the best I can recall.

Mr. Nixon: Do you recall the voice of this fellow Crosley?

Mr. Hiss: I was trying to recall that this morning. It was a low voice. He speaks with a low and rather dramatic roundness. . . .

Mr. Nixon: There are matters which I wish to go into now to which Mr. Chambers has given categorical answers. I am going to put the questions objectively, as you can see. I am not going to try to lead you one way or the other. It will be very helpful as the two records look together to see how accurate he is in this case.

I want to say first of all, so that it won't come up, that I realize that the matters which are covered are matters which third parties could corroborate, and that is the reason we ask these particular questions. Again for the purpose of just checking the veracity of Mr. Chambers and your testimony. It will help us to check it again.

What were the nicknames you and your wife had?

Mr. Hiss: My wife, I have always called her "Prossy."

Mr. Nixon: What does she call you?

Mr. Hiss: Well, at one time she called me quite frequently "Hill," H-i-l-l.

Mr. Nixon: What other name?

Mr. Hiss: "Hilly," with a "y."

Mr. Nixon: What other name did you call her?

Mr. Stripling: What did you say?

Mr. Hiss: She called me "Hill" or "Hilly." I called her "Pross" or "Prossy" almost exclusively. I don't think any other nickname.

Mr. Nixon: Did you ever call her "Dilly"?

Mr. Hiss: No; never.

Mr. Nixon: Never to your knowledge in fun or otherwise?

Mr. Hiss: Never.

Mr. Nixon: What did you call your son?

Mr. Hiss: "Timmy." . . .

Mr. Nixon: If as much as possible we can limit our testimony to the years 1934 to 1937, it will be helpful because there is nothing else at issue. . . .

Mr. Nixon: Where did you spend your vacations during that period?

Mr. Hiss: Normally, I think I didn't begin going to Peacham regularly until either 1937 or 1938; may have been 1937. My son went to a camp over on the Eastern Shore of Maryland. I am partly an Eastern Shore man myself. Part of my family came from there. When he was at camp we spent two summers, I think, during this period in Chestertown, Md.

Mr. Nixon: On the Eastern Shore?

Mr. Hiss: On the Eastern Shore of Maryland. He went to a camp of friends of ours who lived just outside of Chestertown. For two summers we took a small apartment.

Mr. Nixon: Did you have pets?

Mr. Hiss: We had a brown cocker spaniel we had before we came to Washington, was with us all during that period, and lived to be so old she died of old age.

Mr. Nixon: What did you do with the dog when you went on your vacations; do you recall?

Mr. Hiss: I think we took Jenny over on the Eastern Shore. I think we took her on the Eastern Shore when we went there. She did spend some time in the kennels when we were away. . . .

Mr. Nixon: What hobby, if any do you have, Mr. Hiss?

Mr. Hiss: Tennis and amateur ornithology.

Mr. Nixon: Is your wife interested in ornithology?

Mr. Hiss: I also like to swim and also like to sail. My wife is interested in ornithology, as I am, through my interest. Maybe I am using too big a word to say an ornithologist because I am pretty amateur, but I have been interested in it since I was in Boston. I think anybody who knows me would know that.

Mr. McDowell: Did you ever see a prothonotary warbler?

Mr. Hiss: I have right here on the Potomac. Do you know that place?

The Chairman: What is that?

Mr. Nixon: Have you ever seen one?

Mr. Hiss: Did you see it in the same place?

Mr. McDowell: I saw one in Arlington.

Mr. Hiss: They come back and nest in those swamps. Beautiful yellow head, a gorgeous bird. . . .

Mr. Stripling: On this man George Crosley, you say you gave him this car?

Mr. Hiss: Yes, sir.

Mr. Stripling: Did you ever go riding with Crosley in this automobile?

Mr. Hiss: I might very well have.

Mr. Stripling: I mean did you go around with him quite a bit, take rides?

Mr. Hiss: You mean after I gave it to him did he ever give me a ride?

Mr. Stripling: Before or after.

Mr. Hiss: I think I drove him from the Hill to the apartment.

Mr. Stripling: Did you ever take any trips out of town with George Crosley?

Mr. Hiss: No; I don't think so.

Mr. Stripling: Did you ever take him to Pennsylvania?

Mr. Hiss: No. I think I once drove him to New York City when I was going to make a trip to New York City anyway.

Mr. Nixon: Was Mrs. Hiss along?

Mr. Hiss: That I wouldn't recall. She may have been. I think I may have given him a lift when I went to New York.

Mr. Stripling: Did you go to Paoli?

Mr. Hiss: If Mrs. Hiss was along; yes.

The Chairman: Route No. 202?

Mr. Hiss: Route 202 goes through that part of Pennsylvania, and that is the route we would take.

Mr. Nixon: Did you ever drive to Baltimore with Crosley?

Mr. Hiss: I don't recall it. I think he moved to Baltimore from here, as a matter of fact, but I don't recall that I ever drove him.

Mr. Nixon: How did you know that?

Mr. Hiss: I think he told me when he was pulling out. He was in my apartment until the lease expired in September.

Mr. Nixon: What year?

Mr. Hiss: I think it was September 1935 and I think I saw him several times after that, and I think he had told me he moved from here to Baltimore.

Mr. Nixon: Even though he didn't pay his rent you saw him several times?

Mr. Hiss: He was about to pay it and was going to sell his articles. He gave me a payment on account once. He brought a rug over which he said some wealthy patron gave him. I have still got the damned thing.

Mr. Nixon: Did you ever give him anything?

Mr. Hiss: Never anything but a couple of loans; never got paid back.

Mr. Nixon: Never gave him anything else?

Mr. Hiss: Not to my recollection.

Mr. Nixon: Where is he now?

Mr. Hiss: I have no idea. I don't think I have seen him since 1935.

Mr. Nixon: Have you ever heard of him since 1935?

Mr. Hiss: No; never thought of him again until this morning on the train. . . .

TESTIMONY OF WHITTAKER CHAMBERS AND ALGER HISS, AUGUST 17, 1948

Mr. Nixon: Mr. Russell, will you bring Mr. Chambers in?

Mr. Russell: Yes.

(Mr. Russell leaves room and returns accompanied by Mr. Chambers.)

Mr. Nixon: Sit over here, Mr. Chambers.

Mr. Chambers, will you please stand?

And will you please stand, Mr. Hiss?

Mr. Hiss, the man standing here is Mr. Whittaker Chambers. I ask you now if you have ever known that man before.

Mr. Hiss: May I ask him to speak?

Will you ask him to say something?

Mr. Nixon: Yes.

Mr. Chambers, will you tell us your name and your business?

Mr. Chambers: My name is Whittaker Chambers.

(At this point, Mr. Hiss walked in the direction of Mr. Chambers.)

Mr. Hiss: Would you mind opening your mouth wider?

Mr. Chambers: My name is Whittaker Chambers.

Mr. Hiss: I said, would you open your mouth?

You know what I am referring to, Mr. Nixon.

Will you go on talking?

Mr. Chambers: I am senior editor of Time magazine.

Mr. Hiss: May I ask whether his voice, when he testified before, was comparable to this?

Mr. Nixon: His voice?

Mr. Hiss: Or did he talk a little more in a lower key?

Mr. McDowell: I would say it is about the same now as we have heard.

Mr. Hiss: Would you ask him to talk a little more?

Mr. Nixon: Read something, Mr. Chambers. I will let you read from———

Mr. Hiss: I think he is George Crosley, but I would like to hear him talk a little longer.

Mr. McDowell: Mr. Chambers, if you would be more comfortable, you may sit down.

Mr. Hiss: Are you George Crosley?

Mr. Chambers: Not to my knowledge. You are Alger Hiss, I believe.

Mr. Hiss: I certainly am.

Mr. Chambers: That was my recollection. (Reading:)

Since June———

Mr. Nixon (interposing): Just one moment. Since some repartee goes on between these two people, I think Mr. Chambers should be sworn.

Mr. Hiss: That is a good idea.

Mr. McDowell: You do solemnly swear, sir, that the testimony you shall give this committee will be the truth, the whole truth, and nothing but the truth, so help you God?

Mr. Chambers: I do.

Mr. Nixon: Mr. Hiss, may I say something? I suggested that he be sworn, and when I say something like that I want no interruptions from you.

Mr. Hiss: Mr. Nixon, in view of what happened yesterday, I think there is no occasion for you to use that tone of voice in speaking to me, and I hope the record will show what I have just said.

Mr. Nixon: The record shows everything that is being said here today.

Mr. Stripling: You were going to read.

Mr. Chambers (reading from Newsweek magazine):

Tobin for Labor. Since June, Harry S. Truman had been peddling the labor secretaryship left vacant by Lewis B. Schwellenbach's death in hope of gaining the maximum political advantage from the appointment.

Mr. Hiss: May I interrupt?

Mr. McDowell: Yes.

Mr. Hiss: The voice sounds a little less resonant than the voice that I recall of the man I knew as George Crosley. The teeth look to me as though either they have been improved upon or that there has been considerable dental work done since I knew George Crosley, which was some years ago.

I believe I am not prepared without further checking to take an absolute oath that he must be George Crosley.

Mr. Nixon: May I ask a question of Mr. Chambers?

Mr. Hiss: I would like to ask Mr. Chambers, if I may.

Mr. Nixon: I will ask the questions at this time.

Mr. Chambers, have you had any dental work since 1934 of a substantial nature?

Mr. Chambers: Yes; I have.

Mr. Nixon: What type of dental work?

Mr. Chambers: I have had some extractions and a plate.

Mr. Nixon: Have you had any dental work in the front of your mouth?

Mr. Chambers: Yes.

Mr. Nixon: What is the nature of that work?

Mr. Chambers: That is a plate in place of some of the upper dentures.

Mr. Nixon: I see.

Mr. Hiss: Could you ask him the name of the dentist that performed these things? Is that appropriate?

Mr. Nixon: Yes. What is the name?

Mr. Chambers: Dr. Hitchcock, Westminster, Md.

Mr. Hiss: That testimony of Mr. Chambers, if it can be believed, would tend to substantiate my feeling that he represented himself to me in 1934 or 1935 or thereabout as George Crosley, a free lance writer of articles for magazines.

I would like to find out from Dr. Hitchcock if what he has just said is true, because I am relying partly, one of my main recollections of Crosley was the poor condition of his teeth.

Mr. Nixon: Can you describe the condition of your teeth in 1934?

Mr. Chambers: Yes. They were in very bad shape.

Mr. Nixon: The front teeth were?

Mr. Chambers: Yes; I think so.

Mr. Hiss: Mr. Chairman.

Mr. Nixon: Excuse me. Before we leave the teeth, Mr. Hiss, do you feel that you would have to have the dentist tell you just what he did to the teeth before you could tell anything about this man?

Mr. Hiss: I would like a few more questions asked.

I didn't intend to say anything about this, because I feel very strongly that he is Crosley, but he looks very different in girth and in other appearances—hair, forehead, and so on, particularly the jowls.

Mr. Nixon: What was Crosley's wife's name?

Mr. Hiss: I don't think I recall.

Mr. Nixon: You did testify that she on several occasions was in your home overnight.

Mr. Hiss: That is right.

Mr. Nixon: And that you have ridden with her in a car as well as with him.

Mr. Hiss: I don't recall testifying to that.

Mr. Nixon: Do you testify she didn't?

Mr. Hiss: I don't recall.

Mr. Nixon: But she did stay overnight in your home on several occasions?

Mr. Hiss: She did. I don't think I said several occasions.

Mr. Nixon: How many times did you say?

Mr. Hiss: My recollection is that at the time George Crosley subrented my apartment on Twenty-ninth Street his wife and he and infant spent two or three or four consecutive nights in my house because the van had not come with their furniture, and we left only certain pieces of furniture behind to accommodate them.

Mr. Nixon: In regard to the rental agreement that was entered into with Mr. Crosley, do you recall approximately the rental that was charged and agreed to?

Mr. Hiss: My recollection is that I said I would be glad to let him have the apartment for the cost to me. It was a rather moderate rental.

Mr. Nixon: Could you say within certain limits?

Mr. Hiss: My recollection—I can't remember just what I paid for the apartment that far back—my recollection is it was under $75 a month. It was a very reasonable rental. That is one of the reasons I had taken it. . . .

Mr. Nixon: Then the total rental value for the period was, if it was for 2 months, it would have been approximately $150; 3 months, approximately $225.

Mr. Hiss: It was contingent upon the number of months he would occupy the remaining unexpired term under my lease.

Mr. Nixon: How long did he stay there?

Mr. Hiss: As far as I know, he stayed there all summer. He certainly never said he didn't.

Mr. Nixon: Your lease did not run out after the end of the summer?

Mr. Hiss: That is right.

Mr. Nixon: He didn't stay there after that?

Mr. Hiss: Not to my knowledge.

Mr. Nixon: Did he ever pay any rent at all?

Mr. Hiss: My recollection is that he paid no cash, that he once paid in kind.

Mr. Nixon: No cash at all?

Mr. Hiss: He also borrowed some cash in addition.

Mr. Nixon: How much did he borrow, approximately?

Mr. Hiss: I don't think it got over $35 or $40 in different transactions, not all at once. I hope it didn't.

Mr. Nixon: Did you enter into a written contract?

Mr. Hiss: I think it was oral. It wasn't easy to sublet an apartment during the summer in those days in Washington. . . .

Mr. Nixon: You had known Mr. Crosley, your testimony is, for about 8 months before you entered into this agreement?

Mr. Hiss: Five or six months.

Mr. Nixon: Then you had had several conversations with him during that period?

Mr. Hiss: I think I must have seen him as often as I did any other newspaperman who was particularly interested. I think I saw him 10 or 11 times.

Mr. Nixon: Never saw him socially during that period?

Mr. Hiss: Never saw him socially.

Mr. Nixon: Only in the course of your business?

Mr. Hiss: Only in the course of my business.

Mr. Nixon: Then in 1935, the spring of 1935, Mr. Crosley discussed this matter of getting your apartment for the summer with you? . . .

And then there was some conversation about a car. What was that?

Mr. Hiss: There was. Mr. Crosley said that while he was in Washington he wondered if he could get a rented car or something, because he would like to have it while his family were with him, get out week ends, something like that. I said, "You came to just the right place. I would be very glad to throw a car in because I have been trying to get rid of an old car which we have kept solely for sentimental reasons which we couldn't get anything on for trade-in or sale." I would be very glad to let him have the car because we wanted somebody to make real use of it. We had had it sitting on the city streets because we had a new one.

Mr. Nixon: It was a '29 Ford?

Mr. Hiss: One of the first model A Fords.

Mr. Nixon: The year of this transaction would be 1935?

Mr. Hiss: That would be my best recollection.

Mr. Nixon: A 6-year-old Ford?

Mr. Hiss: That is right.

Mr. Nixon: You just gave him the car with this $225 rental?

Mr. Hiss: As part of the total contract. That is my best recollection.

Mr. Nixon: The rent was simply the going rate, as you indicated?

Mr. Hiss: That is right.

Mr. Nixon: And you just threw in this 6-year-old car with it?

Mr. Hiss: That is my best recollection. I don't think it figured as a financial element in the transaction.

Mr. Nixon: Do you know the Blue Book value of a 1929 Ford in 1935?

Mr. Hiss: I certainly don't. I know what the going rate was with sellers of new cars. I think the most I had ever been offered for it was $25 or $30 at that time, a few months before that.

Mr. Nixon: So you gave him this car.

Mr. Hiss: As part of the whole transaction.

Mr. Nixon: Then before he moved into the apartment I understand that you allowed him and his wife to stay with you in your home?

Mr. Hiss: My recollection of that—and this is repetitious———

Mr. Nixon: We are repeating it for his benefit as well as to see if he can recall this incident.

Mr. Hiss: I am glad he has no other way of finding out about it, Mr. Nixon.

My recollection on that point is that Mr. Crosley said since he was only coming down for the summer, he didn't want to bring very many things. I said since we had rented a furnished house, we had more furniture than we really needed. In fact, one of the rooms in 2905 P Street was perpetually used as a storeroom for furniture while we were there.

We left several pieces of furniture in the apartment for several weeks or months, I don't remember how long, and I don't remember which pieces, but there was a bed and a bureau and a table and a couple of chairs.

When the day came when Mr. Crosley was supposed to move in, his moving van hadn't arrived but his wife and baby had. We put them up the way one would be apt to try to be helpful to people you were subletting. You develop a kind of pseudo-friendliness over a transaction of that kind.

Mr. Crosley, his wife, and infant were put up in my house for 2 or 3 days while the moving van was coming; it may have been 4, may have been 2. It was more than one night. I imagine my wife would testify it seemed even longer than that.

Mr. Nixon: Were those the only two apartments in which Mr. Crosley saw you?

Mr. Hiss: To the best of my knowledge, yes.

Mr. Nixon: When did you see him after that period of the rental agreement?

Mr. Hiss: I saw him several times in the fall of 1935, as I recall it. . . .

Mr. Nixon: On these other occasions on which Mr. Crosley stayed with you; did he ever stay overnight?

Mr. Hiss: I wouldn't be sure of my recollection. It is quite possible he may have said that he couldn't get a reservation. Mr. Crosley was apparently in the habit of having difficulties. He may very well have said that he couldn't get a hotel reservation, could I put him up. Mr. Crosley, not being someone who paid his debts, may very well have added to his obligations in that way. That I wouldn't be sure of.

Mr. Nixon: You testified on one occasion you took him on a trip, as I understand it, ferried him to New York.

Mr. Hiss: My recollection is that on one occasion when my wife and I were going to drive to New York in any event, Mr. Crosley asked for a ride. I may have mentioned when I was talking to him that I was going to New York, or he may have said he was going to New York, and I said so was I.

My recollection is I drove him to New York on one occasion. Whether my wife was present or not, I am not sure. I rather think she may have been. I would have to ask her and I haven't asked her.

Mr. Nixon: Was that after the time of this rental agreement?

Mr. Hiss: I am afraid I can't recall.

Mr. Nixon: No further questions of Mr. Hiss at this time.

Mr. Stripling: Mr. Hiss, you say that person you knew as George Crosley, the one feature which you must have to check on to identify him is the dentures. . . .

Mr. Hiss: I saw him at the time I was seeing hundreds of people. Since then I have seen thousands of people. He meant nothing to me except as one I saw under the circumstances I have described.

My recollection of George Crosley, if this man had said he was George Crosley, I would have no difficulty in identification. He denied it right here.

I would like and asked earlier in this hearing if I could ask some further questions to help in identification. I was denied that. . . .

Mr. Stripling: The witness says he was denied the right to ask this witness questions. I believe the record will show you stated "at this time." I think he should be permitted to ask the witness questions now . . . him to determine whether or not this is the individual to whom he is referring.

Mr. Hiss: Right. I would be very happy if I could pursue that. Do I have the Chair's permission?

Mr. McDowell: The Chair will agree to that.

Mr. Hiss: Do I have Mr. Nixon's permission.

Mr. Nixon: Yes.

Mr. McDowell: Here is a very difficult situation.

Mr. Hiss: I will welcome that.

Mr. Nixon: Mr. Chambers, do you have any objection?

Mr. Chambers: No.

Mr. Hiss: Did you ever go under the name of George Crosley?

Mr. Chambers: Not to my knowledge.

Mr. Hiss: Did you ever sublet an apartment on Twenty-ninth Street from me?

Mr. Chambers: No; I did not.

Mr. Hiss: You did not?

Mr. Chambers: No.

Mr. Hiss: Did you ever spend any time with your wife and child in an apartment on Twenty-ninth Street in Washington when I was not there because I and my family were living on P Street?

Mr. Chambers: I most certainly did.

Mr. Hiss: You did or did not?

Mr. Chambers: I did.

Mr. Hiss: Would you tell me how you reconcile your negative answers with this affirmative answer?

Mr. Chambers: Very easily, Alger. I was a Communist and you were a Communist.

Mr. Hiss: Would you be responsive and continue with your answer?

Mr. Chambers: I do not think it is needed.

Mr. Hiss: That is the answer.

Mr. Nixon: I will help you with the answer, Mr. Hiss. The question, Mr. Chambers, is, as I understand it, that Mr. Hiss cannot understand how you would deny that you were George Crosley and yet admit that you spent time in his apartment. Now would you explain the circumstances? I don't want to put that until Mr. Hiss agrees that is one of his questions.

Mr. Hiss: You have the privilege of asking any questions you want. I think that is an accurate phrasing.

Mr. Nixon: Go ahead.

Mr. Chambers: As I have testified before, I came to Washington as a Communist functionary, a functionary of the American Communist Party. I was connected with the underground group of which Mr. Hiss was a member. Mr. Hiss and I became friends. To the best of my knowledge, Mr. Hiss himself suggested that I go there, and I accepted gratefully.

Mr. Hiss: Mr. Chairman.

Mr. Nixon: Just a moment. How long did you stay there?

Mr. Chambers: My recollection was about 3 weeks. It may have been longer. I brought no furniture, I might add.

Mr. Hiss: Mr. Chairman, I don't need to ask Mr. Whittaker Chambers any more questions. I am now perfectly prepared to identify this man as George Crosley. . . .

Mr. McDowell: Well, now, Mr. Hiss, you positively identify———

Mr. Hiss: Positively on the basis of his own statement that he was in my apartment at the time when I say he was there. I have no further questions at all. If he had lost both eyes and taken his nose off, I would be sure.

Mr. McDowell: Then, your identification of George Crosley is complete?

Mr. Hiss: Yes, as far as I am concerned, on his own testimony.

Mr. McDowell: Mr. Chambers, is this the man, Alger Hiss, who was also a member of the Communist Party at whose home you stayed?

Mr. Nixon: According to your testimony.

Mr. McDowell: You make the identification positive?

Mr. Chambers: Positive identification.

(At this point, Mr. Hiss arose and walked in the direction of Mr. Chambers.)

Mr. Hiss: May I say for the record at this point, that I would like to invite Mr. Whittaker Chambers to make those same statements out of the presence of this committee without their being privileged for suit for libel. I challenge you to do it, and I hope you will do it damned quickly. . . .

The Rise of Joe McCarthy

The conviction of Alger Hiss seemed to prove that the trumpeters of the Red Scare were right—that Communists had in fact worked their way into the government. And worse followed. In England, brilliant and trusted young scientists were discovered to have stolen atomic secrets and given them to Soviet agents. In America, proof was found of a wartime spy ring that had operated at the Los Alamos atomic laboratory.

By 1950, hunters of Communists were in full cry. The Un-American Activities Committee was exploiting every lead given it by ex-Communists and other informers. Committees of the Senate were following suit, and committees of various state legislatures were trying to outdo those in Washington.

Federal, state, and municipal agencies frantically conducted investigations of their own. They wanted to get rid of suspect employees before legislative committees descended on them. Men and women were fired for having belonged to organizations that supported Ethiopia in the Italo-Ethiopian War or Spanish Loyalists in the Spanish Civil War, for Communists had been in these organizations. Some lost their jobs just because they had once been acquainted with Communists.

The inquisitions reached beyond the civil service. Private business firms investigated the political backgrounds of their employees. Loyalty oaths were imposed on schoolteachers, college professors, and college students. The nation seemed in the grip of panic, not about the Russians with their huge population, hundreds of divisions, and new atomic arsenal, but about a tiny minority of Americans who were, had been, or had once consorted with members of the Communist party.

These conditions provided a perfect setting for the emergence of a demagogue. Like Mussolini in Italy or Hitler in Germany, a man without conscience or scruple could shout lies and be believed.

Such a man appeared. He was Joseph R. McCarthy, the junior Republican Senator from Wisconsin. In time, he was to change his name and become officially Senator Joe McCarthy. He had risen to his high office by lying about his political opponents and about his own combat record in World War II. As was to be demonstrated later, he accepted bribes from lobbyists while in the Senate. His bizarre career can be followed in Richard Rovere's superb character study, Senator Joe McCarthy *(1959), and in Jack Anderson and R. W. May,* McCarthy *(1952). The facts about his campaign tactics and his acceptance of bribes emerged in Eighty-third Congress, second session, Select Committee to Study Censure Charges,* Hearings on Senate Resolution Number 301.

When the Communist issue emerged, McCarthy was prepared to exploit it to the full. At Wheeling, West Virginia, on February 9, 1950, he declared that 205 known Communists were in the State Department. In subsequent speeches, he kept changing the figure, but each speech captured headlines. The Korean conflict erupted that summer. McCarthy's popularity grew. Though his charges became wilder and wilder, he fast developed a worshipful following among those who were terrified about communism at home.

Shocked by McCarthy's tactics and growing popularity, other Senators decided that a careful investigation of his charges was in order. A special committee was impaneled. Its chairman was one of the most conservative Democratic Senators, Millard Tydings of Maryland. The first document below is the report finally issued by the Tydings committee. It is Eighty-first Congress, second session, Senate Report Number 2108, State Department Employee Loyalty Investigation, *pages 152–155, 167.*

Astonishingly, the report of the Tydings committee had little or no effect on McCarthy's popularity. Those who had been willing to accept McCarthy's accusations were not willing to accept the committee's judgment that they were a "fraud and a hoax."

That autumn, Tydings came up for reelection. McCarthy went into Maryland to fight him. Using a doctored photograph as evidence, McCarthy made the preposterous charge that Tydings had been on intimate terms with onetime Communist presidential candidate Earl Browder. Though earlier thought invulnerable, Tydings was defeated. Thereafter, for years, politicians in both parties were to live in terror of McCarthy and his following.

When the Republican party won a narrow majority in the Senate in 1952, McCarthy was given the chairmanship of the Government Operations Committee. Though this committee existed simply to scrutinize the bookkeeping of the executive branch, McCarthy turned it to hunting Communists.

McCarthy pursued any lead that promised a headline. Subpoenaing newspaper editors who had attacked him, he grilled them on possible past associations with Communists. He went after universities. He attacked the United

States Information Service, claiming to find a deep-laid plot in the fact that a few books by alleged Communist authors (such as mystery-writer Dashiell Hammett) were on the shelves of USIA libraries overseas.

By 1954, McCarthy was concentrating his fire on the Army. The reason may have been that President Eisenhower was a former Army man, and each sally against the Army that passed without rebuke from the White House was a seeming proof of McCarthy's superior power.

On the flimsiest evidence, McCarthy claimed to have found a spy ring at an Army radar laboratory at Fort Monmouth, New Jersey. Then, almost for the first time, he turned up a genuine Communist. The man's name was Irving Peress. A dentist, Peress had held commissioned rank in the Army Dental Corps during World War II. Recalled to active duty during the Korean emergency, Peress had been stationed at Camp Kilmer, New Jersey. Just as his tour of duty was ending, McCarthy came upon him. Acting as a one-man subcommittee, McCarthy subpoenaed Peress. The dentist declined to answer questions about past Communist affiliations. He claimed the privilege, under the Fifth Amendment, of not being forced to incriminate himself. Then, routinely, Peress was released from the Army with an honorable discharge and a terminal leave promotion from captain to major.

McCarthy pretended to see in this discharge the evidence of a monstrous conspiracy. Communists high up in the Army, he claimed, had aided and shielded Peress.

McCarthy summoned before him Brigadier General Ralph W. Zwicker, the commanding officer at Camp Kilmer. Although not exactly an intellectual, Zwicker had a distinguished combat record and was an old friend of President Eisenhower's. McCarthy's treatment of him was brutal. Excerpts from the confrontation between the Senator and General Zwicker comprise the second document below. The other questioner of the general is Roy M. Cohn, a young lawyer who was counsel for McCarthy's committee. The excerpts are taken from Eighty-third Congress, second session, Hearings before a Subcommittee of the Senate Committee on Government Operations, Communist Infiltration in the Army, *pages 145–153.*

"COMMUNISTS IN THE STATE DEPARTMENT": THE TYDINGS COMMITTEE REPORT

1. Despite his denials on the Senate floor, publicly, and before this subcommittee, that he made the statement, we find on the evidence that Senator Joseph R. McCarthy, on February 9, 1950, at Wheeling, W. Va., said:

> Ladies and gentlemen, while I cannot take the time to name all the men in the State Department who have been named as active members of the Communist Party and members of a spy ring, I have here in my hand a list of 205—a list of names that were made known to the Secretary of State as being members of the Communist Party and who nevertheless are still working and shaping policy in the State Department.

Our investigation establishes that the foregoing allegations are false and, particularly, that Senator McCarthy had no such list as alleged and that there is not one member of the Communist Party or of a "spy ring" employed in the State Department known to the Secretary of State or other responsible officials of that Department.

2. We find that on February 20, 1950, at Salt Lake City, Utah, Senator McCarthy said:

> Last night I discussed the Communists in the State Department. I stated that I had the names of 57 card-carrying members of the Communist Party.

Our investigation establishes that Senator McCarthy at no time has had the names of 57 card-carrying members of the Communist Party in the State Department and that during the course of a 4 months' investigation he has been unable to produce competent evidence or to indicate where such evidence is obtainable concerning one member of the Communist Party, card-carrying or otherwise, who is employed in the State Department.

3. We find that on the evening of February 11, 1950, at Reno, Nev., Senator McCarthy again spoke on the question. As reported in the Nevada State Journal:

> Senator McCarthy who had first typed a total of 205 employees of the State Department who could be considered disloyal to the United States and pro-Communists scratched out that number, and mentioned only "57 card-carrying members," whom Acheson should know as well as Members of Congress.

4. We find that in making a speech on the Senate floor on February 20, 1950, Senator McCarthy read what purported to be the speech delivered by him at Wheeling, W. Va.; that the purported speech as read to the Senate was identical with the speech delivered at Wheeling except that he withheld from the Senate the statement actually made, as set forth in conclusion 1 above, and substituted in lieu thereof the following:

> I have in my hand 57 cases of individuals who would appear to be either card-carrying members or certainly loyal to the Communist Party, but who nevertheless are still helping to shape our foreign policy.

The substitution of the foregoing terminology constituted a misrepresentation of the true facts to the Senate.

5. We find that in making his speech on February 20, 1950 . . . Senator McCarthy left the unmistakable inference that he had but recently obtained from unrevealed sources in the State Department the information which he was presenting to the Senate.

Our investigation establishes that the material presented in this speech was data developed in 1947 by the Republican-controlled Eightieth Congress; and that representations indicating it had recently come from "loyal" State Department employees misled and deceived the Senate.

6. We find that the information presented to the Senate on February 20, 1950, by Senator McCarthy, concerning "81" individuals identified by him only by numbers, was a colored and distorted version of material developed by investigators of the House Appropriations Committee in 1947 during the Eightieth Congress.

To the extent that the information was colored and distorted and the source thereof concealed, the Senate was deceived.

7. We find that four separate committees of the Eightieth Congress,

controlled by Senator McCarthy's own party, formally considered the same information relative to the "81" individuals, as that utilized in the Senator's speech, and did not regard such information as sufficiently significant to prepare a report relative to the matter or to cite a single employee of the State Department as disloyal.

In suggesting on February 20, 1950, that the situation as reflected by his information was so gravely disturbing that he felt it his immediate duty to expose it, Senator McCarthy misled the Senate.

8. We find that Senator McCarthy failed to cooperate with the subcommittee or to supply further information concerning the "81" individuals mentioned in his speech of February 20, 1950, after having assured the Senate that he would "be willing, happy, and eager to go before any committee and give the names and all the information available."

Our investigation establishes that the only logical reason for the Senator's noncooperation and failure to supply further information was the fact that he had no information to supply.

9. We find that Senator McCarthy asserted the proof to sustain his charges against the "81" individuals would be found in the loyalty files concerning them.

Our review of these files reveals that they do not contain proof to support the charges; that none of these individuals employed in the State Department is a "card-carrying Communist," a member of the Communist Party; or "loyal to the Communist Party"; and, furthermore, that the Loyalty and Security Board has not in any instance erroneously or improperly granted loyalty or security clearance under existing standards. Amazingly, despite Senator McCarthy's insistence that the loyalty files would prove his case and the clamor that the files be opened after the President made the files available to us, Senator Hickenlooper read only 9 of the files and Senator Lodge only 12.

10. We find that in speaking to the Senate on February 20, 1950, Senator McCarthy said:

> While I consider them all important, there are three big Communists involved (cases 1, 2, and 81) and I cannot possibly conceive of any Secretary of State allowing these three big Communists, who are tremendously important, and of great value to Russia, to remain in the State Department.
>
> * * * I feel that if those individuals are removed from the State Department we shall have gone a considerable distance in breaking the back of the espionage ring in the State Department.
>
> I may also say that I feel very strongly that cases Nos. 1, 2, and 81, should not only be discharged but should be immediately prosecuted. * * *

Our review of the loyalty files concerning each of these three individuals revealed nothing whatever to sustain the foregoing assertion that they are "big Communists"; that they are "tremendously important and of great value to Russia"; "that they are part of an espionage ring in the State Department"; or that they should be "prosecuted." Interestingly, we found that case No. 81 resigned from the State Department on April 2, 1948.

11. We find that on February 20, 1950, Senator McCarthy told the Senate:

> This individual (No. 53) is, in my opinion, Mr. President, one of the most dangerous Communists in the State Department.

Our investigation reveals that No. 53 resigned from the State Department on December 30, 1948.

12. We find that in the period 1945–46, over 12,000 employees of emergency agencies created during the war were transferred by various Executive orders to the State Department; that some of these individuals appeared to warrant investigation as possible loyalty and security risks in the postwar period; and that, through the transfer of such an inordinately large number of employees, the security staff of the Department was confronted with a great problem.

Our investigation establishes that this problem was handled in a capable manner; that disloyal individuals were effectively weeded out; and that continuous effective efforts are being made and procedures followed to insure the security of the Department.

13. Our investigation reveals that the loyalty program is of indispensable value in protecting both the employee and the security of the Federal service and that it is being efficiently administered, specifically:

(A) That the FBI's loyalty investigations are comprehensive and conclusive with respect to the facts.
(B) That the State Department's Security Division is efficiently operated by highly qualified personnel.
(C) That the Loyalty and Security Board of the State Department is made up of high-type individuals of unquestioned loyalty, integrity, and sound judgment.
(D) That the Loyalty Review Board provides an effective and salutary control over the functioning of the loyalty program.

14. Our conclusions with respect to each of the individuals publicly charged by Senator McCarthy are being restated as follows: . . .

24. At a time when American blood is again being shed to preserve our dream of freedom, we are constrained fearlessly and frankly to call the charges, and the methods employed to give them ostensible validity, what they truly are: A fraud and a hoax perpetrated on the Senate of the United States and the American people. They represent perhaps the most nefarious campaign of half-truths and untruth in the history of this Republic. For the first time in our history, we have seen the totalitarian technique of the "big lie" employed on a sustained basis. The result has been to confuse and divide the American people, at a time when they should be strong in their unity, to a degree far beyond the hopes of the Communists themselves whose stock in trade is confusion and division. In such a disillusioning setting, we appreciate as never before our Bill of Rights, a free press, and the heritage of freedom that has made this Nation great.

THE GRILLING OF GENERAL RALPH ZWICKER

Mr. Cohn: General, to see if we can save a little time here, isn't the situation this—by the way, you have been commanding officer at Kilmer since when?

General Zwicker: Since the middle of July last year.

Mr. Cohn: Has the Peress case come to your attention since that time? I am not asking questions about it.

General Zwicker: Yes.
Mr. Cohn: It has come to your attention and you have a familiarity with that case?
General Zwicker: Yes.
Mr. Cohn: Now, general, would you like to be able to tell us exactly what happened in that case, and what steps you took and others took down at Kilmer to take action against Peress a long time before action was finally forced by the committee?
General Zwicker: That is a toughie.
Mr. Cohn: All I am asking you now is if you could, if you were at liberty to do so, would you like to be in a position to tell us that story?
General Zwicker: Well, may I say that if I were in a position to do so, I would be perfectly glad to give the committee any information that they desired.
Mr. Cohn: You certainly feel that that information would not reflect unfavorably on you; is that correct?
General Zwicker: Definitely not.
Mr. Cohn: And would not reflect unfavorably on a number of other people at Kilmer and the First Army?
General Zwicker: Definitely not.
The Chairman: It would reflect unfavorably upon some of them, of course?
General Zwicker: That I can't answer, sir. I don't know.
The Chairman: Well, you know that somebody has kept this man on knowing he was a Communist, do you not?
General Zwicker: No, sir.
The Chairman: You know that somebody has kept him on knowing that he has refused to tell whether he was a Communist, do you not?
General Zwicker: I am afraid that would come under the category of the Executive order, Mr. Chairman.
The Chairman: What?
General Zwicker: I am afraid an answer to that question would come under the category of the Presidential Executive order.
The Chairman: You will be ordered to answer the question.
General Zwicker: Would you repeat the question, please?
Mr. Cohn: Read it to the general.
(The question referred to was read by the reporter.)
General Zwicker: I respectfully decline to answer, Mr. Chairman, on the grounds of the directive, Presidential directive, which, in my interpretation, will not permit me to answer that question.
The Chairman: You know that somebody signed or authorized an honorable discharge for this man, knowing that he was a fifth amendment Communist, do you not?
General Zwicker: I know that an honorable discharge was signed for the man.
The Chairman: The day the honorable discharge was signed, were you aware of the fact that he had appeared before our committee?
General Zwicker: I was.
The Chairman: And had refused to answer certain questions?
General Zwicker: No, sir, not specifically on answering any questions. I knew that he had appeared before your committee.
The Chairman: Didn't you read the news?

General Zwicker: I read the news releases.

The Chairman: And the news releases were to the effect that he had refused to tell whether he was a Communist, and that there was evidence that he had attended Communist leadership schools. It was on all the wire service stories, was it not? You knew generally what he was here for, did you not?

General Zwicker: Yes; indeed.

The Chairman: And you knew generally that he had refused to tell whether he was a Communist, did you not?

General Zwicker: I don't recall whether he refused to tell whether he was a Communist.

The Chairman: Are you the commanding officer there?

General Zwicker: I am the commanding general.

The Chairman: When an officer appears before a committee and refuses to answer, would you not read that story rather carefully?

General Zwicker: I read the press releases.

The Chairman: Then, General, you knew, did you not, that he appeared before the committee and refused, on the grounds of the fifth amendment, to tell about all of his Communist activities? You knew that, did you not?

General Zwicker: I knew everything that was in the press.

The Chairman: Don't be coy with me, General.

General Zwicker: I am not being coy, sir.

The Chairman: Did you have that general picture?

General Zwicker: I believe I remember reading in the paper that he had taken refuge in the fifth amendment to avoid answering questions before the committee.

The Chairman: About communism?

General Zwicker: I am not too certain about that.

The Chairman: Do you mean that you did not have enough interest in the case, General, the case of this major who was in your command, to get some idea of what questions he had refused to answer? Is that correct?

General Zwicker: I think that is not putting it quite right, Mr. Chairman.

The Chairman: You put it right, then.

General Zwicker: I have great interest in all of the officers of my command, with whatever they do.

The Chairman: Let's stick to fifth-amendment Communists, now. Let's stick to him. You told us you read the press releases.

General Zwicker: I did.

The Chairman: But now you indicate that you did not know that he refused to tell about his Communist activities. Is that correct?

General Zwicker: I know that he refused to answer questions for the committee.

The Chairman: Did you know that he refused to answer questions about his Communist activities?

General Zwicker: Specifically, I don't believe so.

The Chairman: Did you have any idea?

General Zwicker: Of course I had an idea.

The Chairman: What do you think he was called down here for?

General Zwicker: For that specific purpose.

The Chairman: Then you knew that those were the questions he was asked, did you not? General, let's try and be truthful. I am going to keep you here as long as you keep hedging and hemming.

General Zwicker: I am not hedging.

The Chairman: Or hawing.

General Zwicker: I am not hawing, and I don't like to have anyone impugn my honesty, which you just about did.

The Chairman: Either your honesty or your intelligence; I can't help impugning one or the other, when you tell us that a major in your command who was known to you to have been before a Senate committee, and of whom you read the press releases very carefully—to now have you sit here and tell us that you did not know whether he refused to answer questions about Communist activities. I had seen all the press releases, and they all dealt with that. So when you do that, General, if you will pardon me, I cannot help but question either your honesty or your intelligence, one or the other. I want to be frank with you on that.

Now, is it your testimony now that at the time you read the stories about Major Peress, that you did not know that he had refused to answer questions before this committee about his Communist activities?

General Zwicker: I am sure I had that impression. . . .

The Chairman: Were you aware that he was being given a discharge on February 2? In other words, the day he was discharged, were you aware of it?

General Zwicker: Yes; yes, sir.

The Chairman: Who ordered his discharge?

General Zwicker: The Department of the Army.

The Chairman: Who in the Department?

General Zwicker: That I can't answer.

Mr. Cohn: That isn't a security matter?

General Zwicker: No. I don't know. Excuse me.

Mr. Cohn: Who did you talk to? You talked to somebody?

General Zwicker: No. I did not. . . .

The Chairman: Let me ask this question: If this man, after the order came up, after the order of the 18th came up, prior to his getting an honorable discharge, were guilty of some crime—let us say that he held up a bank or stole an automobile—and you heard of that the day before—let us say you heard of it the same day that you heard of my letter—could you then have taken steps to prevent his discharge, or would he have automatically been discharged?

General Zwicker: I would have definitely taken steps to prevent discharge.

The Chairman: In other words, if you found that he was guilty of improper conduct, conduct unbecoming an officer, we will say, then you would not have allowed the honorable discharge to go through, would you?

General Zwicker: If it were outside the directive of this order?

The Chairman: Well, yes, let us say it were outside the directive.

General Zwicker: Then I certainly would never have discharged him until that part of the case———

The Chairman: Let us say he went out and stole $50 the night before.

General Zwicker: He wouldn't have been discharged.

The Chairman: Do you think stealing $50 is more serious than being a traitor to the country as part of the Communist conspiracy?

General Zwicker: That, sir, was not my decision.

The Chairman: You said if you learned that he stole $50, you would have prevented his discharge. You did learn something much more serious than that. You learned that he had refused to tell whether he was a Communist. You learned that the chairman of a Senate committee suggested he be court-martialed. And you say if he had stolen $50 he would not have gotten the honorable discharge. But merely being a part of the Communist conspiracy, and the chairman of the committee asking that he be court-martialed, would not give you grounds for holding up his discharge. Is that correct? . . . Do you think you sound a bit ridiculous, General, when you say that for $50, you would prevent his being discharged, but for being a part of the conspiracy to destroy this country you could not prevent his discharge?

General Zwicker: I did not say that, sir.

The Chairman: Let's go over that. You did say if you found out he stole $50 the night before, he would not have gotten an honorable discharge the next morning?

General Zwicker: That is correct.

The Chairman: You did learn, did you not, from the newspaper reports, that this man was part of the Communist conspiracy, or at least that there was strong evidence that he was. Did you not think that was more serious than the theft of $50?

General Zwicker: He has never been tried for that, sir, and there was evidence, Mr. Chairman———

The Chairman: Don't you give me doubletalk. The $50 case, that he had stolen the night before, he has not been tried for that. . . .

The Chairman: Would you tell us, General, why $50 is so much more important to you than being part of the conspiracy to destroy a nation which you are sworn to defend?

General Zwicker: Mr. Chairman, it is not, and you know that as well as I do.

The Chairman: I certainly do. That is why I cannot understand you sitting there, General, a General in the Army, and telling me that you could not, would not, hold up his discharge having received information———

General Zwicker: I could not hold up his discharge.

The Chairman: Why could you not do it in the case of an allegation of membership in a Communist conspiracy, where you could if you merely heard some private's word that he had stolen $50?

General Zwicker: Because, Mr. Senator, any information that appeared in the press or any releases was well known to me and well known to plenty of other people long prior to the time that you ever called this man for investigation, and there were no facts or no allegations, nothing presented from the time that he appeared before your first investigation that was not apparent prior to that time.

The Chairman: In other words, as you sat here this morning and listened to the testimony you heard nothing new?

Mr. Cohn: Nothing substantially new?

General Zwicker: I don't believe so.

The Chairman: So that all of these facts were known at the time he was ordered to receive an honorable discharge?

General Zwicker: I believe they are all on record; yes, sir.

The Chairman: Do you think, General, that anyone who is responsible for giving an honorable discharge to a man who has been named under oath as a member of the Communist conspiracy should himself be removed from the military?

General Zwicker: You are speaking of generalities now, and not on specifics—is that right, sir, not mentioning about any one particular person?

The Chairman: That is right.

General Zwicker: I have no brief for that kind of person, and if there exists or has existed something in the system that permits that, I say that that is wrong.

The Chairman: I am not talking about the system. I am asking you this question, General, a very simple question. . . . You will answer that question, unless you take the fifth amendment. I do not care how long we stay here, you are going to answer it.

General Zwicker: Do you mean how I feel toward Communists?

The Chairman: I mean exactly what I asked you, General; nothing else. And anyone with the brains of a 5-year-old child can understand that question.

The reporter will read it to you as often as you need to hear it so that you can answer it, and then you will answer it.

General Zwicker: Start it over, please.

(The question was reread by the reporter.)

General Zwicker: I do not think he should be removed from the military.

The Chairman: Then, General, you should be removed from any command. Any man who has been given the honor of being promoted to general and who says, "I will protect another general who protected Communists," is not fit to wear that uniform, General. I think it is a tremendous disgrace to the Army to have this sort of thing given to the public. I intend to give it to them. I have a duty to do that. I intend to repeat to the press exactly what you said. So you know that. You will be back here, General. . . .

Herblock on the Red Scare

The outrageous proceedings of McCarthy and other Red-hunters were challenged by a few brave souls—but amazingly few. One of the most consistent and most telling was Herbert Block. Under the pen name, Herblock, he did political cartoons for the Washington Post. *Two examples follow. The first appeared in the* Post *in June, 1949; the second in May, 1950. They are taken from* The Herblock Book *(The Beacon Press, 1952), pages 130 and 139.*

"Fire!"

"We now have new and important evidence"

The Great Red Scare: Ebb

SELECTION 

The Fall of McCarthy

McCarthy's harassment demoralized the State Department, the United States Information Agency, and other civilian groups in the government. By attacking the Army, McCarthy began to injure morale throughout the armed services.

Trying his best to avoid a confrontation, Eisenhower encouraged the Department of the Army to seek an accommodation with the Senator. Though Secretary of the Army Robert T. Stevens and Army Counsel John G. Adams tried to do so, McCarthy was implacable. Eisenhower finally decided that other tactics were called for and authorized the Army to stage a counterattack. The Army began gathering ammunition.

McCarthy's committee counsel and closest collaborator was young Roy Cohn. One of Cohn's closest friends was G. David Schine, for whom Cohn arranged an appointment as consultant to the McCarthy committee. Cohn and Schine made investigating junkets together. When time came for young Schine to be drafted into the Army, Cohn used his influence in an attempt to get Schine a commission. He threatened ruinous investigations of the Army if the commission did not materialize. If it did, he suggested, McCarthy's attention might be diverted to the Navy or Air Force. When Schine failed to get a commission and went into uniform as a recruit, Cohn insisted successfully that Schine be given special privileges and leaves of absence in order, allegedly, to do essential work for McCarthy's committee. All the time, the Department of the Army was keeping notes, recording Cohn's telephone calls, and keeping tabs on Schine's movements.

When the dossier was complete, the Army struck. Secretary Stevens and Counsel Adams filed with McCarthy's committee a formal complaint that Cohn had used improper influence in seeking special favors for Schine.

Infuriated, McCarthy denounced the complaint. He declared that the Department of the Army was simply trying to divert attention from the exposure of Communist sympathizers in its ranks.

Some time earlier, the Democratic members of McCarthy's Government Operations Committee had walked out, protesting his high-handed tactics. Although the Republican members had not protested, they, too, had become inactive. McCarthy had been running a one-man show.

Now the Democrats returned in force and demanded a full investigation of the Army's charges. With prodding from the White House, certain Republicans on the committee seconded the demand. It was arranged that hearings would be conducted by the full committee, with Senator Karl Mundt in the chair and McCarthy on the sidelines.

Because of McCarthy's notoriety and because of the drama promised, the hearings were carried over nationwide television.

Day after day, millions of Americans watched as McCarthy and Cohn tangled with the Department of the Army and its wise, puckish special attorney, Joseph

N. Welch. Slowly, the meretriciousness of McCarthy's "crusade" against communism became evident to all but the blindest onlookers.

The other Senators on the committee gradually lost their terror of McCarthy. They began to goad him about his earlier failure to appear before a Privileges and Elections subcommittee that had asked him to answer charges of accepting bribes.

Trying to rescue himself, McCarthy attacked Welch, suddenly raising a charge that a young lawyer in Welch's Boston law firm was a fellow traveller.

Welch's handling of McCarthy's attack was masterful. It cost the Senator most of whatever public sympathy he retained. When that day ended and McCarthy walked out of the committee room, men shrank away from him. McCarthy's power was finished.

The first document below consists of excerpts from Eighty-third Congress, second session, Hearings before a Special Subcommittee of the Committee on Government Operations, Special Senate Investigation on Charges and Countercharges involving: Secretary of the Army Robert T. Stevens, John G. Adams, H. Struve Hensel and Senator Joe McCarthy, Roy M. Cohn, and Francis P. Carr, *pages 27–28, 31–32, 1886–1888, 1944–1948, 2268–2270, 2330, 2336–2337, 2350–2352, 2385–2389, 2426–2430.*

After the Army-McCarthy hearings, demand arose that the Senate do something about the obstreperous junior Senator from Wisconsin.

The Senate finally responded. A select committee was formed. Its chairman was an impeccably conservative Republican, Arthur V. Watkins of Utah.

With scrupulous care, the Watkins committee inspected the files of all the past committees that had looked into aspects of McCarthy's behavior. It asked him to answer the questions about bribe-taking that he had refused to answer before.

McCarthy was not cooperative. In the press, he attacked the Watkins committee. He declared that it was working in the Communist interest, trying to choke off his investigative activities.

At length, the Watkins committee reported to the Senate. It asked the parent body to condemn McCarthy on several counts, the chief of which was his display of contempt for the select committee. On December 2, 1954, by a vote of 67 to 22, the resolution passed.

This resolution dealt McCarthy the coup de grâce. *It ended almost his last hope of regaining power. Afterward, he gradually slipped out of the headlines. Two and a half years later, he died, probably of alcoholism.*

The second document below is the text of the resolution of condemnation. It is taken from Eighty-third Congress, second session, Congressional Record, *page 16392.*

EXCERPTS FROM THE ARMY-MCCARTHY HEARINGS

The subcommittee met at 10:30 a. m., pursuant to call, in the caucus room of the Senate Office Building, Senator Karl E. Mundt, presiding.

Present: Senator Karl E. Mundt, Republican, South Dakota; Senator Everett McKinley Dirksen, Republican, Illinois; Senator Charles E. Potter, Republican, Michigan; Senator Henry C. Dworshak, Republican, Idaho; Senator John L. McClellan, Democrat, Arkansas; Senator Henry M. Jackson, Democrat, Washington; and Senator Stuart Symington, Democrat, Missouri.

Also present: Ray H. Jenkins, chief counsel to the subcommittee; Thomas R. Prewitt, assistant counsel; and Ruth Y. Watt, chief clerk.

Principal participants: Senator Joseph R. McCarthy, a United States Senator from the State of Wisconsin; Roy M. Cohn, chief counsel to the subcommittee; Francis P. Carr, executive director of the subcommittee; Hon. Robert T. Stevens, Secretary of the Army; John G. Adams, counselor to the Army; H. Struve Hensel, Assistant Secretary of Defense; Joseph N. Welch, special counsel for the Army; and James D. St. Clair, special counsel for the Army.

Proceedings

Senator Mundt: The hearings will now come to order.

It is customary in hearings of this type for the chairman and the ranking member of the committee to make preliminary statements. At this time the Chair will read a brief statement outlining the purposes and procedures and the policies of these hearings. . . .

This Permanent Subcommittee on Investigations of the United States Senate, being a subcommittee of the Senate Committee on Government Operations, has now convened in open session for the purpose of investigating charges heretofore made by Secretary of the Army, Robert T. Stevens, and his counsel, John G. Adams, and formalized in a document dated April 13, 1954, and filed with this subcommittee, and in which a general charge is made that Senator Joseph R. McCarthy as chairman of the Permanent Subcommittee on Investigations, United States Senate, its chief counsel, Roy M. Cohn, as well as other members of its staff, sought by improper means to obtain preferential treatment for one Pvt. G. David Schine, United States Army, formerly a consultant for this subcommittee, and in which numerous specific allegations are made in support of that general charge.

It is the further purpose of this subcommittee to investigate countercharges made by Senator McCarthy, Mr. Cohn, and other members of their staff against Mr. Stevens, Mr. Adams, and Mr. Hensel, the latter of whom, as a result of these countercharges, has been advised by the subcommittee he is considered a party to this controversy with the full rights and prerogatives provided for each participant by our special rules of procedure. These countercharges were formalized in a statement signed and filed with the subcommittee under date of April 10, 1954, in which they generally allege that Mr. Stevens, Mr. Adams, and Mr. Hensel attempted to discredit what is generally referred to as the McCarthy Investigating Committee and to force a discontinuance of further attempts by that committee to expose Communist infiltration in the Army, and in which it is further charged that Mr. Stevens and Mr. Adams made constant attempts to trade off preferential treatment for Private Schine as an inducement to the subcommittee to halt its exposition of the mishandling of Communist infiltration in the military. Specific allegations are made in support of these general charges. . . .

Senator McCarthy: Mr. Chairman, I do not want to take your time unduly, but we have before us as part of the record the specifications, call them what you may, dated April 13, 1954. These specifications were filed after the committee had ordered Mr. Stevens and Mr. Adams to file specifications. I maintain it is a disgrace and reflection upon everyone of the million outstanding men in the Army to let a few civilians who are trying to hold up an investigation of Communists, label themselves as the Department of the Army. . . . I would like to make it very clear that there is no contest between Senator McCarthy and the Department of the Army. All that Senator McCarthy has been trying to do is expose the Communists who have infiltrated the Department of the Army, a very small percent. . . .

Testimony of Roy M. Cohn, June 2, 1954

. . . *Mr. Welch:* Of course, in the summer of 1953, you were anxious to procure a commission for Mr. Schine, weren't you?

Mr. Cohn: I thought he was qualified. Sir, I was one of the references.

Mr. Welch: Would you mind answering the question. You were anxious to procure one?

Mr. Cohn: Sir, you say anxious to procure. I want to tell you this. I thought he was qualified. I recommended him. I was a reference on his application; yes, sir.

Mr. Welch: Is that your answer, you were anxious to procure one for him?

Mr. Cohn: My answer is as I have given it to you.

Mr. Welch: It was simple, yes, sir. You were, weren't you?

Mr. Cohn: I thought he was entitled to that, sir.

Mr. Welch: And you enlisted some pretty high-powered people to help get one, didn't you?

Mr. Cohn: No, sir; I can't agree with your terminology there. That does not give a fair reflection.

Mr. Welch: Well, sir, let's see, Mr. Cohn———

Mr. Cohn: Sticking to your question, you say I enlisted certain high-powered people to help him get it. What happened was this, sir———

Mr. Welch: I didn't ask you what happened. I asked you if you enlisted certain high-powered help. Did you or didn't you?

Mr. Cohn: Sir———

Mr. Welch: Yes or no, did you or didn't you?

Mr. Cohn: Mr. Welch, I want to give you yes or no answers.

Mr. Welch: You don't want to or you do want to?

Mr. Cohn: Mr. Welch, I would like to give you yes or no answers.

Mr. Welch: All right. Let's start again, then.

Mr. Cohn: Mr. Chairman, may I be permitted to complete one sentence?

Mr. Welch: Mr. Chairman, I am going to try to have this witness be responsive in his answers, and I would like to start again, if I may. Could I start again, Mr. Cohn, or would you like to make a speech now?

If you would like to make a speech, make it.

Mr. Cohn: No, sir; all I was going to tell you was this. I would like to give you responsive answers and I would like to give you as many yes or no answers as I can. There are times, sir, when I cannot agree with some of the adjectives which you put into your questions which make it difficult for me to give you the answer I would like to. If you wish to ask me did I think Schine was qualified for a commission and did I recommend him for one, my answer is yes.

Mr. Welch: We have already covered that, when you said you were anxious to get him one, didn't you?

Mr. Cohn: I told you what happened.

Mr. Welch: And you said you were anxious to get him one. Do you want to change that or stay by it?

Mr. Cohn: Sir, I think, my testimony is very clear to the committee as to just what happened and just what I wanted. . . .

Mr. Welch: The first conference that took place in respect to a commission for Schine, took place in the office of a United States Senator, didn't it?

Mr. Cohn: Yes, sir.

Mr. Welch: That is pretty high-powered stuff, isn't it, a Senator? Is that right?

Mr. Cohn: I can't answer that, sir.

Mr. Welch: There was present in that office a general; is that right?

Mr. Cohn: General Reber was there, yes, sir.

Mr. Welch: That is pretty high-powered stuff, isn't it?

Mr. Cohn: Mr. Welch———

Mr. Welch: Yes or no. Is that high powered or not?

Mr. Cohn: Mr. Welch, I want to give you yes or no answers.

Mr. Welch: Do so, then. Just tell me, is that high powered or not, Mr. Cohn———

Senator McCarthy: Mr. Chairman.

Mr. Cohn: Senator, I don't mind this at all.

Senator McCarthy: I don't think it should be called high powered.

Senator Mundt: Mr. Cohn can ask for more details about what is meant by the adjectives if he does not understand.

Mr. Welch: Let's strike out "high powered" and start again. If you had a Senator there, you had a very important public official there, didn't you?

Mr. Cohn: Yes, sir, I think Senator McCarthy———

Mr. Welch: If you had a general there, you had a very important Army official?

Mr. Cohn: Yes, sir.

Mr. Welch: If you had Mr. Roy Cohn there, you had a very important counsel to an important committee there, didn't you?

Mr. Cohn: The committee is important, sir.

Mr. Welch: Right. Do you think, Mr. Cohn, any ordinary little guy from my State of Iowa could demand that sort of attention?

Mr. Cohn: I hope so, sir.

Mr. Welch: Do you think he could?

Mr. Cohn: Yes, sir.

Mr. Welch: Do you think any little old guy off a farm in Iowa who would like a commission now could manage to have a conference between a Senator and a general and you?

Mr. Cohn: Sir, I don't think———

Mr. Welch: Just answer yes or no. Do you think a little boy from the farm can get away with that?

Mr. Cohn: My answer to you, Mr. Welch, is, I think Iowa might exclude me. If a person from Iowa contacted Senator Hickenlooper, I am sure Senator Hickenlooper or someone in his office would call General Reber or someone on his staff and see that the application was given prompt attention; yes, sir.

Mr. Welch: It is a wonder we haven't got all officers and no privates in our Army, isn't it, Mr. Cohn? . . .

Senator McCarthy: Let me ask you this, Mr. Cohn: Had you something to do with the Hiss case, I believe, also; is that right?

Mr. Cohn: I had. What I had to do with the Hiss case is not important enough to mention here, sir.

Senator McCarthy: Enough to do with it so that you are aware of the facts in the case. Let me ask you this: Are you convinced if it had not been for a congressional committee having exposed the facts in the Hiss case, that Alger Hiss today would be free?

Mr. Cohn: Yes, sir. . . .

Senator McCarthy: O.K. I will leave it that way. Just this one question: Mr. Cohn, do you agree with me that, Nc. 1, the administration is certainly heading in the right direction so far as getting rid of Communists are concerned, and, No. 2, that it is ridiculous, a complete waste of time to have these exchanges of statements between the White House and this committee, that there is no reason on earth why there should be any contest between the executive department and this committee insofar as exposing Communists, graft, and corruption is concerned, that we all should be heading the same way, there should be none of this silly bickering, fighting about this exposure, that we should be getting the complete cooperation from the executive and that should be flowing both ways, of course?

Senator Mundt: The Senator's time has expired. You can answer the question.

Senator McCarthy: Let me finish the question. And if that could be accomplished, a great service could be performed for the country?

Mr. Cohn: I am sure of that, sir. . . .

Mr. Welch: Mr. Chairman, ordinarily, with the clock as late as it is, I would call attention to it, but not tonight.

Mr. Cohn, what is the exact number of Communists or subversives that are loose today in these defense plants?

Mr. Cohn: The exact number that is loose, sir?

Mr. Welch: Yes, sir.

Mr. Cohn: I don't know.

Mr. Welch: Roughly how many?

Mr. Cohn: I can only tell you, sir, what we know about it.

Mr. Welch: That is 130, is that right?

Mr. Cohn: Yes, sir. I am going to try to particularize for you, if I can.
Mr. Welch: I am in a hurry. I don't want the sun to go down while they are still in there, if we can get them out.
Mr. Cohn: I am afraid we won't be able to work that fast, sir.
Mr. Welch: I have a suggestion about it, sir. How many are there?
Mr. Cohn: I believe the figure is approximately 130. . . .
Mr. Welch: . . . In how many plants are they?
Mr. Cohn: How many plants?
Mr. Welch: How many plants.
Mr. Cohn: Yes, sir; just 1 minute, sir. I see 16 offhand, sir.
Mr. Welch: Sixteen plants?
Mr. Cohn: Yes, sir.
Mr. Welch: Where are they, sir?
Mr. Cohn: Senator McCarthy———
Mr. Welch: Reel off the cities.
Mr. Cohn: Would you stop me if I am going too far?
Mr. Welch: You can't go too far revealing Communists, Mr. Cohn. Reel off the cities for us.
Mr. Cohn: Schenectady, N. Y.; Syracuse, N. Y.; Rome, N. Y.; Quincy, Mass.; Fitchburg, Mass.; Buffalo, N. Y.; Dunkirk, N. Y.; another at Buffalo, N.Y.; Cambridge, Mass.; New Bedford, Mass.; Boston, Mass.; Quincy, Mass.; Lynn, Mass.; Pittsfield, Mass.; Boston, Mass.
Mr. Welch: Mr. Cohn, you not only frighten me, you make me ashamed when there are so many in Massachusetts. [Laughter.] This is not a laughing matter, believe me. Are you alarmed at that situation, Mr. Cohn?
Mr. Cohn: Yes, sir; I am.
Mr. Welch: Nothing could be more alarming, could it?
Mr. Cohn: It certainly is a very alarming thing.
Mr. Welch: Will you not, before the sun goes down, give those names to the FBI and at least have those men put under surveillance?
Mr. Cohn: Mr. Welch, the FBI———
Senator McCarthy: Mr. Chairman.
Mr. Welch: That is a fair question.
Senator McCarthy: Mr. Chairman, let's not be ridiculous. Mr. Welch knows, as I have told him a dozen times, that the FBI has all of this information. The defense plants have the information. The only thing we can do is to try and publicly expose these individuals and hope that they will be gotten rid of. And you know that, Mr. Welch.
Mr. Welch: I do not know that.
Mr. Cohn, do you mean to tell us that J. Edgar Hoover and the FBI know the names of these men and are doing nothing about them?
Mr. Cohn: No, sir. I mean to say———
Mr. Welch: Do you mean to tell us they are doing something about them?
Mr. Cohn: Yes, sir.
Mr. Welch: What are they doing about them?
Mr. Cohn: Here is what they do about them. They notify the Defense Department and the appropriate security———
Mr. Welch: Don't they put them under surveillance?
Mr. Cohn: Appropriate security agencies involved. The FBI gives them full information. It is then up to them, the places where the information

goes, to decide whether or not they will act on the FBI information. All the FBI can do is give the information. Their powers ends right there.

Mr. Welch: Cannot the FBI put these 130 men under surveillance before sundown tomorrow?

Mr. Cohn: Sir, if there is need for surveillance in the case of espionage or anything like that, I can well assure you that Mr. John Edgar Hoover and his men know a lot better than I, and I quite respectfully suggest, sir, than probably a lot of us, just who should be put under surveillance. I do not propose to tell the FBI how to run its shop. It does it very well.

Mr. Welch: And they do it, don't they, Mr. Cohn?

Mr. Cohn: When the need arises, of course.

Mr. Welch: And will you tell them tonight, Mr. Cohn, that here is a case where the need has arisen, so that it can be done by sundown tomorrow night?

Mr. Cohn: No, sir; there is no need for my telling the FBI what to do about this or anything else.

Mr. Welch: Are you sure they know every one of them?

Mr. Cohn: I would take an oath on it, sir. I think the FBI has complete information about the Communist movement in this country and that would include information about these people.

Mr. Welch: That being true, Mr. Cohn, can you and I both rest easy tonight?

Mr. Cohn: Sir, I certainly agree with you, it is a very disturbing situation.

Mr. Welch: Well, if the FBI has got a firm grasp on these 130 men, I will go to sleep. . . .

Mr. Cohn: Sir, you do not have to nudge the FBI about this or about anything else.

Mr. Welch: Then they have got the whole 130, have they, Mr. Cohn?

Mr. Cohn: I am sure of it, sir, and a lot more.

Mr. Welch: Then what is all the excitement about, if J. Edgar Hoover is on the job chasing these 130 Communists? . . .

Further Testimony by Roy M. Cohn, June 8, 1954

Mr. Welch: Mr. Cohn, when you were under examination by Senator McClellan, the name Peress came up one more time.

Mr. Cohn: Yes, sir.

Mr. Welch: You understand, of course, that Mr. Jenkins has said we can't try that case here.

Mr. Cohn: Yes, sir.

Mr. Welch: I have the temerity to say 1 or 2 things about it, or ask you 1 or 2 things about it, for this reason: I suspect, Mr. Cohn, that there may be people listening on television who think that Peress was right square in the middle of some radar laboratory at Fort Monmouth, about which we have talked so much. Can you see how someone might get that impression, Mr. Cohn?

Mr. Cohn: Well, it depends how much that person has read about the Peress case.

Mr. Welch: Or how carefully they have listened to us.

Mr. Cohn: Yes, sir.

Mr. Welch: Now, that isn't where Peress was?

Mr. Cohn: No. He was in the Dental Corps, sir.

Mr. Welch: I understand. And he wasn't anywhere near this delicate installation at Fort Monmouth?

Mr. Cohn: Actually, he was near it, sir.

Mr. Welch: Well, I mean he wasn't physically———

Mr. Cohn: I can say this, sir. I know of no tieup between Major Peress and the Fort Monmouth situation.

Mr. Welch: And he had no unusual clearances to let him know high secret stuff?

Mr. Cohn: Well, there was no question about clearances. I would say this, Mr. Welch. You are certainly right———

Mr. Welch: If I am right, let's move along. I don't want to spend much time on it. I just want to get it clear before the country that he was not sitting right square in the middle of Fort Monmouth.

Mr. Cohn: You are correct.

Mr. Welch: And you will help me make that, as the Senator says, "crystal clear"?

Mr. Cohn: I will, sir.

Mr. Welch: And secondly he was a dentist, wasn't he?

Mr. Cohn: Yes, sir.

Mr. Welch: And he was a dentist at a point of embarkation where troops came in and moved overseas?

Mr. Cohn: No, sir. Actually, he was stationed at Camp Kilmer, N. J.

Mr. Welch: Well, I understand, and I may be misinformed, that that was a staging camp for overseas troops. Well, I may be wrong.

Mr. Cohn: You may be right.

Mr. Welch: Well, he was, as I have said, a dentist?

Mr. Cohn: Yes, he was. I don't minimize the importance of the Peress case, sir.

Mr. Welch: I don't intend to, sir, myself. Don't misunderstand me, either. I don't like a Communist, even if he is in a dentist chair. Don't misunderstand me. But I do want to get the guy in perspective. Could I say one more faintly humorous thing about him, if it is possible to say a faintly humorous thing about a Communist, in wherever there is a Communist, the fear about them is that they may indoctrinate other soldiers or other people, that is right, isn't it?

Mr. Cohn: That is one of the dangers.

Mr. Welch: Now, whatever you say about indoctrinating other people, it wouldn't be too happy a way to try to drill it into people with a dentist's drill and an aching biscuspid, would it?

Mr. Cohn: It might be an effective way, sir.

Mr. Welch: Well, you don't have the guy's attention very well, if his tooth hurts. Isn't that right, Mr. Cohn? Let's pass it fast.

Mr. Cohn: Well, Mr. Welch, it is hard to pass it fast. You have this situation. You have a man with an open record as a Communist———

Mr. Welch: We understand that Peress is a no good Communist.

Senator Mundt: Mr. Welch, the Chair believes that when you ask the witness a question, you should give him a chance to answer it.

Mr. Cohn: I will be short.

Mr. Welch: All right, let's be short, because I want to get through with Peress as far as this case is concerned.

Mr. Cohn: Here is the importance of the Peress case———

Mr. Welch: I didn't ask you about the importance of the Peress case.

Mr. Cohn: Well, you have asked me a question and I am keeping it short.

Mr. Welch: I want to run this as best I can. If you want me to ask a question over again, I will. This is what I am saying to you, that if you want to catch a young soldier and make a Communist out of him, one pass at him in a dentist's chair isn't much of a pass, is it? Isn't that right?

Mr. Cohn: Sir———

Mr. Welch: Well, the answer is obvious, isn't it?

Senator Mundt: Mr. Welch, I am awfully sorry, but you asked the witness a question, and he started to answer and you won't give him a chance.

Mr. Welch: He scares me because of the way he takes the deep breath. I only want yes or no. One pass at him in the dentist's chair isn't very dangerous, is it, Mr. Cohn?

Mr. Cohn: Well, sir, you have asked me a number of questions which I haven't answered. If I can say a few sentences I can probably give you———

Mr. Welch: Let's just take one sentence.

Senator McCarthy: Let him answer.

Mr. Welch: No. He wants to make a speech. . . .

[One of McCarthy's tactics was to open up new issues whenever occasion presented. Displaying two-and-a-half pages of typescript, he claimed that it was an FBI report on Communists in the army. It had been given him, he said, by a member of the "loyal American underground." He charged that the army had not acted on the FBIs information. (In fact, the document turned out to be spurious.) In addition, McCarthy seized upon scraps of evidence to charge that Senator Symington and another Democrat, Clark Clifford, formerly an aide to President Truman, had tricked the army into making its charges against Cohn and the Committee (*ed.*)]

. . . *Mr. Welch:* Here is the thing about these hearings that begins to somewhat appal me.

Looking at you, Senator McCarthy, you have, I think, something of a genius for creating confusion, throwing in new issues, new accusations, and creating a turmoil in the hearts and minds of the country that I find troublesome. And because of your genius, sir, we keep on, just keep on, as I view it, creating these confusions. Maybe I am overimpressed by them. But I don't think they do the country any good. . . .

Now, Mr. Chairman, I think it is quite clear that this hearing cannot actually resolve and solve some of the things that have been presented in it, to wit, the constitutional issues as I view them, which can only be revealed to the public, and thought about, and settled in the course of the next year or 5 years or 10 years or our lifetime.

Those constitutional issues have actually been revealed. There is no doubt about it.

Lawyers and Senators and executives—members of the executive—can differ as to what the result ought to be, but the issues are revealed.

As to the personal conflicts here of who is saying what, I hesitate to say this but as a lawyer it would seem to me that neither side is bound to have a 100 percent clearcut victory in that. That is going to be left in some kind of balance from the way the committee looks and acts, and probably the way the country reacts. . . .

Senator McCarthy: . . . Mr. Welch made a statement that I want to comment on. He said Mr. McCarthy had a genius for creating confusion. I assume by that he means a genius for bringing out the facts which may disturb the people. . . . I think that confuses people, showing up that Mr. Symington and Mr. Clifford were behind this. That may create confusion, but I have no choice but to bring out those facts.

Mr. Chairman, I think that if we do not limit this as to witnesses, and I frankly hope that we don't, although I will go along with whatever the committee does, I think it is imperative that Senator Symington take the stand. . . .

I think, however, in view of the fact that Mr. Symington—I mean from all the mail I get, people are confused. They know that Stu—Mr. Symington, I mean, and Mr. Clifford, were engineering this deal which called off the hearings of the Communists. I am going to continue urging that he take the stand. I hope that finally public opinion, public pressure, makes him do what he so sanctimoniously told the Republicans they should do, namely, put all the facts on the table. . . .

Senator Symington: Have you finished?

Senator McCarthy: For the time being, yes.

Senator Symington: I will make a deal with you. I will go on the floor of the Senate and make a speech, and then I will take the stand, see, and I will go under oath and let this committee examine me, if you will make a speech and if you will go on the stand on the charges you never answered in 1952. There is your deal, and I will make it with you right now.

Senator McCarthy: Let us first get the record straight. The Senator made a misstatement yesterday when he said I was asked to go on the stand in 1952. That is incorrect.

Senator Symington: You were invited to answer the charges.

Senator McCarthy: I was told that I could go on the stand.

Senator Symington: You were invited to answer the charges.

Senator McCarthy: Let us not have any of this phony stuff.

Senator Symington: Any time you want to pull me, going on the stand—I will make a deal with you right now. I will get on the floor of the Senate and I will give my position in this matter, and I will go under cross-examination by this committee, which would be a very unusual thing for a Senator to do, if you will go under cross-examination with respect to the charges that were made against you by a committee which was unanimously signed by Democrats and Republicans in 1952.

There is your deal. I will make it here, and if you want to, I will make it on television, whichever way you want to do it, or both.

Senator McCarthy: Your deal is to retry the 1952 case.

Senator Symington: There was no retrial, because he never appeared.

Senator Dirksen: Mr. Chairman.

Senator Symington: I am going to answer you just that way, so long as you feel he understands.

I make a motion that these minutes be published today, that they be written up and published today, so everybody will know what we are talking about. . . .

Session of June 9, 1954: Further Testimony of Roy M. Cohn

Senator Symington: . . . Mr. Chairman, I have decided to testify under oath before this committee, and, therefore, I am addressing the following letter to Senator McCarthy and I will read it:

DEAR SENATOR McCARTHY: On yesterday you agreed to take the stand to testify under oath with reference to the matters considered by the Subcommittee on Privileges and Elections of the United States Senate. You will recall that this committee was chaired by Senator Hennings and although requests were made to you to appear before it, you persistently refused. You agreed to do this if I would take the stand with respect to my connections and dealings with Secretary Stevens and Mr. Clark Clifford, which have been testified to in the present proceedings. I have considered your statement, and I present herewith a plan by which it can be carried out.

I believe that I will have performed a public service of overwhelming importance if any action of mine can induce you to answer under oath the allegations formally preferred against you by the Senate subcommittee and to which you have heretofore persistently refused to respond, except to denounce the subcommittee.

Accordingly, I propose that we agree on the following points:

1. You will agree to an investigation by a committee of the Senate to be appointed by the Vice President, upon recommendation of the majority and minority leaders of the Senate, despite your previous refusals you will agree to testify under oath before this committee and to furnish all relevant documents and materials without resort to any immunity or privilege. This investigation will cover the following subjects, all of which are included in the report of the subcommittee:

1. Whether, under the circumstances, it was proper for Senator McCarthy to receive $10,000 from the Lustron Corp.
2. Whether funds supplied to Senator McCarthy to fight communism or for other specific purposes were diverted to his own use.
3. Whether Senator McCarthy used close associates and members of his family to secrete receipts, income, commodity and stock speculations and other financial transactions for ulterior motives.
4. Whether Senator McCarthy's activities on behalf of certain special interest groups such as housing, sugar, and China, were motivated by self-interest.
5. Whether loans or other transactions Senator McCarthy had with Appleton State Bank or others involved violation of the tax and banking laws.
6. Whether Senator McCarthy violated Federal and State corrupt practices act in connection with his 1944–46 senatorial campaigns or in connection with his dealings with Ray Kiermas.

This investigation will commence as soon as the members of the committee are appointed and are available.

If you will agree to the foregoing, I will agree to take the stand in the present proceedings, and to testify as to my conversations and dealings with Secretary Stevens and Mr. Clark Clifford, relating to the events preceding the institution of these hearings. I trust that you will confirm your agreement with this program. If you are in accord, please sign as indicated below.

Senator, here is the letter, and if you will sign it, then we can get this matter settled. [Document handed.]

Senator McCarthy: Mr. Chairman?

Senator Mundt: Senator, may I suggest, if you are going to discuss the letter of Senator Symington———

Senator McCarthy: An important point of personal privilege. . . . This very vicious smear of Mr. Symington's must be answered now as a point of personal privilege. He has raised everything now that the Daily Worker———

Senator Mundt: The Chair feels that if you feel that it is so important———

Senator McCarthy: I think, Mr. Chairman, as a point of privilege, I should be allowed to answer this.

Senator Mundt: There is no question but what your name has been mentioned———

Senator McCarthy: I am glad we are on television. I think the millions of people can see how low a man can sink. I repeat, they can see how low an alleged man can sink. He has been asked here to come before the committee and give the information which he has in regard to this investigation. He retorts by saying that he wants all of the old smears investigated.

Now, may I say this, Mr. Chairman: If that is necessary in order to get Symington on the stand, that will be done. If the Vice President or the Senate wants to appoint a committee to investigate these smears, if they ask me to testify, I will, period. And that is a firm commitment.

I will not sign any of Mr. Symington's letters for him. But let me repeat, while this has nothing to do with this hearing, if, in order to get Symington to be a decent, honest individual, and get on the stand here where the subject of perjury—where he will be made to tell the truth so I can cross-examine him, I will do almost anything in the world. If that includes the creation of a special committee, I will now consent to go before that special committee, and I will be glad to answer any of these smears that appeared in the Daily Worker or any place else.

Mr. Symington, I think, has intelligence enough to know that what he brings up has nothing to do with this hearing. He knows that now it has appeared crystal clear to the American people that he is the individual who got the chief adviser of the Democrat Party underground to deceive an honest Secretary of the Army, who was not used to the rough, dirty politics he might run into. . . .

Now, Symington seems to be deathly afraid of going on the stand and taking the oath. Again I say, Mr. Chairman, if a condition of that is that we will reinvestigate—and I have been investigated about as thoroughly as anyone should be by Mr. Symington's administration, if they had anything against me they certainly would have presented that to a grand jury. They did not.

He now raises the same old smears. As I say, so this will be crystal clear, Mr. Chairman, if it is necessary to form a special committee to reinvestigate those smears, to get Stu Symington on the stand, as I intend to take the stand, as I have taken it, as my Republican colleagues have taken it, I will now make the firm commitment to go before that committee. I will sign no Symington document. . . .

Mr. Welch: Mr. Cohn, I was fascinated with the questions that Senator Jackson was asking you. As I understand it, you got this purloined document in March or April of 1953; is that right?

Mr. Cohn: This what document, sir?

Mr. Welch: This FBI document.

Mr. Cohn: Yes, sir. It was in the spring of 1953.

Mr. Welch: Did you hear the word I applied to it?

Mr. Cohn: I wasn't sure I understood it correctly.

Mr. Welch: Do you want to hear it?

Mr. Cohn: That is your option, Mr. Welch, not mine.

Mr. Welch: Purloined. You got it in March or April; is that right?

Mr. Cohn: Sir, I don't know whether the document was purloined or whether it wasn't. I know that due to that and some other things there are 35 subversives who are out of Fort Monmouth and who were in there before we came along.

Mr. Welch: I understand that. You had a new Secretary of the Army over there, didn't you?

Mr. Cohn: Yes, sir.

Mr. Welch: And this document long antedated his being Secretary?

Mr. Cohn: Yes; some 2 or 3 years.

Mr. Welch: And when you saw it, you must have thought it was a frightening document; is that right?

Mr. Cohn: I thought it was a disturbing situation; yes, sir.

Mr. Welch: And one involving a situation where time is of the essence; is that right?

Mr. Cohn: Any situation, surely.

Mr. Welch: That is right, isn't it?

Mr. Cohn: Surely.

Mr. Welch: And you had a brand new Secretary of the Army, didn't you?

Mr. Cohn: Yes, sir.

Mr. Welch: He was either 4 weeks in office, say, 8 weeks in office, or something like that; is that right?

Mr. Cohn: Yes, sir.

Mr. Welch: Now, with this frightening information in your hands, if you could hail a taxicab, you could get Bob Stevens on the job about these Communists within whatever time it takes to drive from here to the Pentagon; is that right?

Mr. Cohn: No, sir.

Mr. Welch: That is not right?

Mr. Cohn: No, sir.

Mr. Welch: Well, at least you could have gone over. Do you think you would have got near him if you had gone over in the front door of the Pentagon and yelled out loud to some receptionists, "We got a lot of hot dope on Communists in the Army"?

Don't you think that would have taken you right straight to Stevens?

Mr. Cohn: If I had what, sir?

Mr. Welch: If you had gone over to the Pentagon and got inside the door and yelled to the first receptionist you saw, "We got some hot dope on some Communists in the Army" don't you think you would have landed at the top?

Mr. Cohn: Sir, that is not the way I do things.

Mr. Welch: It may not be the way you do things, but you were counsel to the committee, weren't you?

Mr. Cohn: Yes, sir; I was.

Mr. Welch: And the Senator was a Senator?

Mr. Cohn: And a very good one, sir.

Mr. Welch: Yes, sir. And have you the slightest doubt that you could have gotten Bob Stevens' ear the moment you got ahold of that document?

Mr. Cohn: It is perfectly possible I could have, sir.

Mr. Welch: You know you could have, don't you?

Mr. Cohn: I don't dispute it for one minute.

Mr. Welch: And you tell us now that you were busy with hearings in other cases, is that right?

Mr. Cohn: Yes, sir; we were.

Mr. Welch: And although you had this dope and a fresh and ambitious new Secretary of the Army, reachable by the expenditure of one taxicab fare, you never went during March, if you had it in March, did you, is that right?

Mr. Cohn: Mr. Welch———

Mr. Welch: Just answer. You never went near him in March?

Mr. Cohn: No, I———

Mr. Welch: Or April? Did you?

Mr. Cohn: Mr. Welch———

Mr. Welch: Tell me, please.

Mr. Cohn: I am trying, sir.

Mr. Welch: Or April?

Mr. Cohn: No, sir.

Mr. Welch: Or May?

Mr. Cohn: I never went near him, sir.

Mr. Welch: Or June?

Mr. Cohn: The answer is never.

Mr. Welch: Right. Or July?

Mr. Cohn: I communicated———

Mr. Welch: Or July?

Mr. Cohn: No, sir———

Senator Mundt: I think we have covered July.

Mr. Welch: I think it is really dramatic to see how these Communist hunters will sit on this document when they could have brought it to the attention of Bob Stevens in 20 minutes and they let month after month go by without going to the head and saying, "Sic 'em, Stevens."

Mr. Cohn: Senator Mundt———

Mr. Welch: Now, turning back to my other matter.

Mr. Cohn: May I answer that last statement?

Mr. Welch: I only said you didn't say, "Sic 'em, Stevens," and you didn't, did you?

Mr. Cohn: Mr. Welch, you said a few days ago that you wanted to be fair. If you do want to be fair, sir, you will let me correct what is an erroneous impression which you are trying to convey here.

Mr. Welch: I am not trying to convey the impression that you actually said, "Sic 'em, Stevens," you understand that, don't you?

Mr. Cohn: I think I understand what you are trying to do, sir.

Mr. Welch: And I am actually trying to convey the impression that you did not say, "Sic 'em, Stevens," is that right?

Mr. Cohn: Sir———

Mr. Welch: Is that right?

Mr. Cohn: Mr. Welch, if you want to know the way the things work, I will tell you.

Mr. Welch: I don't care how it works. I just want to know if it is right that you did not say, "Sic 'em, Stevens."

Mr. Cohn: No, sir, you are right.

Mr. Welch: I am at long last right once, is that correct?

Mr. Cohn: Mr. Welch, you can always get a laugh. You are probably right a thousand times more often———

Mr. Welch: Mr. Cohn, we are not talking about laughing matters. If there is a laugh, I suggest to you, sir, it is because it is so hard to get you to say that you didn't actually yell, "Sic 'em, Stevens." . . .

Senator McCarthy: An important point of order, Mr. Chairman. Mr. Welch knows that my counsel wouldn't call up and say, "Sic 'em, Stevens."

That may sound funny as all get out here. It may get a laugh. He knows it is ridiculous. He is wasting time doing it. He is trying to create a false impression. . . .

Mr. Chairman, every other witness has been allowed to answer at length. Mr. Cohn, I think, has been answering every question as briefly as any human being could, and as truthfully. Now Mr. Welch has a series of 6 or 7 questions, and answers his own questions, and plays to the gallery here, as though this were a vaudeville show, which it isn't. This is a pretty serious matter, Mr. Chairman. While we are having fun here while Mr. Welch is trying to put on a circus, there are Communists in defense plants handling secret work, there to sabotage the work of this Nation, Communists who may at this very moment be decreeing the death of the sons of some people in this very audience, in this building. . . . I am getting sick of this circus. I am getting sick of this filibustering. I have given up my time so that we could get through with this, and instead of trying to get through, Mr. Welch is trying to create a circus and filibuster. Whether he is intrigued by the television lights or what, I don't know. . . .

Mr. Welch: I don't often say anything on my own behalf. If I have appeared to the Senators in this room or this audience or even on television—of which happily I am generally unaware—as seeking to be a clown or to make a funny joke or to catch a headline, may I disclaim that. I am only trying to dramatize the fact that we had a new Secretary of the Army over there, described in this room as a Communist hater, and it seems to me that it would have been simple to have gone over and gotten his help. If, Senator, in trying to dramatize, it has seemed to you that I was playing for a laugh, I beg of you, believe me, I was not. . . .

Senator McCarthy: Mr. Chairman . . .

Senator Mundt: Have you a point of order?

Senator McCarthy: Not exactly, Mr. Chairman, but in view of Mr. Welch's request that the information be given once we know of anyone who might be performing any work for the Communist Party, I think we should tell him that he has in his law firm a young man named Fisher whom he recommended, incidentally, to do work on this committee, who has been for a number of years a member of an organization which was named, oh, years and years ago, as the legal bulwark of the Communist Party, an organization which always swings to the defense of anyone who dares to expose Communists. I certainly assume that Mr. Welch did not know of this young man at the time he recommended him as the assistant counsel for this committee, but he has such terror and such a great desire to know where anyone is located who may be serving the Communist cause, Mr. Welch, that I thought we should just call to your attention the fact that your Mr. Fisher, who is still in your law firm today, whom you asked to have down here looking over the secret and classified material, is a member of an organization, not named by me but named by various committees, named by the Attorney General, as I recall, and I think I quote this verbatim, as "the legal bulwark of the Communist Party." He belonged to that for a sizable number of years, according to his own admission, and he belonged to it long after it had been exposed as the legal arm of the Communist Party. . . .

I am not asking you at this time to explain why you tried to foist him on this committee. Whether you knew he was a member of that Communist organization or not, I don't know. I assume you did not, Mr. Welch, because I get the impression that, while you are quite an actor, you play for a laugh, I don't think you have any conception of the danger of the Communist Party. I don't think you yourself would ever knowingly aid the Communist cause. I think you are unknowingly aiding it when you try to burlesque this hearing in which we are attempting to bring out the facts, however. . . .

Mr. Welch: Senator McCarthy, I did not know—Senator, sometimes you say "May I have your attention?"

Senator McCarthy: I am listening to you. I can listen with one ear.

Mr. Welch: This time I want you to listen with both.

Senator McCarthy: Yes.

Mr. Welch: Senator McCarthy, I think until this moment———

Senator McCarthy: Jim, will you get the news story to the effect that this man belonged to this Communist-front organization? Will you get the citations showing that this was the legal arm of the Communist Party, and the length of time that he belonged, and the fact that he was recommended by Mr. Welch? I think that should be in the record.

Mr. Welch: You won't need anything in the record when I have finished telling you this.

Until this moment, Senator, I think I never really gaged your cruelty or your recklessness. Fred Fisher is a young man who went to the Harvard Law School and came into my firm and is starting what looks to be a brilliant career with us.

When I decided to work for this committee I asked Jim St. Clair, who sits on my right, to be my first assistant. I said to Jim, "Pick somebody in the firm who works under you that you would like." He chose Fred Fisher and they came down on an afternoon plane. That night, when he had taken a little stab at trying to see what the case was about, Fred Fisher and Jim St. Clair and I went to dinner together. I then said to these two young men, "Boys, I don't know anything about you except I have always liked you, but if there is anything funny in the life of either one of you that would hurt anybody in this case you speak up quick."

Fred Fisher said, "Mr. Welch, when I was in law school and for a period of months after, I belonged to the Lawyers Guild," as you have suggested, Senator. He went on to say, "I am secretary of the Young Republicans League in Newton with the son of Massachusetts' Governor, and I have the respect and admiration of my community and I am sure I have the respect and admiration of the 25 lawyers or so in Hale & Dorr."

I said, "Fred, I just don't think I am going to ask you to work on the case. If I do, one of these days that will come out and go over national television and it will just hurt like the dickens."

So, Senator, I asked him to go back to Boston.

Little did I dream you could be so reckless and so cruel as to do an injury to that lad. It is true he is still with Hale & Dorr. It is true that he will continue to be with Hale & Dorr. It is, I regret to say, equally true that I fear he shall always bear a scar needlessly inflicted by you. If it were in my power to forgive you for your reckless cruelty, I will do so. I like to think I am a gentleman, but your forgiveness will have to come from someone other than me.

Senator McCarthy: Mr. Chairman.

Senator Mundt: Senator McCarthy?

Senator McCarthy: May I say that Mr. Welch talks about this being cruel and reckless. He was just baiting; he has been baiting Mr. Cohn here for hours, requesting that Mr. Cohn, before sundown, get out of any department of Government anyone who is serving the Communist cause.

I just give this man's record, and I want to say, Mr. Welch, that it has been labeled long before he became a member, as early as 1944——

Mr. Welch: Senator, may we not drop this? We know he belonged to the Lawyers Guild, and Mr. Cohn nods his head at me. I did you, I think, no personal injury, Mr. Cohn.

Mr. Cohn: No, sir.

Mr. Welch: I meant to do you no personal injury, and if I did, I beg your pardon.

Let us not assassinate this lad further, Senator. You have done enough. Have you no sense of decency, sir, at long last? Have you left no sense of decency?

Senator McCarthy: I know this hurts you, Mr. Welch. But I may say, Mr. Chairman, on a point of personal privilege, and I would like to finish it——

Mr. Welch: Senator, I think it hurts you, too, sir.

Senator McCarthy: I would like to finish this. . . .

Mr. Welch: Mr. McCarthy, I will not discuss this with you further. You have sat within 6 feet of me, and could have asked me about Fred Fisher. You have brought it out. If there is a God in heaven, it will do neither you nor your cause any good. I will not discuss it further. I will not ask Mr. Cohn any more questions. You, Mr. Chairman, may, if you will, call the next witness. . . .

THE SENATE'S CONDEMNATION OF MCCARTHY, DECEMBER 2, 1954

Resolved, That the Senator from Wisconsin, Mr. MCCARTHY, failed to cooperate with the Subcommittee on Privileges and Elections of the Senate

Committee on Rules and Administration in clearing up matters referred to that subcommittee which concerned his conduct as a Senator and affected the honor of the Senate and, instead, repeatedly abused the subcommittee and its members who were trying to carry out assigned duties, thereby obstructing the constitutional processes of the Senate, and that this conduct of the Senator from Wisconsin, Mr. MCCARTHY, is contrary to senatorial traditions and is hereby condemned.

Sec. 2. The Senator from Wisconsin, Mr. MCCARTHY, in writing to the chairman of the Select Committee To Study Censure Charges (Mr. WATKINS) after the select committee had issued its report and before the report was presented to the Senate charging three members of the select committee with "deliberate deception" and "fraud" for failure to disqualify themselves; in stating to the press on November 4, 1954, that the special Senate session that was to begin November 8, 1954, was a "lynch party"; in repeatedly describing this special Senate session as a "lynch bee" in a nationwide television and radio show on November 7, 1954; in stating to the public press on November 13, 1954, that the chairman of the select committee (Mr. WATKINS) was guilty of "the most unusual, most cowardly thing I've heard of" and stating further: "I expected he would be afraid to answer the questions, but didn't think he'd be stupid enough to make a public statement"; and in characterizing the said committee as the "unwitting handmaiden," "involuntary agent," and "attorneys in fact" of the Communist Party and in charging that the said committee in writing its report "imitated Communist methods—that it distorted, misrepresented, and omitted in its effort to manufacture a plausible rationalization" in support of its recommendations to the Senate, which characterizations and charges were contained in a statement released to the press and inserted in the CONGRESSIONAL RECORD of November 10, 1954, acted contrary to senatorial ethics and tended to bring the Senate into dishonor and disrepute, to obstruct the constitutional processes of the Senate, and to impair its dignity; and such conduct is hereby condemned.

The Supreme Court to the Breach: "Watkins v. the United States"

The downfall of McCarthy was a sign that the Red Scare was ebbing. But it was by no means over. Congressional and state legislative committees continued to chase alleged Communist sympathizers, smirch reputations, and blight careers. An array of stringent security and loyalty tests remained among the statutes and the regulations of government agencies, colleges, schools, and private business firms. Not only among bureaucrats but even among groups of students and artists, acute observers saw signs that fear still prevailed. No one wanted to say anything, join anything, or associate with anyone if the result might be that his name would one day appear on someone's list of suspected subversives. The best summary of the status of the Red Scare after McCarthy's fall is John W. Caughey, In Clear and Present Danger *(1958).*

Slowly, however, the courts began to come to the rescue of civil liberties and the tradition of an open society. Some state courts took part. The Supreme Court of California, for example, voided a special loyalty oath that the state university's board of regents had imposed on professors. The most important decisions naturally were those of the United States Supreme Court. In Commonwealth of Pennsylvania v. Nelson, *in 1956, the Court held that nearly all state antisubversive legislation was unconstitutional. In* Watkins v. the United States, *in 1957, it rebuked and sharply curbed Congress's Communist-hunting committees. In other decisions, the Court held Congress and the Federal prosecutors to rigorous standards of justice and due process in their handling even of admitted Communists.*

The Supreme Court did not crusade against the Red Scare. In other decisions, it upheld congressional committees and other bodies. These decisions are surveyed in Robert G. McCloskey, "Deeds without Doctrines: Civil Rights in the 1960 Term of the Supreme Court," American Political Science Review, *volume 56 (March, 1962), pages 71–89. But the net effect of actions by the Supreme Court, lower Federal courts, and the state courts was to recall Americans to traditional conceptions of justice and, in the long run, to refresh the springs of dissent.*

The document that follows is the Supreme Court's decision in one of the most important civil liberties cases of the late 1950s, Watkins v. the United States. *It was a case that originated with the House Committee on Un-American Activities. In April, 1954, the committee had subpoenaed John T. Watkins, a veteran labor organizer. Watkins had given full testimony about his own career, declaring that while he had never been a Communist he had, during the early 1940s, cooperated with many members of the party. The committee then read Watkins a list of names, asking him to say which ones were Communists. This Watkins refused to do. He told the committee respectfully that he believed it to be asking for testimony to which it was not entitled. The committee took umbrage. Watkins was charged with contempt of Congress. In the lower courts he was found guilty. But the Supreme Court reversed the verdict. The decision, reproduced below, is taken from* United States Supreme Court Reports, *volume 354 (1956–1957), pages 187–188, 195–206, 208–209, 215–216.*

. . . We start with several basic premises on which there is general agreement. The power of the Congress to conduct investigations is inherent in the legislative process. That power is broad. It encompasses inquiries concerning the administration of existing laws as well as proposed or possibly needed statutes. It includes surveys of defects in our social, economic or political system for the purpose of enabling the Congress to remedy them. It comprehends probes into departments of the Federal Government to expose corruption, inefficiency or waste. But, broad as is this power of inquiry, it is not unlimited. There is no general authority to expose the private affairs of individuals without justification in terms of the functions of the Congress. This was freely conceded by the Solicitor General in his argument of this case. Nor is the Congress a law enforcement or trial agency. These are functions of the executive and judicial departments of government. No inquiry is an end in itself; it must be related to, and in furtherance of, a legitimate task of the Congress. Investigations conducted solely for the personal aggrandizement of the investigators or to "punish" those investigated are indefensible.

It is unquestionably the duty of all citizens to cooperate with the Congress in its efforts to obtain the facts needed for intelligent legislative action. It is their unremitting obligation to respond to subpoenas, to respect the dignity of the Congress and its committees and to testify fully with respect to matters within the province of proper investigation. This, of course, assumes that the constitutional rights of witnesses will be respected by the Congress as they are in a court of justice. The Bill of Rights is applicable to investigations as to all forms of governmental action. Witnesses cannot be compelled to give evidence against themselves. They cannot be subjected to unreasonable search and seizure. Nor can the First Amendment freedoms of speech, press, religion, or political belief and association be abridged. . . .

In the decade following World War II, there appeared a new kind of congressional inquiry unknown in prior periods of American history. Principally this was the result of the various investigations into the threat of subversion of the United States Government, but other subjects of congressional interest also contributed to the changed scene. This new phase of legislative inquiry involved a broad-scale intrusion into the lives and affairs of private citizens. It brought before the courts novel questions of the appropriate limits of congressional inquiry. Prior cases . . . had defined the scope of investigative power in terms of the inherent limitations of the sources of that power. In the more recent cases, the emphasis shifted to problems of accommodating the interest of the Government with the rights and privileges of individuals. The central theme was the application of the Bill of Rights as a restraint upon the assertion of governmental power in this form.

It was during this period that the Fifth Amendment privilege against self-incrimination was frequently invoked and recognized as a legal limit upon the authority of a committee to require that a witness answer its questions. Some early doubts as to the applicability of that privilege before a legislative committee never matured. When the matter reached this Court, the Government did not challenge in any way that the Fifth Amendment protection was available to the witness, and such a challenge could not have prevailed. . . .

A far more difficult task evolved from the claim by witnesses that the committees' interrogations were infringements upon the freedoms of the First Amendment. Clearly, an investigation is subject to the command that the Congress shall make no law abridging freedom of speech or press or assembly. While it is true that there is no statute to be reviewed, and that an investigation is not a law, nevertheless an investigation is part of lawmaking. It is justified solely as an adjunct to the legislative process. The First Amendment may be invoked against infringement of the protected freedoms by law or by lawmaking.

Abuses of the investigative process may imperceptibly lead to abridgment of protected freedoms. The mere summoning of a witness and compelling him to testify, against his will, about his beliefs, expressions or associations is a measure of governmental interference. And when those forced revelations concern matters that are unorthodox, unpopular, or even hateful to the general public, the reaction in the life of the witness may be disastrous. This effect is even more harsh when it is past beliefs, expressions or associations that are disclosed and judged by current standards rather than those contemporary with the matters exposed. Nor does the witness alone suffer the consequences. Those who are identified by witnesses and thereby placed in the same glare of publicity are equally subject to public stigma, scorn and obloquy. Beyond that, there is the more subtle and immeasurable effect upon those who tend to adhere to the most orthodox and uncontroversial views and associations in order to avoid a similar fate at some future time. That this impact is partly the result of non-governmental activity by private persons cannot relieve the investigators of their responsibility for initiating the reaction. . . .

Accommodation of the congressional need for particular information with the individual and personal interest in privacy is an arduous and delicate task for any court. We do not underestimate the difficulties that would attend such an undertaking. It is manifest that despite the adverse effects which follow upon compelled disclosure of private matters, not all such inquiries are barred. The critical element is the existence of, and the weight to be ascribed to, the interest of the Congress in demanding disclosures from an unwilling witness. We cannot simply assume, however, that every congressional investigation is justified by a public need that overbalances any private rights affected. To do so would be to abdicate the responsibility placed by the Constitution upon the judiciary to insure that the Congress does not unjustifiably encroach upon an individual's right to privacy nor abridge his liberty of speech, press, religion or assembly.

Petitioner has earnestly suggested that the difficult questions of protecting these rights from infringement by legislative inquiries can be surmounted in this case because there was no public purpose served in his interrogation. His conclusion is based upon the thesis that the Subcommittee was engaged in a program of exposure for the sake of exposure. The sole purpose of the inquiry, he contends, was to bring down upon himself and others the violence of public reaction because of their past beliefs, expressions and associations. In support of this argument, petitioner has marshalled an impressive array of evidence that some Congressmen have believed that such was their duty, or part of it.

We have no doubt that there is no congressional power to expose for the sake of exposure. The public is, of course, entitled to be informed concerning the workings of its government. That cannot be inflated into a general power to expose where the predominant result can only be an invasion of the private rights of individuals. But a solution to our problem is not to be found in testing the motives of committee members for this purpose. Such is not our function. Their motives alone would not vitiate an investigation which had been instituted by a House of Congress if that assembly's legislative purpose is being served.

Petitioner's contentions do point to a situation of particular significance from the standpoint of the constitutional limitations upon congressional investigations. The theory of a committee inquiry is that the committee members are serving as the representatives of the parent assembly in collecting information for a legislative purpose. Their function is to act as the eyes and ears of the Congress in obtaining facts upon which the full legislature can act. To carry out this mission, committees and subcommittees, sometimes one Congressman, are endowed with the full power of the Congress to compel testimony. In this case, only two men exercised that authority in demanding information over petitioner's protest.

An essential premise in this situation is that the House or Senate shall have instructed the committee members on what they are to do with the power delegated to them. It is the responsibility of the Congress, in the first instance, to insure that compulsory process is used only in furtherance of a legislative purpose. That requires that the instructions to an investigating committee spell out that group's jurisdiction and purpose with sufficient particularity. Those instructions are embodied in the authorizing resolution. That document is the committee's charter. Broadly drafted and loosely worded, however, such resolutions can leave tremendous latitude to the discretion of the investigators. The more vague the committee's charter is, the greater becomes the possibility that the committee's specific actions are not in conformity with the will of the parent House of Congress.

The authorizing resolution of the Un-American Activities Committee was adopted in 1938. . . . It defines the Committee's authority as follows:

> The Committee on Un-American Activities, as a whole or by subcommittee, is authorized to make from time to time investigations of (1) the extent, character, and objects of un-American propaganda activities in the United States, (2) the diffusion within the United States of subversive and un-American propaganda that is instigated from foreign countries or of a domestic origin and attacks the principle of the form of government as guaranteed by our Constitution, and (3) all other questions in relation thereto that would aid Congress in any necessary remedial legislation.

It would be difficult to imagine a less explicit authorizing resolution. Who can define the meaning of "un-American"? What is that single, solitary "principle of the form of government as guaranteed by our Constitution"? There is no need to dwell upon the language, however. At one time, perhaps, the resolution might have been read narrowly to confine the Committee to the subject of propaganda. The events that have transpired in the fifteen years before the interrogation of petitioner make such a construction impossible at this date.

The members of the Committee have clearly demonstrated that they did not feel themselves restricted in any way to propaganda in the narrow sense of the word. Unquestionably the Committee conceived of its task in the grand view of its name. Un-American activities were its target, no matter how or where manifested. . . .

Combining the language of the resolution with the construction it has been given, it is evident that the preliminary control of the Committee exercised by the House of Representatives is slight or non-existent. No one could reasonably deduce from the charter the kind of investigation that the Committee was directed to make. As a result, we are asked to engage in a process of retroactive rationalization. Looking backward from the events that transpired, we are asked to uphold the Committee's actions unless it appears that they were clearly not authorized by the charter. As a corollary to this inverse approach, the Government urges that we must view the matter hospitably to the power of the Congress—that if there is any legislative purpose which might have been furthered by the kind of disclosure sought, the witness must be punished for withholding it. No doubt every reasonable indulgence of legality must be accorded to the actions of a coordinate branch of our Government. But such deference cannot yield to an unnecessary and unreasonable dissipation of precious constitutional freedoms.

The Government contends that the public interest at the core of the investigations of the Un-American Activities Committee is the need by the Congress to be informed of efforts to overthrow the Government by force and violence so that adequate legislative safeguards can be erected. From this core, however, the Committee can radiate outward infinitely to any topic thought to be related in some way to armed insurrection. The outer reaches of this domain are known only by the content of "un-American activities." Remoteness of subject can be aggravated by a probe for a depth of detail even farther removed from any basis of legislative action. A third dimension is added when the investigators turn their attention to the past to collect minutiae on remote topics, on the hypothesis that the past may reflect upon the present.

The consequences that flow from this situation are manifold. . . . The Committee is allowed, in essence, to define its own authority, to choose the direction and focus of its activities. In deciding what to do with the power that has been conferred upon them, members of the Committee may act pursuant to motives that seem to them to be the highest. Their decisions, nevertheless, can lead to ruthless exposure of private lives in order to gather data that is neither desired by the Congress nor useful to it. Yet it is impossible in this circumstance, with constitutional freedoms in jeopardy, to declare that the Committee has ranged beyond the area committed to it by its parent assembly because the boundaries are so nebulous.

More important and more fundamental than that, however, it insulates the House that has authorized the investigation from the witnesses who are subjected to the sanctions of compulsory process. There is a wide gulf between the responsibility for the use of investigative power and the actual exercise of that power. This is an especially vital consideration in assuring respect for constitutional liberties. Protected freedoms should not be placed in danger in the absence of a clear determination by the House or the Senate that a particular inquiry is justified by a specific legislative need.

It is, of course, not the function of this Court to prescribe rigid rules for the Congress to follow in drafting resolutions establishing investigating committees. That is a matter peculiarly within the realm of the legislature, and its decisions will be accepted by the courts up to the point where their own duty to enforce the constitutionally protected rights of individuals is affected. An excessively broad charter, like that of the House Un-American Activities Committee, places the courts in an untenable position if they are to strike a balance between the public need for a particular interrogation and the right of citizens to carry on their affairs free from unnecessary governmental interference. It is impossible in such a situation to ascertain whether any legislative purpose justifies the disclosures sought and, if so, the importance of that information to the Congress in furtherance of its legislative function. The reason no court can make this critical judgment is that the House of Representatives itself has never made it. Only the legislative assembly initiating an investigation can assay the relative necessity of specific disclosures. . . .

The problem attains proportion when viewed from the standpoint of the witness who appears before a congressional committee. He must decide at the time the questions are propounded whether or not to answer. . . . An erroneous determination on his part, even if made in the utmost good faith, does not exculpate him if the court should later rule that the questions were pertinent to the question under inquiry.

It is obvious that a person compelled to make this choice is entitled to have knowledge of the subject to which the interrogation is deemed pertinent. That knowledge must be available with the same degree of explicitness and clarity that the Due Process Clause requires in the expression of any element of a criminal offense. The "vice of vagueness" must be avoided here as in all other crimes. There are several sources that can outline the "question under inquiry" in such a way that the rules against vagueness are satisfied. The authorizing resolution, the remarks of the chairman or members of the committee, or even the nature of the proceedings themselves, might sometimes make the topic clear. This case demonstrates, however, that these sources often leave the matter in grave doubt. . . .

We are mindful of the complexities of modern government and the ample scope that must be left to the Congress as the sole constitutional depository of legislative power. Equally mindful are we of the indispensable function, in the exercise of that power, of congressional investigations. The conclusions we have reached in this case will not prevent the Congress, through its committees, from obtaining any information it needs for the proper fulfillment of its role in our scheme of government. The legislature is free to determine the kinds of data that should be collected. It is only those investigations that are conducted by use of compulsory process that give rise to a need to protect the rights of individuals against illegal encroachment. That protection can be readily achieved through procedures which prevent the separation of power from responsibility and which provide the constitutional requisites of fairness for witnesses. A measure of added care on the part of the House and the Senate in authorizing the use of compulsory process and by their committees in exercising that power would suffice. That is a small price to pay if it serves to uphold the principles of limited, constitutional government without constricting the power of the Congress to inform itself.

The judgment of the Court of Appeals is reversed, and the case is remanded to the District Court with instructions to dismiss the indictment.

PART NINE

Restless Opulence

The Great Boom

New Directions

SELECTION **40**

"The Economic Report of the President, 1952 . . . 1957 . . . 1962"

Although the years after World War II were turbulent, anxious years, they were also flush years. The nation did not revert to the depression of the prewar period. On the contrary, it enjoyed an almost uninterrupted boom that raised production figures, incomes, and standards of living to heights that would have seemed incredible in the 1930s.

In the immediate aftermath of the war, President Truman and the Congress had both been fearful of the return of hard times. Truman asked Congress for broad powers to regulate the economy and initiate public works if such an event came to pass. He did not get what he asked. Congress did, however, pass a law with a high-sounding name—the Full Employment Act of 1946. It authorized the President to establish a Council of Economic Advisers with a staff of economists. This council was to collect information on the state of the economy and forecast short-term and long-term prospects. The President himself was charged with the duty of delivering to the Congress an annual Economic Report, summarizing the findings of his economic advisers.

There follow excerpts from one report by Truman, one by Eisenhower, and one by Kennedy. They suggest how the economy looked, at five-year intervals, during this great postwar boom. The first is taken from The Economic Report of the President, 1952 *(Government Printing Office, 1952), pages 1–8, 13–14, 17–20, 24. The second is from* The Economic Report of the President, 1957 *(Government Printing Office, 1957), pages iii–v, vii. The third is from* Public Papers of the Presidents: John F. Kennedy, 1962 *(Government Printing Office, 1963), pages 42–45, 47, 51.*

1952

To the Congress of the United States:

The past year has been marked by great gains in our basic economic strength. These gains have enabled us to move forward toward our security objectives with far less strain upon the economy than would otherwise have been possible.

It is the tragic necessity of our time that we and other peace-loving peoples must devote so large a part of our resources to building up our military strength. But it is because we seek peace—a just and lasting peace—that we have shouldered this burden. If, despite our best efforts, another world conflict should come, the cost would be beyond description. If we succeed in the effort for peace, our productive ability will enable us to achieve a material well-being never before known. . . .

Without continued economic growth, the defense burden could make us weaker year by year. Without economic stability and control of inflation, the resulting hardships could disastrously affect millions of our people. Without agreement on economic fundamentals at home, group conflicts or political conflicts could weaken our ability to withstand the communist threat.

It is only natural that the scope and operation of a program of this magnitude should evoke some disagreement and criticism. This can be constructive. But it would be most unfortunate if, in those economic matters which affect our world security, we were divided by narrow partisanship rather than united by the desire to find the best possible solution.

To agree upon wise policies, it is essential to know and understand the facts. These facts are available, and they are compelling. They show that our basic economic strength is greater than it was a year ago. They point the way to the necessary policies that we should follow. They reveal why all of us can and need to stand upon common ground. . . .

Comparing the year 1947 with the year 1950, before our economy was greatly affected by the new defense program, civilian employment rose from 58 million to 60 million. Unemployment during those years averaged about 2.7 million, which was low by previous peacetime standards. Our total annual output, measured in uniform (1951) prices, rose from about 270 billion dollars to about 300 billion.

This growth in our economy accelerated rapidly after the Korean outbreak. In the year and a half since then, our annual rate of total output, in terms of 1951 prices, has risen by about 30 billion dollars, or 10 percent, to 330 billion dollars. By the end of 1951, civilian employment mounted to about 61 million, and unemployment was about 1.7 million.

Thus, comparing 1947 with the current situation, the annual output of the economy, in constant prices, has risen by about 60 billion dollars. Total civilian employment is now about 3 million higher than 4 years ago.

This expansion of our economy has occurred because the American people have never lost faith in progress. They have rejected the idea that we have reached, or will ever reach, the last frontiers of our growth. Businessmen, workers, and farmers have dared to produce more and more, confident that we had the ingenuity and the imagination to utilize this increasing abundance. They have not been held back by the fear that we would get into a depression by not knowing how to make use of the blessing of full production and full employment.

An expanding economy has paid particularly rich dividends, in helping us to assume new burdens of world responsibility. In 1947, we justly regarded ourselves as having reached remarkable levels of production and productivity, compared with any prewar year. Our total output, measured in 1951 prices, was more than 90 billion dollars higher than in 1939, and more than 100 billion above 1929. But since 1947, the 60-billion-dollar increase in annual output has been greater than the total cost of the security program in 1951. (See chart 1.) The high level of production helped to hold inflation in check during most of 1951, despite a rapidly rising security program. The growth of production during the last few years now enables us to carry the security program without undue impairment of the rest of the economy. Despite the defense burden, the past year witnessed a production of tools, factories, automobiles, housing, household goods, and food that was very high—and, in some cases, record-breaking.

In the light of this experience, we should hold fast to the principle of an expanding economy. During 1952, we can and should lift employment by another 1⅓ million. Some further reduction in unemployment may be possible, despite the fact that additional defense-created unemployment in some local areas appears inevitable. We can and should lift our total output by at least another 5 percent, or by 15 to 20 billion dollars. We should adopt policies which pave the way for a continuation or acceleration of these productive gains in the years further ahead.

BUILDING OUR STRENGTH

GROSS NATIONAL PRODUCT IN 1951 PRICES

In 1952, we should be able to increase total production by about 5 per cent. This will help to meet the needs of the expanding security program.

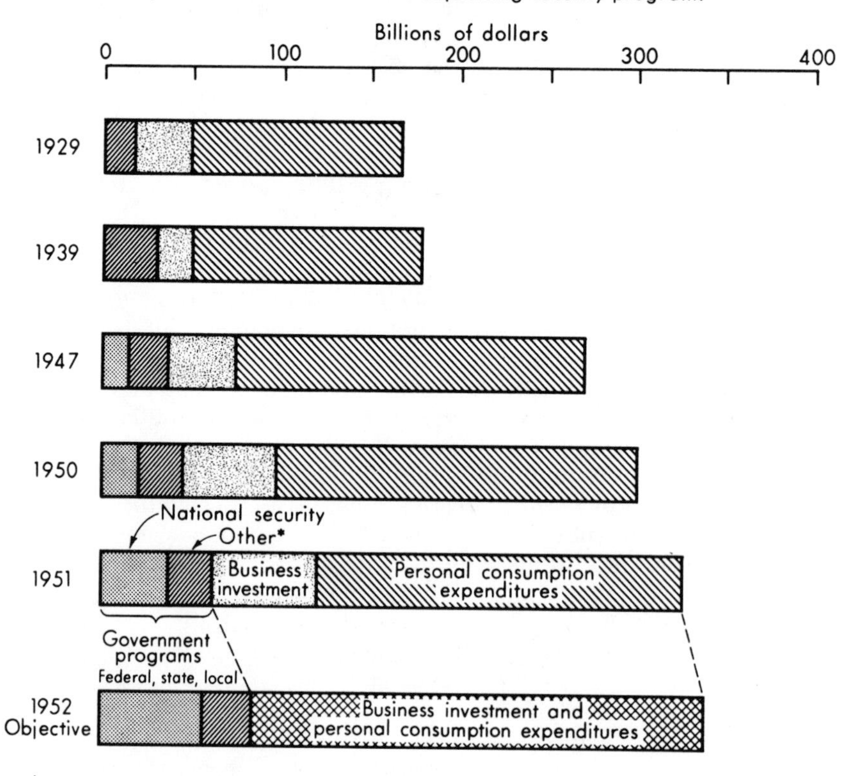

*Development of natural and human resources.

Note: Net foreign investment in all years, and national security in 1929, not shown separately since amounts are relatively very small.

SOURCES: Department of Commerce and Council of Economic Advisers.

Such progress will have many advantages. It will give us even greater strength to meet any aggressor. If the world situation stabilizes, so that we can after 2 or 3 years taper off the defense program, we will then be producing enough to remove many unpleasant controls without risking inflation, and to have a higher standard of living than we had even in 1951. And if we succeed in attaining a durable peace, our expanding economy can double our standard of living within a generation.

Viewing the next 2 hard years, the productive capacity of the United States leaves no room for faintheartedness or defeatism about our ability to carry whatever necessary burdens the international situation may impose upon us. But we cannot afford to be complacent. In moving ahead confidently to what must be done, we should not overlook the points of weakness or vulnerability in our economic system. Our resources are bountiful, but we must make the most of them by careful use.

Economic strength, in these times, is not only a matter of size. If we should devote too much of our productive power to building up our standard of living, while the communists build up their armaments, we could fall far behind despite our immensely greater economic potential. We must use our strength in the right way.

In a total war, our course would be plain. We would build up our striking forces as rapidly as possible, and sacrifice all else to that purpose. In a fully peaceful situation, our course would also be plain. We would reduce armaments, and devote our full resources to the pursuit of what we count as the good things of life. But for the time being, and perhaps for a long time, we must sail a middle course in an uncertain sea.

The whole mobilization effort is based upon the economic strategy of following this middle course. This means keeping strong all three components of our total strength—military, industrial, and civilian. We are making allowance for the possibility that war could come suddenly. But we are also making allowance for the possibility of a long period of international tension without total war. It is a mistake to oversimplify this problem by calling it a conflict between guns and butter. We must strive for the amounts and kinds of "guns," of "tools," and of "butter" which will do most to advance our security and well-being in the long run.

While too slow a defense build-up would imperil the Nation, too rapid a build-up also has dangers. It could burden us with a mass of out-of-date weapons, deplete our economy, and weaken public support for a program which may be needed over a long period.

If the build-up of our industrial capacity were too slow, the very foundation of our economic and military strength would be impaired. But if our industrial build-up were too fast or were made indiscriminately, it could feed an inflationary boom by placing too heavy a demand upon scarce materials.

If we maintained civilian consumption at too lush a level under current world conditions, we would be deceiving ourselves tragically. But excessive cutbacks of civilian supplies and essential public services would weaken the ultimate source of our collective strength—155 million Americans.

The defense mobilization effort thus far has been based upon this rounded concept of total national strength for the long pull. Since the Korean outbreak, the size of our armed forces has more than doubled. Deliveries of military goods, including military construction, have totaled

20 billion dollars. Nearly $5\frac{1}{2}$ million workers are now engaged directly or indirectly in defense production. Government outlays for the major national security programs—the military services, atomic energy, stockpiling, military and economic aid abroad, Defense Production Act programs, civil defense, and merchant marine activities—have increased from an annual rate of 17 billion dollars to about 45 billion.

While increasing these major security programs, we have also been rapidly building up our productive economic strength. Since the Korean outbreak, private investment in producers' equipment and nonresidential construction has averaged 37 billion dollars a year, compared with a 32-billion-dollar rate from 1947 through the middle of 1950, 14 billion in 1939, and 22 billion in 1929, all measured at the 1951 price level. In 1951, steelmaking capacity increased 4 percent and electric power capacity 10 percent, and the year's steel output of 105 million tons exceeded the previous record by 9 percent. Aluminum output at present is running 17 percent higher than during the middle of 1950. Additions to farm equipment and larger use of fertilizers have made it possible to set a realistic 1952 agricultural production goal above any previous year's output, and almost 50 percent higher than the Nation's average farm production in the years before World War II.

This growth in the productive sector of our economy indicates that neither the size of the military build-up, nor the high level of taxation enacted to finance that build-up, has repressed business investment initiative. Instead, the problem has been to hold the expansion down to non-inflationary proportions.

Despite the great demand for resources to enlarge the military build-up and to expand the industrial mobilization base, the year and a half since Korea has witnessed an extremely high level of general civilian supplies. While per capita consumption in constant dollars declined about 3 percent from the pre-Korean level to the final quarter of 1951, this was mainly because of a fall in demand for durable goods. Considering the increase in consumers' stocks of durable goods since the end of the war, and the steady improvement in housing accommodations, it seems clear that living standards have thus far been rising. Compared with 1939, per capita consumption expenditures, after adjustment for price rises, have increased about one-third.

There have been some shortcomings to set off against these evidences of progress. Bottlenecks and shortages, and problems of design, have delayed production of some important military items. Some of the materials expansion programs have not moved forward as rapidly as we had anticipated. As was to be expected in the first stages of a mobilization effort, the development of smoothly operating administrative machinery took time to accomplish. In some areas of the country, although not generally, dislocations have resulted in unemployment and business hardship. Furthermore, particularly during the first months after the Korean aggression, a rapid inflationary upsurge caused undue hardship to many families.

Nonetheless, the facts which have been recited make it clear that the Nation has been gaining steadily and vigorously in economic strength. Moreover, the utilization of our resources, under the mobilization program, has kept the three major components of our strength in reasonably balanced proportion.

But the defense program is still in the build-up stage; the main effort lies ahead. This will impose new strains upon the economy. It calls for improvement in existing programs, and new adjustments to meet new events. . . .

Looking at the situation as a whole, however, the essential security program neither imposes excessive strains upon the economy, nor makes it impossible to contain inflation. If we realize as fully as possible, our productive potential, business investment and real consumption, while curtailed, will still be high, except when measured against the last 2 years—the highest in our history. Certainly these are not large sacrifices, in view of the dangers against which we must protect ourselves. Further, if the people as a whole are willing to avoid excesses and extravagances, the recent containment of inflation can be made more effective during this year. We contained inflation, under more difficult circumstances, during World War II, although we did not do a good enough job of forestalling postwar inflation. We must learn from past mistakes as well as from past successes.

True economy is desirable at all times. It is imperative during a national emergency. But, as shown by the foregoing review of events since 1947, true economy means conserving and expanding the economic strength of the Nation as a whole. It can, therefore, be achieved only by recognizing all the basic factors in that strength—and not neglecting any of them.

When we look at the whole picture, we find that true economy embraces two equally important elements: The first is the avoidance of unnecessary outlays; but the second, and equally important, is the making of necessary outlays. A nation which spent its resources foolishly would dissipate its strength. But a nation which was too timid or miserly in applying its resources to urgent needs would fail to build up its strength.

We must exert every effort—through business action, consumer action, and government action—to avoid unnecessary outlays. But we cannot by this method alone achieve world peace or a highly productive economy. The main reason for not spending on the things that we do not need, is to afford the things that we do need. . . .

Building up our productive capacity is a many-sided operation. The mainspring of this expansion is private initiative and investment. But the Government has had to exercise important responsibilities. It has had to program and guide expansions in various key industries. This has been effected by materials allocations, and by selective aids and inducements such as tax amortization, loans, loan guarantees, and purchase agreements. The authority provided by the Defense Production Act and related legislation to use these aids to expand production has been very valuable, and will continue to be necessary.

A number of public programs play an important role in expanding the total productive capacity of the economy. Roads, other transport facilities, public power developments, and pilot plant research in metals and fuels, are illustrations. The Government is equipping and building certain facilities for the production of war matériel, and is carrying out a large atomic energy program. To support needed expansion of production, certain urgently needed development projects, particularly the St. Lawrence seaway and power projects, should be started now. . . .

In general, the labor force thus far has proved adequate to meet the needs of increased production and a growing military establishment. But in certain categories of skill, and in certain industrial and farm areas, shortages exist. Appropriate measures are being taken to encourage training, recruitment, and the movement of workers when necessary, and to promote efficient use of the labor supply by employers. Manpower problems will probably grow more difficult, as defense production approaches its maximum level. A serious need has already appeared for additional housing and community facilities and services in defense areas. . . .

Farmers are now being asked to produce more than ever before. The "sliding scale" in existing price support legislation has aroused concern in the minds of many farmers, who fear that their cooperation in expanding production to meet the present emergency might later result in serious losses to them. The Government's price support operations obviously should further attainment of production objectives, and they should not penalize producers for their full and patriotic cooperation with the agricultural program. I therefore recommend that the sliding scale provisions of the present agricultural legislation be repealed for this purpose.

We need to strengthen the agricultural program by finding a more effective way of supporting the price of perishable farm commodities. One method is by direct payments to farmers. This and other methods are now being studied by the Congress. I hope that the Congress will provide legislation authorizing a sound and workable program for supporting prices of these perishables. . . .

In determining the national economic policies necessary to maintain stability in the economy in the coming year, the basic fact to take into consideration is that the progress of the security program will involve a steady increase in the requirements of the Government for goods and services. The increase will bring Government demand at the end of the year to a level 20 billion dollars higher than the current annual rate of Government purchases for this purpose, and will entail a corresponding increase in the amount of labor, materials, and other productive resources diverted from the civilian economy to the security program. At the same time, the security program will place large additional buying power in the hands of businessmen and consumers.

Consumer spending is the most uncertain factor determining the general inflationary outlook for 1952. While it is possible to make a reasonably satisfactory estimate of the volume of new business investment in plant and equipment this year, since it will be limited by the allocation of scarce materials, there is no certainty at all in any estimate of consumer spending. For the last three quarters of 1951, consumers have voluntarily elected to buy at a level no higher, in total physical units, than in the period before the initial attack in Korea. Instead, they have added to their personal saving much of the large increases which have taken place since that time in their income after taxes.

The exceptionally high rate of personal saving has not been due to any general lack of goods available to consumers. Even in the case of durable goods which have been cut back in production by allocation orders, such as automobiles and major household appliances, no market pressure has been noticed since the first quarter of 1951. Textiles and some other types of soft goods have been produced at a rate well below capacity, not on account of any shortage of labor or materials, but because consumer demand has fallen off in many lines. Manufacturers and retailers have been struggling with overlarge inventories, which in many cases have not yet been brought down to the levels they desire.

It is impossible to foresee how long this extraordinarily high level of personal saving will continue. It is not even certain that it may not be raised. But national economic policy may safely be based upon these assumptions: the progress of the security program will bring an increase in personal incomes and enlarge the potential market demand of consumers; the longer consumers elect to save rather than to buy goods, the larger will become the accumulated fund of liquid assets; and the fund of liquid assets when coupled with the higher current income of consumers, will add greatly to the potential consumer demand, and may increasingly tend to turn potential demand into abnormally active buying. . . .

The year 1952 is not going to be an easy year for the economy. It is going to be a year of strain. We must expect this, and prepare to bear some inconveniences and hardships. For most of us, the hardships will be minor. There will be plenty of food and other essential commodities, and the higher civilian employment in our history. As the economy becomes adjusted to the new conditions and grows in size, and especially when defense expenditures decline, we may confidently look forward to the relaxation and removal of many kinds of controls and restrictions. In the meantime, all of us must join in the vast effort to safeguard our national security. . . .

DWIGHT D. EISENHOWER

1957

To the Congress of the United States:

. . . The vast productive power of the American economy was demonstrated again in 1956 in a record national output of $412 billion of goods and services.

In addition to providing this material basis for better living, our free economy gives indispensable support to our form of political life and offers unparalleled opportunities to the individual for personal choice and development. . . .

The opportunities which our free economy provides for the improvement of well-being are clearly evident in the record of the last four years. Civilian employment increased by about 3.7 million. Per capita personal income measured in constant dollars rose 10 percent after taxes. Five million homes were built and home ownership became more widespread. Rising incomes enabled consumers to expand their purchases of virtually all types of goods and to make important improvements in their own provisions for financial security. Participation in, and support of, religious, cultural, educational, and civic activities increased significantly.

Great strides were taken in the expansion and improvement of the Nation's productive facilities. Business firms and farmers spent over $150 billion for this purpose. These investment outlays contain the promise of greater national output and better living in the years ahead.

Agriculture has faced difficult problems in this period, resulting chiefly from the persistent tendency for production to exceed commercial demands. Progress has been made, however, toward a better balanced farm economy, and there has been some recent improvement in farm income. To sustain agricultural progress, experience suggests that continued emphasis is needed on the basic objectives of the last four years—wider freedom for our commercial farmers in managing their own enterprises, appropriate shifts in the use of the Nation's cropland, an improved system of price supports, and research into new products, markets, and uses.

The period was marked by economic improvement throughout the free world and by a notable expansion of international trade and finance, including our own exports and imports. Sharp increases have occurred in our exports to industrialized countries with high per capita incomes and to others currently experiencing a rapid rate of economic growth. This fact shows that prosperity elsewhere widens markets for the products of our farms, mines, and factories. . . .

The Nation's aggregate output of goods and services in 1956 was $21.5 billion greater than in 1955, despite a decrease in activity in some sectors of the economy, notably in automobile production and home construction. Heavy expenditures for new plant and equipment by business concerns, increases in foreign trade and investment, a high rate of consumer expenditures, and rising outlays by State and local governments contributed to the expansion. About half of the increase represented a gain in physical output, and the remainder reflected moderately higher prices.

Sizable gains in employment were made in important sectors of the economy; for the year as a whole, there was an increase of 1.8 million over 1955 in total civilian employment. Incomes rose for all major groups of income recipients.

As the year progressed, farm income improved. There were further advances in the value of farm land, in the net worth of farm proprietors, and in agricultural exports. Farm technology continued to improve.

Financial markets and prices were under continuous pressure. Interest rates rose as the demand for credit continued large relative to the supply of funds. The unusually heavy demands of business concerns tended to raise prices of capital goods and related commodities. High costs of raw materials and wage increases that tended to outrun the year's small gain in productivity were pervasive factors making for higher prices. . . .

There are grounds for confidence that the Nation's over-all prosperity will be extended into the months ahead. A moderate rise in business capital outlays is indicated. Construction expenditures and foreign trade and investment should continue to favor economic expansion. The combined expenditures of Federal, State, and local governments are expected to be higher. Consumer expenditures should be sustained by favorable employment conditions and good earnings.

However, uncertainties and problems are always present in the economic situation and require careful attention. These include the present international situation, the upward pressure of costs and prices, factors affecting capital outlays by business, and the provision of an adequate flow of new savings to meet the prospective heavy demands for funds.

These and other uncertainties and problems which inevitably arise in a dynamic economy challenge individuals, economic groups, and Government to meet their respective responsibilities for maintaining stable economic growth. If all live up to these responsibilities, the capacity of our economy to provide the high levels of employment, production, and purchasing power envisaged by the Employment Act, and broadly attained in the past year, will be further enhanced.

DWIGHT D. EISENHOWER

1962

To the Congress of the United States:

I report to you under the provisions of the Employment Act of 1946 at a time when

—the economy has regained its momentum;

—the economy is responding to the Federal Government's efforts, under the Act, "to promote maximum employment, production, and purchasing power;

—the economy is again moving toward the central objective of the Act—to afford "useful employment opportunities, including self-employment, for those able, willing, and seeking to work. . . .

The record of the economy since 1946 is a vast improvement over the prolonged mass unemployment of the 1930's. The Employment Act itself deserves no small part of the credit. Under the mandate and procedures of the Act, both Congress and the Executive have kept the health of the national economy and the economic policies of the Government under constant review. And the national commitment to high employment has enabled business firms and consumers to act and to plan without fear of another great depression.

Though the postwar record is free of major depression, it is marred by four recessions. In the past fifteen years, the economy has spent a total of seven years regaining previous peaks of industrial production. In two months out of three, 4 percent or more of those able, willing, and seeking to work have been unable to find jobs. We must do better in the 1960's. . . .

Last January the economy was in the grip of recession. Nearly 7 percent of the labor force was unemployed. Almost one-fifth of manufacturing capacity lay idle. Actual output was running $50 billion (annual rate) short of the economy's great potential. These figures reflected not only the setback of 1960–61 but the incomplete recovery from the recession of 1957–58. The task before us was to recover not from one but from two recessions.

At the same time, gold was leaving the country at a rate of more than $300 million a month. In the three previous years, the Nation had run a total deficit of $10 billion in its basic international accounts. These large and persistent deficits had weakened confidence in the dollar.

In my message to the Congress on February 2, I stated that this Administration's "realistic aims for 1961 are to reverse the downtrend in our economy, to narrow the gap of unused potential, to abate the waste and misery of unemployment, and at the same time to maintain reasonable stability of the price level." In a message on the balance of payments on February 6, I added a fifth aim, to restore confidence in the dollar and to reduce the deficit in international payments.

These five aims for 1961 have been achieved:

1. The downtrend was reversed. Gross national product (GNP) grew from $501 billion (annual rate) in the first quarter to a record rate of $542 billion in the last quarter. In July, industrial production regained its previous peak, and by the end of the year it showed a total rise of 13 percent.

2. These gains brought into productive use nearly half the plant capacity which was idle at the beginning of the year. The growth of GNP narrowed the over-all gap of unused potential from an estimated 10 percent to 5 percent.

3. Unemployment dropped from 6.8 to 6.1 percent of the labor force. The number of areas of substantial labor surplus declined from 101 in March to 60 in December.

4. Price stability has been maintained during the recovery. Since February, wholesale prices have fallen slightly, and consumer prices have risen only one-half of 1 percent.

5. Confidence in the dollar has been restored. Our gold losses were cut from $1.7 billion in 1960 to less than $0.9 billion in 1961. The deficit in 1961 in our basic international transactions was about one-third as large as in 1960. . . .

The increase of GNP—$41 billion (annual rate) from the first to the fourth quarter—reflected increased purchases of goods and services by consumers, business, and governments:

—Consumers accounted for nearly half. As household incomes rose, consumer expenditure expanded by $18 billion.

—Residential construction and business expenditures for fixed investment responded promptly to the recovery and to favorable credit conditions. By the end of the year, they had risen by $8 billion.

—Business stopped liquidating inventories and started rebuilding them. This shift, which occurred early in the year and helped get recovery off to a flying start, added $8 billion to the demand for goods and services by the fourth quarter.

—Federal, State, and local government purchases rose by $8 billion.

—Although exports were somewhat higher in the fourth quarter than in the first, the rise in imports in response to recovery lowered net exports by $1 billion.

Labor, business, and farm incomes rose as the economy recovered. Wages and salaries increased by $19 billion (annual rate) from the first quarter to the fourth. Corporate profits after taxes recovered sharply, receiving about 15 percent of the gains in GNP. With the help of new programs, farm operators' net income from farming increased from $12 billion in 1960 to $13 billion in 1961, and net income per farm rose by $350. The after-tax incomes of American consumers increased by $21 billion, or $92 per capita, during the year. Since consumer prices rose by only one-half of 1 percent, these gains in income were almost entirely gains in real purchasing power.

One million jobs were added by nonagricultural establishments during the expansion. But employment did not keep pace with production and income. Productivity rose rapidly as capacity was more fully and efficiently utilized. And more workers on part-time jobs were able to work full time.

The record of 1961 demonstrated again the resiliency of the U.S. economy with well-timed support from government policy. Business responded to the expansion of purchasing power by producing more goods and services, not by raising prices. Indeed, the record of price stability in three quarters of expansion was better than in the three preceding quarters of recession. The rates of advance of production and income compared favorably with the two preceding periods of expansion. Production grew rapidly without straining capacity or encountering bottlenecks.

As 1961 ended, actual output was still $25 to $30 billion short of potential, and unemployment was far too high. But much of the industrial manpower, machinery, and plant that lay idle a year ago had been drawn back into productive use. And the momentum of the 1961 recovery should carry the economy further toward full employment and full production in 1962. . . .

The Nation will make further economic progress in 1962. Broad advances are in prospect for the private economy. The gains already achieved have set the stage for further new records in output, employment, personal income, and profits. Rising household incomes brighten the outlook for further increases in consumer buying, particularly of durable goods. Business firms will need larger inventories to support higher sales, and improved profits and expanded markets will lead to rising capital outlays. The outlays of Federal, State, and local governments will continue to increase as we work for peace and progress.

In the first half of 1962, we may therefore expect vigorous expansion in production and incomes, with GNP increasing to a range of $565–570 billion in the second quarter, employment continuing to rise, and the unemployment rate falling further.

In the second half of 1962, business investment in plant and equipment should pick up speed and help maintain the momentum of progress toward full employment—and toward future economic growth. Rising output should push factory operating rates closer to capacity and raise profits still further above previous records. To these incentives for capital expenditures will be added Treasury liberalization of depreciation guidelines and, if the Congress acts favorably, the 8 percent tax credit for machinery and equipment outlays.

For 1962 as a whole, GNP is expected to rise approximately $50 billion above the $521 billion level of 1961. This would be another giant stride toward a fully employed economy. The record of past recoveries and of the U.S. economy's enormous and growing potential indicates that this is a gain we can achieve. In the perspective of our commitments both to our own expanding population and to the world, it is a gain we need to achieve. . . .

Prices and production need not travel together. A number of foreign countries have experienced both rapid growth and stable prices in recent years. We ourselves, in 1961, enjoyed a stable price level during a brisk economic recovery.

While rising prices will not necessarily accompany the expansion we expect in 1962, neither can we rely on chance to keep our price level stable. Creeping inflation in the years 1955–57 weakened our international competitive position. We cannot afford to allow a repetition of that experience.

We do not foresee in 1962 a level of demand for goods and services which will strain the economy's capacity to produce. Neither is it likely that many industries will find themselves pressing against their capacity ceilings. Inflationary pressures from these sources should not be a problem.

But in those sectors where both companies and unions possess substantial market power, the interplay of price and wage decisions could set off a movement toward a higher price level. If this were to occur, the whole Nation would be the victim.

I do not believe that American business or labor will allow this to happen. All of us have learned a great deal from the economic events of the past 15 years. Among both businessmen and workers, there is growing recognition that the road to higher real profits and higher real wages is the road to increased productivity. When better plant and equipment enable the labor force to produce more in the same number of hours, there is more to share among all the contributors to the productive process—and this can happen with no increase in prices. Gains achieved in this manner endure, while gains achieved in one turn of the price-wage spiral vanish on the next.

The Nation must rely on the good sense and public spirit of our business and labor leaders to hold the line on the price level in 1962. If labor leaders in our major industries will accept the productivity benchmark as a guide to wage objectives, and if management in these industries will practice equivalent restraint in their price decisions, the year ahead will be a brilliant chapter in the record of the responsible exercise of freedom. . . .

JOHN F. KENNEDY

The Problem of Automation: Walter P. Reuther

In the rapid growth of the economy, there was cause for national self-congratulation, but there was also cause for concern.

One element in the nation's economic growth was rapid adaptation of new technology. In the past, machines had been developed to do the muscle work of man. But now the vacuum tube and the digital computer made possible the development of machines that could do man's brain work as well. In this fact, there were ominous implications for American workingmen.

One man who perceived these implications clearly was Walter P. Reuther. The head of the United Automobile Workers union, Reuther had succeeded Philip Murray as president of the Congress of Industrial Organizations (CIO). In 1954, after long negotiations, the CIO and the American Federation of Labor (AFL), reunited as the AFL-CIO. One important factor in the merger was Reuther's willingness to let AFL President George Meany be head of the united organization. More often than not, however, it was Reuther rather than Meany who stepped forward as the spokesman for American labor.

The first document below is Reuther's statement on the problem of automation, delivered to the Joint Congressional Committee on the Economic Report in 1955. It is taken from Walter P. Reuther, Selected Papers *(Macmillan, 1961), pages 67–69, 71–79, 98–100.*

. . . One of the essentials of a strong and effective democracy is that we have leaders who attempt to anticipate situations which may arise and prepare in advance to deal with them. Too often in the past, nations have been surprised unnecessarily, by economic and social dislocations. In the eighteenth and nineteenth centuries, for example, the First Industrial Revolution brought untold hardships to millions of families in Great Britain, partly because Britain at that time lacked both the economic knowledge to understand and control the forces at work and the democratic institutions of government through which the people could have called attention to their needs. In our own country, had we understood the economic forces that were eating away at the base of our apparent prosperity in the 1920's, we surely would have been able to build safeguards into our economy that could have protected us from the collapse that followed.

In the spread of automation and the prospective large-scale industrial use of atomic energy—and the possible practical utilization of solar energy, as well—we are faced with mighty forces whose impact on our economy can be vastly beneficial or vastly harmful, depending on whether we succeed or fail in achieving economic and social progress that will keep pace with changing technology.

The willingness of this Committee to study these technological developments, and to look squarely at the potential problems they may create, gives hope that this time we will not be caught unaware. It gives us hope, too, that we may be able to foresee the threat of dislocations and take action in advance to enable us to enjoy the benefits of a new abundance, without first having to pay a heavy price in unemployment and human suffering.

We have been told so often that automation is going to bring on the "Second Industrial Revolution" that there is, perhaps, a danger we may dismiss the warning as a catch phrase, and lose sight of the fact that, not only the technique, but the philosophy of automation is revolutionary, in the truest sense of the word. Automation does not only produce changes in the methods of manufacturing, distribution, many clerical operations, and in the structure of business organization, but the impact of those changes on our economy and our whole society bids fair to prove quite as revolutionary as were those of the First Industrial Revolution.

Through the application of mechanical power to machinery, and the development of new machinery to use this power, the First Industrial Revolution made possible a vast increase in the volume of goods produced for each man-hour of work. Succeeding technological improvements—such as the development of interchangeable parts and the creation of the assembly line, which were essential to the growth of mass production industries—have led to continuous increases in labor productivity. But however much these machines were improved, they still required workers to operate and control them. In some operations, the worker's function was little more than to feed the material in, set the machine in operation, and remove the finished product. In others, proper control of the machine required the exercise of the highest conceivable skills. But whether the required skill was little or great, the presence of a human being, using human judgment, was essential to the operation of the machine.

The revolutionary change produced by automation is its tendency to displace the worker entirely from the direct operation of the machine, through the use of automatic control devices. No one, as far as I know, has yet produced a fully satisfactory definition of automation, but I think John Diebold came close to expressing its essential quality when he described automation as "the integration of machines with each other into fully automatic, and, in some cases, self-regulating systems."

In other words, automation is a technique by which whole batteries of machines, in some cases almost whole factories and offices, can be operated according to predetermined automatic controls. The raw material is automatically fed in, the machine automatically processes it, the product is automatically taken away, often to be fed automatically into still another machine that carries it automatically through a further process. In some cases the machine is self-regulating—that is, it is set to turn out a product within certain tolerances as to size or other factors, and if those tolerances are exceeded, the machine itself detects the variation and automatically adjusts itself to correct it. . . .

One of the important features of automation is that it can be applied not only to long runs of identical operations, but to fairly short-run jobs where instructions given to the machine have to be changed at the end of each job. This is made possible through the use of printed tape, punch cards, etc., on which the instructions are coded, and the machine is given a new set of instructions simply by changing the tape or card. . . .

The use of automation is not restricted to manufacturing plants. Increasingly, so-called "electronic brains" are taking over the functions of office clerks, accountants, and other white-collar workers. . . .

Even automation itself is being automated. One of the bottlenecks, in the use of computers, to which data is fed by punched cards, has been the time required to have the information punched on the cards by trained operators. Now the Burroughs Corporation has produced for the First National City Bank of New York an electronic device which "reads" the serial numbers on travelers' checks and reproduces them on punched cards at a rate of seventy-two hundred checks per hour, doing the work of ten highly skilled operators.

The great variety of applications shown in these few examples illustrates one of the most significant features of the new technology—its wide applicability. That is the real quality that makes automation a genuinely revolutionary force in our economy, rather than just another technological improvement. . . .

What is the attitude of the trade union movement, and specifically of the CIO, to this new technology of automation?

First of all, we fully realize that the potential benefits of automation are great, if properly handled. If only a fraction of what technologists promise for the future is true, within a very few years automation can and should make possible a four-day workweek, longer vacation periods, opportunities for earlier retirement, as well as a vast increase in our material standards of living.

At the same time, automation can bring freedom from the monotonous drudgery of many jobs in which the worker today is no more than a servant of the machine. It can free workers from routine, repetitious tasks which the new machines can be taught to do, and can give to the workers who toil at those tasks the opportunity of developing higher skills.

But in looking ahead to the many benefits which automation can produce, we must not overlook or minimize the many problems which will inevitably arise in making the adjustment to the new technology—problems for individual workers and individual companies, problems for entire communities and regions, problems for the economy as a whole.

What should be done to help the worker who will be displaced from his job, or the worker who will find that his highly specialized skill has been taken over by a machine? What about the businessman who lacks sufficient capital to automate his plant, yet has to face the competition of firms whose resources enable them to build whole new automatic factories? Will automation mean the creation of whole new communities in some areas, while others are turned into ghost towns? How can we increase the market for goods and services sufficiently, and quickly enough, to match greatly accelerated increases in productivity?

Finding the answers to these questions, and many others like them, will not be an easy process, and certainly not an automatic one. Even if the greatest care is taken to foresee and meet these problems, adjustments for many people will prove difficult and even painful. If there is no care and no foresight, if we subscribe to the laissez-faire belief that "these things will work themselves out," untold harm can be done to millions of innocent people and to the whole structure of our economy and our free society.

The CIO insists that we must recognize these problems and face up to them. But our recognition that there will be problems, and serious problems to be solved, does not mean that we are opposed to automation. We are not. We fully recognize the desirability, as well as the inevitability of technological progress. We welcome the potential benefits which automation can and should bring. But we oppose those who would introduce automation blindly and irresponsibility, with no concern for any result except the achievement of the largest possible quick profit for themselves.

When the First Industrial Revolution took place, no effort was made to curb or control greedy, ruthless employers. Businessmen took advantage of unemployment to force workers to labor twelve and fourteen hours a day for a pittance so small that not only wives, but children scarcely out of infancy, had to enter the factories to contribute their mite to the family earnings. The benefits which we today can so readily recognize as the fruits of the First Industrial Revolution were achieved only after decades of privation, misery, and ruthless exploitation for millions of working people.

Most of us find it difficult to believe that the Second Industrial Revolution—the Automation Revolution—can possibly produce similar results. But if vast social dislocations are prevented this time, it will be only because the combined social wisdom of private groups and government will be used to prevent them.

We now know that the greatest good of society is not served by permitting economic forces to operate blindly, regardless of consequences. We now know that economic forces are man-made and subject to controls, that the economic and social consequences of economic decisions can be foreseen, and when the consequences threaten to be harmful, preventive action can be taken. That philosophy is expressed, however imperfectly, in the Employment Act of 1946. We recognize today that it is not only possible, but necessary, for the government to analyze, to foresee, and to give direction to the economic forces that determine whether we shall have prosperity or depression. . . .

Let us consider some of the specific problems that will have to be met. One of the major problems is that no one as yet has made a thorough study of what has been done in the field of automation, what is being planned for the near future, or what impact it has had or will have on our lives. As a result, an exhaustive list of the problems that automation will pose does not yet exist.

There are some problems, however, which can be foreseen. Obviously, there will be problems for the workers who are displaced from their jobs by automation. This is not merely a problem of finding a new job. One point on which most of the writers on automation seem agreed is that, by its very nature, automation will tend to eliminate unskilled and semiskilled jobs, while the new jobs it creates will be at a much higher level of skill. As one spokesman for the Ford Motor Company has put it: "The hand trucker of today replaced by a conveyor belt might become tomorrow's electronics engineer."

That sounds very nice, but it immediately poses the problem: *How* does the hand trucker become an electronics engineer—or a skilled technician? If automation destroys unskilled jobs and creates skilled jobs, means must be found to train large members of unskilled workers in the needed skills.

Another aspect of the same problem is that of the worker with a specialized skill who finds that his skill has been made valueless because a machine has taken over his job—such as the skilled machine operator displaced by a self-operating lathe or the bookkeeper whose job is taken over by an electronic "brain."

You can easily see that if automation is going to displace any substantial number of workers in either of these two ways, we will need a carefully organized retraining program to give them the opportunity of acquiring the skills they will need. Such a program must take into account the needs of the workers, the fact that most of them will be mature men and women to whom the learning of new skills may not come easily, and that they have to live and support their families while they are acquiring these skills. The program will require not merely training facilities and expert vocational guidance. It will have to include provisions for training allowances to replace lost wages during the training period.

Without such a program, there may be a job as an electronics engineer for the hand trucker's son, but the hand trucker himself may have to join the ranks of the unemployed—one of a "lost generation" of workers who will have been scrapped as ruthlessly as so many items of obsolete equipment.

An alternative solution will have to be found in the case of older workers, not old enough for normal retirement, but too old to learn new skills or to adjust to the demands of the new technology. A single instance will be enough to point up the problem. This is from a report in the *New York Post:*

> Then there are workers who can't keep up with automation. Such as Stanley Tylak. Tylak, 61 and for 27 years a job setter at Ford, was shifted from the River Rouge foundry machine shop to the new automated engine plant. He was given a chance to work at a big new automatic machine.
>
> Simply, straightforwardly, he told his story: "The machine had about 80 drills and 22 blocks going through. You had to watch all the time. Every few minutes you had to watch to see everything was all right. And the machines had so many lights and switches—about 90 lights. It sure is hard on your mind.
>
> "If there's a break in the machine the whole line breaks down. But sometimes you make a little mistake, and it's no good for you, no good for the foreman, no good for the company, no good for the union."
>
> And so Stanley Tylak, baffled by the machine he couldn't keep up with, had to take another job—at lower pay.

This was a case where automation resulted in downgrading—not the upgrading so widely heralded by industry spokesmen as one of the fruits of automation. Yet, in one sense, Stanley Tylak was lucky. He at least was able to take another job. In many cases, there will be no other jobs available for a man in his sixties, or even younger. Perhaps if Stanley Tylak had been given more than just a chance to work at the new machine, perhaps if he had been given careful training for the job, taking into account the difficulties of adjustment to a new job at his age, he could have learned to do it even at sixty-one. But for those older workers who cannot adjust, I think we must be prepared to offer the opportunity of early retirement with the assurance of an adequate pension. . . .

We in the CIO do not pretend to have the answers to all the problems posed by automation. We are quite sure, in fact, that no one can have all the answers at present. Not nearly enough is known yet about the current achievements of automation, the planned progress of automation, or the precise impact that automation will have on productivity, on employment, and on the national economy. . . .

The results of these hearings and ensuing studies should lead to positive recommendation from this Committee to the Congress. Such recommendations should cover the problems of displaced workers, industry migrations, stranded communities, small business and education requirements. Above all, such recommendations should promote national economic policies, designed to expand consumer purchasing power, with sufficient speed so that we shall be able to buy and consume the vast flood of goods and services made available by automation. Such policy recommendations should be aimed at taking full advantage of the opportunities presented by rapid productivity increases—to improve federal, state, and local facilities in health, housing, education, natural resources, and other fields of public activity.

We must do all in our power to make sure that the potential abundance of the new technology will be used with social wisdom to improve standards of living and welfare and to provide increased leisure for all Americans.

These are great tasks. In the years that lie immediately ahead, we shall have to undertake these tasks, because the new technology confronts us with a tremendous challenge. If we refuse to accept that challenge, if we fail to solve the problems that will probably crowd upon us, we may be forced to undergo shattering economic dislocations that could threaten our whole economy and our free society.

If we accept the challenge of the new technology, if we use foresight and act wisely and vigorously, we can help to usher in an age of abundance and freedom, the like of which the world has never known.

SELECTION 42

The Problem of Poverty: From Michael Harrington, "The Other America"

A second economic problem was the existence of lingering poverty in an economy characterized by general prosperity. The fact that many Americans were not participating in the postwar boom was pointed out by Harvard economist John Kenneth Galbraith in The Affluent Society *(1958). More often cited than read, Galbraith's book was taken as a description of prosperity. His title was borrowed as a label for boom-time America. His point about the extent of poverty won wide acceptance only after it was popularized by journalist Michael Harrington in a striking book entitled* The Other America *(Macmillan, 1962). The document below is taken from pages 1–7 of Harrington's book.*

There is a familiar America. It is celebrated in speeches and advertised on television and in the magazines. It has the highest mass standard of living the world has ever known.

In the 1950's this America worried about itself, yet even its anxieties were products of abundance. The title of a brilliant book was widely misinterpreted, and the familiar America began to call itself "the affluent society." There was introspection about Madison Avenue and tail fins; there was discussion of the emotional suffering taking place in the suburbs. In all this, there was an implicit assumption that the basic grinding economic problems had been solved in the United States. In this theory the nation's problems were no longer a matter of basic human needs, of food, shelter, and clothing. Now they were seen as qualitative, a question of learning to live decently amid luxury.

While this discussion was carried on, there existed another America. In it dwelt somewhere between 40,000,000 and 50,000,000 citizens of this land. They were poor. They still are.

To be sure, the other America is not impoverished in the same sense as those poor nations were where millions cling to hunger as a defense against starvation. This country has escaped such extremes. That does not change the fact that tens of millions of Americans are, at this very moment, maimed in body and spirit, existing at levels beneath those necessary for human decency. If these people are not starving, they are hungry, and sometimes fat with hunger, for that is what cheap foods do. They are without adequate housing and education and medical care.

The Government has documented what this means to the bodies of the poor, and the figures will be cited throughout this book. But even more basic, this poverty twists and deforms the spirit. The American poor are pessimistic and defeated, and they are victimized by mental suffering to a degree unknown in Suburbia.

This book is a description of the world in which these people live; it is about the other America. Here are the unskilled workers, the migrant farm workers, the aged, the minorities, and all the others who live in the economic underworld of American life. In all this, there will be statistics, and that offers the opportunity for disagreement among honest and sincere men. I would ask the reader to respond critically to every assertion, but not to allow statistical quibbling to obscure the huge, enormous, and intolerable fact of poverty in America. For, when all is said and done, that fact is unmistakable, whatever its exact dimensions, and the truly human reaction can only be outrage. As W. H. Auden wrote:

> Hunger allows no choice
> To the citizen or the police;
> We must love one another or die.

I

The millions who are poor in the United States tend to become increasingly invisible. Here is a great mass of people, yet it takes an effort of the intellect and will even to see them.

I discovered this personally in a curious way. After I wrote my first article on poverty in America, I had all the statistics down on paper. I had proved to my satisfaction that there were around 50,000,000 poor in this country. Yet, I realized I did not believe my own figures. The poor existed in the Government reports; they were percentages and numbers in long, close columns, but they were not part of my experience. I could prove that the other America existed, but I had never been there.

My response was not accidental. It was typical of what is happening to an entire society, and it reflects profound social changes in this nation. The other America, the America of poverty, is hidden today in a way that it never was before. Its millions are socially invisible to the rest of us. No wonder that so many misinterpreted Galbraith's title and assumed that "the affluent society" meant that everyone had a decent standard of life. The misinterpretation was true as far as the actual day-to-day lives of two-thirds of the nation were concerned. Thus, one must begin a description of the other America by understanding why we do not see it.

There are perennial reasons that make the other America an invisible land.

Poverty is often off the beaten track. It always has been. The ordinary tourist never left the main highway, and today he rides interstate turnpikes. He does not go into the valleys of Pennsylvania where the towns look like movie sets of Wales in the thirties. He does not see the company houses in rows, the rutted roads (the poor always have bad roads whether they live in the city, in towns, or on farms), and everything is black and dirty. And even if he were to pass through such a place by accident, the tourist would not meet the unemployed men in the bar or the women coming home from a runaway sweatshop.

Then, too, beauty and myths are perennial masks of poverty. The traveler comes to the Appalachians in the lovely season. He sees the hills, the streams, the foliage—but not the poor. Or perhaps he looks at a rundown mountain house and, remembering Rousseau rather than seeing with his eyes, decides that "those people" are truly fortunate to be living the way they are and that they are lucky to be exempt from the strains and tensions of the middle class. The only problem is that "those people," the quaint inhabitants of those hills, are undereducated, underprivileged, lack medical care, and are in the process of being forced from the land into a life in the cities, where they are misfits.

These are normal and obvious causes of the invisibility of the poor. They operated a generation ago; they will be functioning a generation hence. It is more important to understand that the very development of American society is creating a new kind of blindness about poverty. The poor are increasingly slipping out of the very experience and consciousness of the nation.

If the middle class never did like ugliness and poverty, it was at least aware of them. "Across the tracks" was not a very long way to go. There were forays into the slums at Christmas time; there were charitable organizations that brought contact with the poor. Occasionally, almost everyone passed through the Negro ghetto or the blocks of tenements, if only to get downtown to work or to entertainment.

Now the American city has been transformed. The poor still inhabit the miserable housing in the central area, but they are increasingly isolated from contact with, or sight of, anybody else. Middle-class women coming in from Suburbia on a rare trip may catch the merest glimpse of the other America on the way to an evening at the theater, but their children are segregated in suburban schools. The business or professional man may drive along the fringes of slums in a car or bus, but it is not an important experience to him. The failures, the unskilled, the disabled, the aged, and the minorities are right there, across the tracks, where they have always been. But hardly anyone else is.

In short, the very development of the American city has removed poverty from the living, emotional experience of millions upon millions of middle-class Americans. Living out in the suburbs, it is easy to assume that ours is, indeed, an affluent society.

This new segregation of poverty is compounded by a well-meaning ignorance. A good many concerned and sympathetic Americans are aware that there is much discussion of urban renewal. Suddenly, driving through the city, they notice that a familiar slum has been torn down and that there are towering, modern buildings where once there had been tenements or hovels. There is a warm feeling of satisfaction, of pride in the way things are working out: the poor, it is obvious, are being taken care of.

The irony in this . . . is that the truth is nearly the exact opposite to the impression. The total impact of the various housing programs in postwar America has been to squeeze more and more people into existing slums. More often than not, the modern apartment in a towering building rents at $40 a room or more. For, during the past decade and a half, there has been more subsidization of middle- and upper-income housing than there has been of housing for the poor.

Clothes make the poor invisible too: America has the best-dressed poverty the world has ever known. For a variety of reasons, the benefits of mass production have been spread much more evenly in this area than in many others. It is much easier in the United States to be decently dressed than it is to be decently housed, fed, or doctored. Even people with terribly depressed incomes can look prosperous.

This is an extremely important factor in defining our emotional and existential ignorance of poverty. In Detroit the existence of social classes became much more difficult to discern the day the companies put lockers in the plants. From that moment on, one did not see men in work clothes on the way to the factory, but citizens in slacks and white shirts. This process has been magnified with the poor throughout the country. There are tens of thousands of Americans in the big cities who are wearing shoes, perhaps even a stylishly cut suit or dress, and yet are hungry. It is not a matter of planning, though it almost seems as if the affluent society had given out costumes to the poor so that they would not offend the rest of society with the sight of rags.

Then, many of the poor are the wrong age to be seen. A good number of them (over 8,000,000) are sixty-five years years of age or better; an even larger number are under eighteen. The aged members of the other America are often sick, and they cannot move. Another group of them live out their lives in loneliness and frustration: they sit in rented rooms, or else they stay close to a house in a neighborhood that has completely changed from the old days. Indeed, one of the worst aspects of poverty among the aged is that these people are out of sight and out of mind, and alone.

The young are somewhat more visible, yet they too stay close to their neighborhoods. Sometimes they advertise their poverty through a lurid tabloid story about a gang killing. But generally they do not disturb the quiet streets of the middle class.

And finally, the poor are politically invisible. It is one of the cruelest ironies of social life in advanced countries that the dispossessed at the bottom of society are unable to speak for themselves. The people of the other America do not, by far and large, belong to unions, to fraternal organizations, or to political parties. They are without lobbies of their own; they put forward no legislative program. As a group, they are atomized. They have no face; they have no voice.

Thus, there is not even a cynical political motive for caring about the poor, as in the old days. Because the slums are no longer centers of powerful political organizations, the politicians need not really care about their inhabitants. The slums are no longer visible to the middle class, so much of the idealistic urge to fight for those who need help is gone. Only the social agencies have a really direct involvement with the other America, and they are without any great political power.

To the extent that the poor have a spokesman in American life, that role is played by the labor movement. The unions have their own particular idealism, an ideology of concern. More than that, they realize that the existence of a reservoir of cheap, unorganized labor is a menace to wages and working conditions throughout the entire economy. Thus, many union legislative proposals—to extend the coverage of minimum wage and social security, to organize migrant farm laborers—articulate the needs of the poor.

That the poor are invisible is one of the most important things about them. They are not simply neglected and forgotten as in the old rhetoric of reform; what is much worse, they are not seen. . . .

Questions of Values

During the post-World War II boom, questions began to rise about the impact of prosperity on American life and values. In The Lonely Crowd *(1950) lawyer-sociologist David Riesman suggested that Americans were becoming much more conformist. William H. Whyte, Jr., enlarged on this theme. In a widely read and widely quoted book, he developed a label for the type of American emerging in a society characterized by prosperity and progress toward automation—"the organization man." The first document below is an excerpt from this book,* The Organization Man *(Simon and Schuster, 1956), pages 3–9.*

Meanwhile, however, there was a minority in America that made a religion out of nonconformity. These men and women, mostly young, were called "beatniks." Insofar as they articulated a philosophy, it was simply that life was too short and uncertain to be spent purposefully. They devoted themselves to such self-gratification as could be obtained with a minimum of work. In effect, they became bums, living from hand to mouth and earning just enough for drink, food, and the roughest kind of wardrobe. The bulk of their time was spent in such occupations as listening to or playing jazz or folk music or seeking self-expression in wild works of poetry or art. The value system of the beatniks is suggested in the second document below. An excerpt from a novel by a one-time beatnik, it is taken from Jack Kerouac, On the Road *(The Viking Press, 1957), pages 238–242, 309–310.*

PROTEST AGAINST CONFORMITY: FROM WILLIAM H. WHYTE, JR., "THE ORGANIZATION MAN"

This book is about the organization man. If the term is vague, it is because I can think of no other way to describe the people I am talking about. They are not the workers, nor are they the white-collar people in the usual, clerk sense of the word. These people only work for The Organization. The ones I am talking about *belong* to it as well. They are the ones of our middle class who have left home, spiritually as well as physically, to take the vows of organization life, and it is they who are the mind and soul of our great self-perpetuating institutions. Only a few are top managers or ever will be. In a system that makes such hazy terminology as "junior executive" psychologically necessary, they are of the staff as much as the line, and most are destined to live poised in a middle area that still awaits a satisfactory euphemism. But they are the dominant members of our society nonetheless. They have not joined together into a recognizable elite—our country does not stand still long enough for that—but it is from their ranks that are coming most of the first and second echelons of our leadership, and it is their values which will set the American temper.

The corporation man is the most conspicuous example, but he is only one, for the collectivization so visible in the corporation has affected almost every field of work. Blood brother to the business trainee off to join Du Pont is the seminary student who will end up in the church hierarchy, the doctor headed for the corporate clinic, the physics Ph.D. in a government laboratory, the intellectual on the foundation-sponsored team project, the engineering graduate in the huge drafting room at Lockheed, the young apprentice in a Wall Street law factory.

They are all, as they so often put it, in the same boat. Listen to them talk to each other over the front lawns of their suburbia and you cannot help but be struck by how well they grasp the common denominators which bind them. Whatever the differences in their organization ties, it is the common problems of collective work that dominate their attentions, and when the Du Pont man talks to the research chemist or the chemist to the army man, it is these problems that are uppermost. The word *collective* most of them can't bring themselves to use—except to describe foreign countries or organizations they don't work for—but they are keenly aware of how much more deeply beholden they are to organization than were their elders. They are wry about it, to be sure; they talk of the "treadmill," the "rat race," of the inability to control one's direction. But they have no great sense of plight; between themselves and organization they believe they see an ultimate harmony and, more than most elders recognize, they are building an ideology that will vouchsafe this trust.

It is the growth of this ideology, and its practical effects, that is the thread I wish to follow in this book. America has paid much attention to the economic and political consequences of big organization—the concentration of power in large corporations, for example, the political power of the civil-service bureaucracies, the possible emergence of a managerial hierarchy that might dominate the rest of us. These are proper concerns, but no less important is the principal impact that organization life has had on the individuals within it. A collision has been taking place—indeed, hundreds of thousands of them, and in the aggregate they have been producing what I believe is a major shift in American ideology.

Officially, we are a people who hold to the Protestant Ethic. Because of the denominational implications of the term many would deny its relevance to them, but let them eulogize the American Dream, however, and they virtually define the Protestant Ethic. Whatever the embroidery, there is almost always the thought that pursuit of individual salvation through hard work, thrift, and competitive struggle is the heart of the American achievement.

But the harsh facts of organization life simply do not jibe with these precepts. This conflict is certainly not a peculiarly American development. In their own countries such Europeans as Max Weber and Durkheim many years ago foretold the change, and though Europeans now like to see their troubles as an American export, the problems they speak of stem from a bureaucratization of society that has affected every Western country.

It is in America, however, that the contrast between the old ethic and current reality has been most apparent—and most poignant. Of all peoples it is we who have led in the public worship of individualism. One hundred years ago De Tocqueville was noting that though our special genius—and failing—lay in co-operative action, we talked more than others of personal independence and freedom. We kept on, and as late as the twenties, when big organization was long since a fact, affirmed the old faith as if nothing had really changed at all.

Today many still try, and it is the members of the kind of organization most responsible for the change, the corporation, who try the hardest. It is the corporation man whose institutional ads protest so much that Americans speak up in town meeting, that Americans are the best inventors because Americans don't care that other people scoff, that Americans are the best soldiers because they have so much initiative and native ingenuity, that the boy selling papers on the street corner is the prototype of our business society. Collectivism? He abhors it, and when he makes his ritualistic attack on Welfare Statism, it is in terms of a Protestant Ethic undefiled by change—the sacredness of property, the enervating effect of security, the virtues of thrift, of hard work and independence. Thanks be, he says, that there are some people left—e.g., businessmen—to defend the American Dream.

He is not being hypocritical, only compulsive. He honestly wants to believe he follows the tenets he extols, and if he extols them so frequently it is, perhaps, to shut out a nagging suspicion that he, too, the last defender of the faith, is no longer pure. Only by using the language of individualism to describe the collective can he stave off the thought that he himself is in a collective as pervading as any ever dreamed of by the reformers, the intellectuals, and the utopian visionaries he so regularly warns against.

The older generation may still convince themselves; the younger generation does not. When a young man says that to make a living these days you must do what somebody else wants you to do, he states it not only as a fact of life that must be accepted but as an inherently good proposition. If the American Dream deprecates this for him, it is the American Dream that is going to have to give, whatever its more elderly guardians may think. People grow restive with a mythology that is too distant from the way things actually are, and as more and more lives have been encompassed by the organization way of life, the pressures for an accompanying ideological shift have been mounting. The pressures of the group, the frustrations of individual creativity, the anonymity of achievement: are these defects to struggle against—or are they virtues in disguise? The organization man seeks a redefinition of his place on earth—a faith that will satisfy him that what he must endure has a deeper meaning than appears on the surface. He needs, in short, something that will do for him what the Protestant Ethic did once. And slowly, almost imperceptibly, a body of thought has been coalescing that does that.

I am going to call it a Social Ethic. With reason it could be called an organization ethic, or a bureaucratic ethic; more than anything else it rationalizes the organization's demands for fealty and gives those who offer it wholeheartedly a sense of dedication in doing so—*in extremis,* you might say, it converts what would seem in other times a bill of no rights into a restatement of individualism.

But there is a real moral imperative behind it, and whether one inclines to its beliefs or not he must acknowledge that this moral basis, not mere expediency, is the source of its power. Nor is it simply an opiate for those who must work in big organizations. The search for a secular faith that it represents can be found throughout our society—and among those who swear they would never set foot in a corporation or a government bureau. Though it has its greatest applicability to the organization man, its ideological underpinnings have been provided not by the organization man but by intellectuals he knows little of and toward whom, indeed, he tends to be rather suspicious.

Any groove of abstraction, Whitehead once remarked, is bound to be an inadequate way of describing reality, and so with the concept of the Social Ethic. It is an attempt to illustrate an underlying consistency in what in actuality is by no means an orderly system of thought. No one says, "I believe in the social ethic," and though many would subscribe wholeheartedly to the separate ideas that make it up, these ideas have yet to be put together in the final, harmonious synthesis. But the unity is there.

In looking at what might seem dissimilar aspects of organization society, it is this unity I wish to underscore. The "professionalization" of the manager, for example, and the drive for a more practical education are parts of the same phenomenon; just as the student now feels technique more vital than content, so the trainee believes managing an end in itself, an *expertise* relatively independent of the content of what is being managed. And the reasons are the same. So too in other sectors of our society; for all the differences in particulars, dominant is a growing accommodation to the needs of society—and a growing urge to justify it.

Let me now define my terms. By Social Ethic I mean that contemporary body of thought which makes morally legitimate the pressures of society against the individual. Its major propositions are three: a belief in the group as the source of creativity; a belief in "belongingness" as the ultimate need of the individual; and a belief in the application of science to achieve the belongingness.

. . . I think the gist can be paraphrased thus: Man exists as a unit of society. Of himself, he is isolated, meaningless; only as he collaborates with others does he become worth while, for by sublimating himself in the group, he helps produce a whole that is greater than the sum of its parts. There should be, then, no conflict between man and society. What we think are conflicts are misunderstandings, breakdowns in communication. By applying the methods of science to human relations we can eliminate these obstacles to consensus and create an equilibrium in which society's needs and the needs of the individual are one and the same.

Essentially, it is a utopian faith. Superficially, it seems dedicated to the practical problems of organization life, and its proponents often use the word *hard* (versus *soft*) to describe their approach. But it is the long-range promise that animates its followers, for it relates techniques to the vision of a finite, achievable harmony. It is quite reminiscent of the beliefs of utopian communities of the 1840s. As in the Owen communities, there is the same idea that man's character is decided, almost irretrievably, by his environment. As in the Fourier communities, there is the same faith that there need be no conflict between the individual's aspirations and the community's wishes, because it is the natural order of things that the two be synonymous.

Like the utopian communities, it interprets society in a fairly narrow, immediate sense. One can believe man has a social obligation and that the individual must ultimately contribute to the community without believing that group harmony is the test of it. In the Social Ethic I am describing, however, man's obligation is in the here and now; his duty is not so much to the community in a broad sense but to the actual, physical one about him, and the idea that in isolation from it—or active rebellion against it—he might eventually discharge the greater service is little considered. In practice, those who most eagerly subscribe to the Social Ethic worry very little over the long-range problems of society. It is not that they don't care but rather that they tend to assume that the ends of organization and morality coincide, and on such matters as social welfare they give their proxy to the organization.

It is possible that I am attaching too much weight to what, after all, is something of a mythology. Those more sanguine than I have argued that this faith is betrayed by reality in some key respects and that because it cannot long hide from organization man that life is still essentially competitive the faith must fall of its own weight. They also maintain that the Social Ethic is only one trend in a society which is a prolific breeder of counter-trends. The farther the pendulum swings, they believe, the more it must eventually swing back.

I am not persuaded. We are indeed a flexible people, but society is not a clock and to stake so much on counter-trends is to put a rather heavy burden on providence. Let me get ahead of my story a bit with two examples of trend vs. counter-trend. One is the long-term swing to the highly vocational business-administration courses. Each year for seven years I have collected all the speeches by businessmen, educators, and others on the subject, and invariably each year the gist of them is that this particular pendulum has swung much too far and that there will shortly be a reversal. Similarly sanguine, many academic people have been announcing that they discern the beginnings of a popular swing back to the humanities. Another index is the growth of personality testing. Regularly year after year many social scientists have assured me that this bowdlerization of psychology is a contemporary aberration soon to be laughed out of court.

Meanwhile, the organization world grinds on. Each year the number of business-administration majors has increased over the last year—until, in 1954, they together made up the largest single field of undergraduate instruction outside of the field of education itself. Personality testing? Again, each year the number of people subjected to it has grown, and the criticism has served mainly to make organizations more adept in sugar-coating their purpose. No one can say whether these trends will continue to outpace the counter-trends, but neither can we trust that an equilibrium-minded providence will see to it that excesses will cancel each other out. Counter-trends there are. There always have been, and in the sweep of ideas ineffectual many have proved to be.

It is also true that the Social Ethic is something of a mythology, and there is a great difference between mythology and practice. An individualism as stringent, as selfish as that often preached in the name of the Protestant Ethic would never have been tolerated, and in reality our predecessors co-operated with one another far more skillfully than nineteenth-century oratory would suggest. Something of the obverse is true of the Social Ethic; so complete a denial of individual will won't work either, and even the most willing believers in the group harbor some secret misgivings, some latent antagonism toward the pressures they seek to deify.

But the Social Ethic is no less powerful for that, and though it can never produce the peace of mind it seems to offer, it will help shape the nature of the quest in the years to come. The old dogma of individualism betrayed reality too, yet few would argue, I dare say, that it was not an immensely powerful influence in the time of its dominance. So I argue of the Social Ethic; call it mythology, if you will, but it is becoming the dominant one.

THE BEATNIK WAY: FROM JACK KEROUAC, "ON THE ROAD"

. . . "Oh, man," said Dean to me as we stood in front of a bar, "dig the street of life, the Chinamen that cut by in Chicago. What a weird town. . . . Whee. Sal, we gotta go and never stop going till we get there."

"Where we going, man?"

"I don't know but we gotta go." Then here came a gang of young bop musicians carrying their instruments out of cars. They piled right into a saloon and we followed them. They set themselves up and started blowing. There we were! The leader was a slender, drooping, curly-haired, pursy-mouthed tenorman, thin of shoulder, draped loose in a sports shirt, cool in the warm night, self-indulgence written in his eyes, who picked up his horn and frowned in it and blew cool and complex and was dainty stamping his foot to catch ideas, and ducked to miss others—and said, "Blow," very quietly when the other boys took solos. Then there was Prez, a husky, handsome blond like a freckled boxer, meticulously wrapped inside his sharkskin plaid suit with the long drape and the collar falling back and the tie undone for exact sharpness and casualness, sweating and hitching up his horn and writhing into it, and a tone just like Lester Young himself. "You see, man, Prez has the technical anxieties of a money-making musician, he's the only one who's well dressed, see him grow worried when he blows a clinker, but the leader, that cool cat, tells him not to worry and just blow and blow—the mere sound and serious exuberance of the music is all *he* cares about. He's an artist. He's teaching young Prez the boxer. Now the others dig!!" The third sax was an alto, eighteen-year-old cool, contemplative young Charlie-Parker-type Negro from high school, with a broadgash mouth, taller than the rest, grave. He raised his horn and blew into it quietly and thoughtfully and elicited birdlike phrases and and architectural Miles Davis logics. These were the children of the great bop innovators.

Once there was Louis Armstrong blowing his beautiful top in the muds of New Orleans; before him the mad musicians who had paraded on official days and broke up their Sousa marches into ragtime. Then there was swing, and Roy Eldridge, vigorous and virile, blasting the horn for everything it had in waves of power and logic and subtlety—leaning to it with glittering eyes and a lovely smile and sending it out broadcast to rock the jazz world. Then had come Charlie Parker, a kid in his mother's woodshed in Kansas City, blowing his taped-up alto among the logs, practicing on rainy days, coming out to watch the old swinging Basie and Benny Moten band that had Hot Lips Page and the rest—Charlie Parker leaving home and coming to Harlem, and meeting mad Thelonius Monk and madder Gillespie—Charlie Parker in his early days when he was flipped and walked around in a circle while playing. Somewhat younger than Lester

Young, also from KC, that gloomy, saintly goof in whom the history of jazz was wrapped; for when he held his horn high and horizontal from his mouth he blew the greatest; and as his hair grew longer and he got lazier and stretched-out, his horn came down halfway; till it finally fell all the way and today as he wears his thick-soled shoes so that he can't feel the sidewalks of life his horn is held weakly against his chest, and he blows cool and easy getout phrases. Here were the children of the American bop night.

Stranger flowers yet—for as the Negro alto mused over everyone's head with dignity, the young, tall, slender, blond kid from Curtis Street, Denver, jeans and studded belt, sucked on his mouthpiece while waiting for the others to finish; and when they did he started, and you had to look around to see where the solo was coming from, for it came from angelical smiling lips upon the mouthpiece and it was a soft, sweet, fairy-tale solo on an alto. Lonely as America, a throatpierced sound in the night.

What of the others and all the soundmaking? There was the bass-player, wiry redhead with wild eyes, jabbing his hips at the fiddle with every driving slap, at hot moments his mouth hanging open trancelike. "Man, there's a cat who can really *bend* his girl!" The sad drummer, like our white hipster in Frisco Folsom Street, completely goofed, staring into space, chewing gum, wide-eyed, rocking the neck with Reich kick and complacent ecstasy. The piano—a big husky Italian truck-driving kid with meaty hands, a burly and thoughtful joy. They played an hour. Nobody was listening. Old North Clark bums lolled at the bar, whores screeched in anger. Secret Chinamen went by. Noises of hootchy-kootchy interfered. They went right on. Out on the sidewalk came an apparition—a sixteen-year-old kid with a goatee and a trombone case. Thin as rickets, mad-faced, he wanted to join this group and blow with them. They knew him and didn't want to bother with him. He crept into the bar and surreptitiously undid his trombone and raised it to his lips. No opening. Nobody looked at him. They finished, packed up, and left for another bar. He wanted to jump, skinny Chicago kid. He slapped on his dark glasses, raised the trombone to his lips alone in the bar, and went "Baugh!" Then he rushed out after them. They wouldn't let him play with them, just like the sandlot football team in back of the gas tank. "All these guys live with their grandmothers just like Tom Snark and our Carlo Marx alto," said Dean. We rushed after the whole gang. They went into Anita O'Day's club and there unpacked and played till nine o'clock in the morning. Dean and I were there with beers. . . .

Suddenly Dean stared into the darkness of a corner beyond the bandstand and said, "Sal, God has arrived."

I looked. *George Shearing.* And as always he leaned his blind head on his pale hand, all ears opened like the ears of an elephant, listening to the American sounds and mastering them for his own English summer's-night use. Then they urged him to get up and play. He did. He played innumerable choruses with amazing chords that mounted higher and higher till the sweat splashed all over the piano and everybody listened in awe and fright. They led him off the stand after an hour. He went back to his dark corner, old God Shearing, and the boys said, "There ain't nothing left after that."

But the slender leader frowned. "Let's blow anyway."

Something would come of it yet. There's always more, a little further—

it never ends. They sought to find new phrases after Shearing's explorations; they tried hard. They writhed and twisted and blew. Every now and then a clear harmonic cry gave new suggestions of a tune that would someday be the only tune in the world and would raise men's souls to joy. They found it, they lost, they wrestled for it, they found it again, they laughed, they moaned—and Dean sweated at the table and told them to go, go, go. At nine o'clock in the morning everybody—musicians, girls in slacks, bartenders, and the one little skinny, unhappy trombonist—staggered out of the club into the great roar of Chicago day to sleep until the wild bop night again. . . .

So in America when the sun goes down and I sit on the old broken-down river pier watching the long, long skies over New Jersey and sense all that raw land that rolls in one unbelievable huge bulge over to the West Coast, and all that road going, all the people dreaming in the immensity of it, and in Iowa I know by now the children must be crying in the land where they let the children cry, and tonight the stars'll be out, and don't you know that God is Pooh Bear? the evening star must be drooping and shedding her sparkler dims on the prairie, which is just before the coming of complete night that blesses the earth, darkens all rivers, cups the peaks and folds the final shore in, and nobody, nobody knows what's going to happen to anybody besides the forlorn rags of growing old. . . .

SELECTION 44

The Civil Rights Revolution

In the 1950s, American Negroes began more loudly than in the past to assert their claim to equality. Through most of the ninety years since emancipation, they had benefited only meagerly from the economic and social advance of the rest of the nation. In the North and West, they had poor housing, poor schooling, and poor jobs. In the South, they were segregated, living in conditions halfway between slavery and freedom.

With increasing vigor, Negro leaders protested the Negro's second-class status. The National Association for the Advancement of Colored People and the Urban League grew in strength and numbers. Then, in 1954, the United States Supreme Court took a bold step which, as it turned out, liberated all the energies that the Negro community had quietly been gathering.

The Supreme Court received a case that involved segregation of Negro children in an all-Negro school. The case arose not in the South but in Topeka, Kansas. In the past, the Court had turned away such cases. It had abided by an 1896 ruling, in Plessy v. Ferguson, *that constitutional rights were not impaired if states, counties, or municipalities provided Negroes with facilities that were "separate but equal." Now, the Court decided to reexamine this doctrine. It heard arguments not only on the Topeka case but on other, similar cases rising in Southern states. On May 17, 1954, Chief Justice Earl Warren delivered the opinion of a unanimous Court, overturning the* Plessy *precedent and declaring that school segregation deprived Negroes of the equal protection of the law. The Court's opinion is the first document below. It is* Brown et al. v. Board of Education of Topeka et al. *from* United States Supreme Court Reports, *volume 347 (1953–1954), pages 486–488, 492–495.*

After the school desegregation decision, Negroes organized to demand an end to other kinds of segregation. In Montgomery, Alabama, in December, 1955, a boycott of the city bus system was organized. Negroes there demanded that they no longer be required by law to sit on the back seats and to stand while white passengers sat. Through a period of many months, the Negroes maintained the boycott, in spite of legal reprisals and other measures of coercion adopted by Montgomery's whites. The United States Supreme Court finally upheld the Negroes' position, and Montgomery's buses were desegregated.

In the meantime, Negroes of the South and of the nation had found a leader and a doctrine. The chief organizer of the Montgomery boycott, the Rev. Dr. Martin Luther King, Jr., became a hero to Negroes and to white antisegregationists the nation over. In Montgomery, King had preached a doctrine of nonviolent resistance. It had worked, and to millions it seemed the solution to the problem of how the Negro was to win his rights without a bloody revolution. The second document below is an excerpt from King's account of the Montgomery bus boycott. It includes his exposition of the doctrine of nonviolent resistance. It is taken from Martin Luther King, Jr., Stride toward Freedom: The Montgomery Story *(Ballantine, 1958), pages 32–38, 43–44, 81–86, 115–116, 121–122, and 130–132.*

After Montgomery, the pace of the Negro rights movement quickened. Acting together, young Negroes and young whites campaigned to end segregation at lunch counters in the South. They conducted "sit-ins." Sitting down and refusing to leave until served, they forced lunch-counter owners either to desegregate or shut down. Though subjected to violence by hostile whites, the young crusaders obeyed King's doctrine. And they won. In many cities throughout the South, racial barriers were lifted. Negroes became able to eat alongside whites.

Groups of "freedom riders" then challenged segregation at bus terminals in the South. Traveling in groups by bus or car, they disregarded the ordinances that assigned whites and Negroes to separate waiting rooms and rest rooms. In places, violence resulted. But again it was violence on the part of white segregationists.

As time passed, the Federal government was drawn more and more into the Negroes' battle for equality. When Southerners resisted desegregation of schools or colleges, Federal troops or Federal marshals were sometimes needed to force their compliance. President Eisenhower used troops at Little Rock, Arkansas; President Kennedy at Oxford, Mississippi. Federal forces were also required on occasion to protect freedom riders and, as in Alabama in 1965, to safeguard the rights of groups conducting demonstrations.

The protest movement was by no means confined to the South. Demonstrations against "de facto *segregation" erupted in New York, Philadelphia, San Francisco, Los Angeles, and other Northern and Western cities. But the most important immediate aim remained desegregation in the South, and leaders in the movement became more and more urgent in asking stronger Federal law for use against recalcitrant Southern officials.*

In 1957 and 1960, Congress responded mildly. Congress passed civil rights acts that made it slightly less difficult for Negroes in the South to vote. Leaders of the protest movement clamored for more. In 1964, they were at last rewarded with a strong Civil Rights Act which stiffened the guarantees of the Negro's right to vote and made unlawful any segregation in places of public accommodation.

The third document below is the Civil Rights Act of 1964. It is taken from United States Statutes at Large, *volume 78 (1964), pages 241–268.*

SCHOOL DESEGREGATION: BROWN v. TOPEKA BOARD OF EDUCATION

Mr. Chief Justice Warren delivered the opinion of the Court.

These cases come to us from the States of Kansas, South Carolina, Virginia, and Delaware. They are premised on different facts and different local conditions, but a common legal question justifies their consideration together in this consolidated opinion.

In each of the cases, minors of the Negro race, through their legal representatives, seek the aid of the courts in obtaining admission to the public schools of their community on a nonsegregated basis. In each instance, they had been denied admission to schools attended by white children under laws requiring or permitting segregation according to race. This segregation was alleged to deprive the plaintiffs of the equal protection of the laws under the Fourteenth Amendment. In each of the cases other than the Delaware case, a three-judge federal district court denied relief to the plaintiffs on the so-called "separate but equal" doctrine announced by this Court in *Plessy* v. *Ferguson,* 163 U. S. 537 [1896 (*ed.*)]. Under that doctrine, equality of treatment is accorded when the races are provided substantially equal facilities, even though these facilities be separate. In the Delaware case, the Supreme Court of Delaware adhered to that doctrine, but ordered that the plaintiffs be admitted to the white schools because of their superiority to the Negro schools.

The plaintiffs contend that segregated public schools are not "equal" and cannot be made "equal," and that hence they are deprived of the equal protection of the laws. Because of the obvious importance of the question presented, the Court took jurisdiction. . . .

In approaching this problem, we cannot turn the clock back to 1868 when the Amendment was adopted, or even to 1896 when *Plessy* v. *Ferguson* was written. We must consider public education in the light of its full development and its present place in American life throughout the Nation. Only in this way can it be determined if segregation in public schools deprives these plaintiffs of the equal protection of the laws.

Today, education is perhaps the most important function of state and local governments. Compulsory school attendance laws and the great expenditures for education both demonstrate our recognition of the importance of education to our democratic society. It is required in the performance of our most basic public responsibilities, even service in the armed forces. It is the very foundation of good citizenship. Today it is a principal instrument in awakening the child to cultural values, in preparing him for later professional training, and in helping him to adjust normally to his environment. In these days, it is doubtful that any child may reasonably be expected to succeed in life if he is denied the opportunity of an education. Such an opportunity, where the state has undertaken to provide it, is a right which must be made available to all on equal terms.

We come then to the question presented: Does segregation of children in public schools solely on the basis of race, even though the physical facilities and other "tangible" factors may be equal, deprive the children of the minority group of equal educational opportunities? We believe that it does.

In finding that a segregated law school for Negroes could not provide them equal educational opportunities, this Court relied in large part on "those qualities which are incapable of objective measurement but which make for greatness in a law school." In . . . requiring that a Negro admitted to a white graduate school be treated like all other students, [the Court] again resorted to intangible considerations: " . . . his ability to study, to engage in discussions and exchange views with other students, and, in general, to learn his profession." Such considerations apply with added force to children in grade and high schools. To separate them from others of similar age and qualifications solely because of their race generates a feeling of inferiority as to their status in the community that may affect their hearts and minds in a way unlikely ever to be undone. The effect of this separation on their educational opportunities was well stated by a finding in the Kansas case by a court which nevertheless felt compelled to rule against the Negro plaintiffs:

> Segregation of white and colored children in public schools has a detrimental effect upon the colored children. The impact is greater when it has the sanction of the law; for the policy of separating the races is usually interpreted as denoting the inferiority of the negro group. A sense of inferiority affects the motivation of a child to learn. Segregation with the sanction of law, therefore, has a tendency to [retard] the educational and mental development of negro children and to deprive them of some of the benefits they would receive in a racial[ly] integrated school system.

Whatever may have been the extent of psychological knowledge at the time of *Plessy* v. *Ferguson,* this finding is amply supported by modern authority. Any language in *Plessy* v. *Ferguson* contrary to this finding is rejected.

We conclude that in the field of public education the doctrine of "separate but equal" has no place. Separate educational facilities are inherently unequal. Therefore, we hold that the plaintiffs and others similarly situated for whom the actions have been brought are, by reason of the segregation complained of, deprived of the equal protection of the laws guaranteed by the Fourteenth Amendment. . . .

NONVIOLENT PROTEST: FROM MARTIN LUTHER KING, JR., "STRIDE TOWARD FREEDOM"

. . . The racial peace which had existed in Montgomery was not a Christian peace. It was a pagan peace and it had been bought at too great a price.

One place where the peace had long been precarious was on the citywide buses. Here the Negro was daily reminded of the indignities of segregation. There were no Negro drivers, and although some of the white men who drove the buses were courteous, all too many were abusive and vituperative. It was not uncommon to hear them referring to Negro passengers as "niggers," "black cows," and "black apes." Frequently Negroes paid their fares at the front door, and then were forced to get off and reboard the bus at the rear. Often the bus pulled off with the Negro's dime in the box before he had had time to reach the rear door.

An even more humiliating practice was the custom of forcing Negroes to stand over empty seats reserved for "whites only." Even if the bus had no white passengers, and Negroes were packed throughout, they were prohibited from sitting in the first four seats (which held ten persons). But the practice went further. If white passengers were already occupying all of their reserved seats and additional white people boarded the bus, Negroes sitting in the unreserved section immediately behind the whites were asked to stand so that the whites could be seated. If the Negroes refused to stand and move back, they were arrested. In most instances the Negroes submitted without protest. Occasionally, however, there were those, like Vernon Johns, who refused.

A few months after my arrival a fifteen-year-old high school girl, Claudette Colvin, was pulled off a bus, handcuffed, and taken to jail because she refused to give up her seat for a white passenger. This atrocity seemed to arouse the Negro community. There was talk of boycotting the buses in protest. A citizens committee was formed to talk with the manager of the bus company and the City Commission, demanding a statement of policy on seating and more courtesy from the drivers.

I was asked to serve on this committee. We met one afternoon in March 1955 in the office of J. E. Bagley, manager of the Montgomery City Lines. Dave Birmingham, the police commissioner at the time, represented the city commission. Both men were quite pleasant, and expressed deep concern over what had happened. Bagley went so far as to admit that the bus operator was wrong in having Miss Colvin arrested, and promised to reprimand him. Commissioner Birmingham agreed to have the city attorney give a definite statement on the seating policy of the city. We left the meeting hopeful; but nothing happened. The same old patterns of humiliation continued. The city attorney never clarified the law. Claudette Colvin was convicted with a suspended sentence.

But despite the fact that the city commission and the bus company did not act, something else had begun to happen. The long repressed feelings of resentment on the part of the Negroes had begun to stir. The fear and apathy which had for so long cast a shadow on the life of the Negro community were gradually fading before a new spirit of courage and self-respect. The inaction of the city and bus officials after the Colvin case would make it necessary for them in a few months to meet another committee, infinitely more determined. Next time they would face a committee supported by the longings and aspirations of nearly 50,000 people, tired people who had come to see that it is ultimately more honorable to walk the streets in dignity than to ride the buses in humiliation.

On December 1, 1955, an attractive Negro seamstress, Mrs. Rosa Parks, boarded the Cleveland Avenue Bus in downtown Montgomery. She was returning home after her regular day's work in the Montgomery Fair—a leading department store. Tired from long hours on her feet, Mrs. Parks sat down in the first seat behind the section reserved for whites. Not long after she took her seat, the bus operator ordered her, along with three other Negro passengers, to move back in order to accommodate boarding white passengers. By this time every seat in the bus was taken. This meant that if Mrs. Parks followed the driver's command she would have to stand while a white male passenger, who had just boarded the bus, would sit. The other three Negro passengers immediately complied with the driver's request. But Mrs. Parks quietly refused. The result was her arrest.

There was to be much speculation about why Mrs. Parks did not obey the driver. Many people in the white community argued that she had been "planted" by the NAACP in order to lay the groundwork for a test case, and at first glance that explanation seemed plausible, since she was a former secretary of the local branch of the NAACP. So persistent and persuasive was this argument that it convinced many reporters from all over the country. Later on, when I was having press conferences three times a week—in order to accommodate the reporters and journalists who came to Montgomery from all over the world—the invariable first question was: "Did the NAACP start the bus boycott?"

But the accusation was totally unwarranted, as the testimony of both Mrs. Parks and the officials of the NAACP revealed. Actually, no one can understand the action of Mrs. Parks unless he realizes that eventually the cup of endurance runs over, and the human personality cries out, "I can take it no longer." Mrs. Parks's refusal to move back was her intrepid affirmation that she had had enough. It was an individual expression of a timeless longing for human dignity and freedom. She was not "planted" there by the NAACP, or any other organization; she was planted there by her personal sense of dignity and self-respect. She was anchored to that seat by the accumulated indignities of days gone by and the boundless aspirations of generations yet unborn. She was a victim of both the forces of history and the forces of destiny. She had been tracked down by the *Zeitgeist*—the spirit of the time.

Fortunately, Mrs. Parks was ideal for the role assigned to her by history. She was a charming person with a radiant personality, soft spoken and calm in all situations. Her character was impeccable and her dedication deep-rooted. All of these traits together made her one of the most respected people in the Negro community.

Only E. D. Nixon—the signer of Mrs. Parks's bond—and one or two other persons were aware of the arrest when it occurred early Thursday evening. Later in the evening the word got around to a few influential women of the community, mostly members of the Women's Political Council. After a series of telephone calls back and forth they agreed that the Negroes should boycott the buses. They immediately suggested the idea to Nixon, and he readily concurred. In his usual courageous manner he agreed to spearhead the idea.

Early Friday morning, December 2, Nixon called me. He was so caught up in what he was about to say that he forgot to greet me with the usual "hello" but plunged immediately into the story of what had happened to Mrs. Parks the night before. I listened, deeply shocked, as he described the humiliating incident. "We have taken this type of thing too long already," Nixon concluded, his voice trembling. "I feel that the time has come to boycott the buses. Only through a boycott can we make it clear to the white folks that we will not accept this type of treatment any longer."

I agreed at once that some protest was necessary, and that the boycott method would be an effective one. . . .

By early afternoon the arrest of Mrs. Parks was becoming public knowledge. Word of it spread around the community like uncontrolled fire. Telephones began to ring in almost rhythmic succession. By two o'clock an enthusiastic group had mimeographed leaflets concerning the arrest and the proposed boycott, and by evening these had been widely circulated.

As the hour for the evening meeting arrived, I approached the doors of the church with some apprehension, wondering how many of the leaders would respond to our call. Fortunately, it was one of those pleasant winter nights of unseasonable warmth, and to our relief, almost everybody who had been invited was on hand. More than forty people, from every segment of Negro life, were crowded into the large church meeting room. I saw physicians, schoolteachers, lawyers, businessmen, postal workers, union leaders, and clergymen. Virtually every organization of the Negro community was represented.

The largest number there was from the Christian ministry. Having left so many civic meetings in the past sadly disappointed by the dearth of ministers participating, I was filled with joy when I entered the church and found so many of them there; for then I knew that something unusual was about to happen. . . .

The meeting opened around seven-thirty with H. H. Hubbard leading a brief devotional period. Then Bennett moved into action, explaining the purpose of the gathering. With excited gestures he reported on Mrs. Parks's resistance and her arrest. He presented the proposal that the Negro citizens of Montgomery should boycott the buses on Monday in protest. "Now is the time to move," he concluded. "This is no time to talk; it is time to act."

So seriously did Bennett take his "no time to talk" admonition that for quite a while he refused to allow anyone to make a suggestion or even raise a question, insisting that we should move on and appoint committees to implement the proposal. This approach aroused the opposition of most of those present, and created a temporary uproar. For almost forty-five minutes the confusion persisted. Voices rose high, and many people threatened to leave if they could not raise questions and offer suggestions. It looked for a time as though the movement had come to an end before it began. But finally, in the face of this blistering protest, Bennett agreed to open the meeting to discussion.

Immediately questions began to spring up from the floor. Several people wanted further clarification of Mrs. Parks's actions and arrest. Then came the more practical questions. How long would the protest last? How would the idea be further disseminated throughout the community? How would the people be transported to and from their jobs?

As we listened to the lively discussion, we were heartened to notice that, despite the lack of coherence in the meeting, not once did anyone question the validity or desirability of the boycott itself. It seemed to be the unanimous sense of the group that the boycott should take place.

The ministers endorsed the plan with enthusiasm, and promised to go to their congregations on Sunday morning and drive home their approval of the projected one-day protest. Their coöperation was significant, since virtually all of the influential Negro ministers of the city were present. It was decided that we should hold a city-wide mass meeting on Monday night, December 5, to determine how long we would abstain from riding the buses. Rev. A. W. Wilson—minister of the Holt Street Baptist Church—offered his church, which was ideal as a meeting place because of its size and central location. The group agreed that additional leaflets should be distributed on Saturday, and the chairman appointed a committee, including myself, to prepare the statement.

Our committee went to work while the meeting was still in progress. The final message was shorter than the one that had appeared on the first leaflets, but the substance was the same. It read as follows:

> Don't ride the bus to work, to town, to school, or any place Monday, December 5.
>
> Another Negro woman has been arrested and put in jail because she refused to give up her bus seat.
>
> Don't ride the buses to work, to town, to school, or anywhere on Monday. If you work, take a cab, or share a ride, or walk.
>
> Come to a mass meeting, Monday at 7:00 P.M., at the Holt Street Baptist Church for further instruction.

* * *

My wife and I awoke earlier than usual on Monday morning. We were up and fully dressed by five-thirty. The day for the protest had arrived, and we were determined to see the first act of this unfolding drama. I was still saying that if we could get 60 per cent coöperation the venture would be a success.

Fortunately, a bus stop was just five feet from our house. This meant that we could observe the opening stages from our front window. The first bus was to pass around six o'clock. And so we waited through an interminable half hour. I was in the kitchen drinking my coffee when I heard Coretta cry, "Martin, Martin, come quickly!" I put down my cup and ran toward the living room. As I approached the front window Coretta pointed joyfully to a slowly moving bus: "Darling, it's empty!" I could hardly believe what I saw. I knew that the South Jackson line, which ran past our house, carried more Negro passengers than any other line in Montgomery, and that this first bus was usually filled with domestic workers going to their jobs. Would all of the other buses follow the pattern that had been set by the first? Eagerly we waited for the next bus. In fifteen minutes it rolled down the street, and, like the first, it was empty. A third bus appeared, and it too was empty of all but two white passengers.

I jumped in my car and for almost an hour I cruised down every major street and examined every passing bus. During this hour, at the peak of the morning traffic, I saw no more than eight Negro passengers riding the buses. By this time I was jubilant. Instead of the 60 per cent coöperation we had hoped for, it was becoming apparent that we had reached almost 100 per cent. A miracle had taken place. The once dormant and quiescent Negro community was now fully awake.

All day long it continued. At the afternoon peak the buses were still as empty of Negro passengers as they had been in the morning. Students of Alabama State College, who usually kept the South Jackson bus crowded, were cheerfully walking or thumbing rides. Job holders had either found other means of transportation or made their way on foot. While some rode in cabs or private cars, others used less conventional means. Men were seen riding mules to work, and more than one horse-drawn buggy drove the streets of Montgomery that day.

During the rush hours the sidewalks were crowded with laborers and domestic workers, many of them well past middle age, trudging patiently to their jobs and home again, sometimes as much as twelve miles. They knew why they walked, and the knowledge was evident in the way they carried themselves. And as I watched them I knew that there is nothing more majestic than the determined courage of individuals willing to suffer and sacrifice for their freedom and dignity. . . .

* * *

In 1954 I ended my formal training with all of these relatively divergent intellectual forces converging into a positive social philosophy. One of the main tenets of this philosophy was the conviction that nonviolent resistance was one of the most potent weapons available to oppressed people in their quest for social justice. At this time, however, I had merely an intellectual understanding and appreciation of the position, with no firm determination to organize it in a socially effective situation.

When I went to Montgomery as a pastor, I had not the slightest idea that I would later become involved in a crisis in which nonviolent resistance would be applicable. I neither started the protest nor suggested it. I simply responded to the call of the people for a spokesman. When the protest began, my mind, consciously or unconsciously, was driven back to the Sermon on the Mount, with its sublime teachings on love, and the Gandhian method of nonviolent resistance. As the days unfolded, I came to see the power of nonviolence more and more. Living through the actual experience of the protest, nonviolence became more than a method to which I gave intellectual assent; it became a commitment to a way of life. Many of the things that I had not cleared up intellectually concerning nonviolence were now solved in the sphere of practical action.

Since the philosophy of nonviolence played such a positive role in the Montgomery Movement, it may be wise to turn to a brief discussion of some basic aspects of this philosophy.

First, it must be emphasized that nonviolent resistance is not a method for cowards; it does resist. If one uses this method because he is afraid or merely because he lacks the instruments of violence, he is not truly nonviolent. This is why Gandhi often said that if cowardice is the only alternative to violence, it is better to fight. He made this statement conscious of the fact that there is always another alternative: no individual or group need submit to any wrong, nor need they use violence to right the wrong; there is the way of nonviolent resistance. This is ultimately the way of the strong man. It is not a method of stagnant passivity. The phrase "passive resistance" often gives the false impression that this is a sort of "do-nothing method" in which the resister quietly and passively accepts evil. But nothing is further from the truth. For while the nonviolent resister is passive in the sense that he is not physically aggressive toward his opponent, his mind and emotions are always active, constantly seeking to persuade his opponent that he is wrong. The method is passive physically, but strongly active spiritually. It is not passive nonresistance to evil, it is active nonviolent resistance to evil.

A second basic fact that characterizes nonviolence is that it does not seek to defeat or humiliate the opponent, but to win his friendship and understanding. The nonviolent resister must often express his protest through noncoöperation or boycotts, but he realizes that these are not ends themselves; they are merely means to awaken a sense of moral shame in the opponent. The end is redemption and reconciliation. The aftermath of nonviolence is the creation of the beloved community, while the aftermath of violence is tragic bitterness.

A third characteristic of this method is that the attack is directed against forces of evil rather than against persons who happen to be doing the evil. It is evil that the nonviolent resister seeks to defeat, not the persons victimized by evil. If he is opposing racial injustice, the nonviolent resister has the vision to see that the basic tension is not between races. As I like to say to the people in Montgomery: "The tension in this city is not between white people and Negro people. The tension is, at bottom, between justice and injustice, between the forces of light and the forces of darkness. And if there is a victory, it will be a victory not merely for fifty thousand Negroes, but a victory for justice and the forces of light. We are out to defeat injustice and not white persons who may be unjust."

A fourth point that characterizes nonviolent resistance is a willingness to accept suffering without retaliation, to accept blows from the opponent without striking back. "Rivers of blood may have to flow before we gain our freedom, but it must be our blood," Gandhi said to his countrymen. The nonviolent resister is willing to accept violence if necessary, but never to inflict it. He does not seek to dodge jail. If going to jail is necessary, he enters it "as a bridegroom enters the bride's chamber."

One may well ask: "What is the nonviolent resister's justification for this ordeal to which he invites men, for this mass political application of the ancient doctrine of turning the other cheek?" The answer is found in the realization that unearned suffering is redemptive. Suffering, the nonviolent resister realizes, has tremendous educational and transforming possibilities. "Things of fundamental importance to people are not secured by reason alone, but have to be purchased with their suffering," said Gandhi. He continues: "Suffering is infinitely more powerful than the law of the jungle for converting the opponent and opening his ears which are otherwise shut to the voice of reason."

A fifth point concerning nonviolent resistance is that it avoids not only external physical violence but also internal violence of spirit. The nonviolent resister not only refuses to shoot his opponent but he also refuses to hate him. At the center of nonviolence stands the principle of love. The nonviolent resister would contend that in the struggle for human dignity, the oppressed people of the world must not succumb to the temptation of becoming bitter or indulging in hate campaigns. To retaliate in kind would do nothing but intensify the existence of hate in the universe. Along the way of life, someone must have sense enough and morality enough to cut off the chain of hate. This can only be done by projecting the ethic of love to the center of our lives.

In speaking of love at this point, we are not referring to some sentimental or affectionate emotion. It would be nonsense to urge men to love their oppressors in an affectionate sense. Love in this connection means understanding, redemptive good will. Here the Greek language comes to our aid. . . . We speak of a love which is expressed in the Greek word *agape*. *Agape* means understanding, redeeming good will for all men. It is an overflowing love which is purely spontaneous, unmotivated, groundless, and creative. It is not set in motion by any quality or function of its object. It is the love of God operating in the human heart.

Agape is disinterested love. It is a love in which the individual seeks not his own good, but the good of his neighbor (I Cor. 10:24). *Agape* does not begin by discriminating between worthy and unworthy people, or any qualities people possess. It begins by loving others *for their sakes*. It is an entirely "neighbor-regarding concern for others," which discovers the neighbor in every man it meets. Therefore, *agape* makes no distinction between friend and enemy; it is directed toward both. If one loves an individual merely on account of his friendliness, he loves him for the sake of the benefits to be gained from the friendship, rather than for the friend's own sake. Consequently, the best way to assure oneself that Love is disinterested is to have love for the enemy-neighbor from whom you can expect no good in return, but only hostility and persecution.

Another basic point about *agape* is that it springs from the *need* of the other person—his need for belonging to the best in the human family. The Samaritan who helped the Jew on the Jericho Road was "good" because he responded to the human need that he was presented with. God's love is eternal and fails not because man needs his love. St. Paul assures us that the loving act of redemption was done "while we were yet sinners"—that is, at the point of our greatest need for love. Since the white man's personality is greatly distorted by segregation, and his soul is greatly scarred, he needs the love of the Negro. The Negro must love the white man, because the white man needs his love to remove his tensions, insecurities, and fears.

Agape is not a weak, passive love. It is love in action. *Agape* is love seeking to preserve and create community. It is insistence on community even when one seeks to break it. *Agape* is a willingness to sacrifice in the interest of mutuality. *Agape* is a willingness to go to any length to restore community. It doesn't stop at the first mile, but it goes the second mile to restore community. It is a willingness to forgive, not seven times, but seventy times seven to restore community. The cross is the eternal expression of the length to which God will go in order to restore broken community. The resurrection is a symbol of God's triumph over all the forces that seek to block community. The Holy Spirit is the continuing community creating reality that moves through history. He who works against community is working against the whole of creation. Therefore, if I respond to hate with a reciprocal hate I do nothing but intensify the cleavage in broken community. I can only close the gap in broken community by meeting hate with love. If I meet hate with hate, I become depersonalized, because creation is so designed that my personality can only be fulfilled in the context of community. Booker T. Washington was right: "Let no man pull you so low as to make you hate him." When he pulls you that low he brings you to the point of working against community; he drags you to the point of defying creation, and thereby becoming depersonalized.

In the final analysis, *agape* means a recognition of the fact that all life is interrelated. All humanity is involved in a single process, and all men are brothers. To the degree that I harm my brother, no matter what he is doing to me, to that extent I am harming myself. For example, white men often refuse federal aid to education in order to avoid giving the Negro his rights; but because all men are brothers they cannot deny Negro children without harming their own. They end, all efforts to the contrary, by hurting themselves. Why is this? Because men are brothers. If you harm me, you harm yourself.

Love, *agape,* is the only cement that can hold this broken community together. When I am commanded to love, I am commanded to restore community, to resist injustice, and to meet the needs of my brothers.

A sixth basic fact about nonviolent resistance is that it is based on the conviction that the universe is on the side of justice. Consequently, the believer in nonviolence has deep faith in the future. This faith is another reason why the nonviolent resister can accept suffering without retaliation. For he knows that in his struggle for justice he has cosmic companionship. It is true that there are devout believers in nonviolence who find it difficult to believe in a personal God. But even these persons believe in the existence of some creative force that works for universal wholeness. Whether we call it an unconscious process, an impersonal Brahman, or a Personal Being of matchless power and infinite love, there is a creative force in this universe that works to bring the disconnected aspects of reality into a harmonious whole.

* * *

When the opposition discovered that violence could not block the protest, they resorted to mass arrests. As early as January 9, a Montgomery attorney had called the attention of the press to an old state law against boycotts. He referred to Title 14, Section 54, which provides that when two or more persons enter into a conspiracy to prevent the operation of a lawful business, without just cause or legal excuse, they shall be guilty of a misdemeanor. On February 13 the Montgomery County Grand Jury was called to determine whether Negroes who were boycotting the buses were violating this law. After about a week of deliberations, the jury, composed of seventeen whites and one Negro, found the boycott illegal and indicted more than one hundred persons. My name, of course, was on the list. . . .

On Thursday afternoon, March 22, both sides rested. All eyes were turned toward Judge Carter, as with barely a pause he rendered his verdict; "I declare the defendant guilty of violating the state's anti-boycott law." The penalty was a fine of $500 and court costs, or 386 days at hard labor in the County of Montgomery. Then Judge Carter announced that he was giving a minimum penalty because of what I had done to prevent violence. In the cases of the other Negroes charged with the same violation—the number had now boiled down to 89—Judge Carter entered a continuance until a final appeal was complete in my case.

In a few minutes several friends had come up to sign my bond, and the lawyers had notified the judge that the case would be appealed. Many people stood around the courtroom in tears. Others walked out with their heads bowed. I came to the end of my trial with a feeling of sympathy for Judge Carter in his dilemma. To convict me he had to face the condemnation of the nation and world opinion; to acquit me he had to face the condemnation of the local community and those voters who kept him in office. Throughout the proceedings he had treated me with great courtesy, and he had rendered a verdict which he probably thought was the best way out. After the trial he left town for a "welcomed rest."

I left the courtroom with my wife at my side and a host of friends following. In front of the courthouse hundreds of Negroes and whites, including television cameramen and photographers, were waiting. As I waved my hand, they shouted: "God bless you," and began to sing, "We ain't gonna ride the buses no more."

Ordinarily, a person leaving a courtroom with a conviction behind him would wear a somber face. But I left with a smile. I knew that I was a convicted criminal, but I was proud of my crime. It was the crime of joining my people in a nonviolent protest against injustice. It was the crime of seeking to instill within my people a sense of dignity and self-respect. It was the crime of desiring for my people the unalienable rights of life. liberty, and the pursuit of happiness. It was above all the crime of seeking to convince my people that noncoöperation with evil is just as much a moral duty as is coöperation with good.

So ended another effort to halt the protest. Instead of stopping the movement, the opposition's tactics had only served to give it greater momentum, and to draw us closer together. What the opposition failed to see was that our mutual sufferings had wrapped us all in a single garment of destiny. What happened to one happened to all.

On that cloudy afternoon in March, Judge Carter had convicted more than Martin Luther King, Jr., Case No. 7399; he had convicted every Negro in Montgomery. It is no wonder that the movement couldn't be stopped. It was too large to be stopped. Its links were too well bound together in a powerfully effective chain. There is amazing power in unity. Where there is true unity, every effort to disunite only serves to strengthen the unity. This is what the opposition failed to see.

The members of the opposition had also revealed that they did not know the Negroes with whom they were dealing. They thought they were dealing with a group who could be cajoled or forced to do whatever the white man wanted them to do. They were not aware that they were dealing with Negroes who had been freed from fear. And so every move they made proved to be a mistake. It could not be otherwise, because their methods were geared to the "old Negro," and they were dealing with a "new Negro."

* * *

. . . I read these words: "The United States Supreme Court today affirmed a decision of a special three-judge U. S. District Court in declaring Alabama's state and local laws requiring segregation on buses unconstitutional. The Supreme Court acted without listening to any argument; it simply said 'the motion to affirm is granted and the Judgment is affirmed.' "

At this moment my heart began to throb with an inexpressible joy. The darkest hour of our struggle had indeed proved to be the first hour of victory. . . . The faces of the Negroes showed that they had heard. "God Almighty has spoken from Washington, D.C.," said one joyful bystander. . . .

I rushed home and notified the press that I was calling the Negro citizens together on Wednesday night, November 14, to decide whether to call off the protest. In order to accommodate as many people as possible, two simultaneous meetings were scheduled, one on each side of town, with the speakers traveling from one meeting to the other. In the meantime, the executive board decided, on the advice of counsel, to recommend that the official protest be ended immediately, but that the return to the buses be delayed until the mandatory order arrived from the Supreme Court in Washington. It was expected in a few days.

The eight thousand men and women who crowded in and around the two churches were in high spirits. At the first meeting it was clear that the news of the decision had spread fast, and the opening hymn had a special note of joy. Reading the Scripture that night was Bob Graetz, who had chosen Paul's famous letter to the Corinthians: "Though I have all faith, so that I could remove mountains, and have not love, I am nothing. . . . Love suffereth long, and is kind. . . ."

When the slender blond minister came to the words: "When I was a child, I spoke as a child, I understood as a child, I thought as a child: but when I became a man, I put away childish things," the congregation burst into applause. Soon they were shouting and cheering and waving their handkerchiefs, as if to say that they knew they had come of age, had won new dignity. When Bob Graetz concluded: "And now abideth faith, hope, love, but the greatest of these is love," there was another spontaneous outburst. Only a people who had struggled to love in the midst of bitter conflict could have reacted in this fashion. I knew then that nonviolence, for all its difficulties, had won its way into our hearts.

Later Ralph Abernathy spoke. He told how a white newspaperman had reproached him for this outburst on the part of the congregation.

"Isn't it a little peculiar," the journalist had asked, "for people to interrupt the Scripture in that way?"

"Yes it is," Abernathy quoted himself in reply. "Just as it is peculiar for people to walk in the snow and rain when there are empty buses available; just as it is peculiar for people to pray for those who persecute them; just as it is peculiar for the Southern Negro to stand up and look a white man in the face as an equal." At this his audience laughed and shouted and applauded. . . .

THE CIVIL RIGHTS ACT OF 1964

Sec. 101. Section 2004 of the Revised Statutes (42 U.S.C. 1971), as amended by section 131 of the Civil Rights Act of 1957 (71 Stat. 637), and as further amended by section 601 of the Civil Rights Act of 1960 (74 Stat. 90), is further amended as follows:

(a) Insert "1" after "(a)" in subsection (a) and add at the end of subsection (a) the following new paragraphs:

"(2) No person acting under color of law shall—

"(A) in determining whether any individual is qualified under State law or laws to vote in any Federal election, apply any standard, practice, or procedure different from the standards, practices, or procedures applied under such law or laws to other individuals within the same county, parish, or similar political subdivision who have been found by State officials to be qualified to vote;

"(B) deny the right of any individual to vote in any Federal election because of an error or omission on any record or paper relating to any application, registration, or other act requisite to voting, if such error or omission is not material in determining whether such individual is qualified under State law to vote in such election; or

"(C) employ any literacy test as a qualification for voting in any Federal election unless (i) such test is administered to each individual and is conducted wholly in writing, and (ii) a certified copy of the test and of the answers given by the individual is furnished to him within twenty-five days of the submission of his request made within the period of time during which records and papers are required to be retained and preserved pursuant to title III of the Civil Rights Act of 1960. . . .

(b) Insert immediately following the period at the end of the first sentence of subsection (c) the following new sentence: "If in any such proceeding literacy is a relevant fact there shall be a rebuttable presumption that any person who has not been adjudged an incompetent and who has completed the sixth grade in a public school in, or a private school accredited by, any State or territory, the District of Columbia, or the Commonwealth of Puerto Rico where instruction is carried on predominantly in the English language, possesses sufficient literacy, comprehension, and intelligence to vote in any Federal election."

(c) Add the following subsection "(f)" and designate the present subsection "(f)" as subsection "(g)":

"(f) When used in subsection (a) or (c) of this section, the words 'Federal election' shall mean any general, special, or primary election held solely or in part for the purpose of electing or selecting any candidate for the office of President, Vice President, presidential elector, Member of the Senate, or Member of the House of Representatives."

(d) Add the following subsection "(h)":

"(h) In any proceeding instituted by the United States in any district court of the United States under this section in which the Attorney General requests a finding of a pattern or practice of discrimination pursuant to subsection (e) of this section the Attorney General, at the time he files the complaint, or any defendant in the proceeding, within twenty days after service upon him of the complaint, may file with the clerk of such court a request that a court of three judges be convened to hear and determine the entire case. A copy of the request for a three-judge court shall be immediately furnished by such clerk to the chief judge of the circuit (or in his absence, the presiding circuit judge of the circuit) in which the case is pending. Upon receipt of the copy of such request it shall be the duty of the chief judge of the circuit or the presiding circuit judge, as the case may be, to designate immediately three judges in such circuit, of whom at least one shall be a circuit judge and another of whom shall be a district judge of the court in which the proceeding was instituted, to hear and determine such case, and it shall be the duty of the judges so designated to assign the case for hearing at the earliest practicable date, to participate in the hearing and determination thereof, and to cause the case to be in every way expedited. An appeal from the final judgment of such court will lie to the Supreme Court. . . .

"It shall be the duty of the judge designated pursuant to this section to assign the case for hearing at the earliest practicable date and to cause the case to be in every way expedited."

Title II—Injunctive Relief against Discrimination in Places of Public Accommodation

Sec. 201. (a) All persons shall be entitled to the full and equal enjoyment of the goods, services, facilities, privileges, advantages, and accommodations of any place of public accommodation, as defined in this section, without discrimination or segregation on the ground of race, color, religion, or national origin.

(b) Each of the following establishments which serves the public is a place of public accommodation within the meaning of this title if its operations affect commerce, or if discrimination or segregation by it is supported by State action:

(1) any inn, hotel, motel, or other establishment which provides lodging to transient guests, other than an establishment located within a building which contains not more than five rooms for rent or hire and which is actually occupied by the proprietor of such establishment as his residence;

(2) any restaurant, cafeteria, lunchroom, lunch counter, soda fountain, or other facility principally engaged in selling food for consumption on the premises, including, but not limited to, any such facility located on the premises of any retail establishment; or any gasoline station;

(3) any motion picture house, theater, concert hall, sports arena, stadium or other place of exhibition or entertainment; and

(4) any establishment (A) (i) which is physically located within the premises of any establishment otherwise covered by this subsection, or (ii) within the premises of which is physically located any such covered establishment, and (B) which holds itself out as serving patrons of such covered establishment.

(c) The operations of an establishment affect commerce within the meaning of this title if (1) it is one of the establishments described in paragraph (1) of subsection (b); (2) in the case of an establishment described in paragraph (2) of subsection (b), it serves or offers to serve interstate travelers or a substantial portion of the food which it serves, or gasoline or other products which it sells, has moved in commerce; (3) in the case of an establishment described in paragraph (3) of subsection (b), it customarily presents films, performances, athletic teams, exhibitions, or other sources of entertainment which move in commerce; and (4) in the case of an establishment described in paragraph (4) of subsection (b), it is physically located within the premises of, or there is physically located within its premises, an establishment the operations of which affect commerce within the meaning of this subsection. For purposes of this section, "commerce" means travel, trade, traffic, commerce, transportation, or communication among the several States, or between the District of Columbia and any State, or between any foreign country or any territory or possession and any State or the District of Columbia, or between points in the same State but through any other State or the District of Columbia or a foreign country.

(d) Discrimination or segregation by an establishment is supported by State action within the meaning of this title if such discrimination or segregation (1) is carried on under color of any law, statute, ordinance, or regulation; or (2) is carried on under color of any custom or usage required or enforced by officials of the State or political subdivision thereof; or (3) is required by action of the State or political subdivision thereof.

(e) The provisions of this title shall not apply to a private club or other establishment not in fact open to the public, except to the extent that the facilities of such establishment are made available to the customers or patrons of an establishment within the scope of subsection (b).

Sec. 202. All persons shall be entitled to be free, at any establishment or place, from discrimination or segregation of any kind on the ground of race, color, religion, or national origin, if such discrimination or segregation is or purports to be required by any law, statute, ordinance, regulation, rule, or order of a State or any agency or political subdivision thereof.

Sec. 203. No person shall (a) withhold, deny, or attempt to withhold or deny, or deprive or attempt to deprive, any person of any right or privilege secured by section 201 or 202, or (b) intimidate, threaten, or coerce, or attempt to intimidate, threaten, or coerce any person with the purpose of interfering with any right or privilege secured by section 201 or 202, or (c) punish or attempt to punish any person for exercising or attempting to exercise any right or privilege secured by section 201 or 202.

Sec. 204. (a) Whenever any person has engaged or there are reasonable grounds to believe that any person is about to engage in any act or practice prohibited by section 203, a civil action for preventive relief, including an application for a permanent or temporary injunction, restraining order, or other order, may be instituted by the person aggrieved and, upon timely application, the court may, in its discretion, permit the Attorney General to intervene in such civil action if he certifies that the case is of general public importance. Upon application by the complainant and in such circumstances as the court may deem just, the court may appoint an attorney for such complainant and may authorize the commencement of the civil action without the payment of fees, costs, or security. . . .

Sec. 206. (a) Whenever the Attorney General has reasonable cause to believe that any person or group of persons is engaged in a pattern or practice of resistance to the full enjoyment of any of the rights secured by this title, and that the pattern or practice is of such a nature and is intended to deny the full exercise of the rights herein described, the Attorney General may bring a civil action in the appropriate district court of the United States by filing with it a complaint (1) signed by him (or in his absence the Acting Attorney General), (2) setting forth facts pertaining to such pattern or practice, and (3) requesting such preventive relief, including an application for a permanent or temporary injunction, restraining order or other order against the person or persons responsible for such pattern or practice, as he deems necessary to insure the full enjoyment of the rights herein described. . . .

Title III—Desegregation of Public Facilities

Sec. 301. (a) Whenever the Attorney General receives a complaint in writing signed by an individual to the effect that he is being deprived of or threatened with the loss of his right to the equal protection of the laws, on account of his race, color, religion, or national origin, by being denied equal utilization of any public facility which is owned, operated, or managed by or on behalf of any State or subdivision thereof, other than a public school or public college as defined in section 401 of title IV hereof, and the Attorney General believes the complaint is meritorious and certifies that the signer or signers of such complaint are unable, in his judgment, to initiate and maintain appropriate legal proceedings for relief and that the institution of an action will materially further the orderly progress of desegregation in public facilities, the Attorney General is authorized to institute for or in the name of the United States a civil action in any appropriate district court of the United States against such parties and for such relief as may be appropriate, and such court shall have and shall exercise jurisdiction of proceedings instituted pursuant to this section. The Attorney General may implead as defendants such additional parties as are or become necessary to the grant of effective relief hereunder.

(b) The Attorney General may deem a person or persons unable to initiate and maintain appropriate legal proceedings within the meaning of subsection (a) of this section when such person or persons are unable, either directly or through other interested persons or organizations, to bear the expense of the litigation or to obtain effective legal representation; or whenever he is satisfied that the institution of such litigation would jeopardize the personal safety, employment, or economic standing of such person or persons, their families, or their property. . . .

Title VI—Nondiscrimination in Federally Assisted Programs

Sec. 601. No person in the United States shall, on the ground of race, color, or national origin, be excluded from participation in, be denied the benefits of, or be subjected to discrimination under any program or activity receiving Federal financial assistance.

Sec. 602. Each Federal department and agency which is empowered to extend Federal financial assistance to any program or activity, by way of grant, loan, or contract other than a contract of insurance or guaranty, is authorized and directed to effectuate the provisions of section 601 with respect to such program or activity by issuing rules, regulations, or orders of general applicability which shall be consistent with achievement of the objectives of the statute authorizing the financial assistance in connection with which the action is taken. No such rule, regulation, or order shall become effective unless and until approved by the President. Compliance with any requirement adopted pursuant to this section may be effected (1) by the termination of or refusal to grant or to continue assistance under such program or activity to any recipient as to whom there has been an express finding on the record, after opportunity for hearing, of a failure to comply with such requirement, but such termination or refusal shall be limited to the particular political entity, or part thereof, or other recipient as to whom such a finding has been made and, shall be limited in its effect to the particular program, or part thereof, in which such noncompliance has been so found, or (2) by any other means authorized by law: *Provided, however,* That no such action shall be taken until the department or agency concerned has advised the appropriate person or persons of the failure to comply with the requirement and has determined that compliance cannot be secured by voluntary means. In the case of any action terminating, or refusing to grant or continue, assistance because of failure to comply with a requirement imposed pursuant to this section, the head of the Federal department or agency shall file with the committees of the House and Senate having legislative jurisdiction over the program or activity involved a full written report of the circumstances and the grounds for such action. No such action shall become effective until thirty days have elapsed after the filing of such report.

Sec. 603. Any department or agency action taken pursuant to section 602 shall be subject to such judicial review as may otherwise be provided by law for similar action taken by such department or agency on other grounds. In the case of action, not otherwise subject to judicial review, terminating or refusing to grant or to continue financial assistance upon a finding of failure to comply with any requirement imposed pursuant to section 602, any person aggrieved (including any State or political subdivision thereof and any agency of either) may obtain judicial review of such action in accordance with section 10 of the Administrative Procedure Act, and such action shall not be deemed committed to unreviewable agency discretion within the meaning of that section.

Sec. 604. Nothing contained in this title shall be construed to authorize action under this title by any department or agency with respect to any employment practice of any employer, employment agency, or labor organization except where a primary objective of the Federal financial assistance is to provide employment.

Sec. 605. Nothing in this title shall add to or detract from any existing authority with respect to any program or activity under which Federal financial assistance is extended by way of a contract of insurance or guaranty.

Title VII—Equal Employment Opportunity

* * *

Sec. 703. (a) It shall be an unlawful employment practice for an employer—

(1) to fail or refuse to hire or to discharge any individual, or otherwise to discriminate against any individual with respect to his compensation, terms, conditions, or privileges of employment, because of such individual's race, color, religion, sex, or national origin; or

(2) to limit, segregate, or classify his employees in any way which would deprive or tend to deprive any individual of employment opportunities or otherwise adversely affect his status as an employee, because of such individual's race, color, religion, sex, or national origin.

(b) It shall be an unlawful employment practice for an employment agency to fail or refuse to refer for employment, or otherwise to discriminate against, any individual because of his race, color, religion, sex, or national origin, or to classify or refer for employment any individual on the basis of his race, color, religion, sex, or national origin.

(c) It shall be an unlawful employment practice for a labor organization—

(1) to exclude or to expel from its membership, or otherwise to discriminate against, any individual because of his race, color, religion, sex, or national origin;

(2) to limit, segregate, or classify its membership, or to classify or fail to refuse to refer for employment any individual, in any way which would deprive or tend to deprive any individual of employment opportunities, or would limit such employment opportunities or otherwise adversely affect his status as an employee or as an applicant for employment, because of such individual's race, color, religion, sex, or national origin; or

(3) to cause or attempt to cause an employer to discriminate against an individual in violation of this section. . . .

(j) Nothing contained in this title shall be interpreted to require any employer, employment agency, labor organization, or joint labor-management committee subject to this title to grant preferential treatment to any individual or to any group because of the race, color, religion, sex, or national origin of such individual or group on account of an imbalance which may exist with respect to the total number or percentage of persons of any race, color, religion, sex, or national origin employed by any employer, referred or classified for employment by any employment agency or labor organization, admitted to membership or classified by any labor organization, or admitted to, or employed in, any apprenticeship or other training program, in comparison with the total number or percentage of persons of such race, color, religion, sex, or national origin in any community, State, section, or other area, or in the available work force in any community, State, section, or other area. . . .

Sec. 707. (a) Whenever the Attorney General has reasonable cause to believe that any person or group of persons is engaged in a pattern or practice of resistance to the full enjoyment of any of the rights secured by this title, and that the pattern or practice is of such a nature and is intended to deny the full exercise of the rights herein described, the Attorney General may bring a civil action in the appropriate district court of the United States by filing with it a complaint (1) signed by him (or in his absence the Acting Attorney General), (2) setting forth facts pertaining to such pattern or practice, and (3) requesting such relief, including an application for a permanent or temporary injunction, restraining order or other order against the person or persons responsible for such pattern or practice, as he deems necessary to insure the full enjoyment of the rights herein described. . . .

Title XI—Miscellaneous

Sec. 1101. In any proceeding for criminal contempt arising under title II, III, IV, V, VI, or VII of this Act, the accused, upon demand therefor, shall be entitled to a trial by jury, which shall conform as near as may be to the practice in criminal cases. Upon conviction, the accused shall not be fined more than $1,000 or imprisoned for more than six months. . . .

SELECTION 45

The Vision of the Great Society: Lyndon B. Johnson, State of the Union Address, 1965

After being elected to the Presidency in his own right in 1964, Lyndon B. Johnson outlined his vision of what the rich, restless American nation should try to become in the future. This sketch of what he called "The Great Society" emerged in his 1965 State of the Union address, the text of which follows. It is taken from The New York Times, *Jan. 2, 1965.*

We are entering the third century of the pursuit of American Union. Two hundred years ago, in 1765, nine assembled colonies first joined together to demand freedom from arbitrary power.

For the first century we struggled to hold together the first continental union of democracy in the history of man. One hundred years ago, in 1865, following a terrible test of blood and fire, the compact of union was finally sealed.

For a second century we labored to establish a unity of purpose and interest among the many groups which make up the American community.

That struggle has often brought pain and violence. It is not yet over. But we have achieved a unity of interest among our people unmatched in the history of freedom.

And now, in 1965, we begin a new quest for union. We seek the unity of man with the world he has built—with the knowledge that can save or destroy him—with the cities which can stimulate or stifle him—with the wealth and machines which can enrich or menace his spirit.

We seek to establish a harmony between man and society which will allow each of us to enlarge the meaning of his life and all of us to elevate the quality of our civilization.

But the unity we seek cannot realize its full promise in isolation. For today the state of the Union depends, in large measure, upon the state of the world.

Our concern and interest, compassion and vigilance, extend to every corner of a dwindling planet.

Yet, it is not merely our concern but the concern of all free men. We will not, and should not, assume it is the task of Americans alone to settle all the conflicts of a torn and troubled world.

Let the foes of freedom take no comfort from this. For in concert with other nations, we shall help men defend their freedom.

Our first aim remains the safety and well-being of our own country.

We are prepared to live as good neighbors with all, but we cannot be indifferent to acts designed to injure our interests, our citizens, or our establishments abroad. The community of nations requires mutual respect. We shall extend it—and we shall expect it.

In our relations with the world we shall follow the example of Andrew

Jackson, who said: "I intend to ask for nothing that is not clearly right and to submit to nothing that is wrong."

And he promised, "The honor of my country shall never be stained by an apology from me for the statement of truth or the performance of duty." That was our policy in the 1830's and that is our policy today.

Our own freedom and growth have never been the final goal of the American dream.

We were never meant to be an oasis of liberty and abundance in a world-wide desert of disappointed dreams. Our nation was created to help strike away the chains of ignorance and misery and tyranny wherever they keep man less than God means him to be.

We are moving toward that destiny, never more rapidly than in the last four years.

In this period we have built a military power strong enough to meet any threat and destroy any adversary. And that superiority will continue to grow so long as this office is mine—and you sit on Capitol Hill.

In this period no new nation has become Communist, and the unity of the Communist empire has begun to crumble.

In this period we have resolved in friendship our disputes with our neighbors of the hemisphere, and joined in an Alliance for Progress toward economic growth and political democracy.

In this period we have taken more steps toward peace—including the test ban treaty—that at any time since the cold war began.

In this period we have relentlessly pursued our advances toward the conquest of space.

Most important of all, in this period, the United States has re-emerged into the fullness of its self-confidence and purpose. No longer are we called upon to get America moving. We are moving. No longer do we doubt our strength or resolution. We are strong and we have proven our resolve.

No longer can anyone wonder whether we are in the grip of historical decay. We know that history is ours to make. And if there is great danger, there is now also the excitement of great expectations.

Yet we still live in a troubled and perilous world. There is no longer a single threat. There are many. They differ in intensity and danger. They require different attitudes and different answers.

With the Soviet Union we seek peaceful understanding that can lessen the danger to freedom.

Last fall I asked the American people to choose that course.

I will carry forward their command.

If we are to live together in peace, we must come to know each other better.

I am sure the American people would welcome a chance to listen to the Soviet leaders on our television—as I would like the Soviet people to hear our leaders.

I hope the new Soviet leaders can visit America so they can learn about this country at first hand.

In Eastern Europe restless nations are slowly beginning to assert their identity. Your Government, assisted by leaders in labor and business, is exploring ways to increase peaceful trade with these countries and the Soviet Union. I will report our conclusions to the Congress.

In Asia, Communism wears a more aggressive face.

We see that in Vietnam.

Why are we there?

We are there, first, because a friendly nation has asked us for help against Communist aggression. Ten years ago we pledged our help. Three Presidents have supported that pledge. We will not break it.

Second, our own security is tied to the peace of Asia. Twice in one generation we have had to fight against aggression in the Far East. To ignore aggression would only increase the danger of a larger war.

Our goal is peace in Southeast Asia. That will come only when aggressors leave their neighbors in peace.

What is at stake is the cause of freedom. In that cause we shall never be found wanting.

But Communism is not the only source of trouble and unrest. There are older and deeper sources—in the misery of nations and in man's irrepressible ambition for liberty and a better life.

With the free republics of Latin America I have always felt—and my country has always felt—special ties of interest and affection. It will be the purpose of this Administration to strengthen these ties.

Together we share and shape the destiny of the New World. In the coming year I hope to pay a visit to Latin America. And I will steadily enlarge our commitment to the Alliance for Progress as the instrument of our war against poverty and injustice in the Hemisphere.

In the Atlantic community we continue to pursue our goal of 20 years—a Europe growing in strength, unity and cooperation with America. A great unfinished task is the reunification of Germany through self-determination.

This European policy is not based on any abstract design. It is based on the realities of common interests and common values, common dangers and common expectations. These realities will continue to have their way—especially in our expanding trade and our common defense.

Free Americans have shaped the policies of the United States. And because we know these realities, those policies have been, and will be, in the interest of Europe.

Free Europeans must shape the course of Europe. And, for the same reasons, that course has been, and will be, in our interest and the interest of freedom.

I found this truth confirmed in my talks with European leaders in the last year. I hope to repay these visits to some of our friends in Europe this year.

In Africa and Asia we are witnessing the turbulent unfolding of new nations and continents.

We welcome them to the society of nations.

We are committed to help those seeking to strengthen their own independence, and to work most closely with those governments dedicated to the welfare of all their people.

We seek not fidelity to an iron faith, but a diversity of belief as varied as man himself. We seek not to extend the power of America but the progress of humanity. We seek not to dominate others but to strengthen the freedom of all.

I will seek new ways to use our knowledge to help deal with the explosion in world population and the growing scarcity of world resources.

Finally, we renew our commitment to the continued growth and effectiveness of the United Nations. The frustrations of the United Nations are a product of the world we live in, not of the institution which gives them voice.

It is far better to throw these differences open to the assembly of nations than permit them to fester in silent danger.

These are some of the goals of the American nation in the world.

For ourselves we seek neither praise nor blame, gratitude nor obedience.

We seek peace.

We seek freedom.

We seek to enrich the life of man.

For that is the world in which we will flourish.

That is the world we mean for all men to have.

World affairs will continue to call upon our energy and courage.

But today we can turn increased attention to the character of American life.

We are in the midst of the greatest upward surge of economic well-being in the history of any nation.

Our flourishing progress has been marked by price stability unequalled in the world. Our balance of payments deficit has declined and the soundness of our dollar is unquestioned. I pledge to keep it that way. I urge business and labor to cooperate to that end.

We worked for two centuries to climb this peak of prosperity.

But we are only at the beginning of the road to the Great Society. Ahead now is a summit where freedom from the wants of the body can help fulfill the needs of the spirit.

We built this nation to serve its people.

We want to grow and build and create, but we want progress to be the servant and not the master of man.

We do not intend to live—in the midst of abundance—isolated from neighbors and nature, confined by blighted cities and bleak suburbs, stunted by a poverty of learning and an emptiness of leisure.

The Great Society asks not only how much, but how good; not only how to create wealth but how to use it; not only how fast we are going, but where we are headed.

It proposes as the first test for a nation: the quality of its people.

This kind of society will not flower spontaneously from swelling riches and surging power.

It will not be the gift of Government or the creation of Presidents.

It will require of every American, for many generations, both faith in the destination and the fortitude to make the journey.

Like freedom itself, it will always be challenge and not fulfillment.

Tonight we accept that challenge.

I propose we begin a program in education to ensure every American child the fullest development of his mind and skills.

I propose we begin a massive attack on crippling and killing diseases.

I propose we launch a national effort to make the American city a better and more stimulating place to live.

I propose we increase the beauty of America and end the poisoning of our rivers and the air we breathe.

I propose we carry out a new program to develop regions of our country now suffering from distress and depression.

I propose we make new efforts to control and prevent crime and delinquency.

I propose we eliminate every remaining obstacle to the right and opportunity to vote.

I propose we honor and support the achievements of thought and the creation of art.

I propose we make an all-out campaign against waste and inefficiency.

Our basic task is three fold:

1. To keep our economy growing.
2. To open for all Americans the opportunities now enjoyed by most Americans.
3. To improve the quality of life for all.

In the next six weeks I will submit special messages with detailed proposals for national action in each of these areas.

Tonight I would like briefly to explain some of my major recommendations in the three main areas of national need.

First, we must keep our nation prosperous. We seek full employment opportunity for every American. I will present a budget designed to move the economy forward. More money will be left in the hands of the consumer by a substantial cut in excise taxes. We will continue along the path toward a balanced budget and a balanced economy.

I confidently predict—what every economic sign now tells us—the continued flourishing of the American economy.

But we must remember that fear of a recession can contribute to the fact of a recession. The knowledge that our Government will, and can, move swiftly will strengthen the confidence of investors and business.

Congress can reinforce this confidence by insuring that its procedures permit rapid action on temporary income tax cuts. And special funds for job-creating public programs should be made available for immediate use if recession threatens.

Our continued prosperity demands continued price stability. Business, labor and the consumer all have a high stake in keeping wages and prices within the framework of the guideposts that have already served the nation so well.

Finding new markets abroad for our goods depends on the initiative of American business. But we stand ready—with credit and other help—to assist the flow of trade which will benefit the entire nation.

Our economy owes much to the efficiency of our farmers. We must continue to assure them the opportunity to earn a fair reward. I have instructed the Secretary of Agriculture to lead a major effort to find new approaches to reduce the heavy cost of our farm programs and to direct more of our effort to the small farmer who needs help most.

We can help insure continued prosperity through:

1. A regional recovery program to assist development of stricken areas left behind by our national progress.
2. Further efforts to provide our workers with the skills demanded by modern technology, for the laboring man is an indispensable force in the American system.

3. Extension of the minimum wage to more than two million unprotected workers.
4. Improvement and modernization of the unemployment compensation system.

As pledged in our 1960 and 1964 Democratic platforms, I will propose to Congress changes in the Taft-Hartley Act including section 14-B. I will do so hoping to reduce conflicts that for several years have divided Americans in various states.

In a country that spans a continent modern transportation is vital to continued growth.

I will recommend heavier reliance on competition in transportation and a new policy for our Merchant Marine.

I will ask for funds to study high-speed rail transportation between urban centers. We will begin with test projects between Boston and Washington. On high-speed trains, passengers could travel this distance in less than four hours.

Second, we must open opportunity to all our people.

Most Americans tonight enjoy a good life. But far too many are still trapped in poverty, idleness and fear.

Let a just nation throw open to them the city of promise:

1. To the elderly, by providing hospital care under Social Security and by raising benefit payments to those struggling to maintain the dignity of their later years.
2. To the poor, through doubling the war against poverty this year.
3. To Negro Americans, through enforcement of the Civil Rights Law and elimination of barriers to the right to vote.
4. To those in other lands seeking the promise of America, through an immigration law based on the work a man can do and not where he was born or how he spells his name.

Our third goal is to improve the quality of American life.

We begin with learning.

Every child must have the best education our nation can provide.

Thomas Jefferson said no nation can be both ignorant and free. Today no nation can be both ignorant and great.

In addition to our existing programs, I will recommend a new program for schools and students with a first-year authorization of one billion, 500 million dollars.

It will help at every stage along the road to learning.

For the pre-school years we will help needy children become aware of the excitement of learning.

For the primary and secondary school years we will aid public schools serving low-income families and assist students in both public and private schools.

For the college years we will provide scholarships to high school students of the greatest promise and greatest need and guaranteed low interest loans to students continuing their college studies.

New laboratories and centers will help our schools lift their standards of excellence and explore new methods of teaching. These centers will provide special training for those who need and deserve special treatment.

Greatness requires not only an educated people but a healthy people.

Our goal is to match the achievements of our medicine to the afflictions of our people.

We already carry on a large program for research and health.

In addition, regional medical centers can provide the most advanced diagnosis and treatment for heart disease, cancer, stroke and other major diseases.

New support for medical and dental education will provide the trained men to apply our knowledge.

Community centers can help the mentally ill and improve health care for school-age children from poor families, including services for the mentally retarded.

An educated and healthy people require surroundings in harmony with their hopes.

In our urban areas the central problem today is to protect and restore man's satisfaction in belonging to a community where he can find security and significance.

The first step is to break old patterns—to begin to think, work and plan for the development of entire metropolitan areas. We will take this step with new programs of help for basic community facilities and neighborhood centers of health and recreation.

New and existing programs will be open to those cities which work together to develop unified long-range policies for metropolitan areas.

We must also make important changes in our housing programs if we are to pursue these same basic goals.

A department of housing and urban development will be needed to spearhead this effort in our cities.

Every citizen has the right to feel secure in his home and on the streets of his community.

To help control crime, we will recommend programs:

1. To train local enforcement officers.
2. To put the best techniques of modern science at their disposal.
3. To discover the causes of crime and better ways to prevent it.

I will soon assemble a panel of outstanding experts to search out answers to the national problem of crime and delinquency.

For over three centuries the beauty of America has sustained our spirit and enlarged our vision. We must act now to protect this heritage.

In a fruitful new partnership with the states and cities the next decade should be a conservation milestone. We must make a massive effort to save the countryside and establish—as a green legacy for tomorrow—more large and small parks, more seashores and open spaces than have been created during any period in our history.

A new and substantial effort must be made to landscape highways and provide places of relaxation and recreation wherever our roads run.

Within our cities imaginative programs are needed to landscape streets and transform open areas into places of beauty and recreation.

We will seek legal power to prevent pollution of our air and water before it happens. We will step up our effort to control harmful wastes, giving first priority to the clean-up of our most contaminated rivers. We will increase research to learn more about control of pollution.

We hope to make the Potomac a model of beauty and recreation for the entire country—and preserve unspoiled stretches of some of our waterways with a wild rivers bill.

More ideas for a beautiful America will emerge from a White House conference on natural beauty which I will soon call.

We must also recognize and encourage those who can be pathfinders for the nation's imagination and understanding.

To help promote and honor creative achievements, I will propose a national foundation of the arts.

To develop knowledge which will enrich our lives and ensure our progress, I will recommend programs to encourage basic science, particularly in the universities—and to bring closer the day when the oceans will supply our growing need for fresh water.

For Government to serve these goals it must be modern in structure, efficient in action and ready for any emergency.

I am currently reviewing the structure of the Executive Branch. I hope to reshape and reorganize it to meet more effectively the tasks of today.

Wherever waste is found, I will eliminate it.

Last year we saved almost 3.5 billion dollars by eliminating waste.

I intend to do better this year.

And I will soon report to you on our progress and on new economies we plan to make.

Even the best of Government is subject to the worst of hazards.

I will propose laws to ensure the necessary continuity of leadership should the President become disabled or die.

In addition, I will propose reforms in the Electoral College—leaving undisturbed the vote by states—but making sure no elector can substitute his will for that of the people.

Last year I spoke to you after 33 years of public service—most of them on this Hill.

This year I speak after one year as President of the United States.

Many of you in this chamber are among my oldest friends. We have shared many happy moments and many hours of work, and we have watched many Presidents together. Yet, only in the White House can you finally know the full weight of this office.

The greatest burden is not running the huge operations of Government—or meeting daily troubles, large and small—or even working with the Congress.

A President's hardest task is not to do what is right, but to know what is right.

Yet the Presidency brings no special gift or prophecy or foresight. You take an oath—step into an office—and must then help guide a great democracy.

The answer was waiting for me in the land where I was born.

It was once barren land. The angular hills were covered with scrub cedar and a few live oaks. Little would grow in the harsh caliche soil. And each spring the Pedernales River would flood the valley.

But men came and worked and endured and built.

Today that country is abundant with fruit, cattle, goats and sheep. There are pleasant homes and lakes, and the floods are gone.

Why did men come to that once forbidding land?

They were restless, of course, and had to be moving on. But there was more than that. There was a dream—a dream of a place where a free man could build for himself, and raise his children to a better life—a dream of a continent to be conquered, a world to be won, a nation to be made.

Remembering this, I knew the answer.

A President does not shape a new and personal vision of America.

He collects it from the scattered hopes of the American past.

It existed when the first settlers saw the coast of a new world, and when the first pioneers moved westward.

It has guided us every step of the way.

It sustains every President. But it is also your inheritance and it belongs equally to the people we serve.

It must be interpreted anew by each generation for its own needs; as I have tried, in part, to do today.

It shall lead us as we enter this third century of the search for "a more perfect Union."

This, then, is the State of the Union: free, restless, growing and full of hope.

So it was in the beginning.

So it shall always be, while God is willing, and we are strong enough to keep the faith.